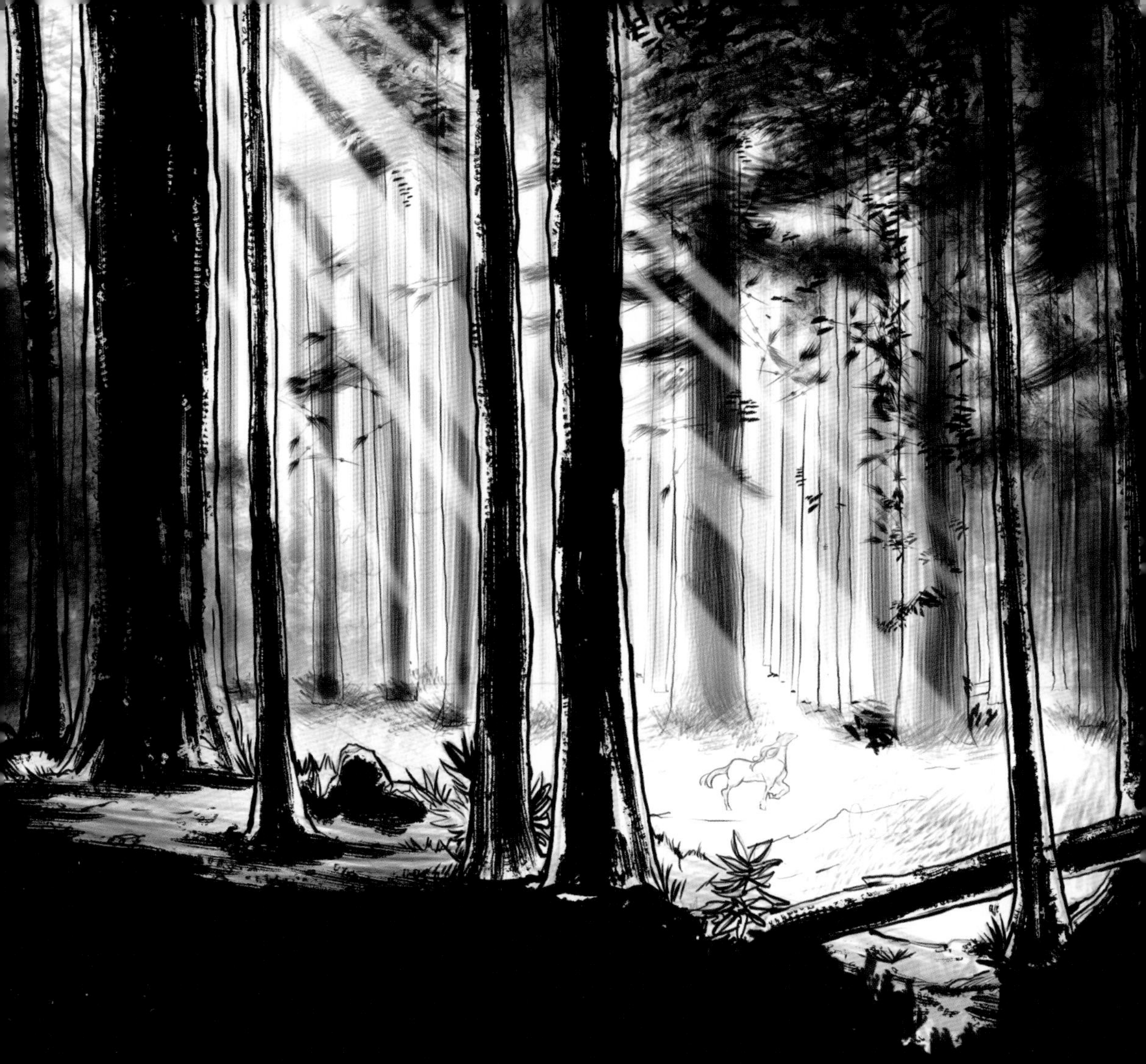

The Last Unicorn

Peter S. Beagle

ORIGINAL STORY BY
PETER S. BEAGLE

ADAPTATION BY
PETER B. GILLIS

ART BY
RENAE DE LIZ

INKS AND COLORS BY
RAY DILLON

LETTERING BY
ROBBIE ROBBINS,
NEIL UYETAKE,
CHRIS MOWRY,
AND SHAWN LEE

ORIGINAL SERIES EDITS BY
MARIAH HUEHNER

COLLECTION EDITS BY
JUSTIN EISINGER
AND MARIAH HUEHNER

COLLECTION DESIGN BY
SHAWN LEE

Special thanks to Connor Cochran, Terri Kempton, David Roudebush, Johnsie Cagle, Chris Ryall, Greg Goldstein, and AnnaMaria White for their invaluable assistance.

www.**IDWPUBLISHING**.com   ISBN: 978-1-60010-851-8   15 14 13 12   2 3 4 5

IDW Publishing is: Operations: Ted Adams, CEO & Publisher • Greg Goldstein, Chief Operating Officer • Matthew Ruzicka, CPA, Chief Financial Officer • Alan Payne, VP of Sales • Lorelei Bunjes, Director of Digital Services • Jeff Webber, Director of ePublishing • AnnaMaria White, Dir., Marketing and Public Relations • Dirk Wood, Dir., Retail Marketing • Marci Hubbard, Executive Assistant • Alonzo Simon, Shipping Manager • Angela Loggins, Staff Accountant • Cherrie Go, Assistant Web Designer • Editorial: Chris Ryall, Chief Creative Officer, Editor-In-Chief • Scott Dunbier, Senior Editor, Special Projects • Andy Schmidt, Senior Editor • Justin Eisinger, Senior Editor, Books • Kris Oprisko, Editor/Foreign Lic. • Denton J. Tipton, Editor • Tom Waltz, Editor • Mariah Huehner, Editor • Carlos Guzman, Assistant Editor • Bobby Curnow, Assistant Editor • Design: Robbie Robbins, EVP/Sr. Graphic Artist • Neil Uyetake, Senior Art Director • Chris Mowry, Senior Graphic Artist • Amauri Osorio, Graphic Artist • Gilberto Lazcano, Production Assistant • Shawn Lee, Graphic Artist

When I was four years old, my mother—she was a schoolteacher—brought me into her classroom one day and I wound up telling her students a story about unicorns. Once I was done, according to her, I very formally said to all of them, "Thank you. I will come back and tell you more about unicorns someday." I like to think that when I wrote *The Last Unicorn*, two decades later, I was finally keeping that promise.

And I like to think that earnest young version of me would have loved *this*. Because comic books were a big part of my kid years. 1940s, war over, comics ten cents a shot... I mostly read the DC stuff, with *Batman* far and away my favorite; no competition from *Green Lantern*, mighty-muscled *Hawkman*, or even *Wonder Woman*. But I also read a few *Classic Comics*, like *Moby Dick* and *A Tale Of Two Cities*, plus a handful of Fawcetts, especially sexy Nyoka the Jungle Girl (those shorts!) and Captain Marvel, the Big Red Cheese himself. Unlike many of my contemporaries, I can't honestly blame my mother for throwing all my old comics out, because I was never any sort of a collector, not even of matchbooks, like my cousin Ezra. I didn't save comic books to reread: every one I finished I traded for a new one I hadn't seen yet, bartering with my closest friends and the other kids who lived around Gunhill Road, in the Bronx. That went on until around 1950 or so. I don't recall reading comics much after that—I discovered baseball and science-fiction around then, so there you are.

Now I'm approaching 71, and I find myself with the unexpected task of introducing a six-issue comic book of *The Last Unicorn*, thanks to the splendid artwork of Renae De Liz and Ray Dillon; the remarkable adaptation by Peter Gillis (which I could never conceivably have created); the impossible energy and plain doggedness of Connor Cochran; the sharp editorial eye of Mariah Huehner; and the gracious support and belief of IDW's Chris Ryall and Greg Goldstein. My thanks to them all, because for once in my life I get to sit back and preen myself and simply *marvel*, as I'm sure you reading this will marvel too. May you enjoy it as much as I do.

It's the newest incarnation—after animated movie and stage—of a book I wrote when I was a much younger man. I'm impressed that both it and I have survived this long; and I hope you'll think that the story, at least, has worn well.

— Peter S. Beagle
Oakland, California
7 February 2010

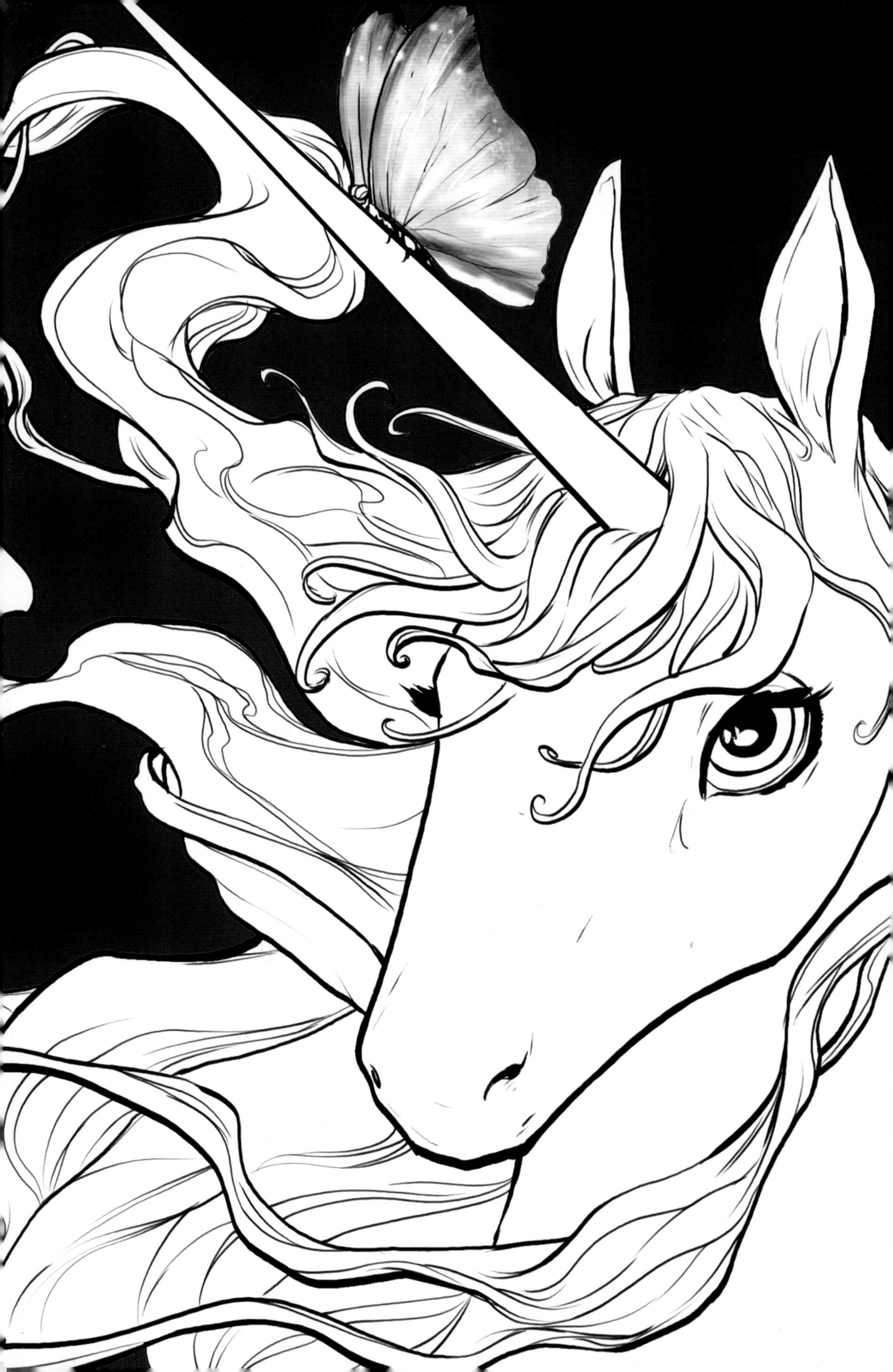

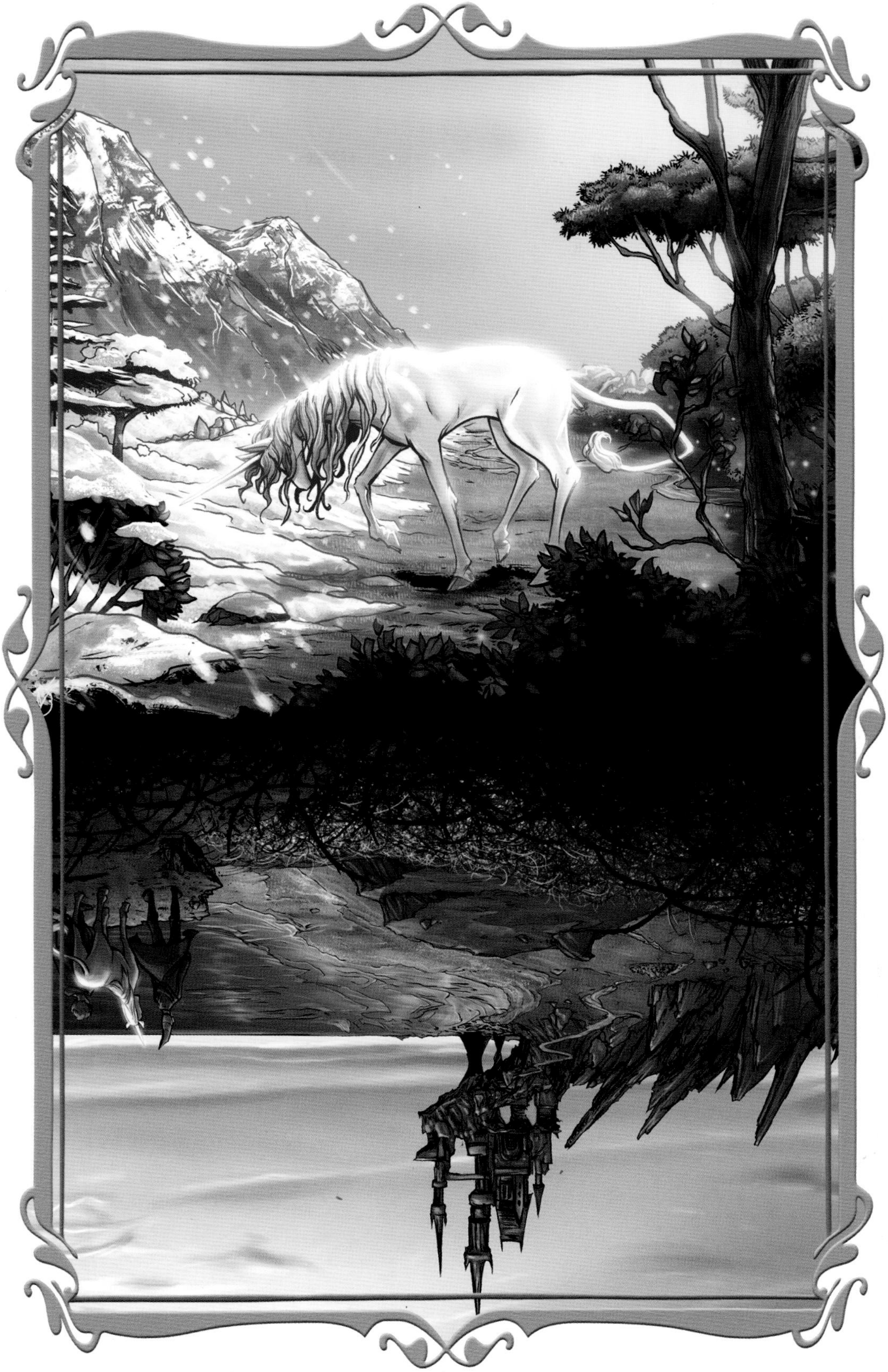

CHAPTER ONE

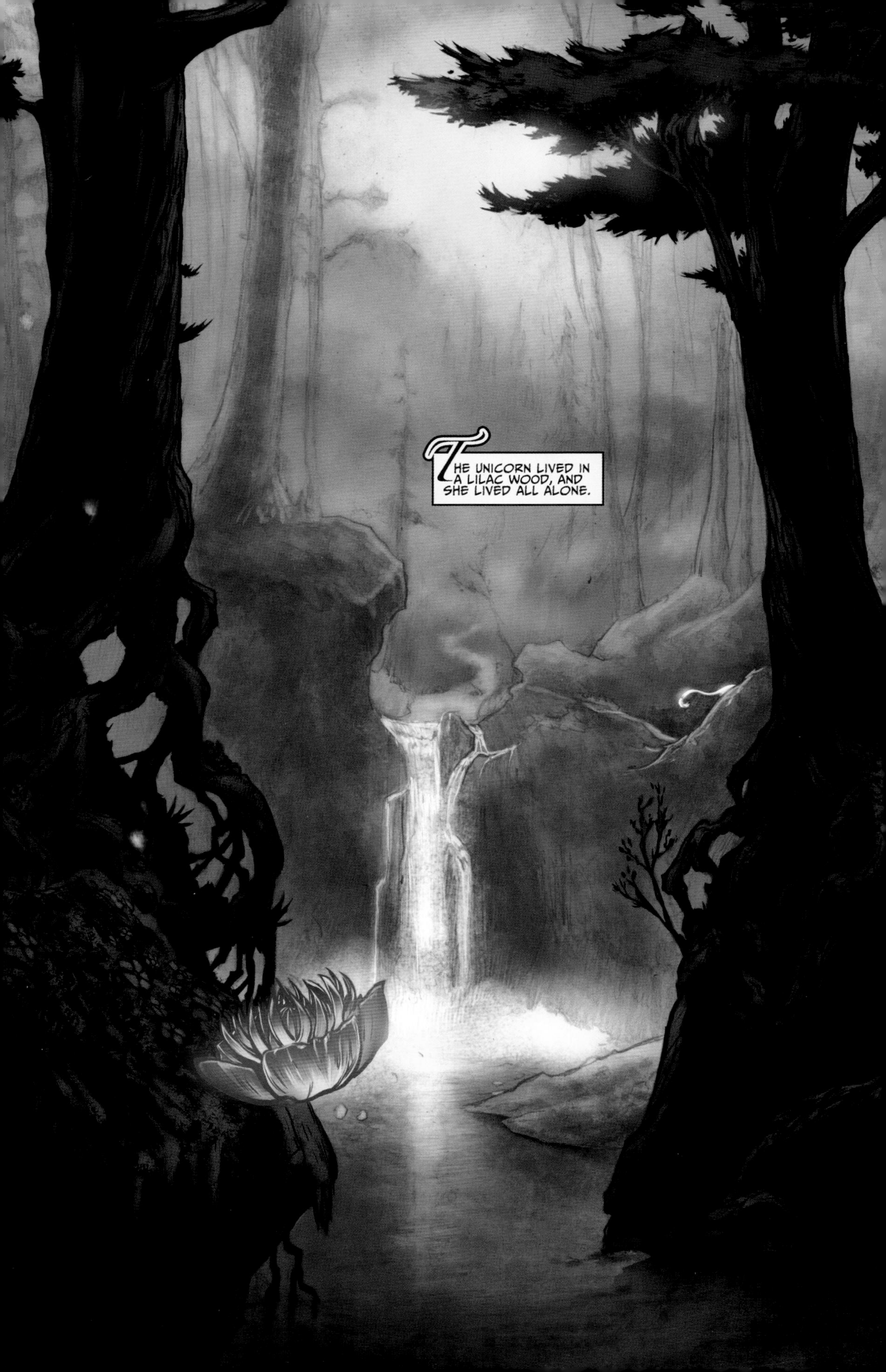
THE UNICORN LIVED IN A LILAC WOOD, AND SHE LIVED ALL ALONE.

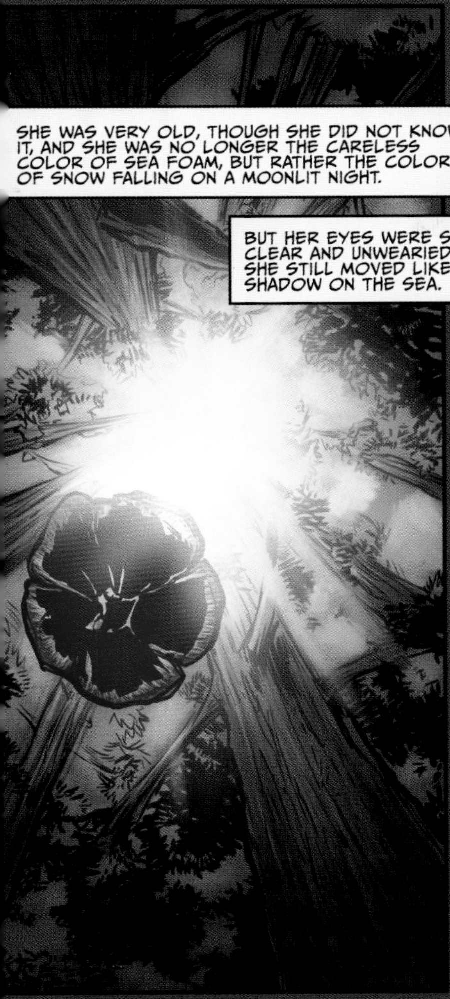
SHE WAS VERY OLD, THOUGH SHE DID NOT KNOW IT, AND SHE WAS NO LONGER THE CARELESS COLOR OF SEA FOAM, BUT RATHER THE COLOR OF SNOW FALLING ON A MOONLIT NIGHT.
BUT HER EYES WERE STILL CLEAR AND UNWEARIED, AND SHE STILL MOVED LIKE A SHADOW ON THE SEA.

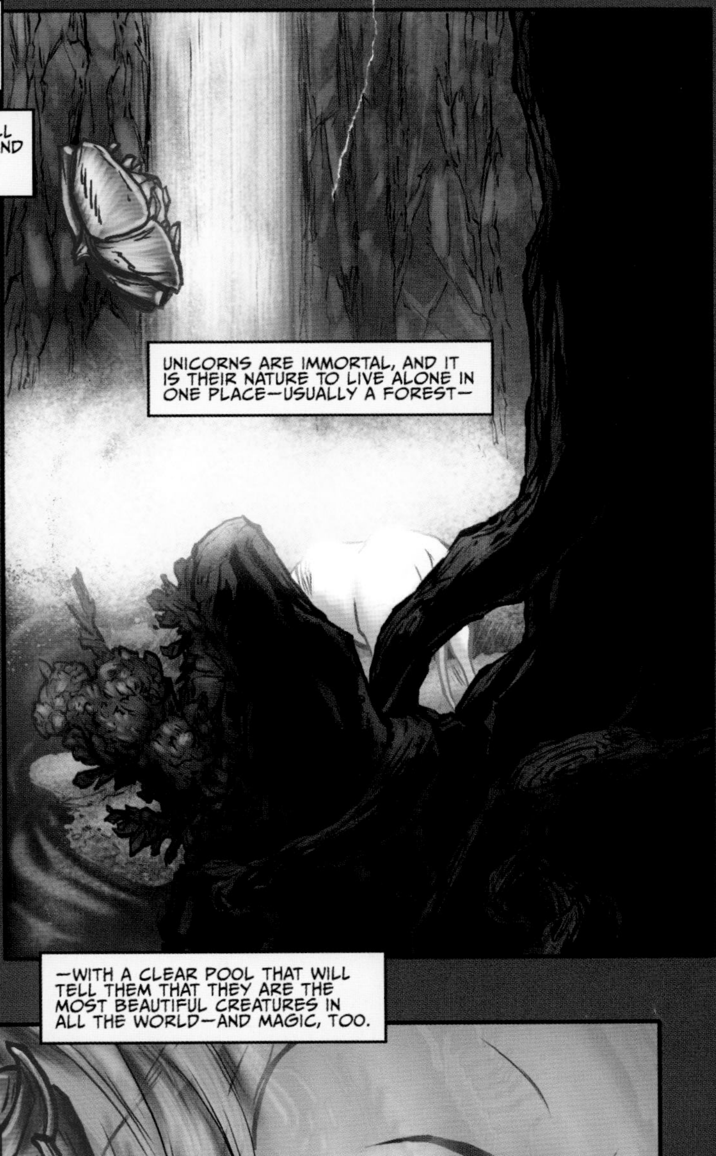
UNICORNS ARE IMMORTAL, AND IT IS THEIR NATURE TO LIVE ALONE IN ONE PLACE—USUALLY A FOREST—

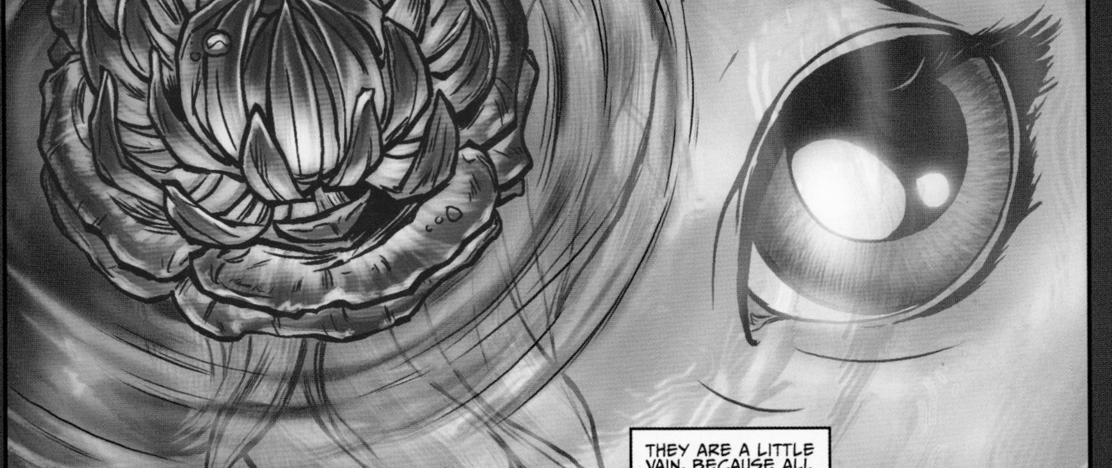
—WITH A CLEAR POOL THAT WILL TELL THEM THAT THEY ARE THE MOST BEAUTIFUL CREATURES IN ALL THE WORLD—AND MAGIC, TOO.
THEY ARE A LITTLE VAIN, BECAUSE ALL OF THAT IS TRUE.

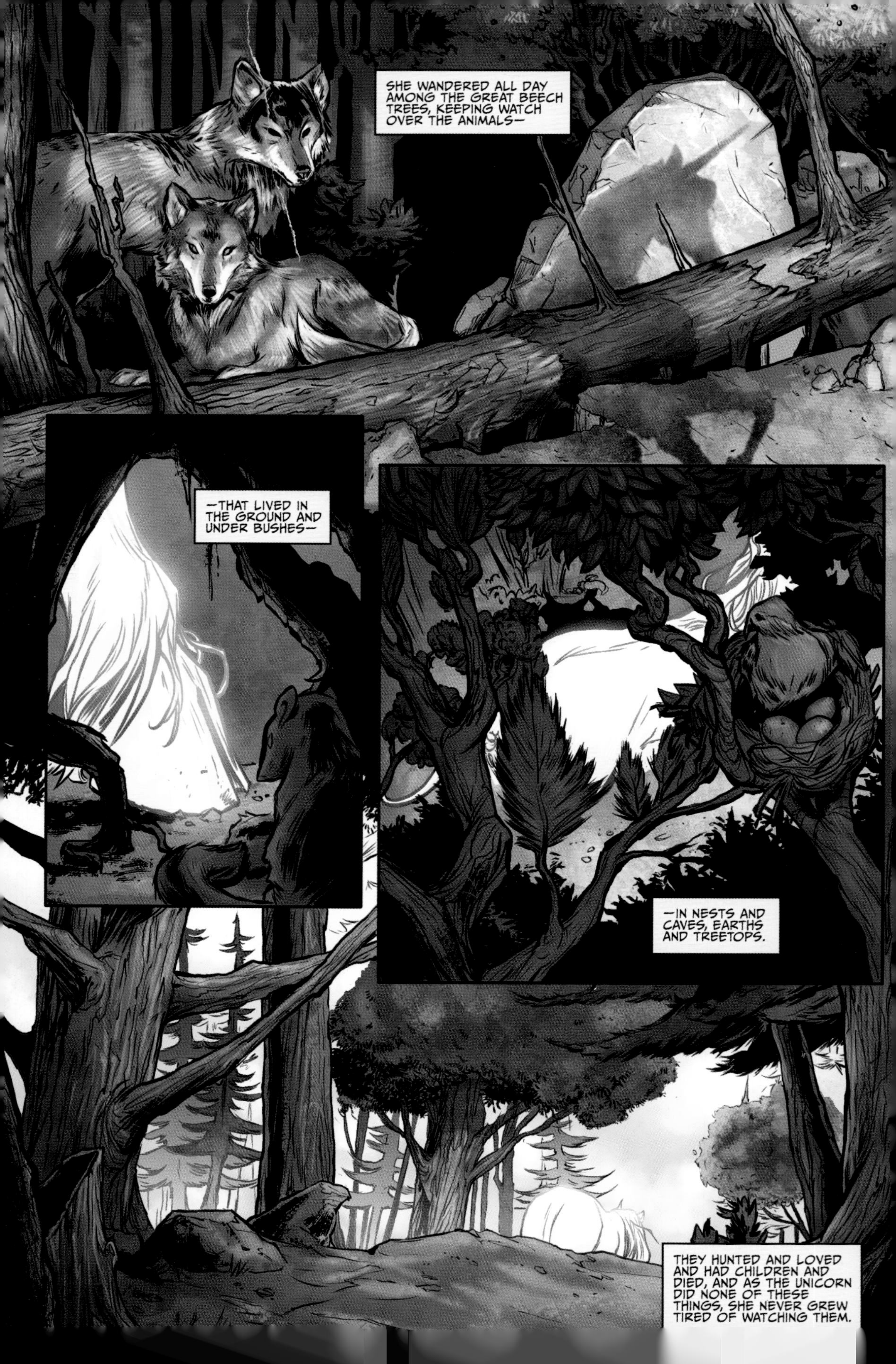
SHE WANDERED ALL DAY AMONG THE GREAT BEECH TREES, KEEPING WATCH OVER THE ANIMALS—
—THAT LIVED IN THE GROUND AND UNDER BUSHES—
—IN NESTS AND CAVES, EARTHS AND TREETOPS.
THEY HUNTED AND LOVED AND HAD CHILDREN AND DIED, AND AS THE UNICORN DID NONE OF THESE THINGS, SHE NEVER GREW TIRED OF WATCHING THEM.

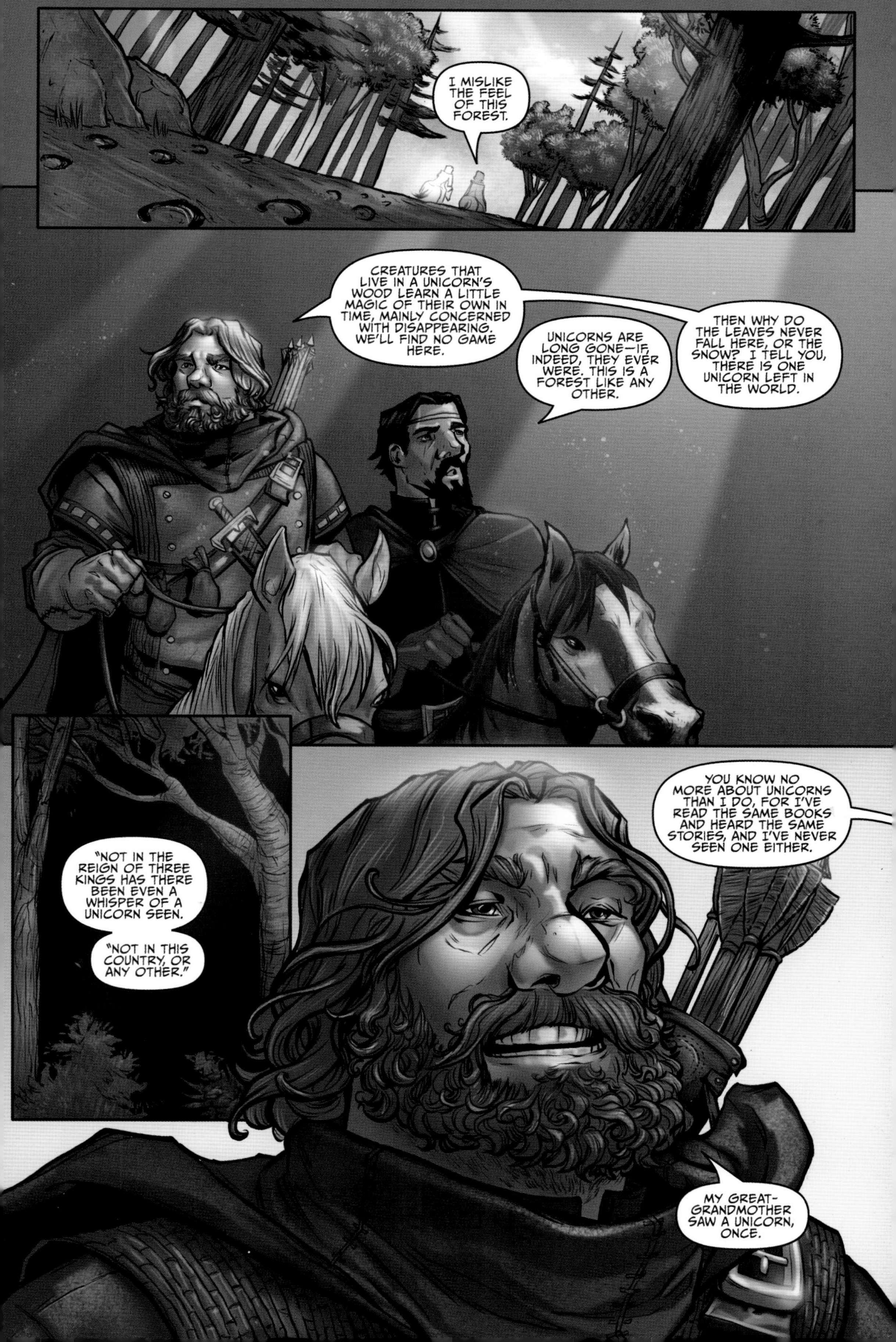
I MISLIKE THE FEEL OF THIS FOREST.
CREATURES THAT LIVE IN A UNICORN'S WOOD LEARN A LITTLE MAGIC OF THEIR OWN IN TIME, MAINLY CONCERNED WITH DISAPPEARING. WE'LL FIND NO GAME HERE.
UNICORNS ARE LONG GONE—IF, INDEED, THEY EVER WERE. THIS IS A FOREST LIKE ANY OTHER.
THEN WHY DO THE LEAVES NEVER FALL HERE, OR THE SNOW? I TELL YOU, THERE IS ONE UNICORN LEFT IN THE WORLD.
"NOT IN THE REIGN OF THREE KINGS HAS THERE BEEN EVEN A WHISPER OF A UNICORN SEEN.
"NOT IN THIS COUNTRY, OR ANY OTHER."
YOU KNOW NO MORE ABOUT UNICORNS THAN I DO, FOR I'VE READ THE SAME BOOKS AND HEARD THE SAME STORIES, AND I'VE NEVER SEEN ONE EITHER.
MY GREAT-GRANDMOTHER SAW A UNICORN, ONCE.

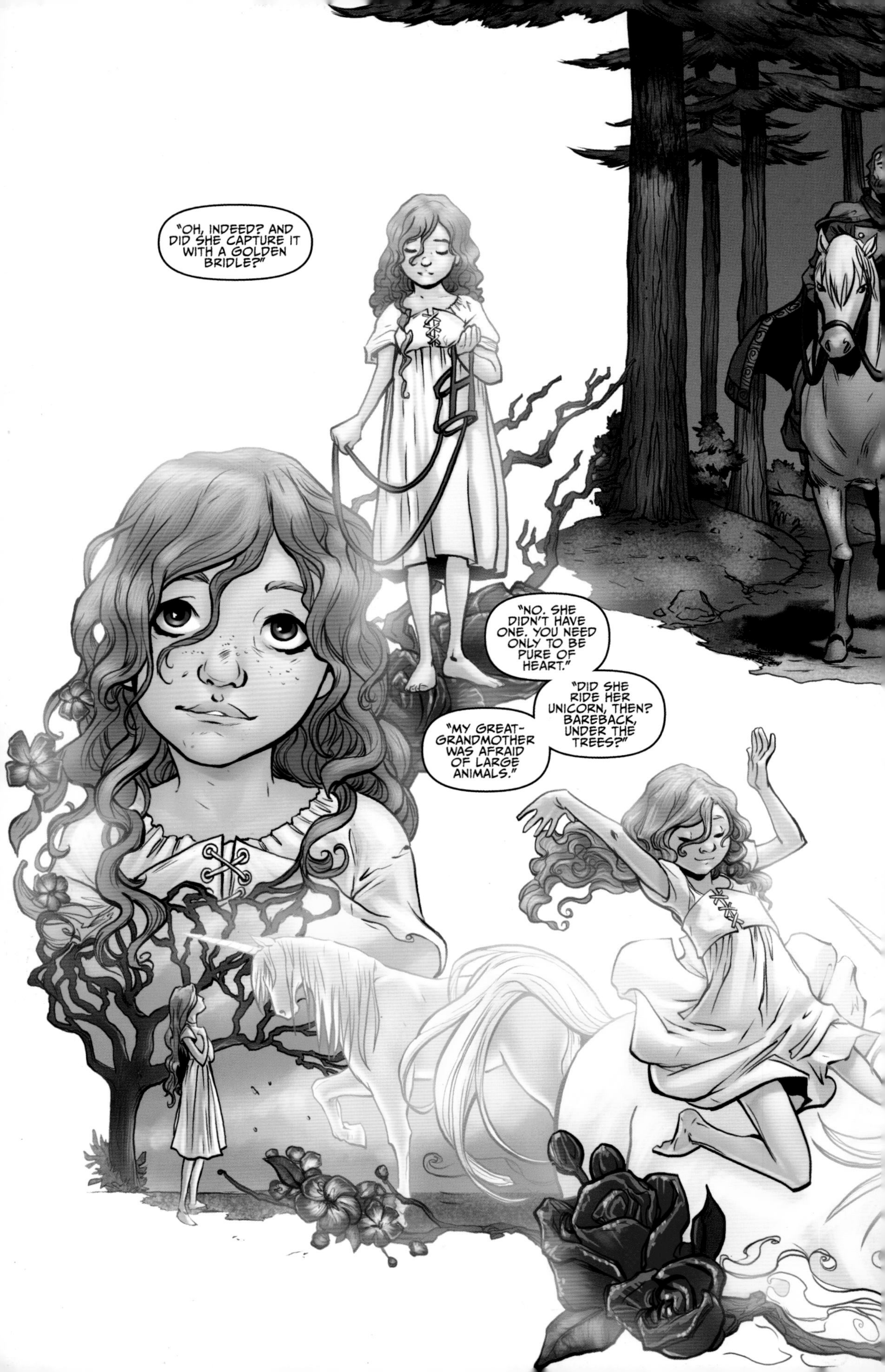
"OH, INDEED? AND DID SHE CAPTURE IT WITH A GOLDEN BRIDLE?"
"NO. SHE DIDN'T HAVE ONE. YOU NEED ONLY TO BE PURE OF HEART."
"DID SHE RIDE HER UNICORN, THEN? BAREBACK, UNDER THE TREES?"
"MY GREAT-GRANDMOTHER WAS AFRAID OF LARGE ANIMALS."

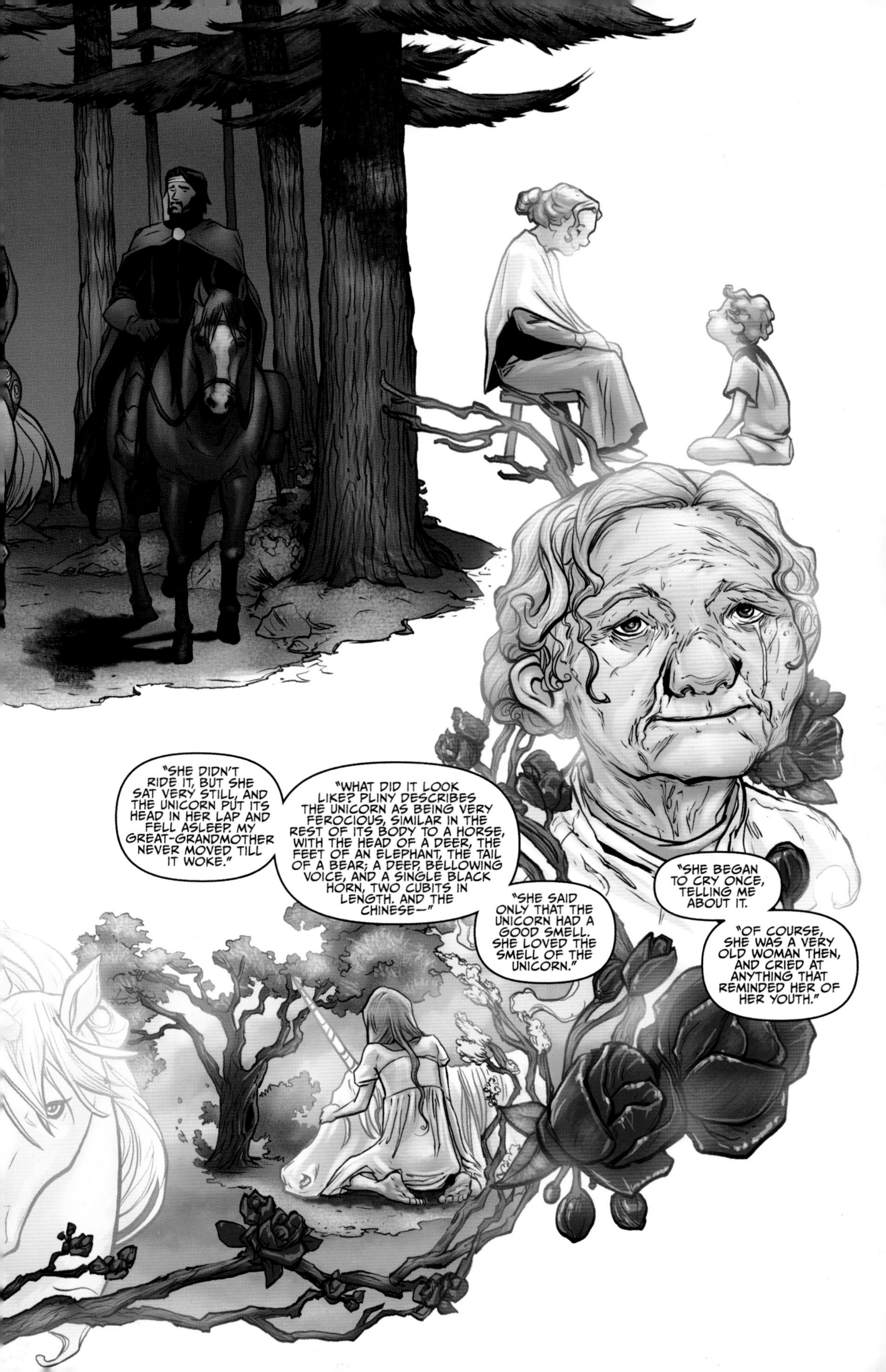
"SHE DIDN'T RIDE IT, BUT SHE SAT VERY STILL, AND THE UNICORN PUT ITS HEAD IN HER LAP AND FELL ASLEEP. MY GREAT-GRANDMOTHER NEVER MOVED TILL IT WOKE."
"WHAT DID IT LOOK LIKE? PLINY DESCRIBES THE UNICORN AS BEING VERY FEROCIOUS, SIMILAR IN THE REST OF ITS BODY TO A HORSE, WITH THE HEAD OF A DEER, THE FEET OF AN ELEPHANT, THE TAIL OF A BEAR; A DEEP, BELLOWING VOICE, AND A SINGLE BLACK HORN, TWO CUBITS IN LENGTH. AND THE CHINESE--"
"SHE SAID ONLY THAT THE UNICORN HAD A GOOD SMELL. SHE LOVED THE SMELL OF THE UNICORN."
"SHE BEGAN TO CRY ONCE, TELLING ME ABOUT IT.
"OF COURSE, SHE WAS A VERY OLD WOMAN THEN, AND CRIED AT ANYTHING THAT REMINDED HER OF HER YOUTH."

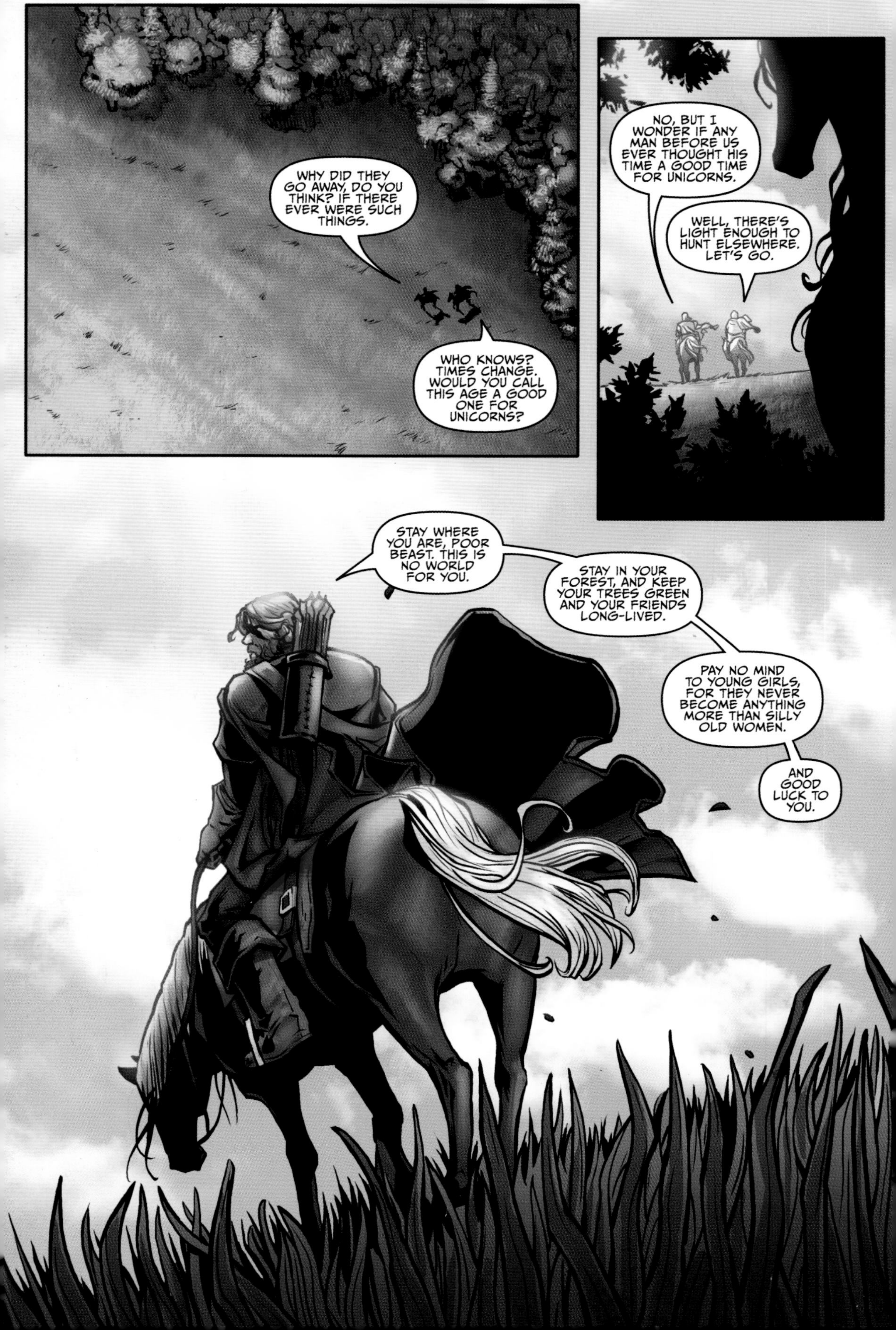
WHY DID THEY GO AWAY, DO YOU THINK? IF THERE EVER WERE SUCH THINGS.
WHO KNOWS? TIMES CHANGE. WOULD YOU CALL THIS AGE A GOOD ONE FOR UNICORNS?
NO, BUT I WONDER IF ANY MAN BEFORE US EVER THOUGHT HIS TIME A GOOD TIME FOR UNICORNS.
WELL, THERE'S LIGHT ENOUGH TO HUNT ELSEWHERE. LET'S GO.
STAY WHERE YOU ARE, POOR BEAST. THIS IS NO WORLD FOR YOU.
STAY IN YOUR FOREST, AND KEEP YOUR TREES GREEN AND YOUR FRIENDS LONG-LIVED.
PAY NO MIND TO YOUNG GIRLS, FOR THEY NEVER BECOME ANYTHING MORE THAN SILLY OLD WOMEN.
AND GOOD LUCK TO YOU.

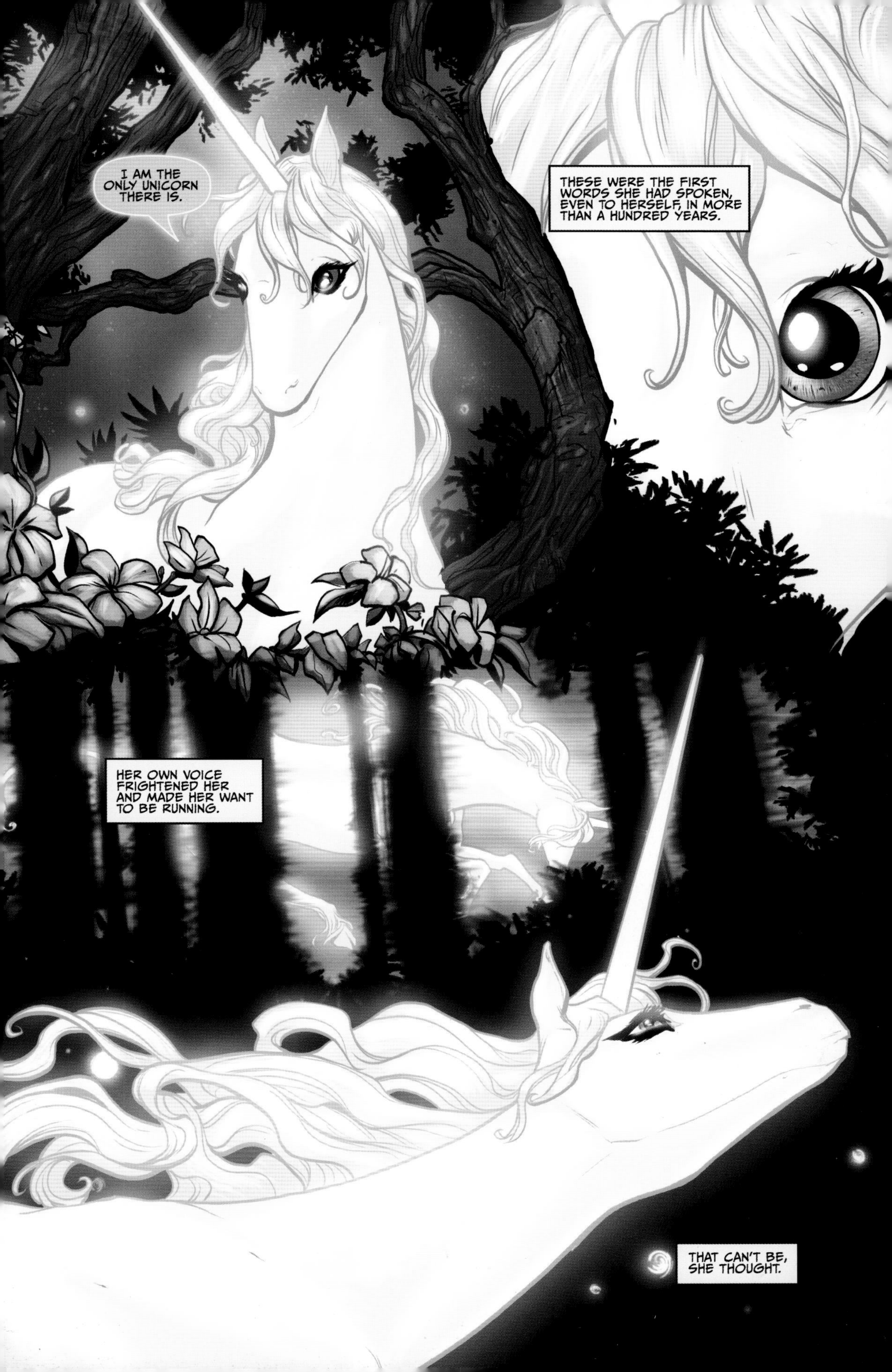
I AM THE ONLY UNICORN THERE IS.
THESE WERE THE FIRST WORDS SHE HAD SPOKEN, EVEN TO HERSELF, IN MORE THAN A HUNDRED YEARS.
HER OWN VOICE FRIGHTENED HER AND MADE HER WANT TO BE RUNNING.
THAT CAN'T BE, SHE THOUGHT.

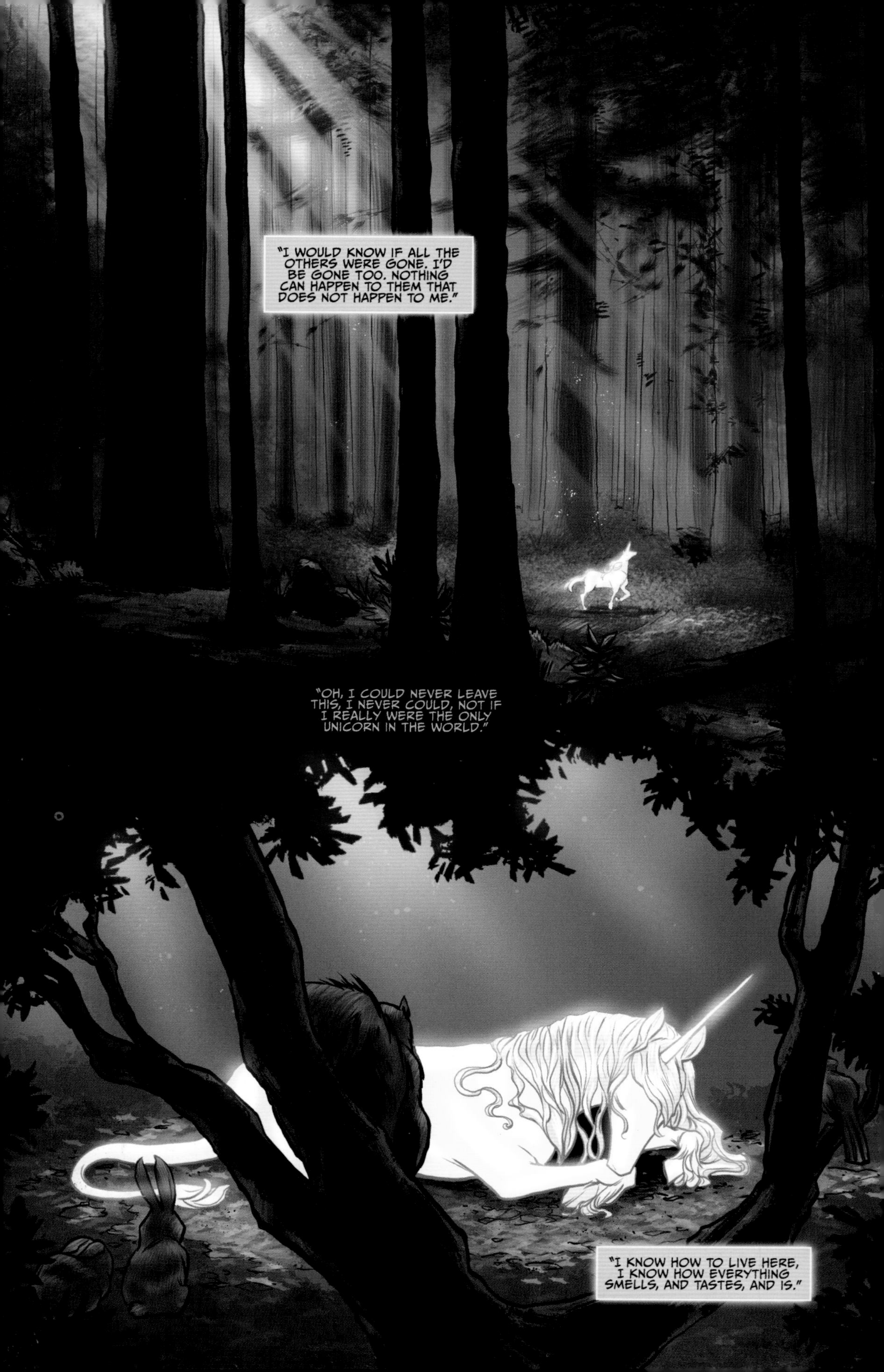
"I WOULD KNOW IF ALL THE OTHERS WERE GONE. I'D BE GONE TOO. NOTHING CAN HAPPEN TO THEM THAT DOES NOT HAPPEN TO ME."
"OH, I COULD NEVER LEAVE THIS, I NEVER COULD, NOT IF I REALLY WERE THE ONLY UNICORN IN THE WORLD."
"I KNOW HOW TO LIVE HERE, I KNOW HOW EVERYTHING SMELLS, AND TASTES, AND IS."

"WHAT COULD I EVER SEARCH FOR IN THE WORLD, EXCEPT THIS AGAIN?"
"BUT SUPPOSE THEY ARE HIDING TOGETHER, SOMEWHERE FAR AWAY? WHAT IF THEY ARE HIDING AND WAITING FOR ME?"
"I WILL NOT GO. BECAUSE MEN HAVE SEEN NO UNICORNS FOR A WHILE DOES NOT MEAN THEY HAVE ALL VANISHED. EVEN IF IT WERE TRUE, I WOULD NOT GO."
"I LIVE HERE."

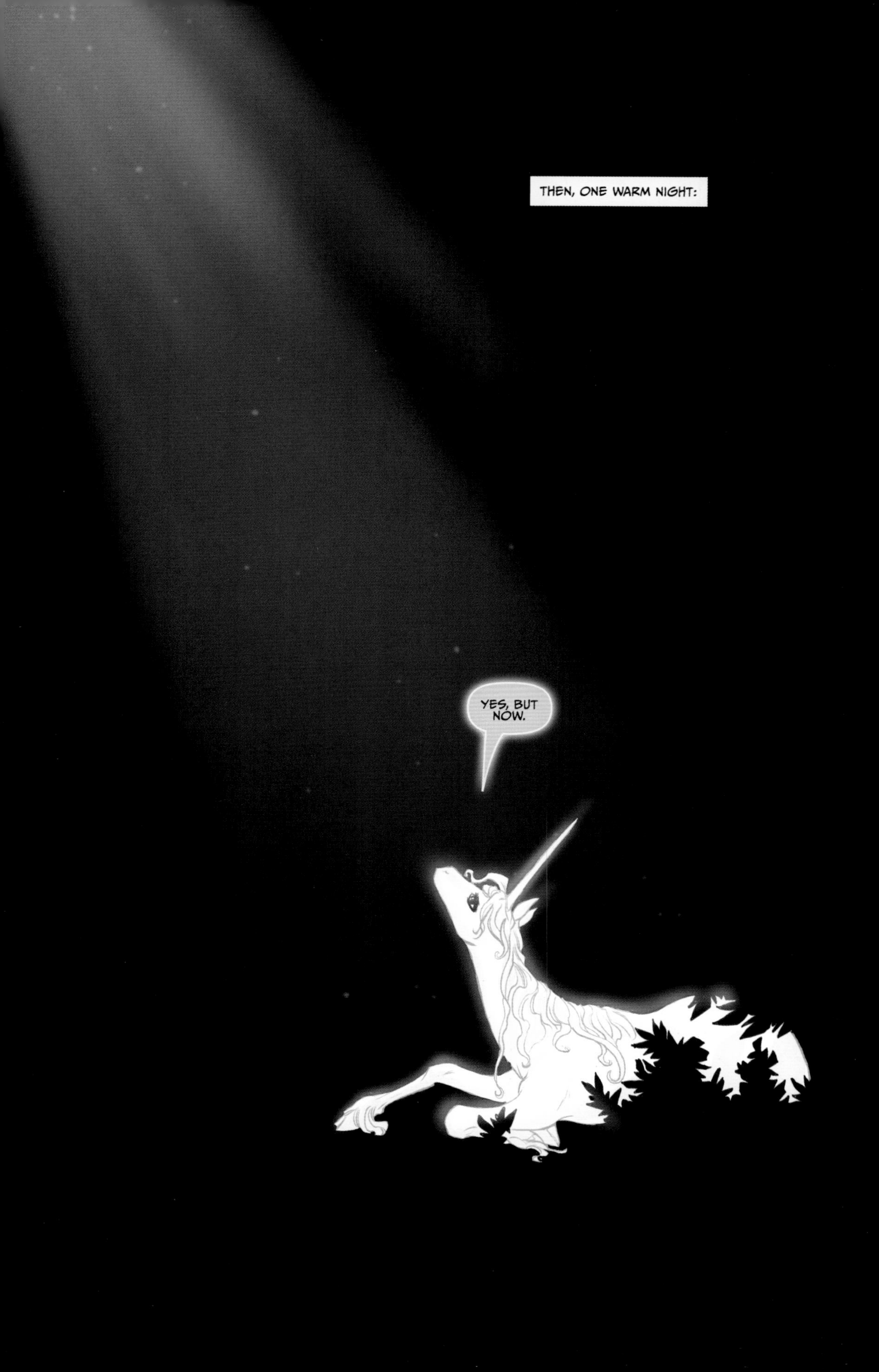
THEN, ONE WARM NIGHT:
YES, BUT NOW.

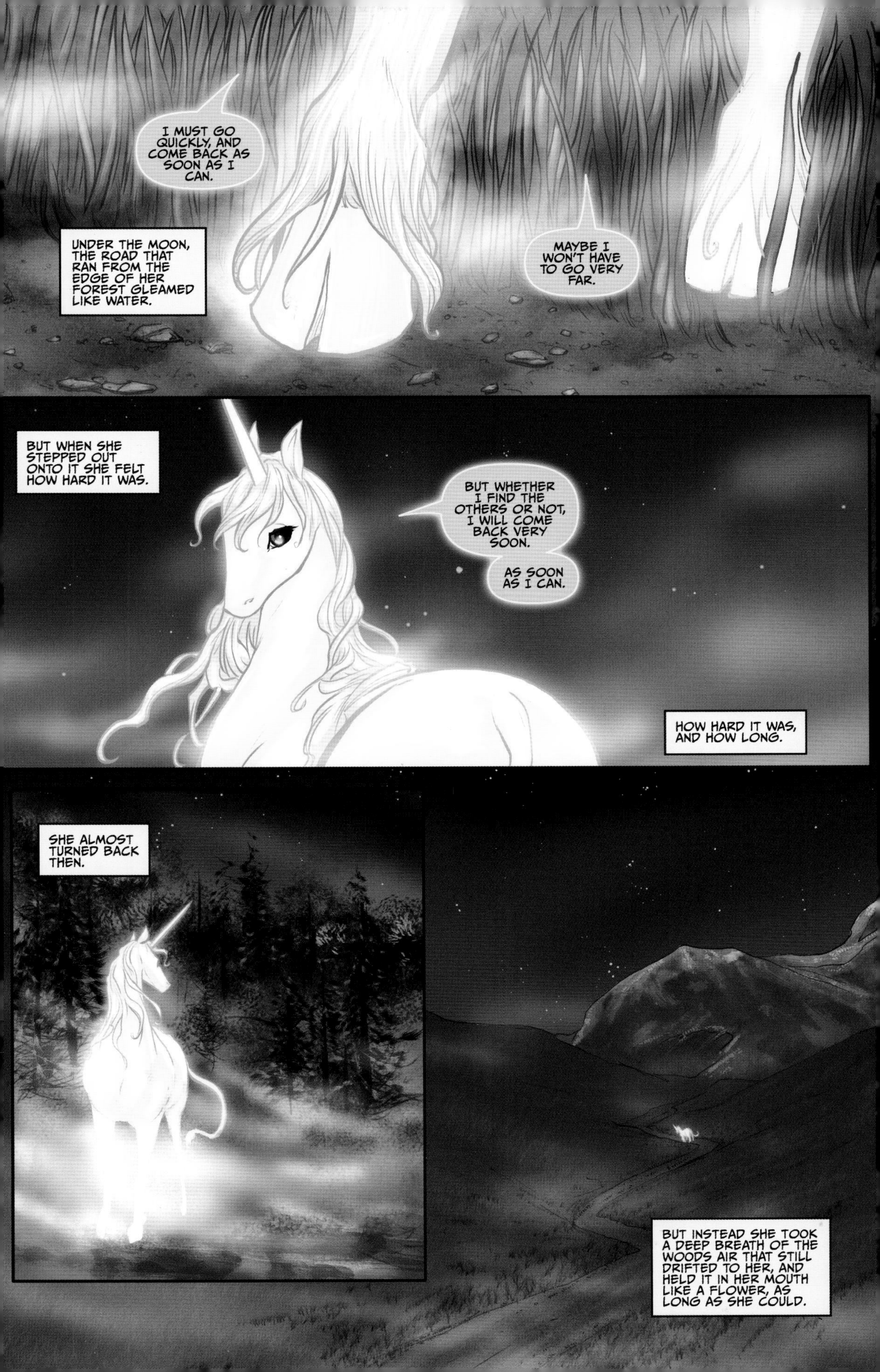
I MUST GO QUICKLY, AND COME BACK AS SOON AS I CAN.
UNDER THE MOON, THE ROAD THAT RAN FROM THE EDGE OF HER FOREST GLEAMED LIKE WATER.
MAYBE I WON'T HAVE TO GO VERY FAR.
BUT WHEN SHE STEPPED OUT ONTO IT SHE FELT HOW HARD IT WAS.
BUT WHETHER I FIND THE OTHERS OR NOT, I WILL COME BACK VERY SOON.
AS SOON AS I CAN.
HOW HARD IT WAS, AND HOW LONG.
SHE ALMOST TURNED BACK THEN.
BUT INSTEAD SHE TOOK A DEEP BREATH OF THE WOODS AIR THAT STILL DRIFTED TO HER, AND HELD IT IN HER MOUTH LIKE A FLOWER, AS LONG AS SHE COULD.

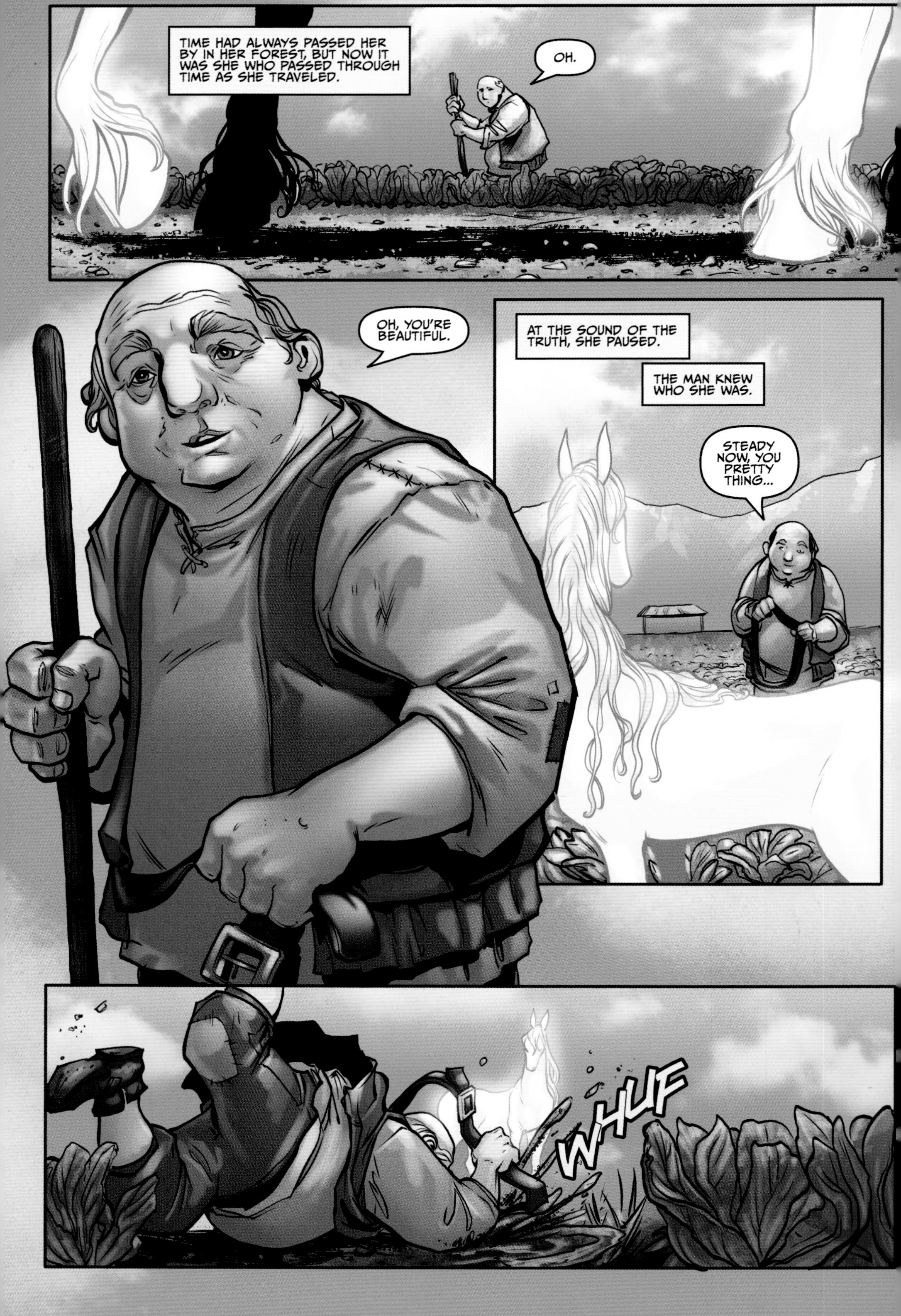
TIME HAD ALWAYS PASSED HER BY IN HER FOREST, BUT NOW IT WAS SHE WHO PASSED THROUGH TIME AS SHE TRAVELED.
OH.
OH, YOU'RE BEAUTIFUL.
AT THE SOUND OF THE TRUTH, SHE PAUSED.
THE MAN KNEW WHO SHE WAS.
STEADY NOW, YOU PRETTY THING...
WHUF

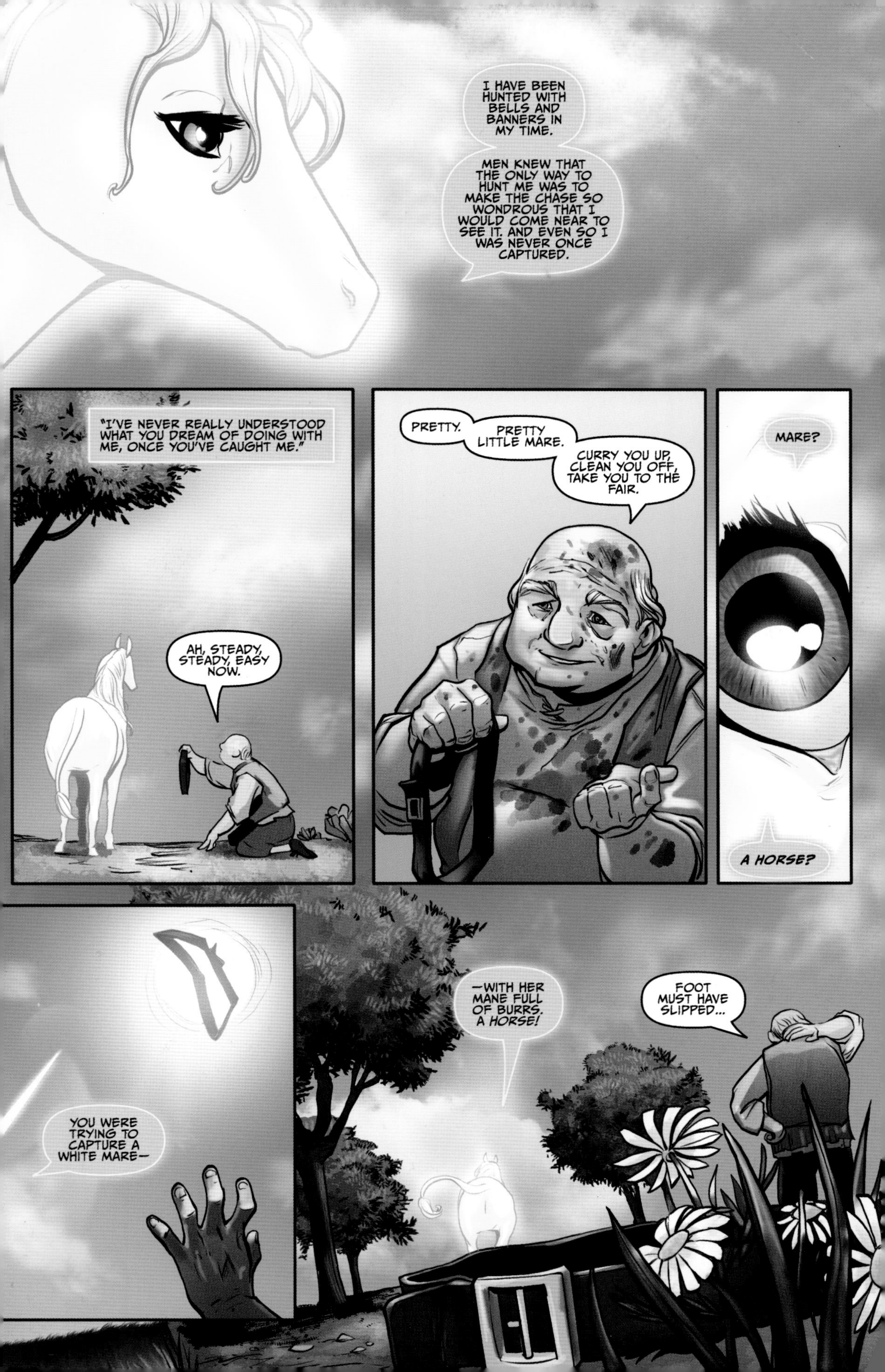
I HAVE BEEN HUNTED WITH BELLS AND BANNERS IN MY TIME.
MEN KNEW THAT THE ONLY WAY TO HUNT ME WAS TO MAKE THE CHASE SO WONDROUS THAT I WOULD COME NEAR TO SEE IT. AND EVEN SO I WAS NEVER ONCE CAPTURED.
"I'VE NEVER REALLY UNDERSTOOD WHAT YOU DREAM OF DOING WITH ME, ONCE YOU'VE CAUGHT ME."
AH, STEADY, STEADY, EASY NOW.
PRETTY.
PRETTY LITTLE MARE.
CURRY YOU UP, CLEAN YOU OFF, TAKE YOU TO THE FAIR.
MARE?
A HORSE?
YOU WERE TRYING TO CAPTURE A WHITE MARE—
—WITH HER MANE FULL OF BURRS. A HORSE!
FOOT MUST HAVE SLIPPED...

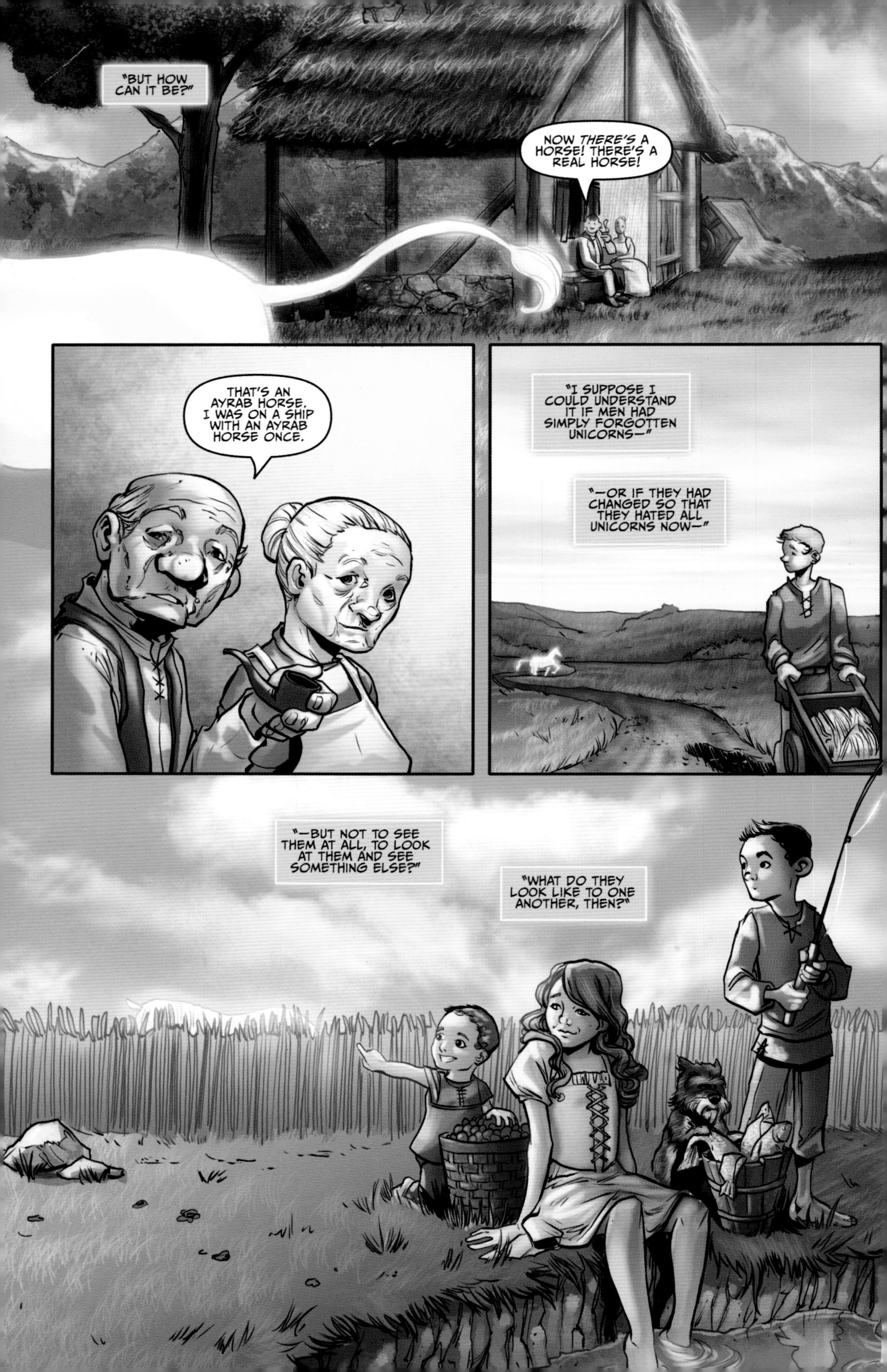
"BUT HOW CAN IT BE?"
NOW THERE'S A HORSE! THERE'S A REAL HORSE!
THAT'S AN AYRAB HORSE. I WAS ON A SHIP WITH AN AYRAB HORSE ONCE.
"I SUPPOSE I COULD UNDERSTAND IT IF MEN HAD SIMPLY FORGOTTEN UNICORNS—"
"—OR IF THEY HAD CHANGED SO THAT THEY HATED ALL UNICORNS NOW—"
"—BUT NOT TO SEE THEM AT ALL, TO LOOK AT THEM AND SEE SOMETHING ELSE?"
"WHAT DO THEY LOOK LIKE TO ONE ANOTHER, THEN?"

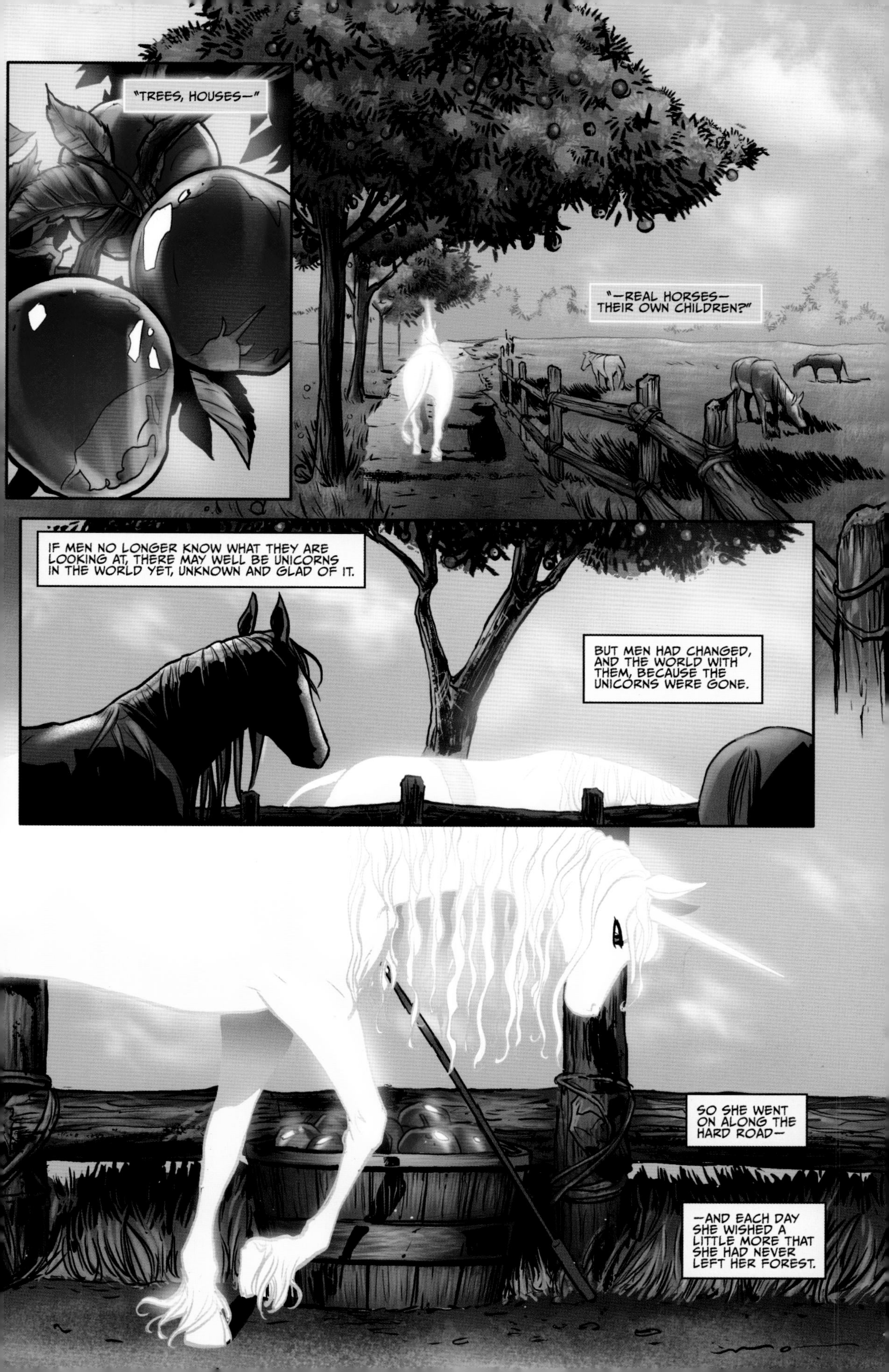
"TREES, HOUSES—"
"—REAL HORSES— THEIR OWN CHILDREN?"
IF MEN NO LONGER KNOW WHAT THEY ARE LOOKING AT, THERE MAY WELL BE UNICORNS IN THE WORLD YET, UNKNOWN AND GLAD OF IT.
BUT MEN HAD CHANGED, AND THE WORLD WITH THEM, BECAUSE THE UNICORNS WERE GONE.
SO SHE WENT ON ALONG THE HARD ROAD—
—AND EACH DAY SHE WISHED A LITTLE MORE THAT SHE HAD NEVER LEFT HER FOREST.

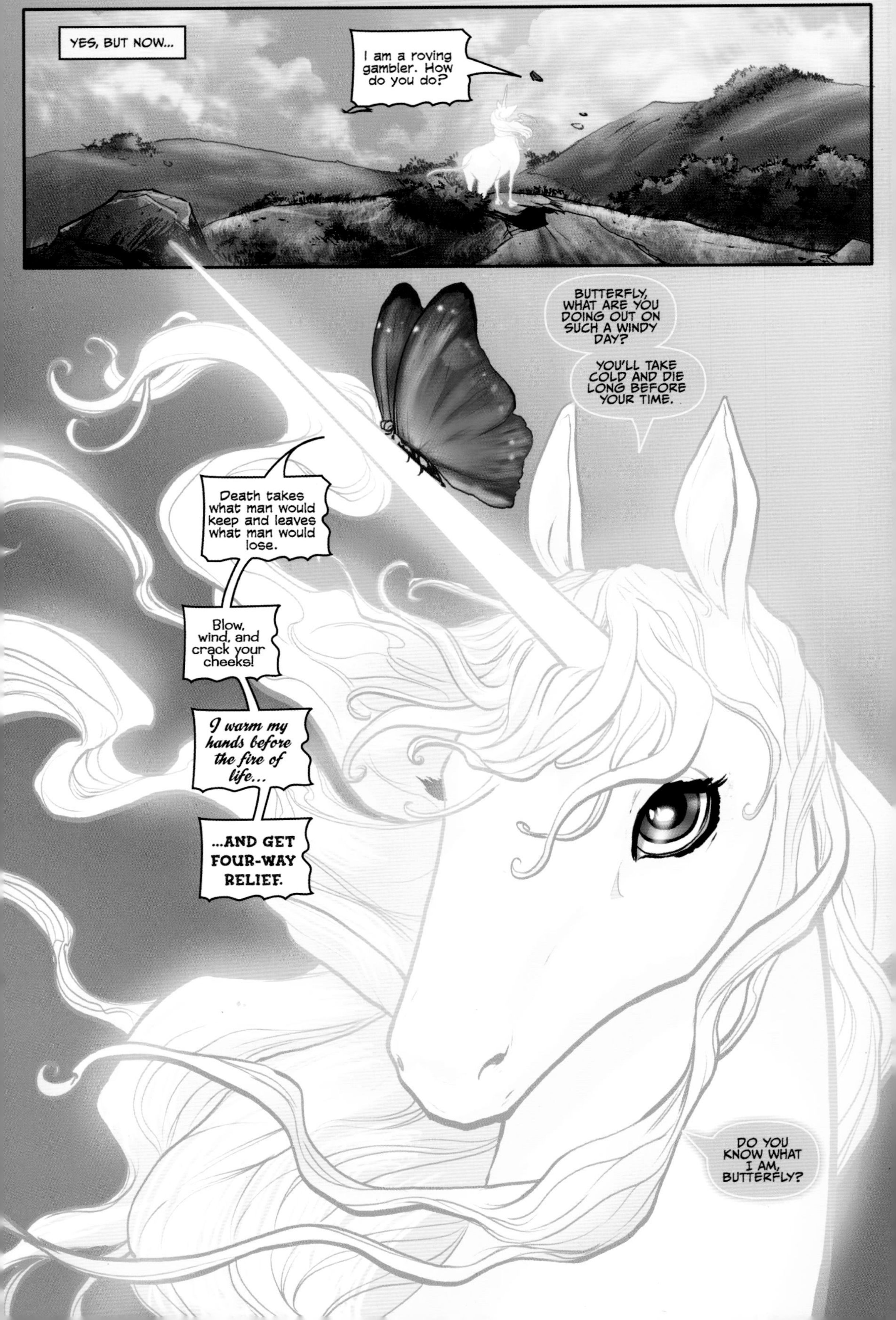
YES, BUT NOW...
I am a roving gambler. How do you do?
BUTTERFLY, WHAT ARE YOU DOING OUT ON SUCH A WINDY DAY?
YOU'LL TAKE COLD AND DIE LONG BEFORE YOUR TIME.
Death takes what man would keep and leaves what man would lose.
Blow, wind, and crack your cheeks!
I warm my hands before the fire of life...
...AND GET FOUR-WAY RELIEF.
DO YOU KNOW WHAT I AM, BUTTERFLY?

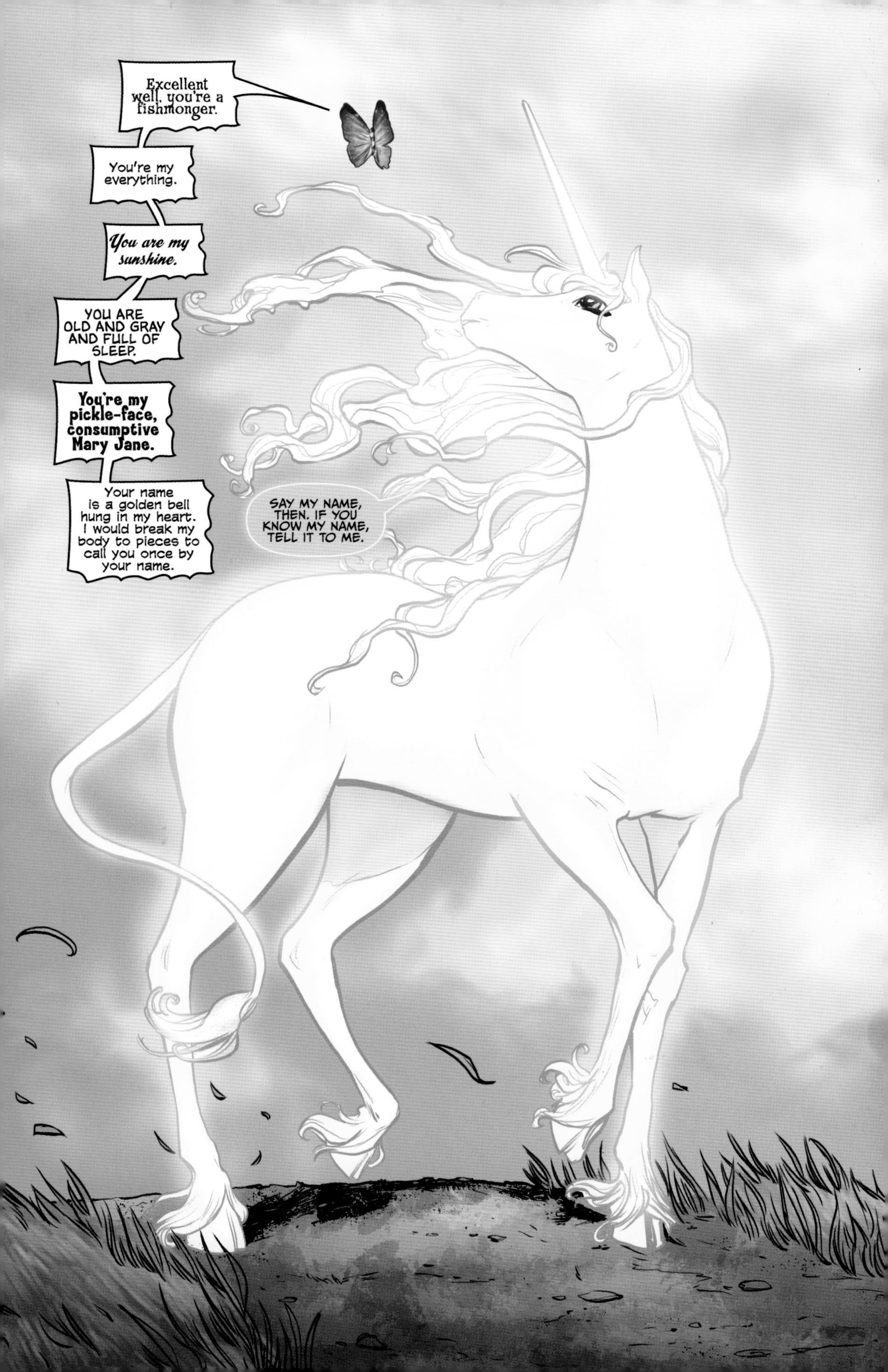
Excellent well, you're a fishmonger.
You're my everything.
You are my sunshine.
YOU ARE OLD AND GRAY AND FULL OF SLEEP.
You're my pickle-face, consumptive Mary Jane.
Your name is a golden bell hung in my heart. I would break my body to pieces to call you once by your name.
SAY MY NAME, THEN. IF YOU KNOW MY NAME, TELL IT TO ME.

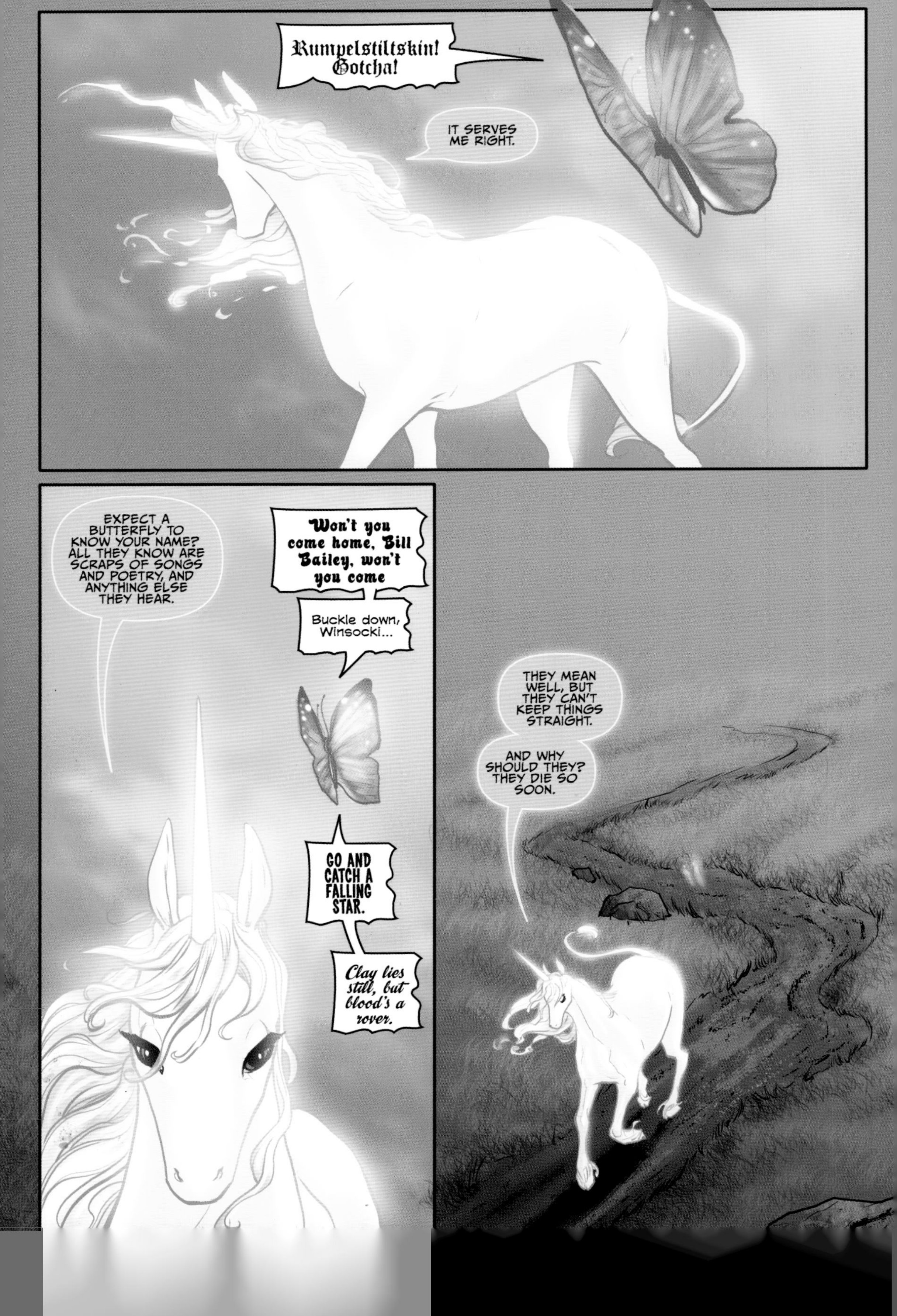
Rumpelstiltskin! Gotcha!
IT SERVES ME RIGHT.
EXPECT A BUTTERFLY TO KNOW YOUR NAME? ALL THEY KNOW ARE SCRAPS OF SONGS AND POETRY, AND ANYTHING ELSE THEY HEAR.
Won't you come home, Bill Bailey, won't you come
Buckle down, Winsocki...
GO AND CATCH A FALLING STAR.
Clay lies still, but blood's a rover.
THEY MEAN WELL, BUT THEY CAN'T KEEP THINGS STRAIGHT.
AND WHY SHOULD THEY? THEY DIE SO SOON.

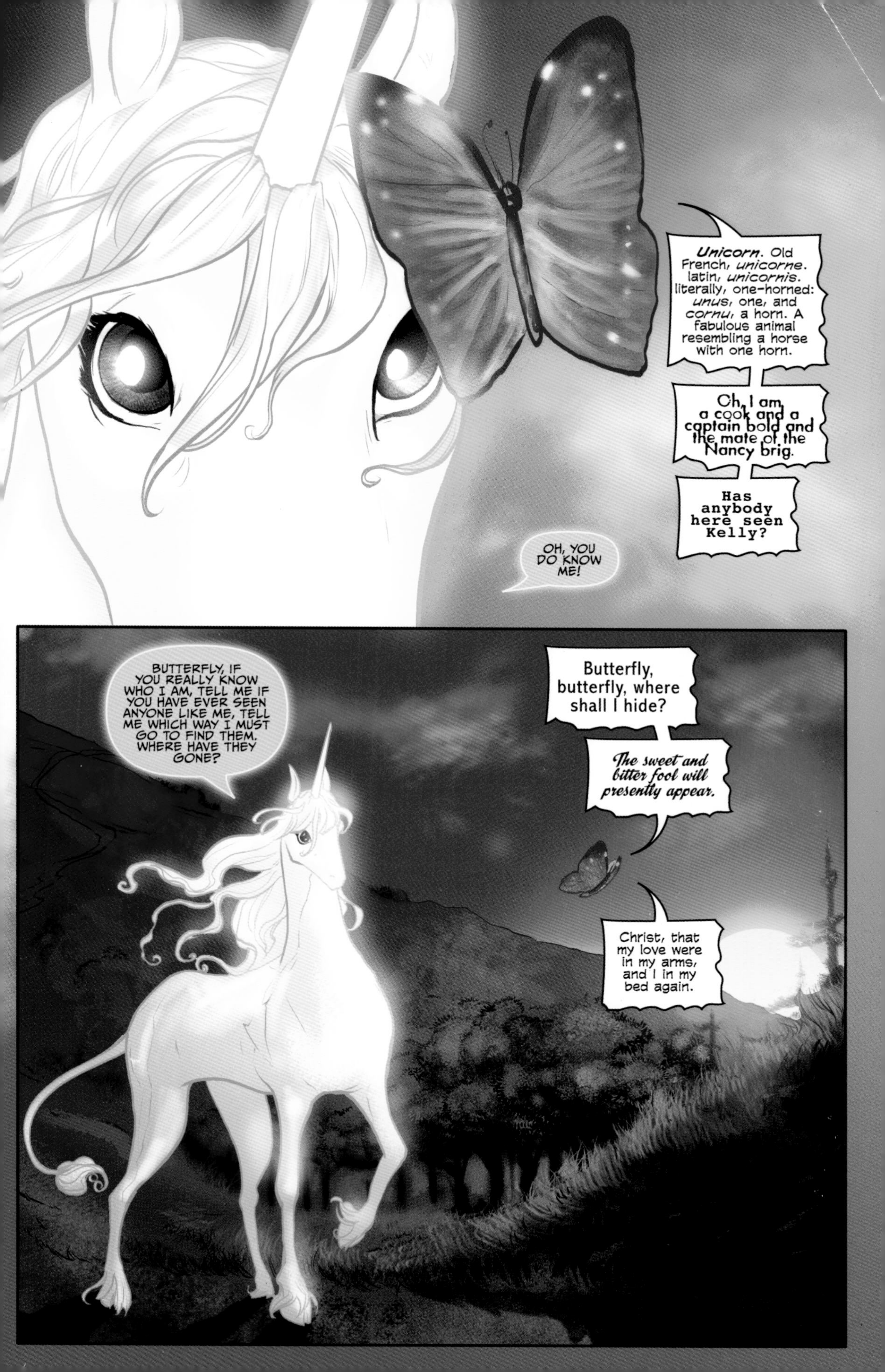
Unicorn. Old French, unicorne. latin, unicornis. literally, one-horned: unus, one, and cornu, a horn. A fabulous animal resembling a horse with one horn.
Oh, I am a cook and a captain bold and the mate of the Nancy brig.
Has anybody here seen Kelly?
OH, YOU DO KNOW ME!
BUTTERFLY, IF YOU REALLY KNOW WHO I AM, TELL ME IF YOU HAVE EVER SEEN ANYONE LIKE ME, TELL ME WHICH WAY I MUST GO TO FIND THEM. WHERE HAVE THEY GONE?
Butterfly, butterfly, where shall I hide?
The sweet and bitter fool will presently appear.
Christ, that my love were in my arms, and I in my bed again.

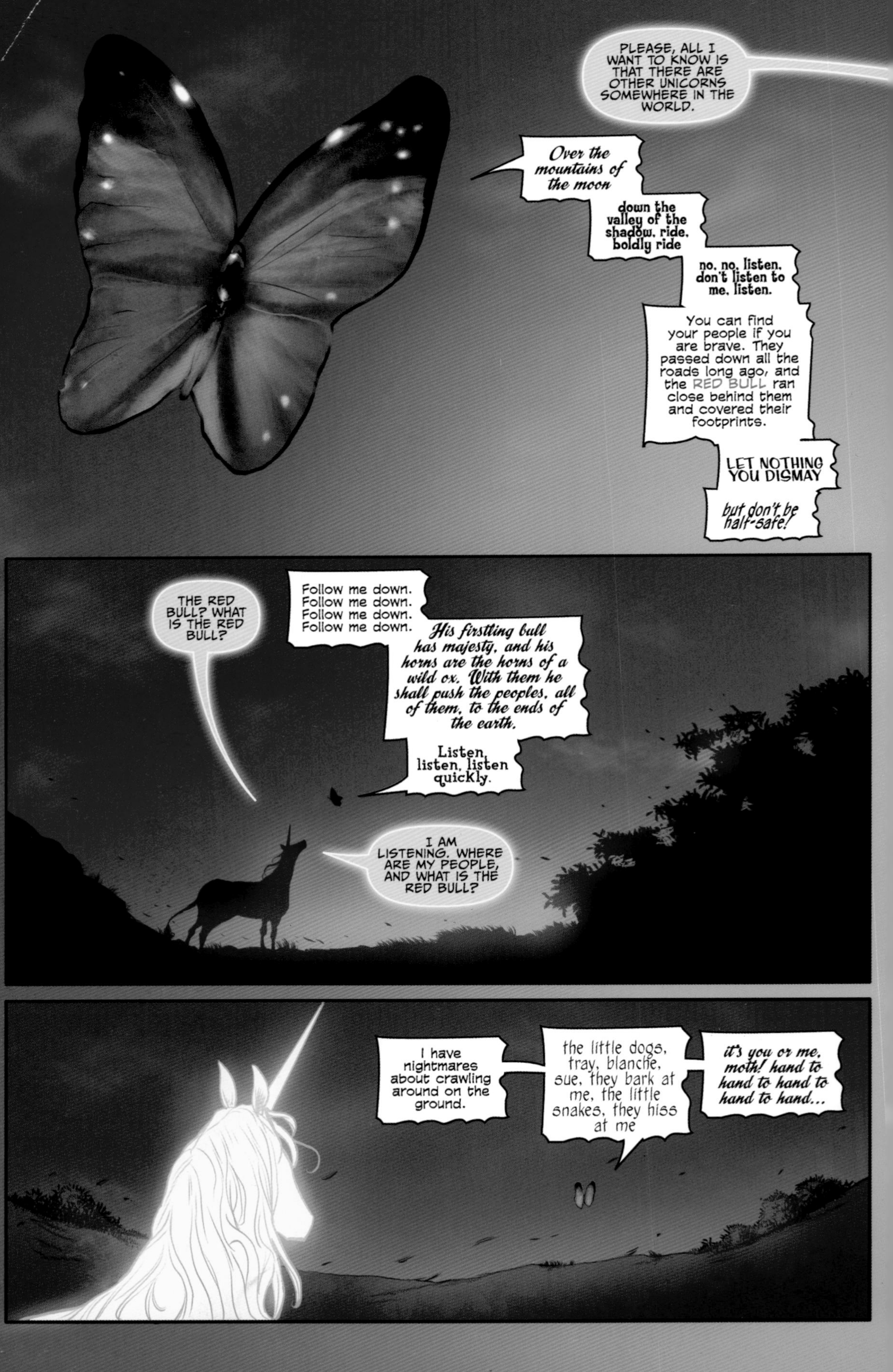
PLEASE, ALL I WANT TO KNOW IS THAT THERE ARE OTHER UNICORNS SOMEWHERE IN THE WORLD.
Over the mountains of the moon
down the valley of the shadow, ride, boldly ride
no, no, listen, don't listen to me, listen.
You can find your people if you are brave. They passed down all the roads long ago, and the RED BULL ran close behind them and covered their footprints.
LET NOTHING YOU DISMAY
but don't be half-safe!
THE RED BULL? WHAT IS THE RED BULL?
Follow me down. Follow me down. Follow me down. Follow me down.
His firstling bull has majesty, and his horns are the horns of a wild ox. With them he shall push the peoples, all of them, to the ends of the earth.
Listen, listen, listen quickly.
I AM LISTENING. WHERE ARE MY PEOPLE, AND WHAT IS THE RED BULL?
I have nightmares about crawling around on the ground.
the little dogs, tray, blanche, sue, they bark at me, the little snakes, they hiss at me
it's you or me, moth! hand to hand to hand to hand to hand...

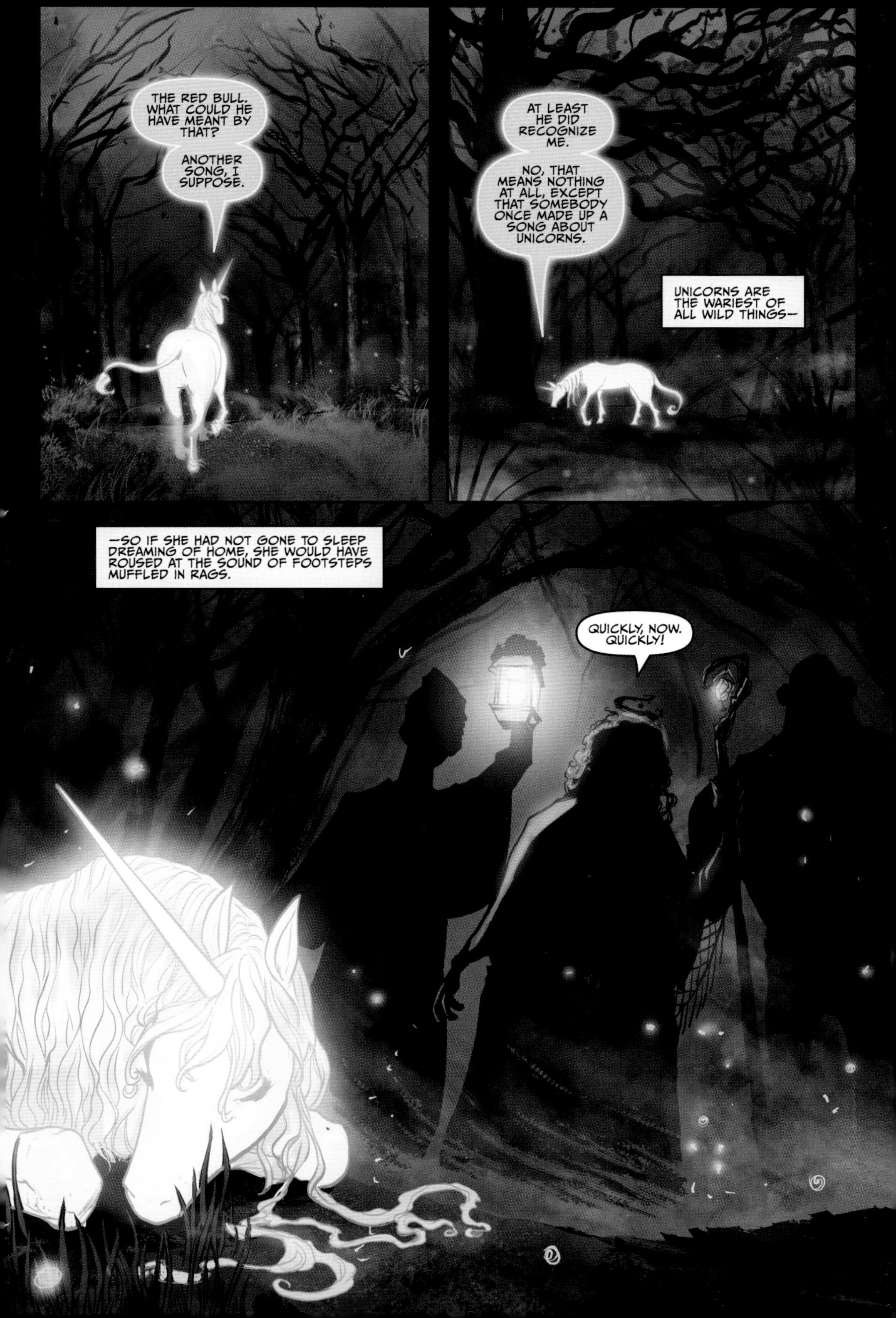
THE RED BULL. WHAT COULD HE HAVE MEANT BY THAT?
ANOTHER SONG, I SUPPOSE.
AT LEAST HE DID RECOGNIZE ME.
NO, THAT MEANS NOTHING AT ALL, EXCEPT THAT SOMEBODY ONCE MADE UP A SONG ABOUT UNICORNS.
UNICORNS ARE THE WARIEST OF ALL WILD THINGS—
—SO IF SHE HAD NOT GONE TO SLEEP DREAMING OF HOME, SHE WOULD HAVE ROUSED AT THE SOUND OF FOOTSTEPS MUFFLED IN RAGS.
QUICKLY, NOW. QUICKLY!

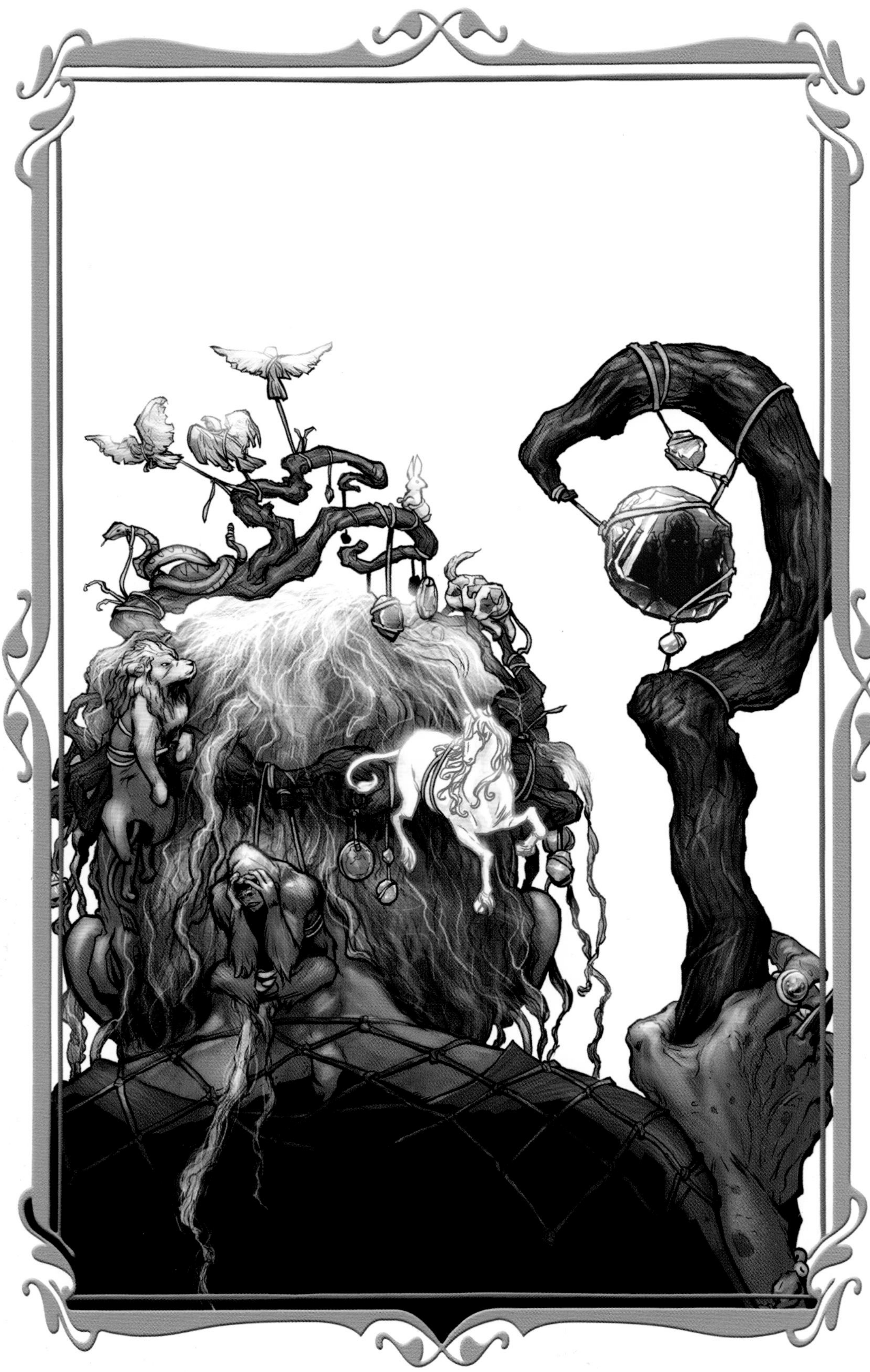

CHAPTER TWO

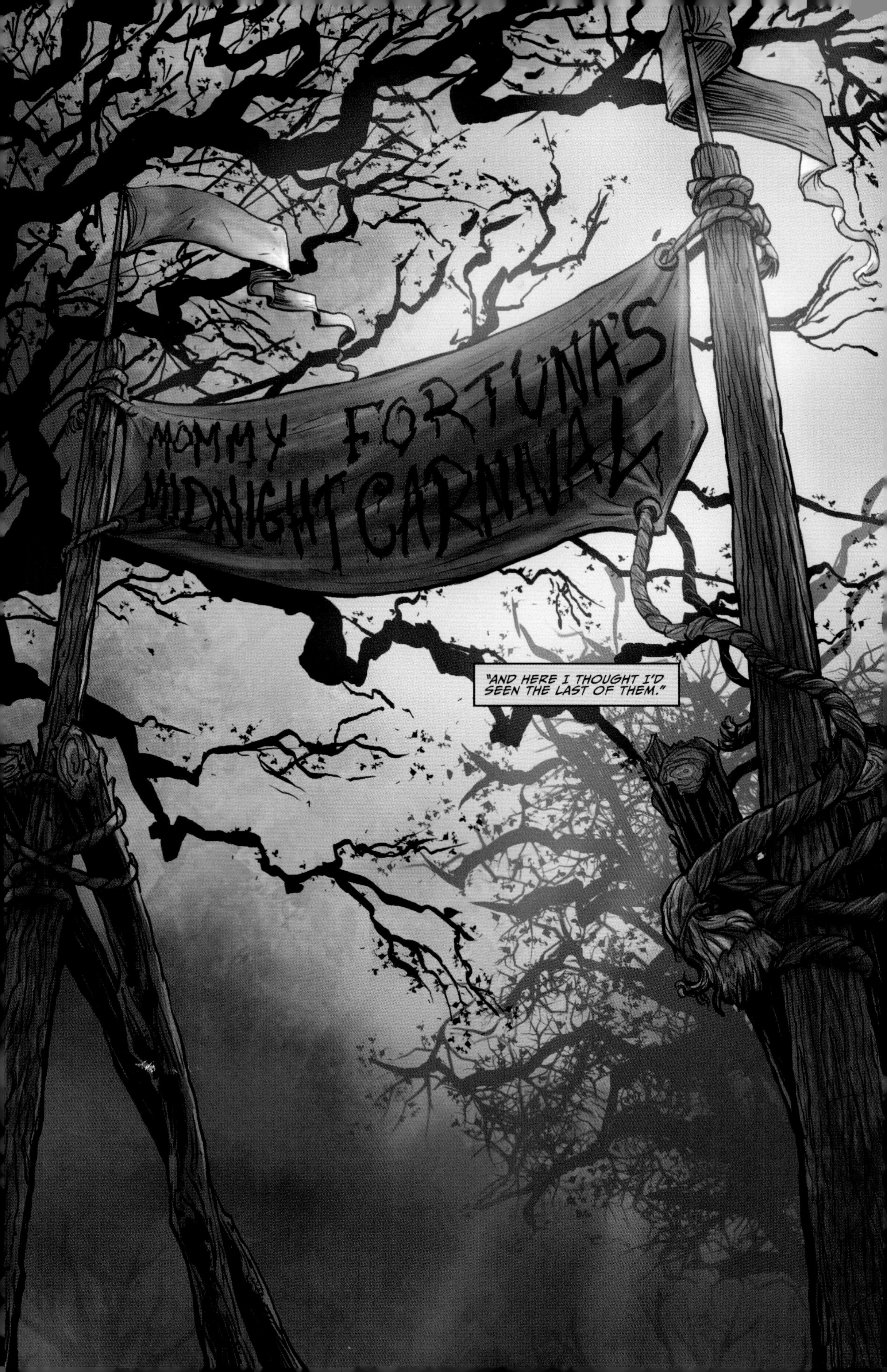
MOMMY FORTUNA'S
MIDNIGHT CARNIVAL
"AND HERE I THOUGHT I'D SEEN THE LAST OF THEM."

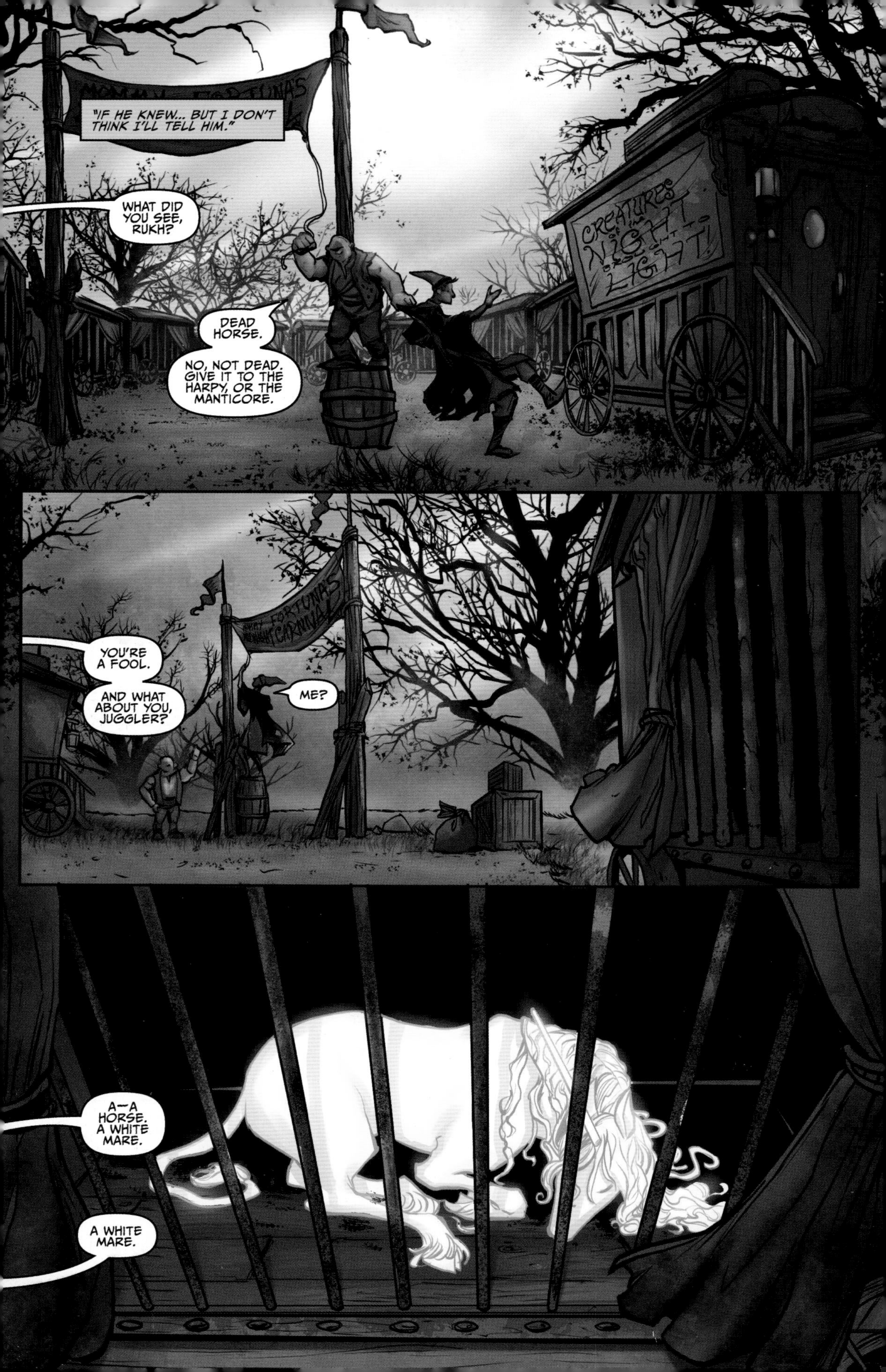

"IF HE KNEW... BUT I DON'T THINK I'LL TELL HIM."
WHAT DID YOU SEE, RUKH?
DEAD HORSE.
NO, NOT DEAD. GIVE IT TO THE HARPY, OR THE MANTICORE.
CREATURES
NIGHT
LIGHT!
FORTUNA'S
CARNIVAL
YOU'RE A FOOL.
AND WHAT ABOUT YOU, JUGGLER?
ME?
A—A HORSE. A WHITE MARE.
A WHITE MARE.

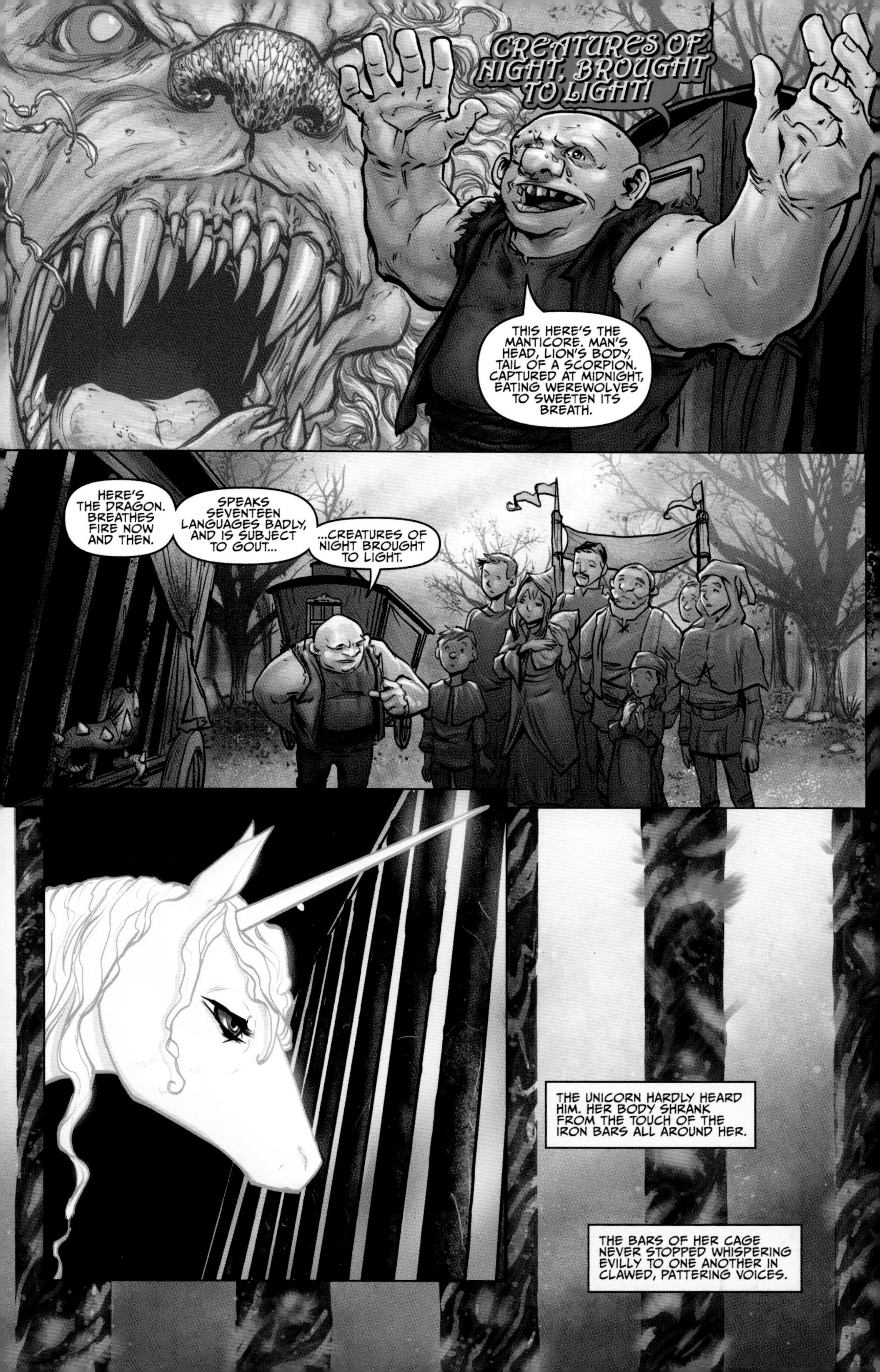
CREATURES OF NIGHT, BROUGHT TO LIGHT!
THIS HERE'S THE MANTICORE. MAN'S HEAD, LION'S BODY, TAIL OF A SCORPION. CAPTURED AT MIDNIGHT, EATING WEREWOLVES TO SWEETEN ITS BREATH.
HERE'S THE DRAGON. BREATHES FIRE NOW AND THEN.
SPEAKS SEVENTEEN LANGUAGES BADLY, AND IS SUBJECT TO GOUT...
...CREATURES OF NIGHT BROUGHT TO LIGHT.
THE UNICORN HARDLY HEARD HIM. HER BODY SHRANK FROM THE TOUCH OF THE IRON BARS ALL AROUND HER.
THE BARS OF HER CAGE NEVER STOPPED WHISPERING EVILLY TO ONE ANOTHER IN CLAWED, PATTERING VOICES.

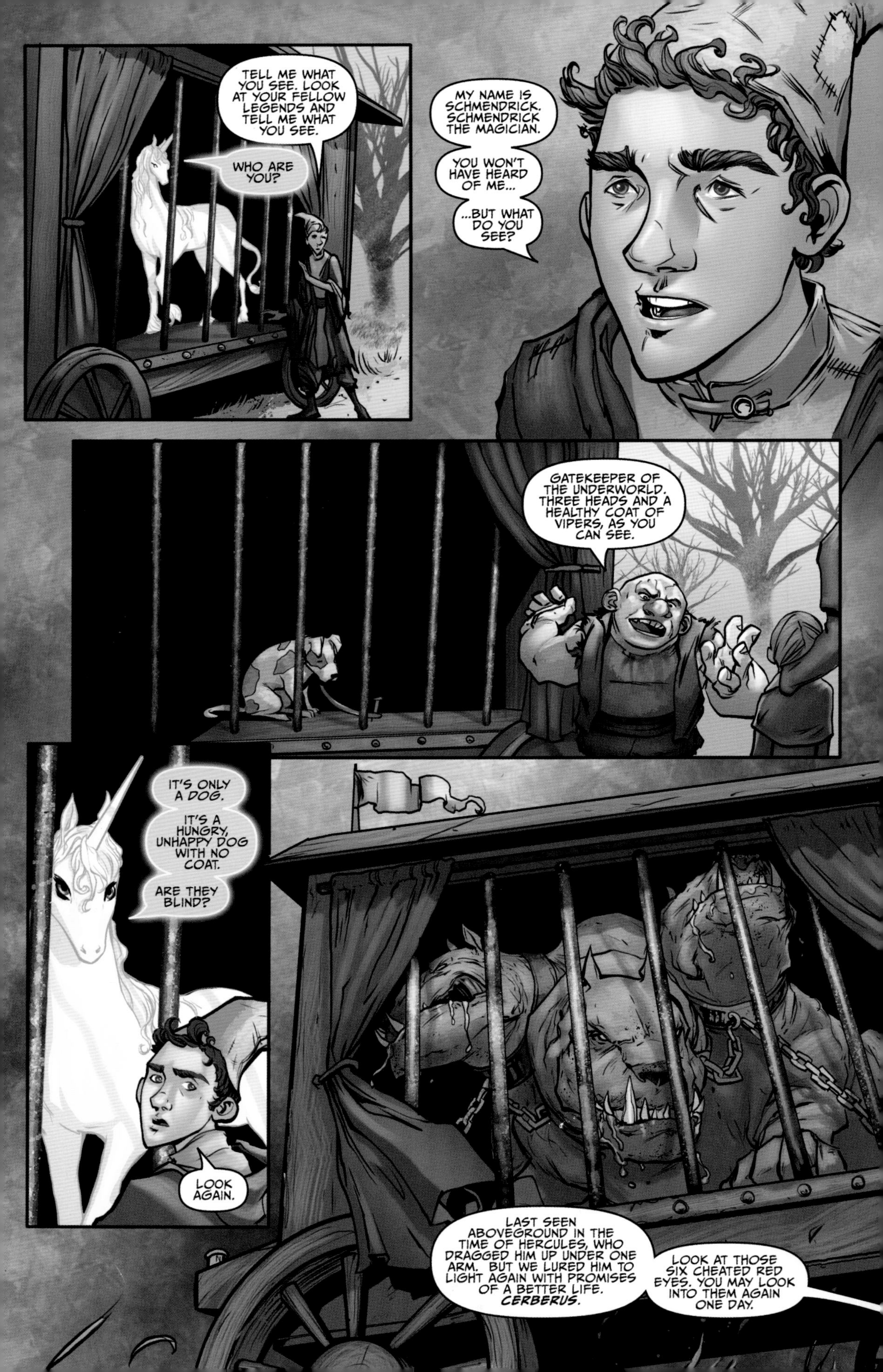
TELL ME WHAT YOU SEE. LOOK AT YOUR FELLOW LEGENDS AND TELL ME WHAT YOU SEE.
WHO ARE YOU?
MY NAME IS SCHMENDRICK. SCHMENDRICK THE MAGICIAN.
YOU WON'T HAVE HEARD OF ME...
...BUT WHAT DO YOU SEE?
GATEKEEPER OF THE UNDERWORLD. THREE HEADS AND A HEALTHY COAT OF VIPERS, AS YOU CAN SEE.
IT'S ONLY A DOG.
IT'S A HUNGRY, UNHAPPY DOG WITH NO COAT.
ARE THEY BLIND?
LOOK AGAIN.
LAST SEEN ABOVEGROUND IN THE TIME OF HERCULES, WHO DRAGGED HIM UP UNDER ONE ARM. BUT WE LURED HIM TO LIGHT AGAIN WITH PROMISES OF A BETTER LIFE. *CERBERUS*.
LOOK AT THOSE SIX CHEATED RED EYES. YOU MAY LOOK INTO THEM AGAIN ONE DAY.

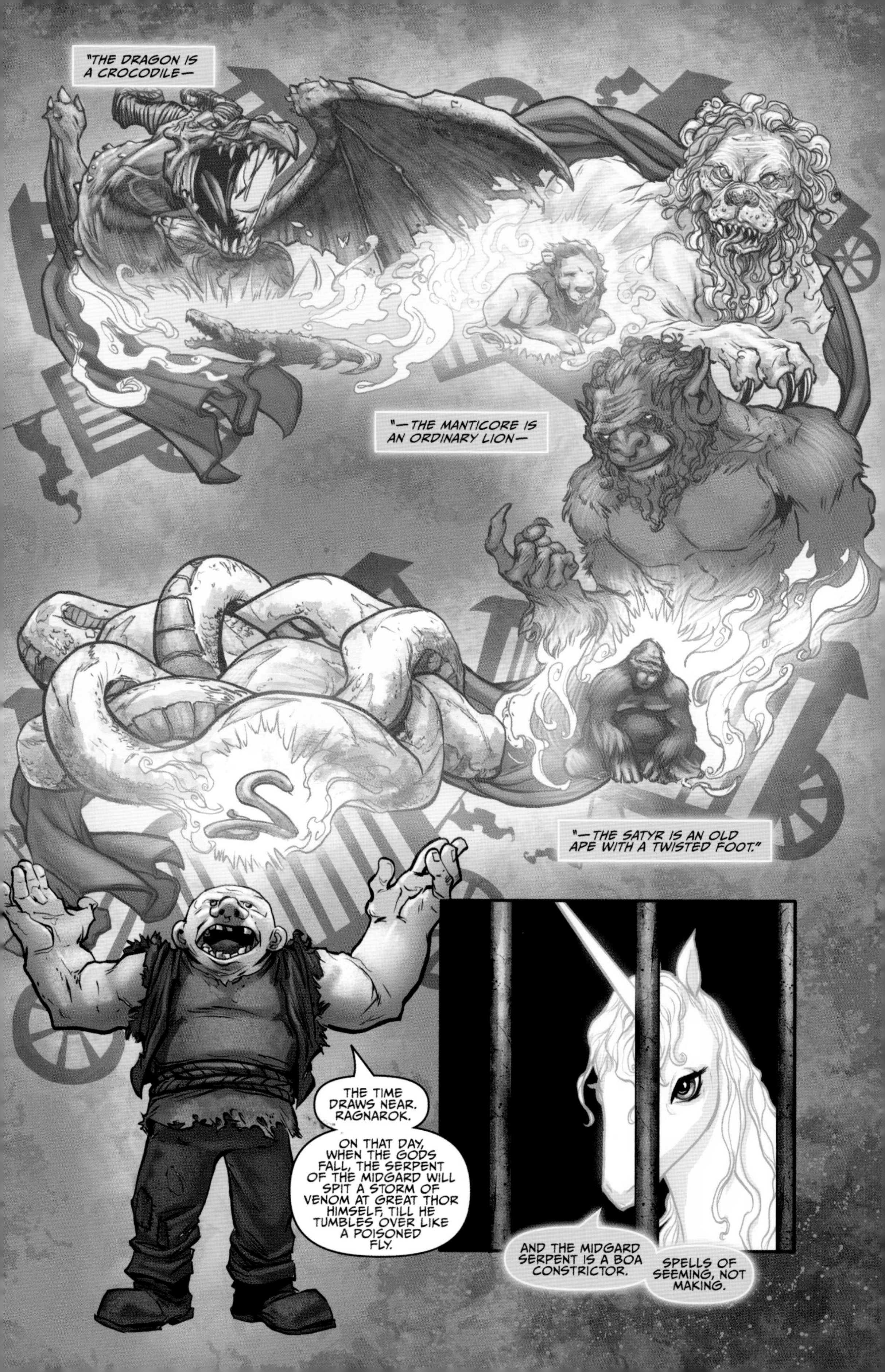
"THE DRAGON IS A CROCODILE—
"—THE MANTICORE IS AN ORDINARY LION—
"—THE SATYR IS AN OLD APE WITH A TWISTED FOOT."
THE TIME DRAWS NEAR. RAGNAROK.
ON THAT DAY, WHEN THE GODS FALL, THE SERPENT OF THE MIDGARD WILL SPIT A STORM OF VENOM AT GREAT THOR HIMSELF, TILL HE TUMBLES OVER LIKE A POISONED FLY.
AND THE MIDGARD SERPENT IS A BOA CONSTRICTOR.
SPELLS OF SEEMING, NOT MAKING.

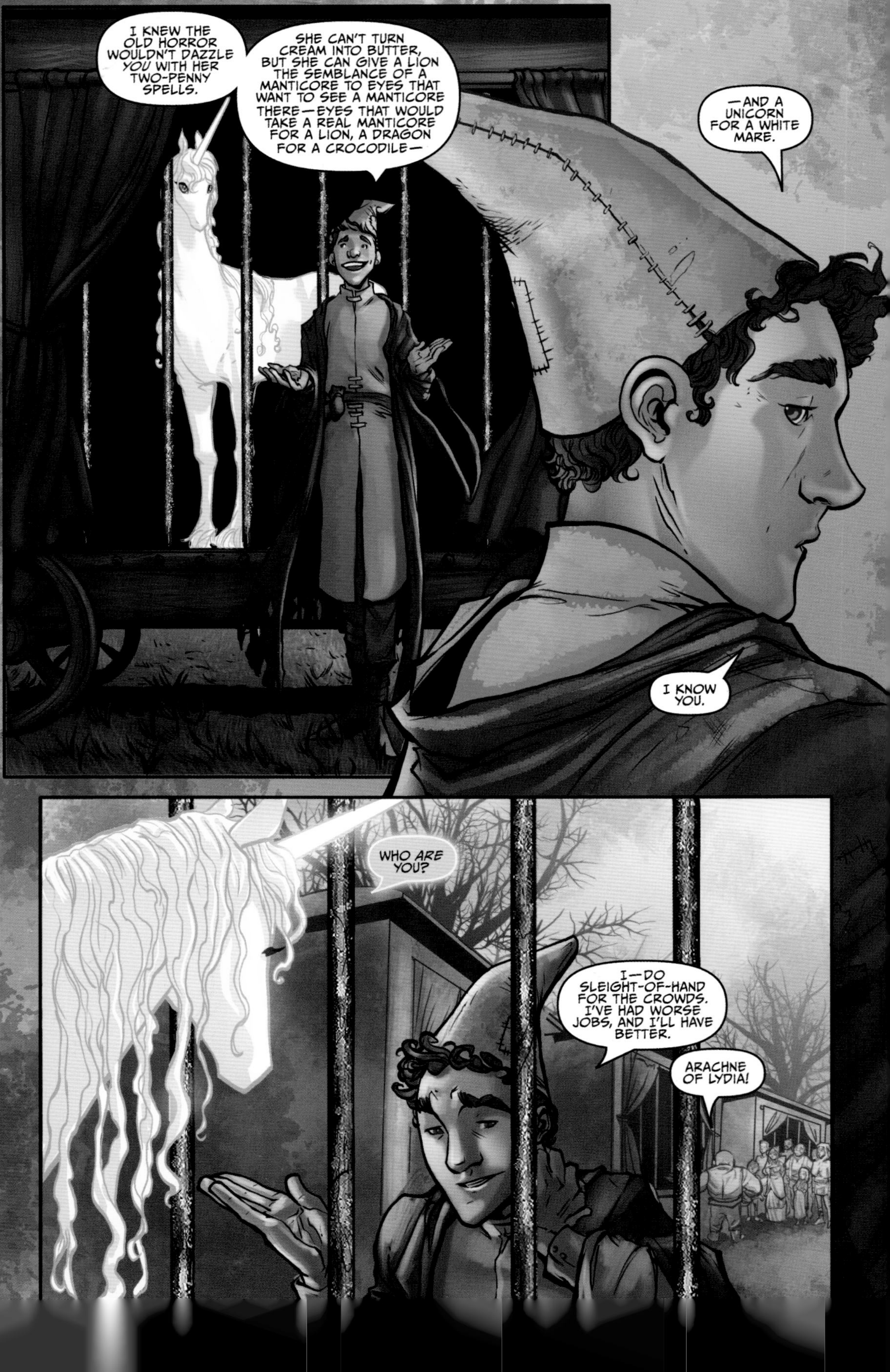
I KNEW THE OLD HORROR WOULDN'T DAZZLE *YOU* WITH HER TWO-PENNY SPELLS.
SHE CAN'T TURN CREAM INTO BUTTER, BUT SHE CAN GIVE A LION THE SEMBLANCE OF A MANTICORE TO EYES THAT WANT TO SEE A MANTICORE THERE—EYES THAT WOULD TAKE A REAL MANTICORE FOR A LION, A DRAGON FOR A CROCODILE—
—AND A UNICORN FOR A WHITE MARE.
I KNOW YOU.
WHO *ARE* YOU?
I—DO SLEIGHT-OF-HAND FOR THE CROWDS. I'VE HAD WORSE JOBS, AND I'LL HAVE BETTER.
ARACHNE OF LYDIA!

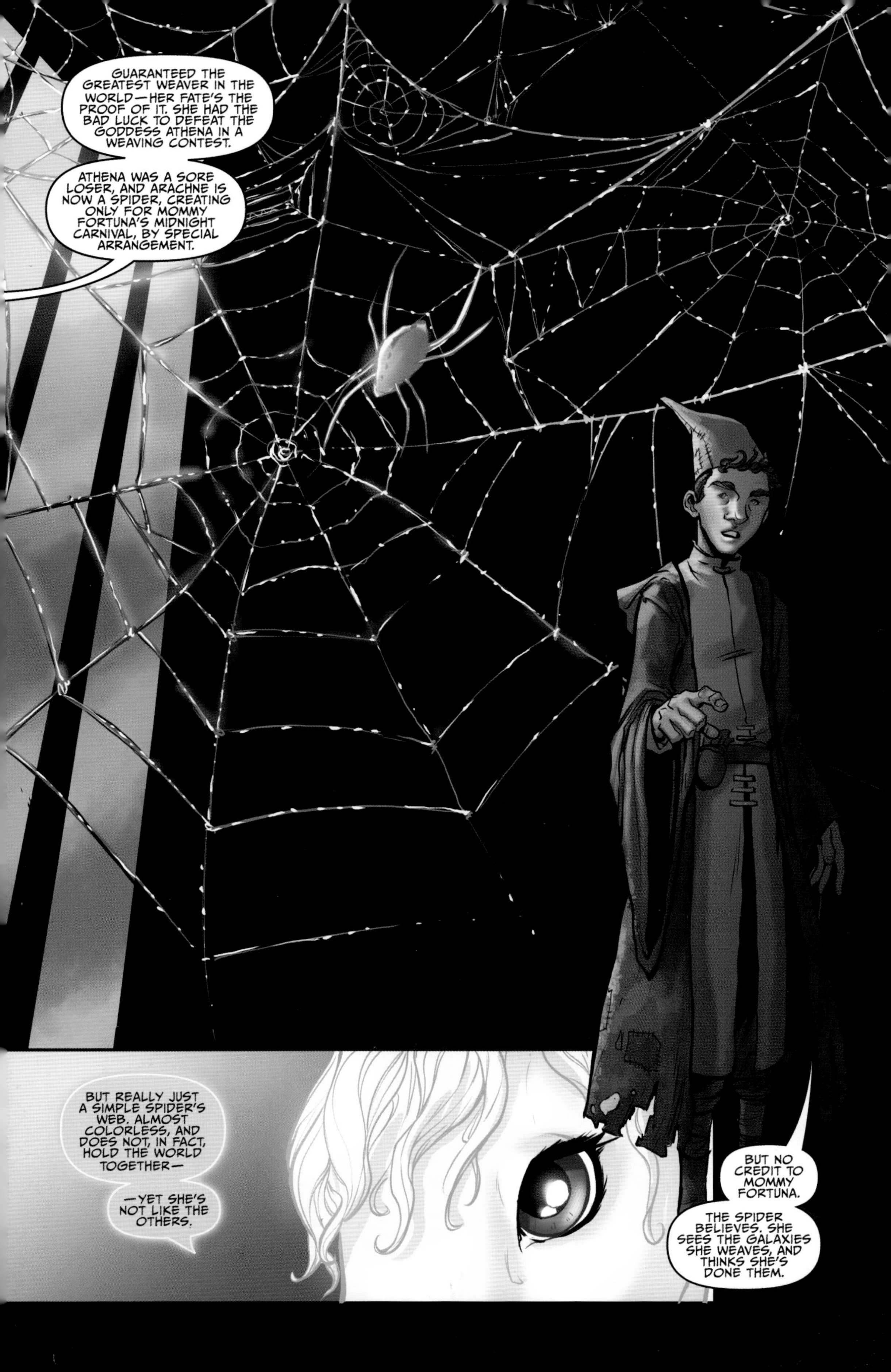

GUARANTEED THE GREATEST WEAVER IN THE WORLD—HER FATE'S THE PROOF OF IT. SHE HAD THE BAD LUCK TO DEFEAT THE GODDESS ATHENA IN A WEAVING CONTEST.
ATHENA WAS A SORE LOSER, AND ARACHNE IS NOW A SPIDER, CREATING ONLY FOR MOMMY FORTUNA'S MIDNIGHT CARNIVAL, BY SPECIAL ARRANGEMENT.
BUT REALLY JUST A SIMPLE SPIDER'S WEB. ALMOST COLORLESS, AND DOES NOT, IN FACT, HOLD THE WORLD TOGETHER—
—YET SHE'S NOT LIKE THE OTHERS.
BUT NO CREDIT TO MOMMY FORTUNA.
THE SPIDER BELIEVES. SHE SEES THE GALAXIES SHE WEAVES, AND THINKS SHE'S DONE THEM.

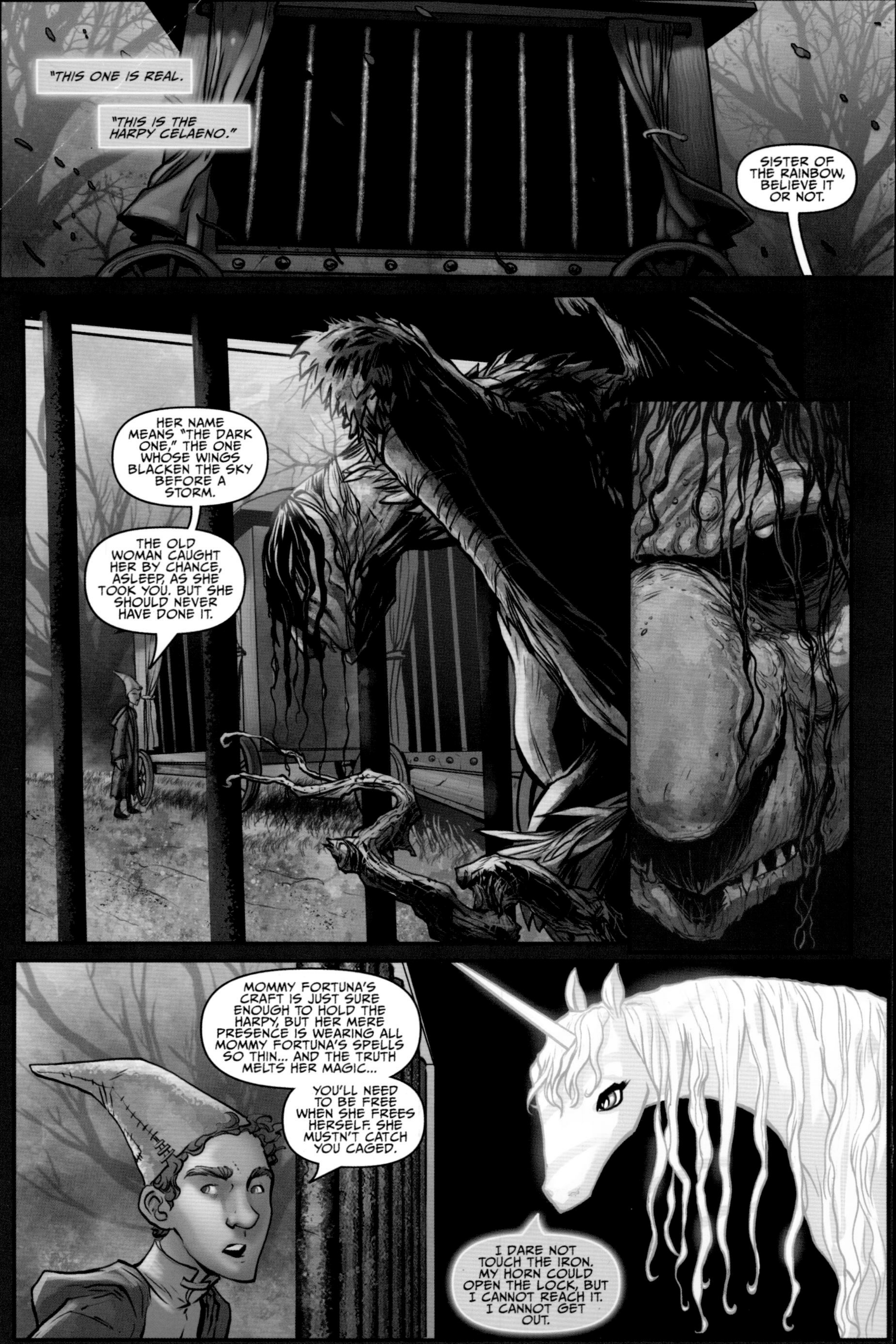
"THIS ONE IS REAL.
"THIS IS THE HARPY CELAENO."
SISTER OF THE RAINBOW, BELIEVE IT OR NOT.
HER NAME MEANS "THE DARK ONE," THE ONE WHOSE WINGS BLACKEN THE SKY BEFORE A STORM.
THE OLD WOMAN CAUGHT HER BY CHANCE, ASLEEP, AS SHE TOOK YOU. BUT SHE SHOULD NEVER HAVE DONE IT.
MOMMY FORTUNA'S CRAFT IS JUST SURE ENOUGH TO HOLD THE HARPY, BUT HER MERE PRESENCE IS WEARING ALL MOMMY FORTUNA'S SPELLS SO THIN... AND THE TRUTH MELTS HER MAGIC...
YOU'LL NEED TO BE FREE WHEN SHE FREES HERSELF. SHE MUSTN'T CATCH YOU CAGED.
I DARE NOT TOUCH THE IRON. MY HORN COULD OPEN THE LOCK, BUT I CANNOT REACH IT. I CANNOT GET OUT.

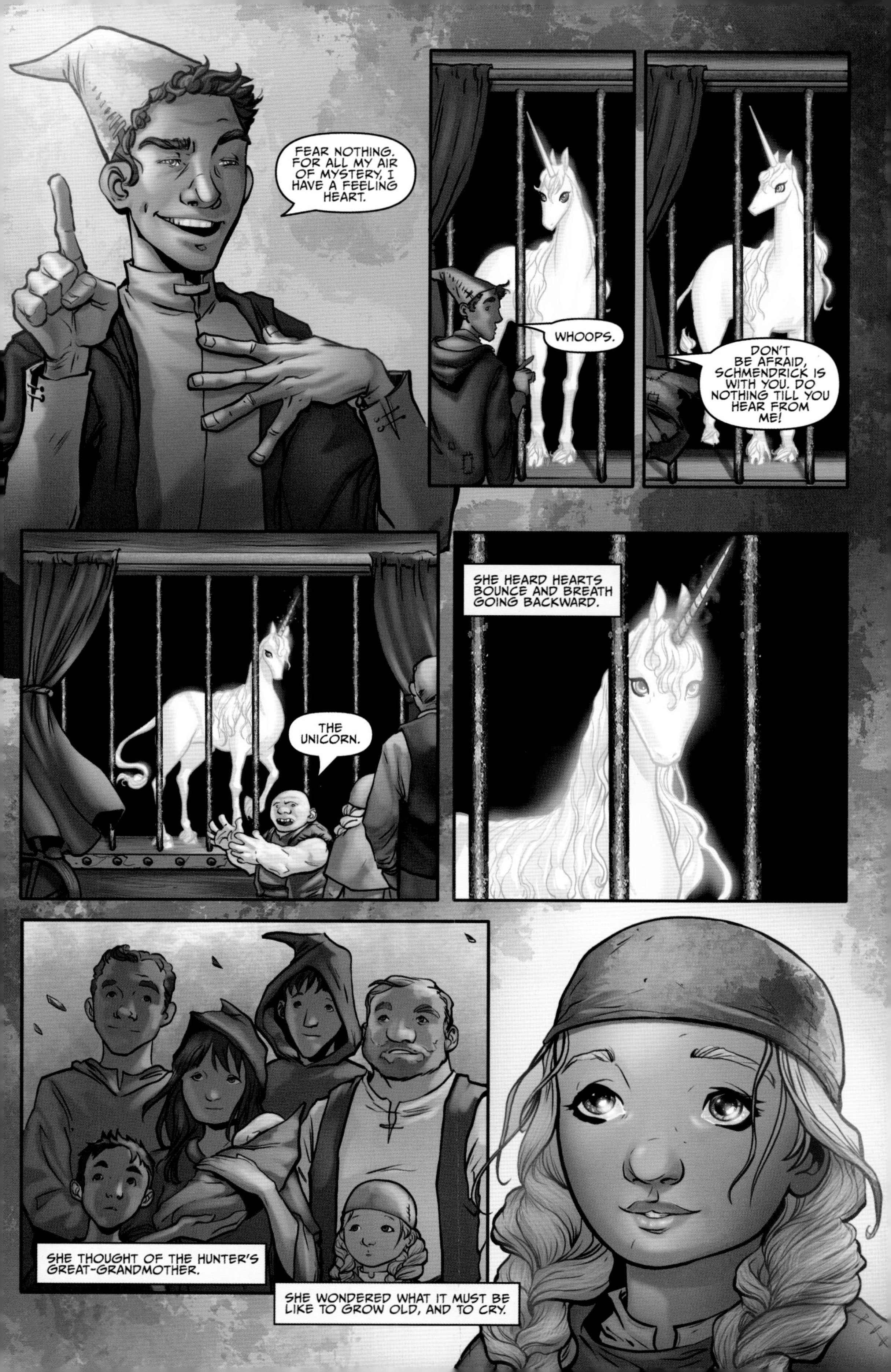
FEAR NOTHING. FOR ALL MY AIR OF MYSTERY, I HAVE A FEELING HEART.
WHOOPS.
DON'T BE AFRAID, SCHMENDRICK IS WITH YOU. DO NOTHING TILL YOU HEAR FROM ME!
THE UNICORN.
SHE HEARD HEARTS BOUNCE AND BREATH GOING BACKWARD.
SHE THOUGHT OF THE HUNTER'S GREAT-GRANDMOTHER.
SHE WONDERED WHAT IT MUST BE LIKE TO GROW OLD, AND TO CRY.

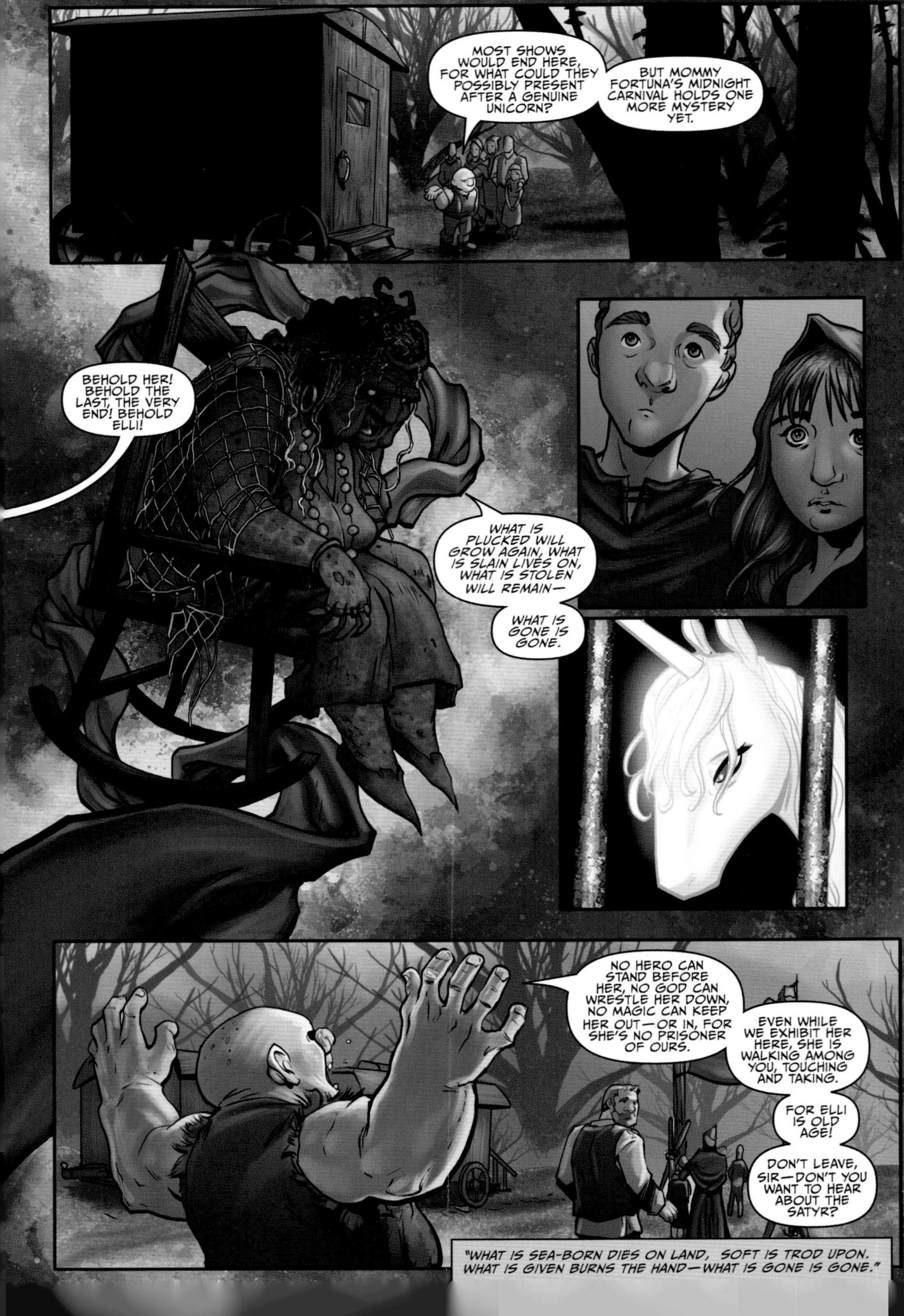
MOST SHOWS WOULD END HERE, FOR WHAT COULD THEY POSSIBLY PRESENT AFTER A GENUINE UNICORN?
BUT MOMMY FORTUNA'S MIDNIGHT CARNIVAL HOLDS ONE MORE MYSTERY YET.
BEHOLD HER! BEHOLD THE LAST, THE VERY END! BEHOLD ELLI!
WHAT IS PLUCKED WILL GROW AGAIN, WHAT IS SLAIN LIVES ON, WHAT IS STOLEN WILL REMAIN—
WHAT IS GONE IS GONE.
NO HERO CAN STAND BEFORE HER, NO GOD CAN WRESTLE HER DOWN, NO MAGIC CAN KEEP HER OUT—OR IN, FOR SHE'S NO PRISONER OF OURS.
EVEN WHILE WE EXHIBIT HER HERE, SHE IS WALKING AMONG YOU, TOUCHING AND TAKING.
FOR ELLI IS OLD AGE!
DON'T LEAVE, SIR—DON'T YOU WANT TO HEAR ABOUT THE SATYR?
"WHAT IS SEA-BORN DIES ON LAND, SOFT IS TROD UPON. WHAT IS GIVEN BURNS THE HAND—WHAT IS GONE IS GONE."

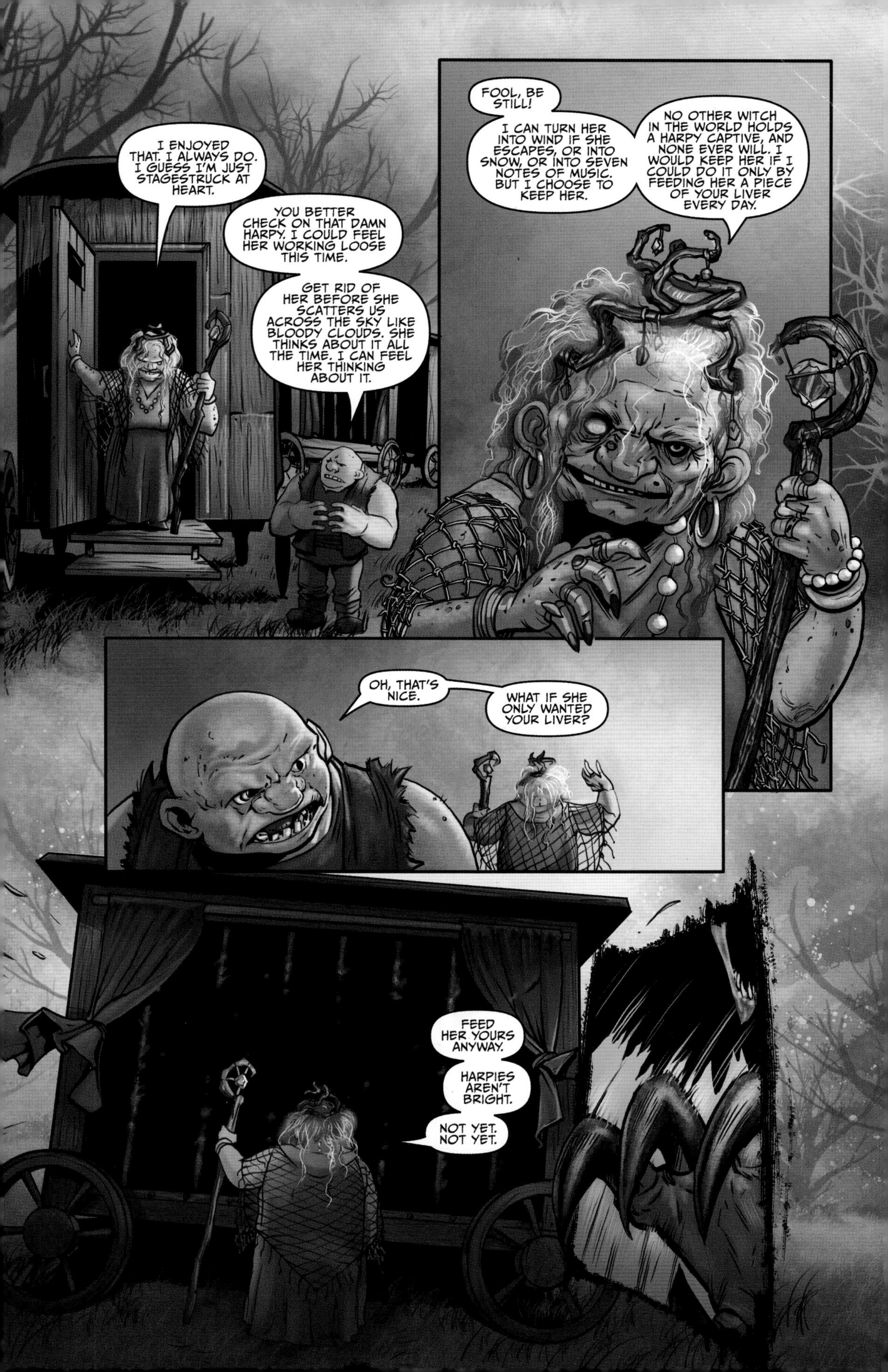
I ENJOYED THAT. I ALWAYS DO. I GUESS I'M JUST STAGESTRUCK AT HEART.
YOU BETTER CHECK ON THAT DAMN HARPY. I COULD FEEL HER WORKING LOOSE THIS TIME.
GET RID OF HER BEFORE SHE SCATTERS US ACROSS THE SKY LIKE BLOODY CLOUDS. SHE THINKS ABOUT IT ALL THE TIME. I CAN FEEL HER THINKING ABOUT IT.
FOOL, BE STILL!
I CAN TURN HER INTO WIND IF SHE ESCAPES, OR INTO SNOW, OR INTO SEVEN NOTES OF MUSIC. BUT I CHOOSE TO KEEP HER.
NO OTHER WITCH IN THE WORLD HOLDS A HARPY CAPTIVE, AND NONE EVER WILL. I WOULD KEEP HER IF I COULD DO IT ONLY BY FEEDING HER A PIECE OF YOUR LIVER EVERY DAY.
OH, THAT'S NICE.
WHAT IF SHE ONLY WANTED YOUR LIVER?
FEED HER YOURS ANYWAY.
HARPIES AREN'T BRIGHT.
NOT YET. NOT YET.

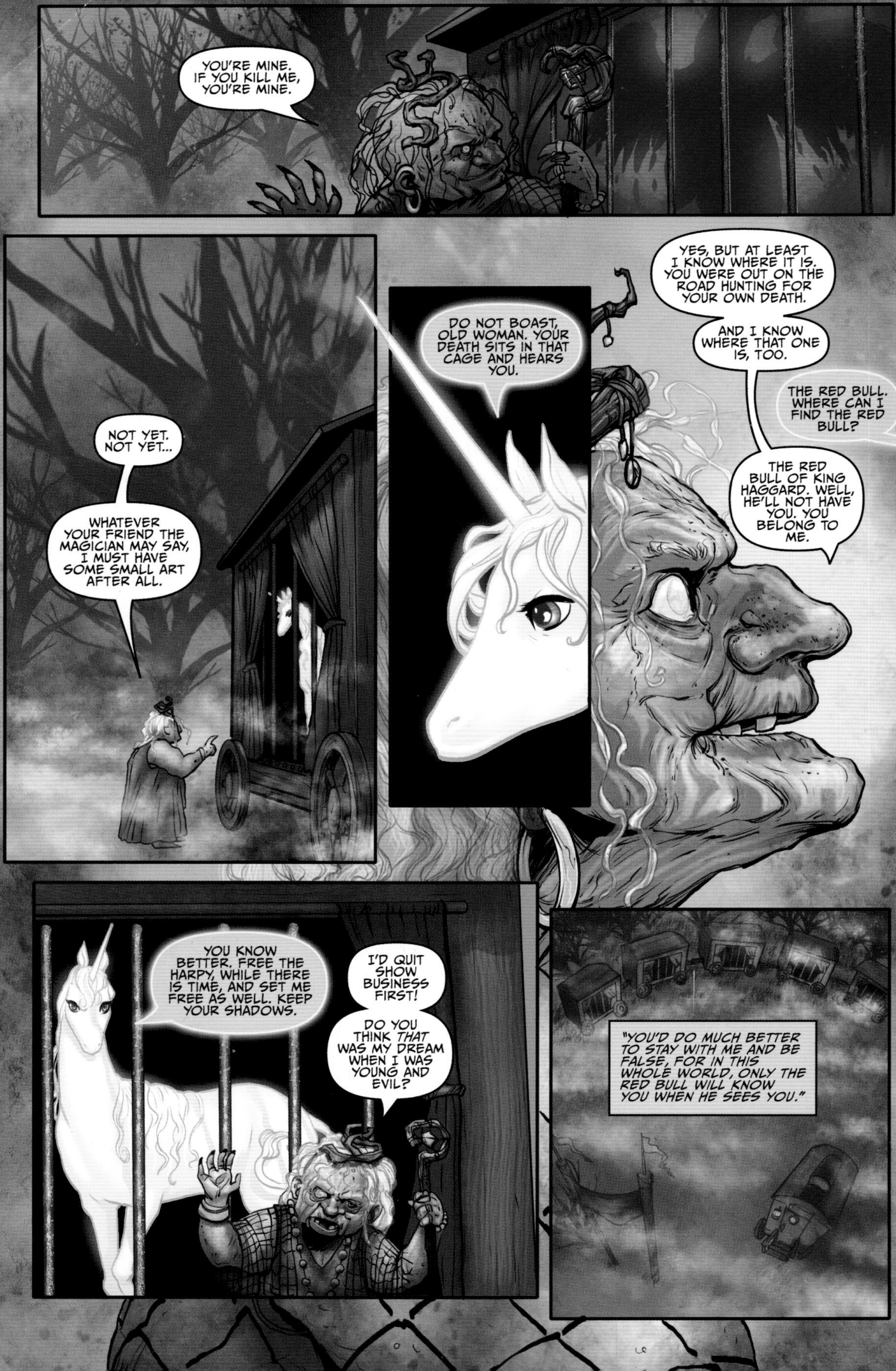
YOU'RE MINE. IF YOU KILL ME, YOU'RE MINE.
NOT YET. NOT YET...
WHATEVER YOUR FRIEND THE MAGICIAN MAY SAY, I MUST HAVE SOME SMALL ART AFTER ALL.
DO NOT BOAST, OLD WOMAN. YOUR DEATH SITS IN THAT CAGE AND HEARS YOU.
YES, BUT AT LEAST I KNOW WHERE IT IS. YOU WERE OUT ON THE ROAD HUNTING FOR YOUR OWN DEATH.
AND I KNOW WHERE THAT ONE IS, TOO.
THE RED BULL. WHERE CAN I FIND THE RED BULL?
THE RED BULL OF KING HAGGARD. WELL, HE'LL NOT HAVE YOU. YOU BELONG TO ME.
YOU KNOW BETTER. FREE THE HARPY, WHILE THERE IS TIME, AND SET ME FREE AS WELL. KEEP YOUR SHADOWS.
I'D QUIT SHOW BUSINESS FIRST!
DO YOU THINK *THAT* WAS MY DREAM WHEN I WAS YOUNG AND EVIL?
"YOU'D DO MUCH BETTER TO STAY WITH ME AND BE FALSE, FOR IN THIS WHOLE WORLD, ONLY THE RED BULL WILL KNOW YOU WHEN HE SEES YOU."

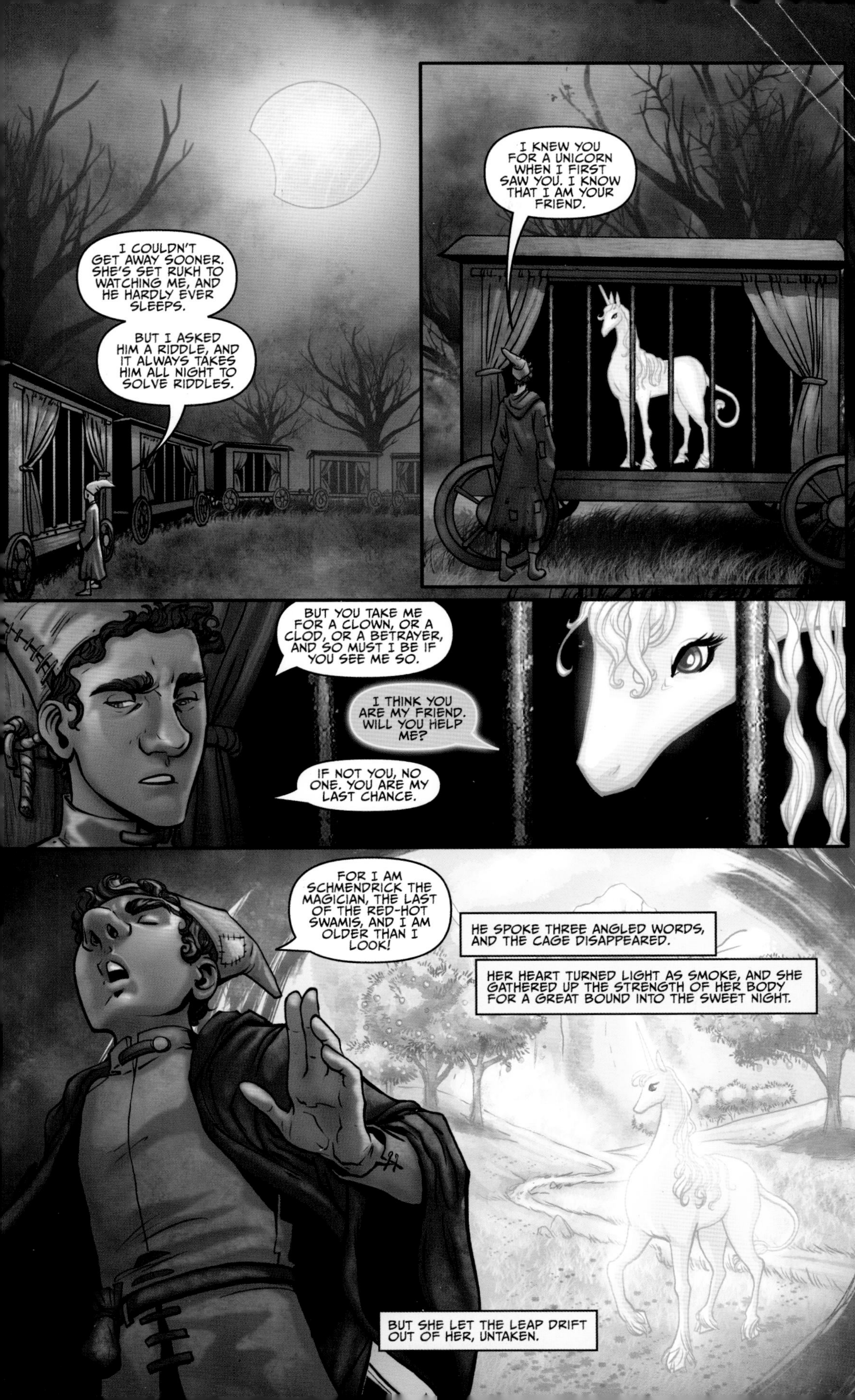
I COULDN'T GET AWAY SOONER. SHE'S SET RUKH TO WATCHING ME, AND HE HARDLY EVER SLEEPS.
BUT I ASKED HIM A RIDDLE, AND IT ALWAYS TAKES HIM ALL NIGHT TO SOLVE RIDDLES.
I KNEW YOU FOR A UNICORN WHEN I FIRST SAW YOU. I KNOW THAT I AM YOUR FRIEND.
BUT YOU TAKE ME FOR A CLOWN, OR A CLOD, OR A BETRAYER, AND SO MUST I BE IF YOU SEE ME SO.
I THINK YOU ARE MY FRIEND. WILL YOU HELP ME?
IF NOT YOU, NO ONE. YOU ARE MY LAST CHANCE.
FOR I AM SCHMENDRICK THE MAGICIAN, THE LAST OF THE RED-HOT SWAMIS, AND I AM OLDER THAN I LOOK!
HE SPOKE THREE ANGLED WORDS, AND THE CAGE DISAPPEARED.
HER HEART TURNED LIGHT AS SMOKE, AND SHE GATHERED UP THE STRENGTH OF HER BODY FOR A GREAT BOUND INTO THE SWEET NIGHT.
BUT SHE LET THE LEAP DRIFT OUT OF HER, UNTAKEN.

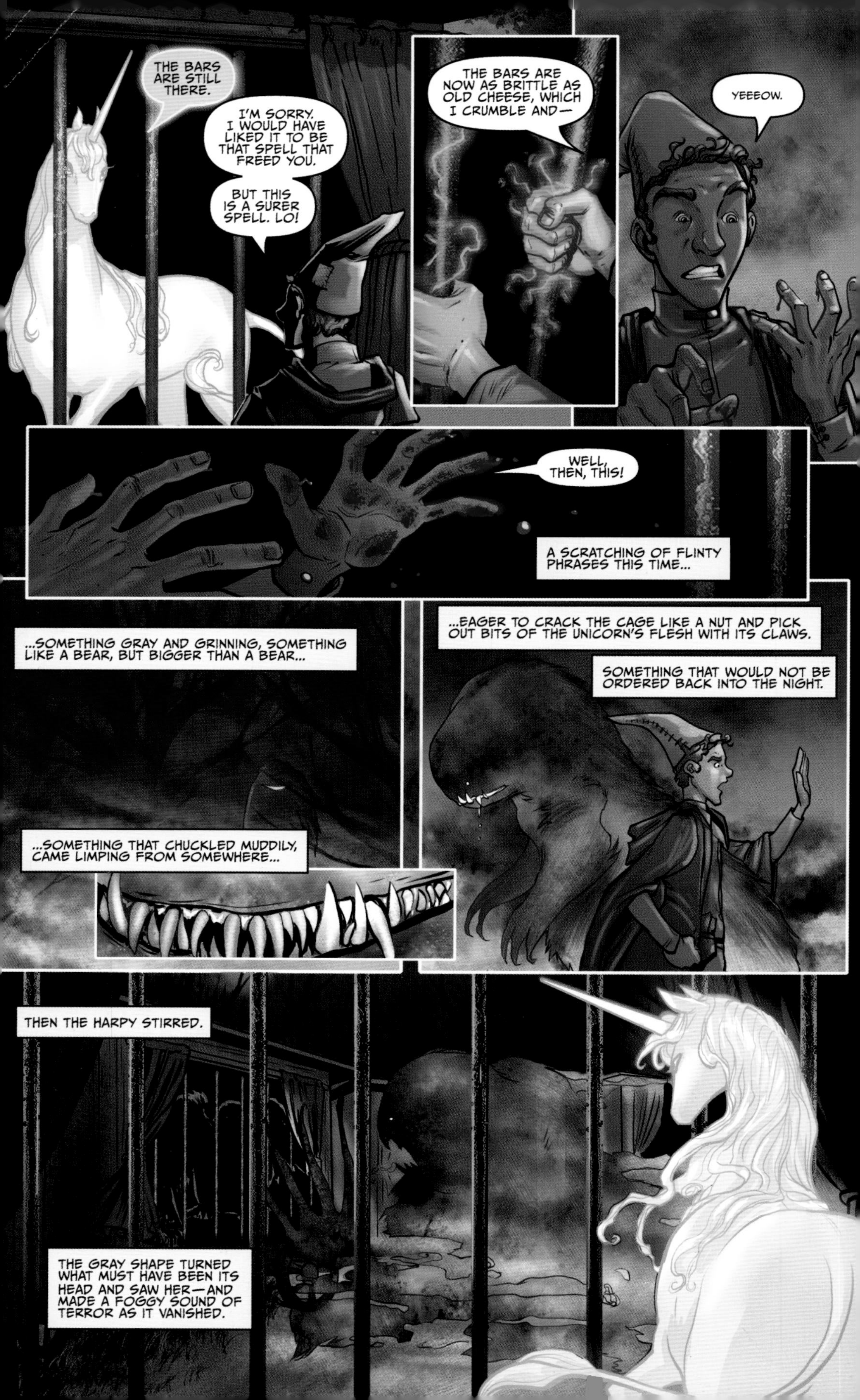
THE BARS ARE STILL THERE.
I'M SORRY. I WOULD HAVE LIKED IT TO BE THAT SPELL THAT FREED YOU.
BUT THIS IS A SURER SPELL. LO!
THE BARS ARE NOW AS BRITTLE AS OLD CHEESE, WHICH I CRUMBLE AND—
YEEEOW.
WELL, THEN, THIS!
A SCRATCHING OF FLINTY PHRASES THIS TIME...
...SOMETHING GRAY AND GRINNING, SOMETHING LIKE A BEAR, BUT BIGGER THAN A BEAR...
...SOMETHING THAT CHUCKLED MUDDILY, CAME LIMPING FROM SOMEWHERE...
...EAGER TO CRACK THE CAGE LIKE A NUT AND PICK OUT BITS OF THE UNICORN'S FLESH WITH ITS CLAWS.
SOMETHING THAT WOULD NOT BE ORDERED BACK INTO THE NIGHT.
THEN THE HARPY STIRRED.
THE GRAY SHAPE TURNED WHAT MUST HAVE BEEN ITS HEAD AND SAW HER—AND MADE A FOGGY SOUND OF TERROR AS IT VANISHED.

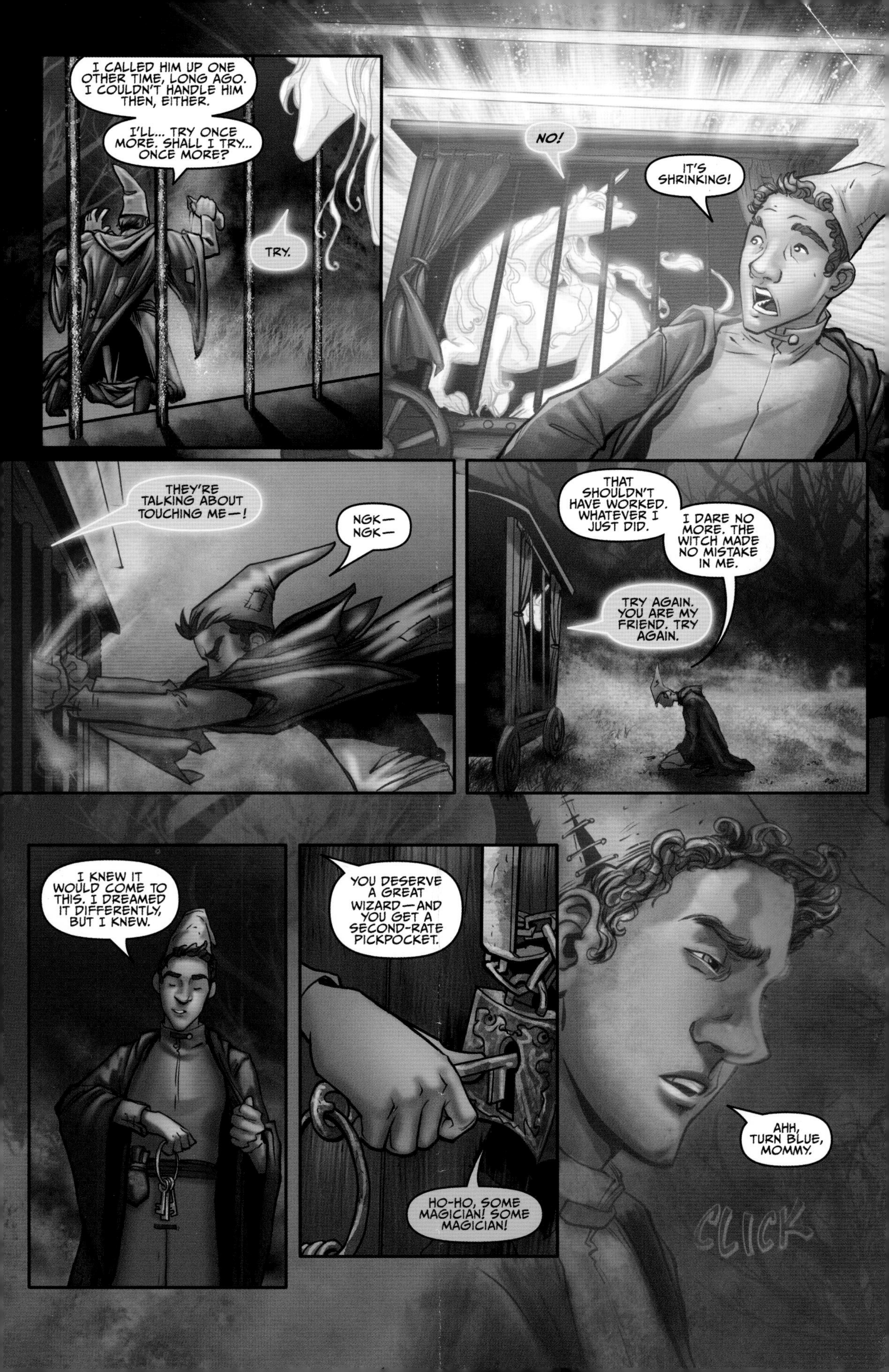

I CALLED HIM UP ONE OTHER TIME, LONG AGO. I COULDN'T HANDLE HIM THEN, EITHER.
I'LL... TRY ONCE MORE. SHALL I TRY... ONCE MORE?
TRY.
NO!
IT'S SHRINKING!
THEY'RE TALKING ABOUT TOUCHING ME—!
NGK— NGK—
THAT SHOULDN'T HAVE WORKED. WHATEVER I JUST DID.
I DARE NO MORE. THE WITCH MADE NO MISTAKE IN ME.
TRY AGAIN. YOU ARE MY FRIEND. TRY AGAIN.
I KNEW IT WOULD COME TO THIS. I DREAMED IT DIFFERENTLY, BUT I KNEW.
YOU DESERVE A GREAT WIZARD—AND YOU GET A SECOND-RATE PICKPOCKET.
HO-HO, SOME MAGICIAN! SOME MAGICIAN!
AHH, TURN BLUE, MOMMY.
CLICK

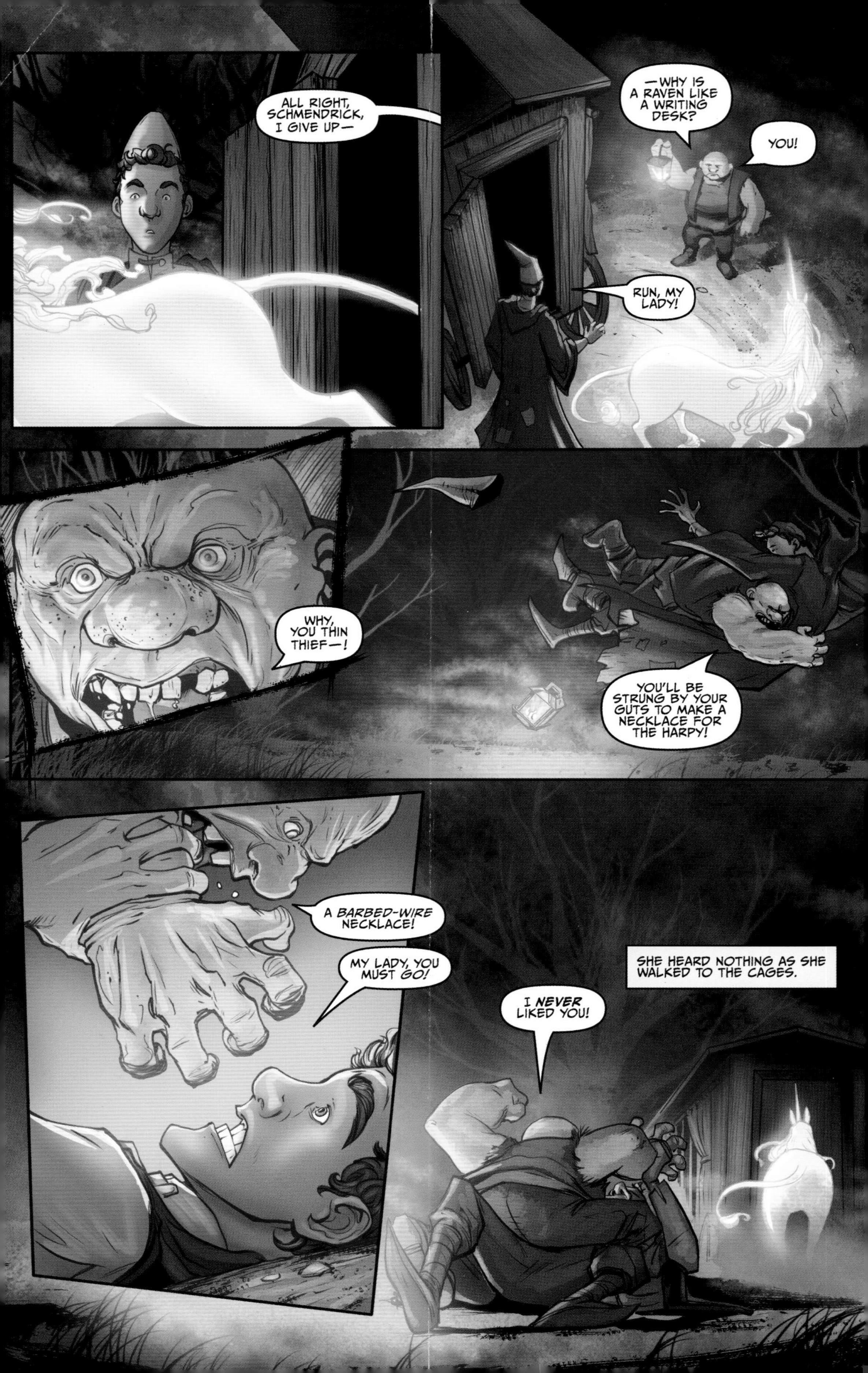
ALL RIGHT, SCHMENDRICK, I GIVE UP—
—WHY IS A RAVEN LIKE A WRITING DESK?
YOU!
RUN, MY LADY!
WHY, YOU THIN THIEF—!
YOU'LL BE STRUNG BY YOUR GUTS TO MAKE A NECKLACE FOR THE HARPY!
A *BARBED-WIRE* NECKLACE!
MY LADY, YOU MUST *GO*!
I ***NEVER*** LIKED YOU!
SHE HEARD NOTHING AS SHE WALKED TO THE CAGES.

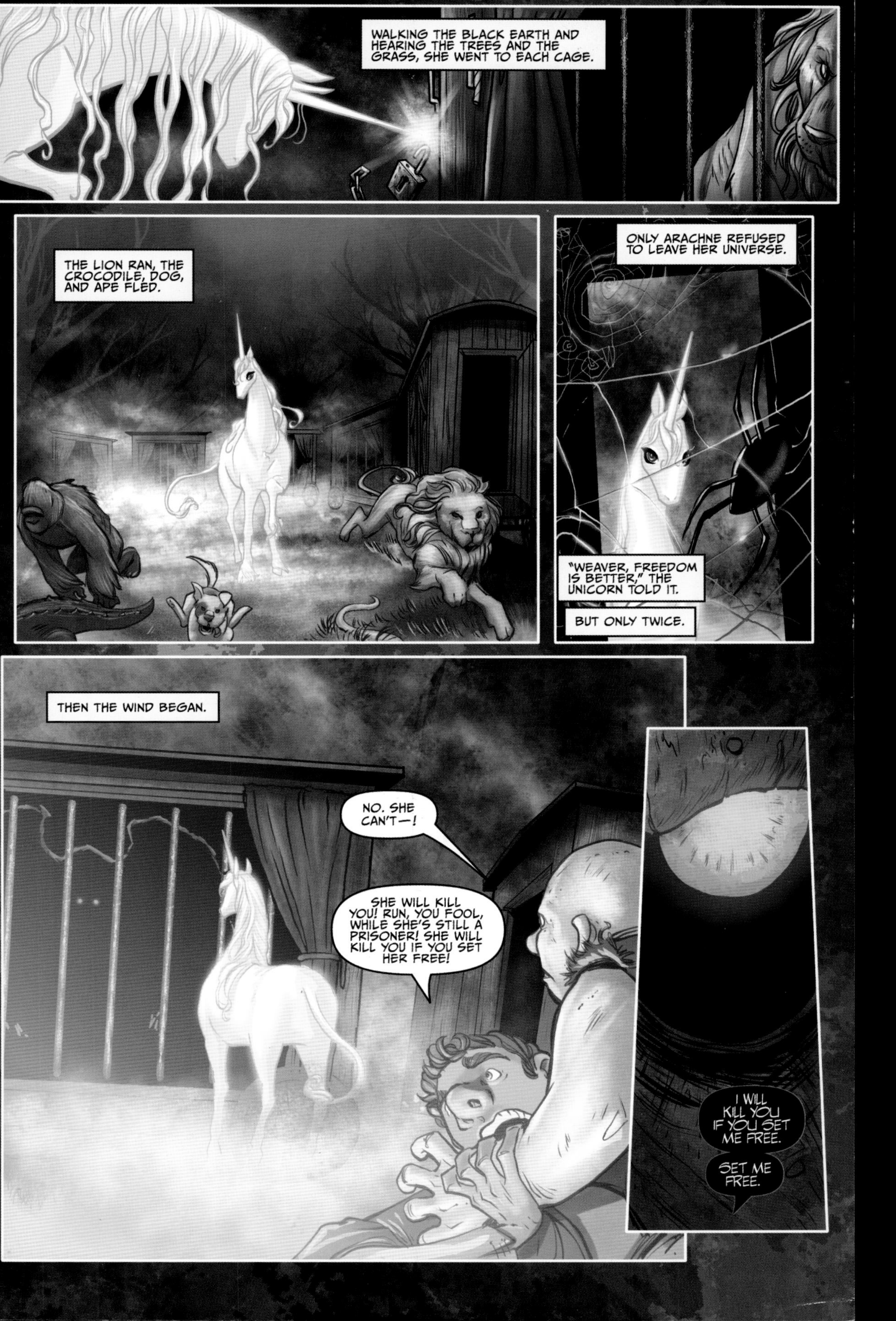
WALKING THE BLACK EARTH AND HEARING THE TREES AND THE GRASS, SHE WENT TO EACH CAGE.
THE LION RAN, THE CROCODILE, DOG, AND APE FLED.
ONLY ARACHNE REFUSED TO LEAVE HER UNIVERSE.
"WEAVER, FREEDOM IS BETTER," THE UNICORN TOLD IT.
BUT ONLY TWICE.
THEN THE WIND BEGAN.
NO. SHE CAN'T—!
SHE WILL KILL YOU! RUN, YOU FOOL, WHILE SHE'S STILL A PRISONER! SHE WILL KILL YOU IF YOU SET HER FREE!
I WILL KILL YOU IF YOU SET ME FREE.
SET ME FREE.

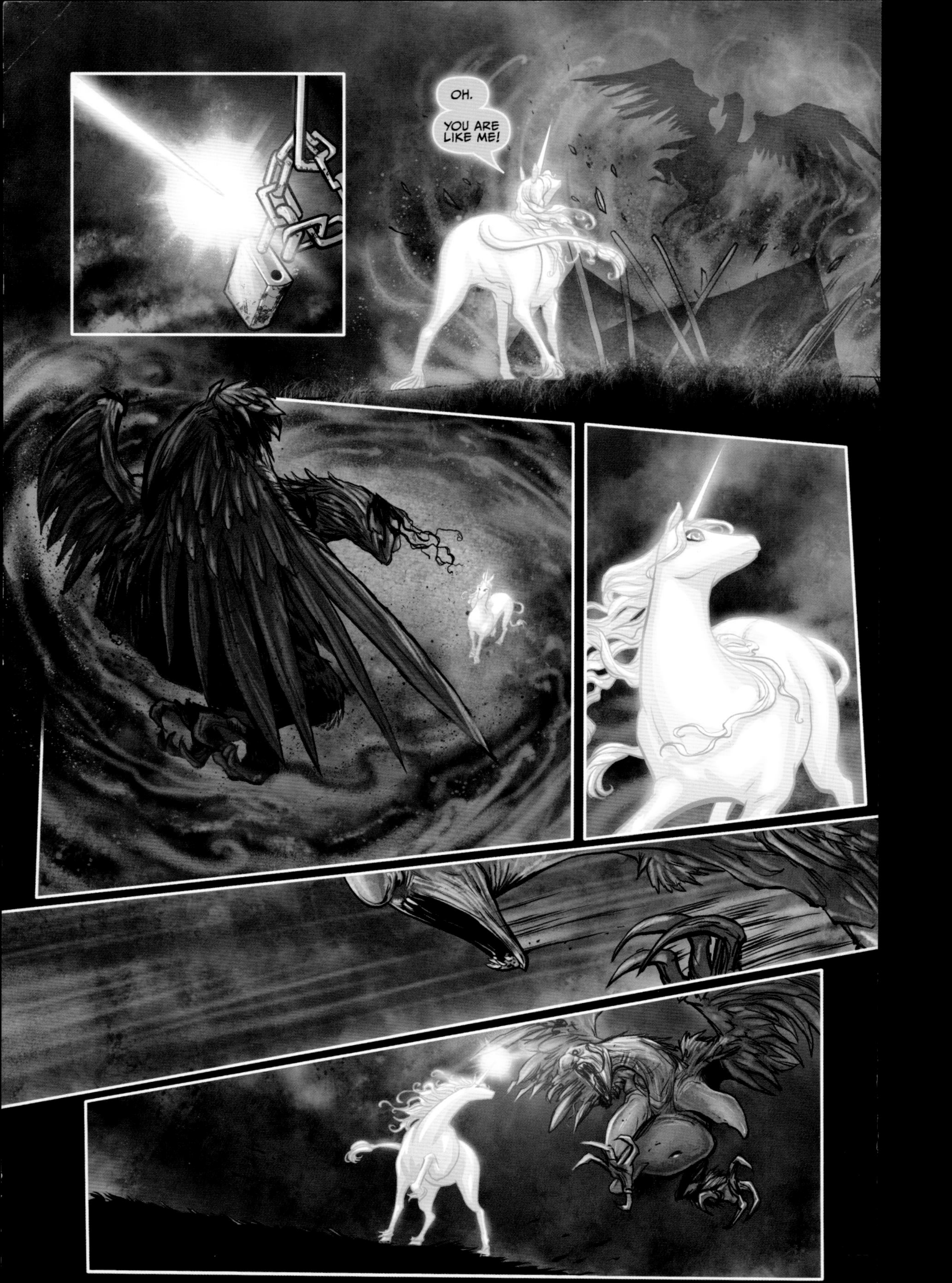
OH.
YOU ARE LIKE ME!

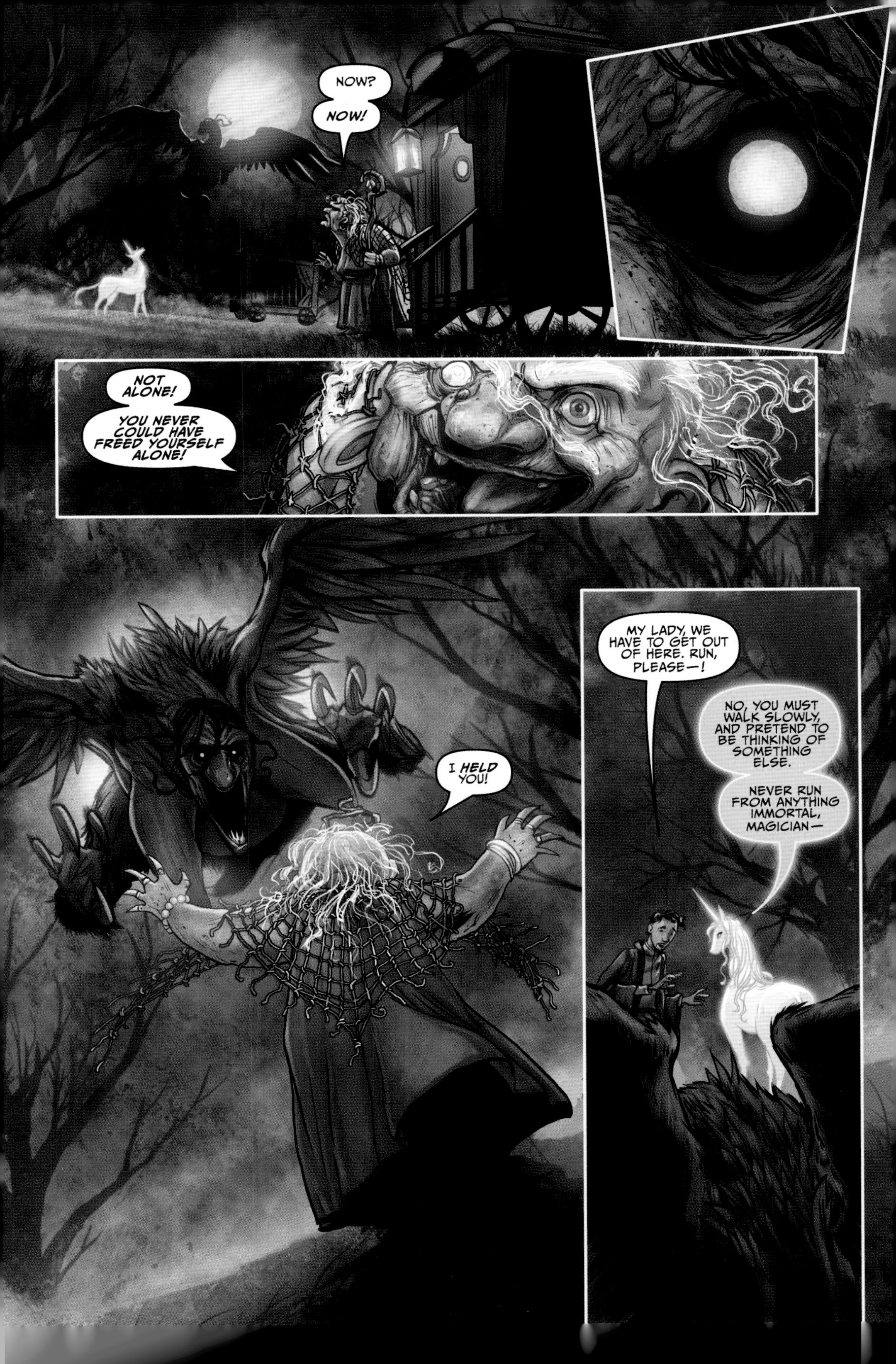
NOW?
NOW!
NOT ALONE!
YOU NEVER COULD HAVE FREED YOURSELF ALONE!
I HELD YOU!
MY LADY, WE HAVE TO GET OUT OF HERE. RUN, PLEASE—!
NO, YOU MUST WALK SLOWLY, AND PRETEND TO BE THINKING OF SOMETHING ELSE.
NEVER RUN FROM ANYTHING IMMORTAL, MAGICIAN—

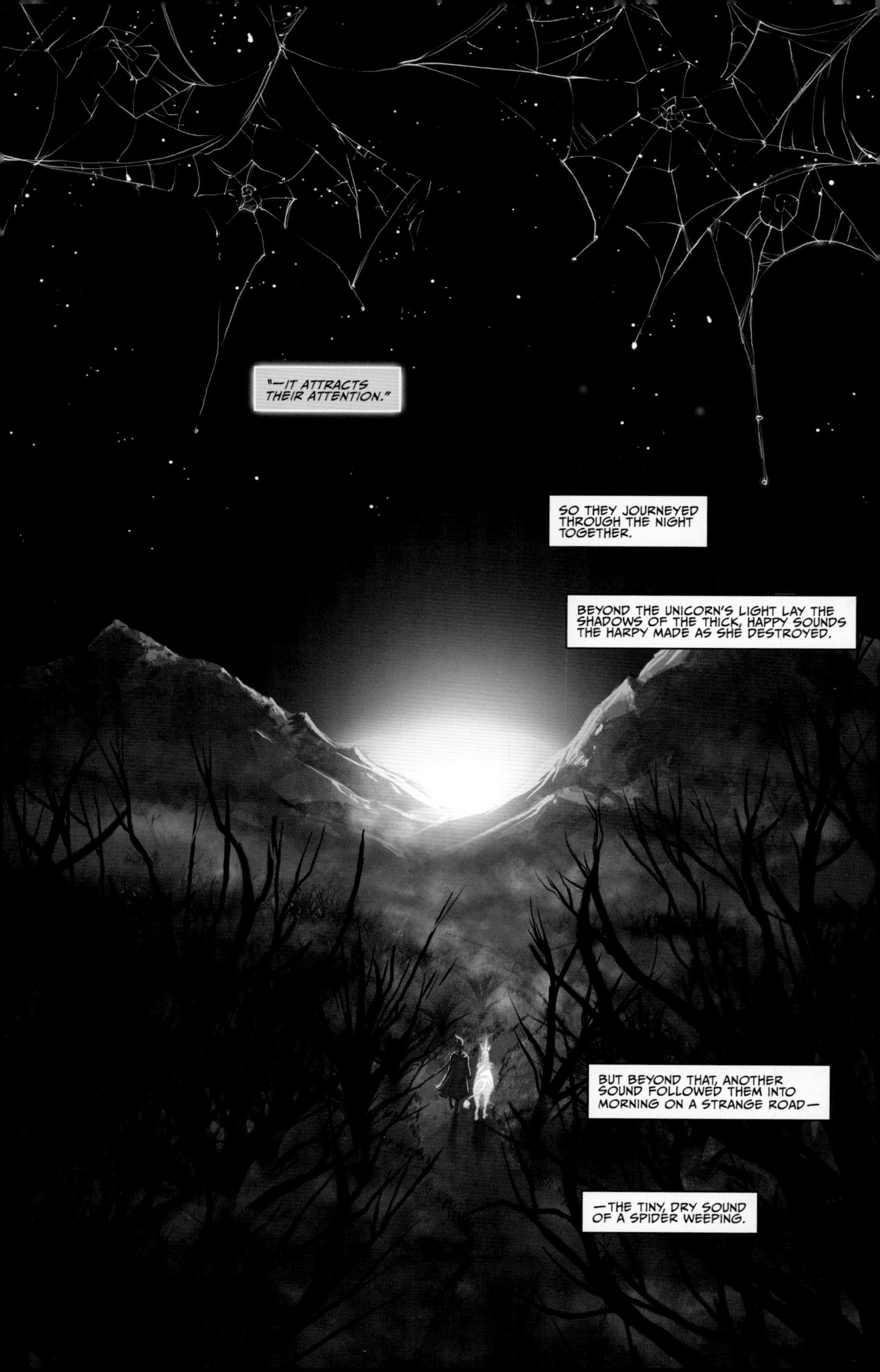
"—IT ATTRACTS THEIR ATTENTION."
SO THEY JOURNEYED THROUGH THE NIGHT TOGETHER.
BEYOND THE UNICORN'S LIGHT LAY THE SHADOWS OF THE THICK, HAPPY SOUNDS THE HARPY MADE AS SHE DESTROYED.
BUT BEYOND THAT, ANOTHER SOUND FOLLOWED THEM INTO MORNING ON A STRANGE ROAD—
—THE TINY, DRY SOUND OF A SPIDER WEEPING.

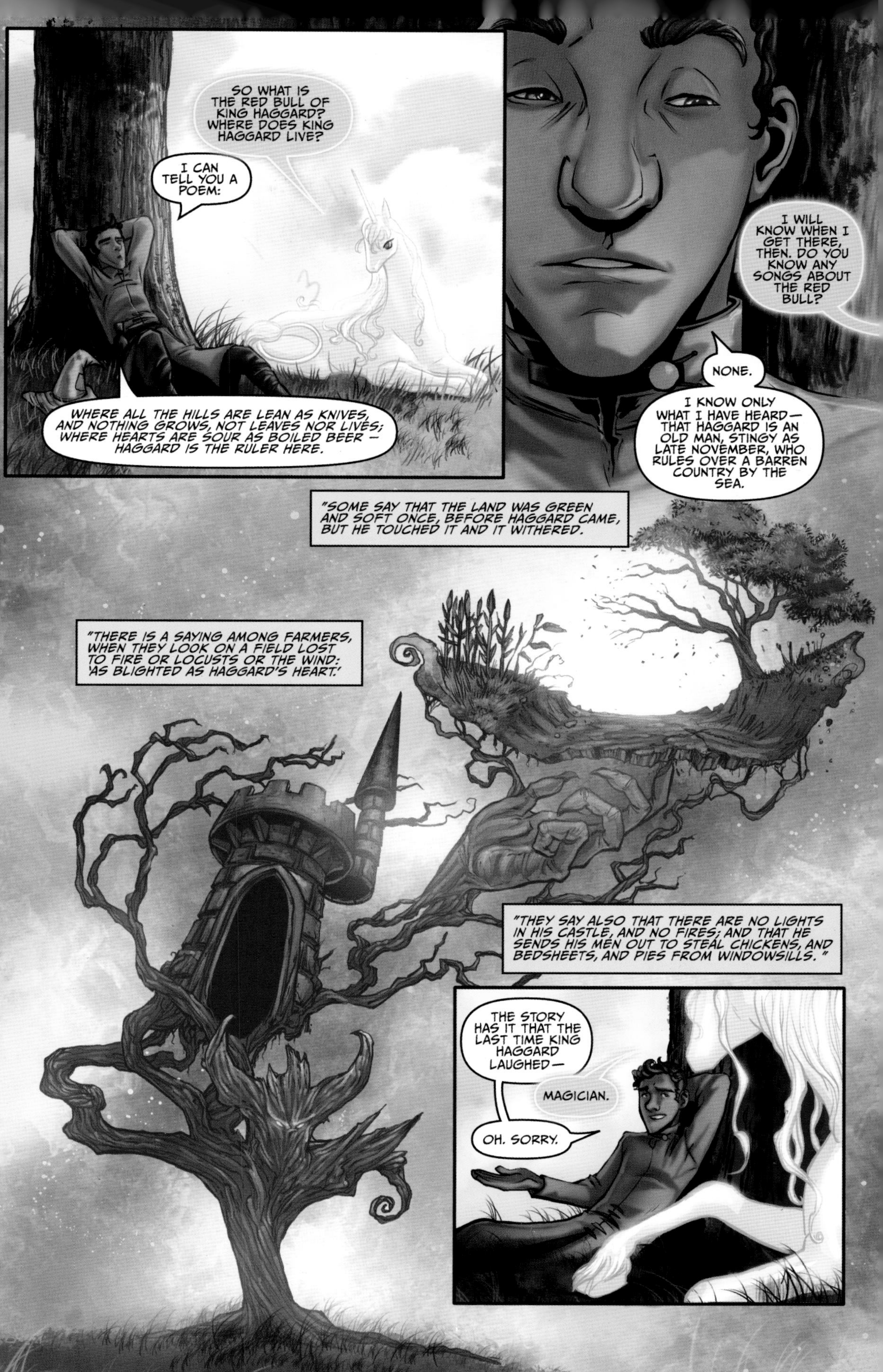
SO WHAT IS THE RED BULL OF KING HAGGARD? WHERE DOES KING HAGGARD LIVE?
I CAN TELL YOU A POEM:
WHERE ALL THE HILLS ARE LEAN AS KNIVES, AND NOTHING GROWS, NOT LEAVES NOR LIVES; WHERE HEARTS ARE SOUR AS BOILED BEER — HAGGARD IS THE RULER HERE.
I WILL KNOW WHEN I GET THERE, THEN. DO YOU KNOW ANY SONGS ABOUT THE RED BULL?
NONE.
I KNOW ONLY WHAT I HAVE HEARD— THAT HAGGARD IS AN OLD MAN, STINGY AS LATE NOVEMBER, WHO RULES OVER A BARREN COUNTRY BY THE SEA.
"SOME SAY THAT THE LAND WAS GREEN AND SOFT ONCE, BEFORE HAGGARD CAME, BUT HE TOUCHED IT AND IT WITHERED.
"THERE IS A SAYING AMONG FARMERS, WHEN THEY LOOK ON A FIELD LOST TO FIRE OR LOCUSTS OR THE WIND: 'AS BLIGHTED AS HAGGARD'S HEART.'
"THEY SAY ALSO THAT THERE ARE NO LIGHTS IN HIS CASTLE, AND NO FIRES; AND THAT HE SENDS HIS MEN OUT TO STEAL CHICKENS, AND BEDSHEETS, AND PIES FROM WINDOWSILLS."
THE STORY HAS IT THAT THE LAST TIME KING HAGGARD LAUGHED—
MAGICIAN.
OH. SORRY.

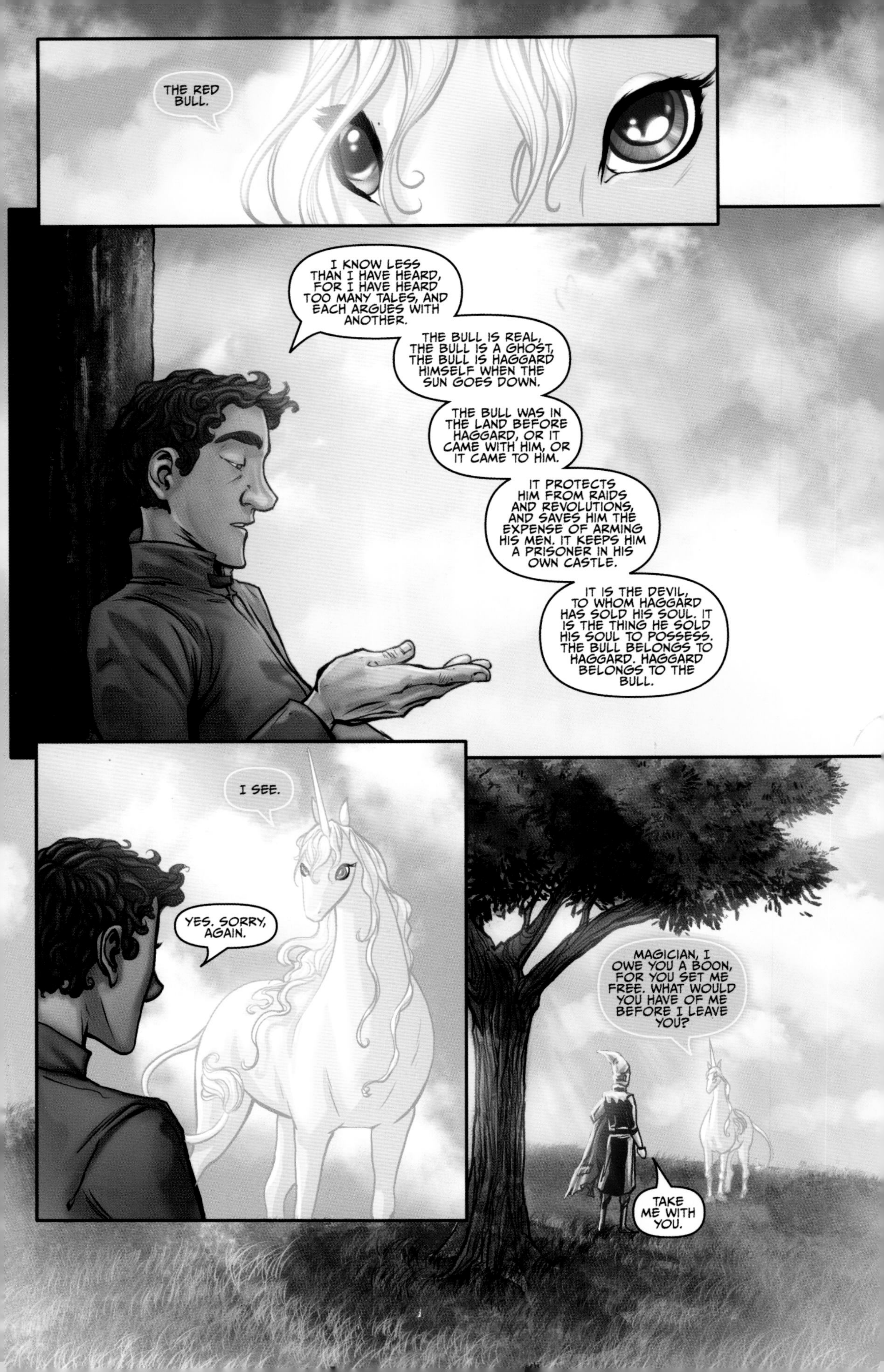
THE RED BULL.
I KNOW LESS THAN I HAVE HEARD, FOR I HAVE HEARD TOO MANY TALES, AND EACH ARGUES WITH ANOTHER.
THE BULL IS REAL, THE BULL IS A GHOST, THE BULL IS HAGGARD HIMSELF WHEN THE SUN GOES DOWN.
THE BULL WAS IN THE LAND BEFORE HAGGARD, OR IT CAME WITH HIM, OR IT CAME TO HIM.
IT PROTECTS HIM FROM RAIDS AND REVOLUTIONS, AND SAVES HIM THE EXPENSE OF ARMING HIS MEN. IT KEEPS HIM A PRISONER IN HIS OWN CASTLE.
IT IS THE DEVIL, TO WHOM HAGGARD HAS SOLD HIS SOUL. IT IS THE THING HE SOLD HIS SOUL TO POSSESS. THE BULL BELONGS TO HAGGARD. HAGGARD BELONGS TO THE BULL.
I SEE.
YES. SORRY, AGAIN.
MAGICIAN, I OWE YOU A BOON, FOR YOU SET ME FREE. WHAT WOULD YOU HAVE OF ME BEFORE I LEAVE YOU?
TAKE ME WITH YOU.

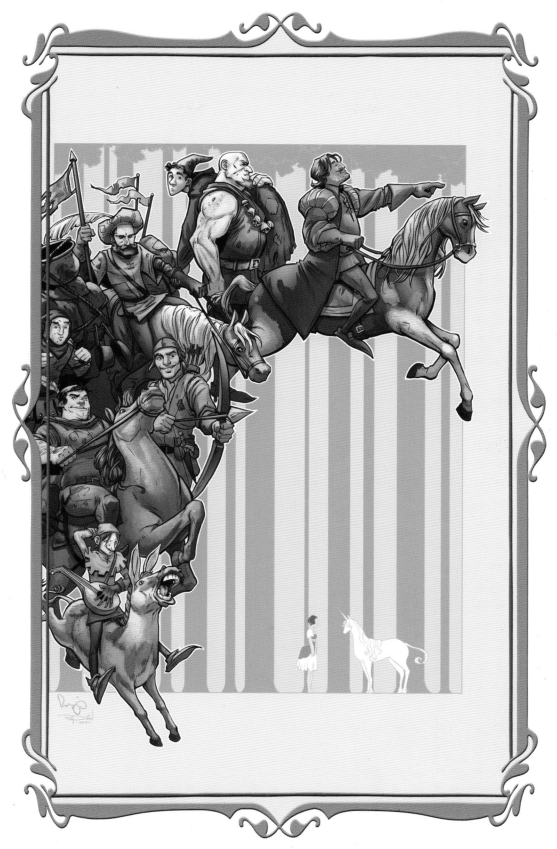

CHAPTER THREE

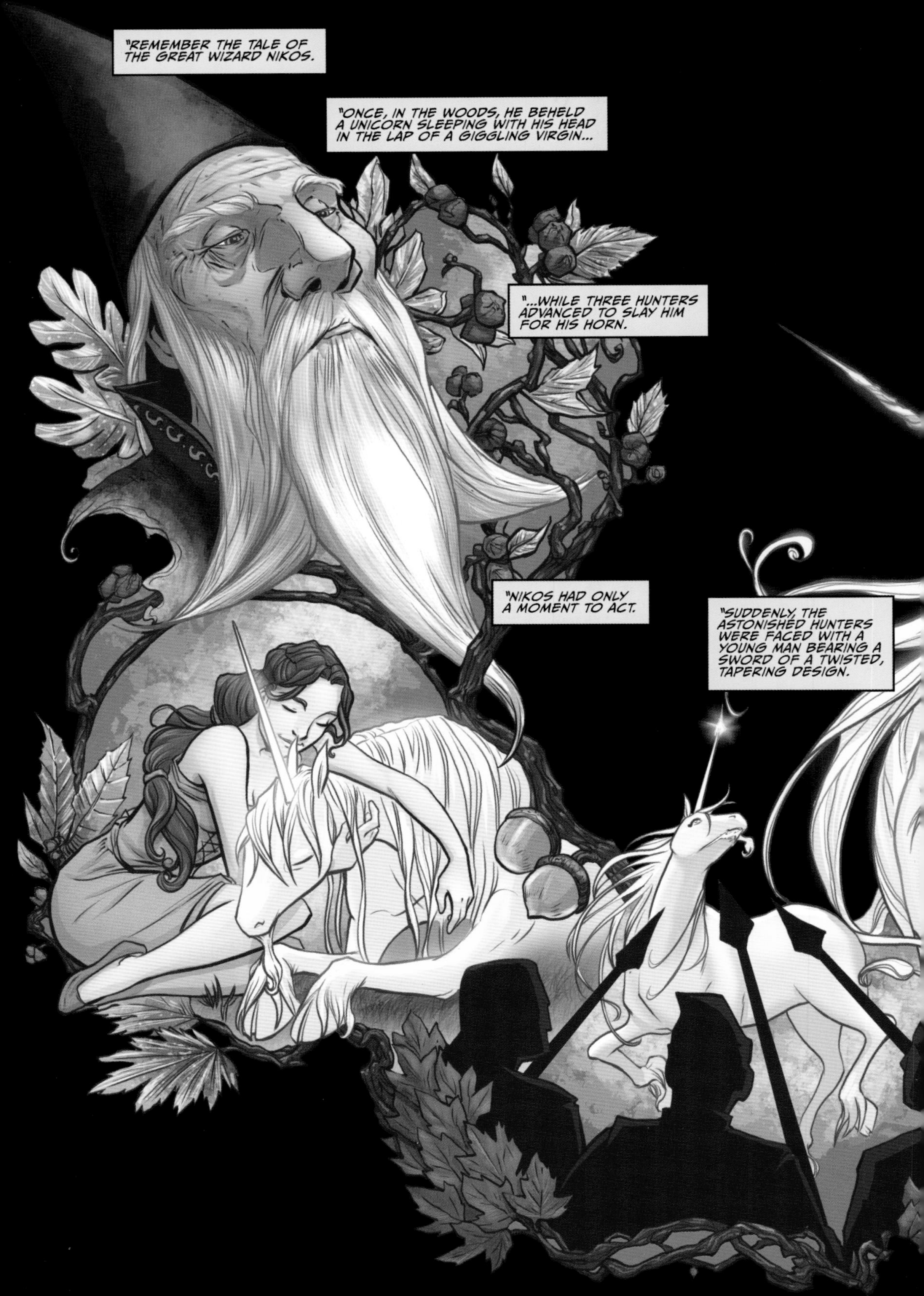
"REMEMBER THE TALE OF THE GREAT WIZARD NIKOS.
"ONCE, IN THE WOODS, HE BEHELD A UNICORN SLEEPING WITH HIS HEAD IN THE LAP OF A GIGGLING VIRGIN...
"...WHILE THREE HUNTERS ADVANCED TO SLAY HIM FOR HIS HORN.
"NIKOS HAD ONLY A MOMENT TO ACT.
"SUDDENLY, THE ASTONISHED HUNTERS WERE FACED WITH A YOUNG MAN BEARING A SWORD OF A TWISTED, TAPERING DESIGN.

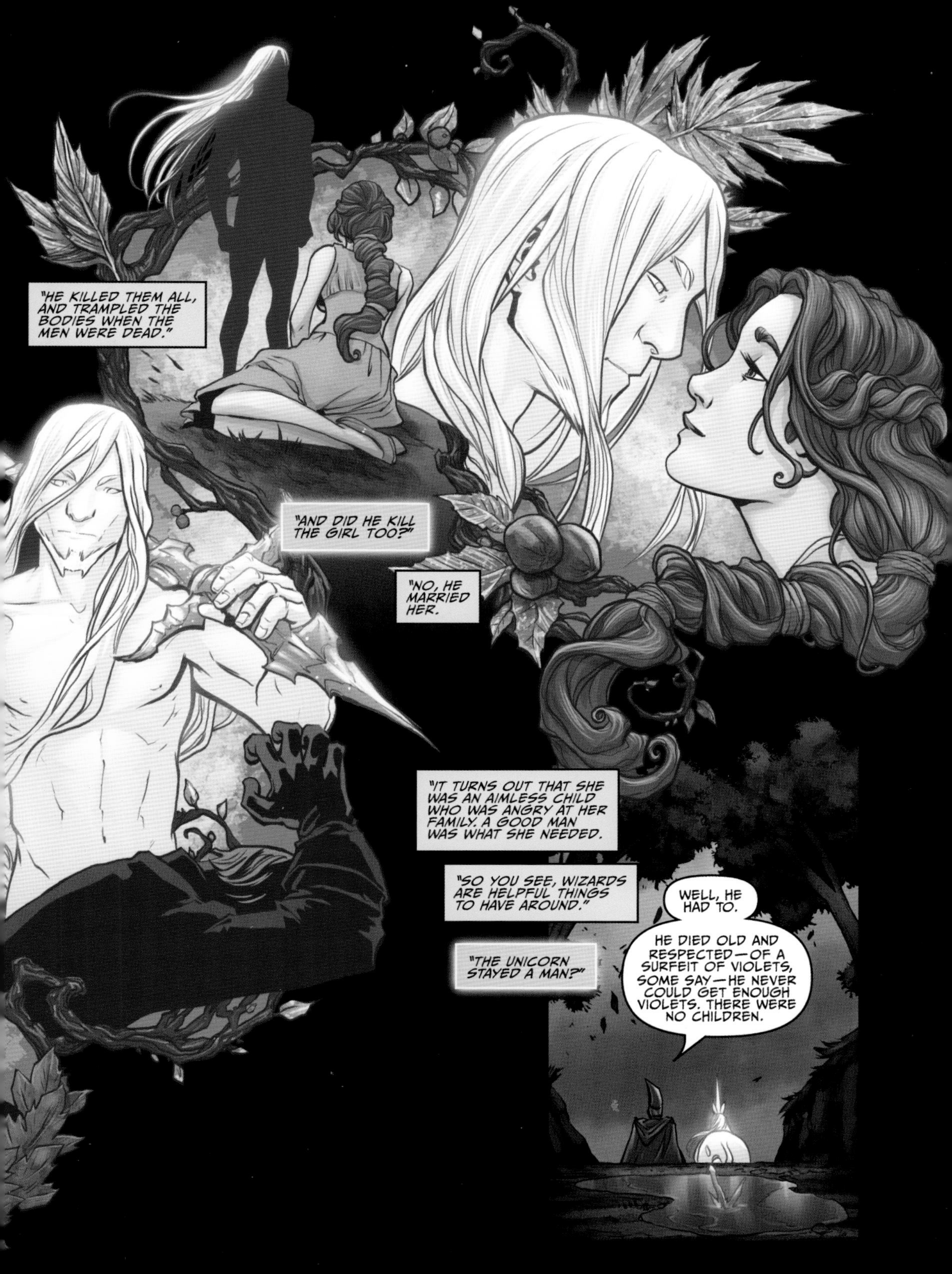
"HE KILLED THEM ALL, AND TRAMPLED THE BODIES WHEN THE MEN WERE DEAD."
"AND DID HE KILL THE GIRL TOO?"
"NO, HE MARRIED HER.
"IT TURNS OUT THAT SHE WAS AN AIMLESS CHILD WHO WAS ANGRY AT HER FAMILY. A GOOD MAN WAS WHAT SHE NEEDED.
"SO YOU SEE, WIZARDS ARE HELPFUL THINGS TO HAVE AROUND."
"THE UNICORN STAYED A MAN?"
WELL, HE HAD TO.
HE DIED OLD AND RESPECTED—OF A SURFEIT OF VIOLETS, SOME SAY—HE NEVER COULD GET ENOUGH VIOLETS. THERE WERE NO CHILDREN.

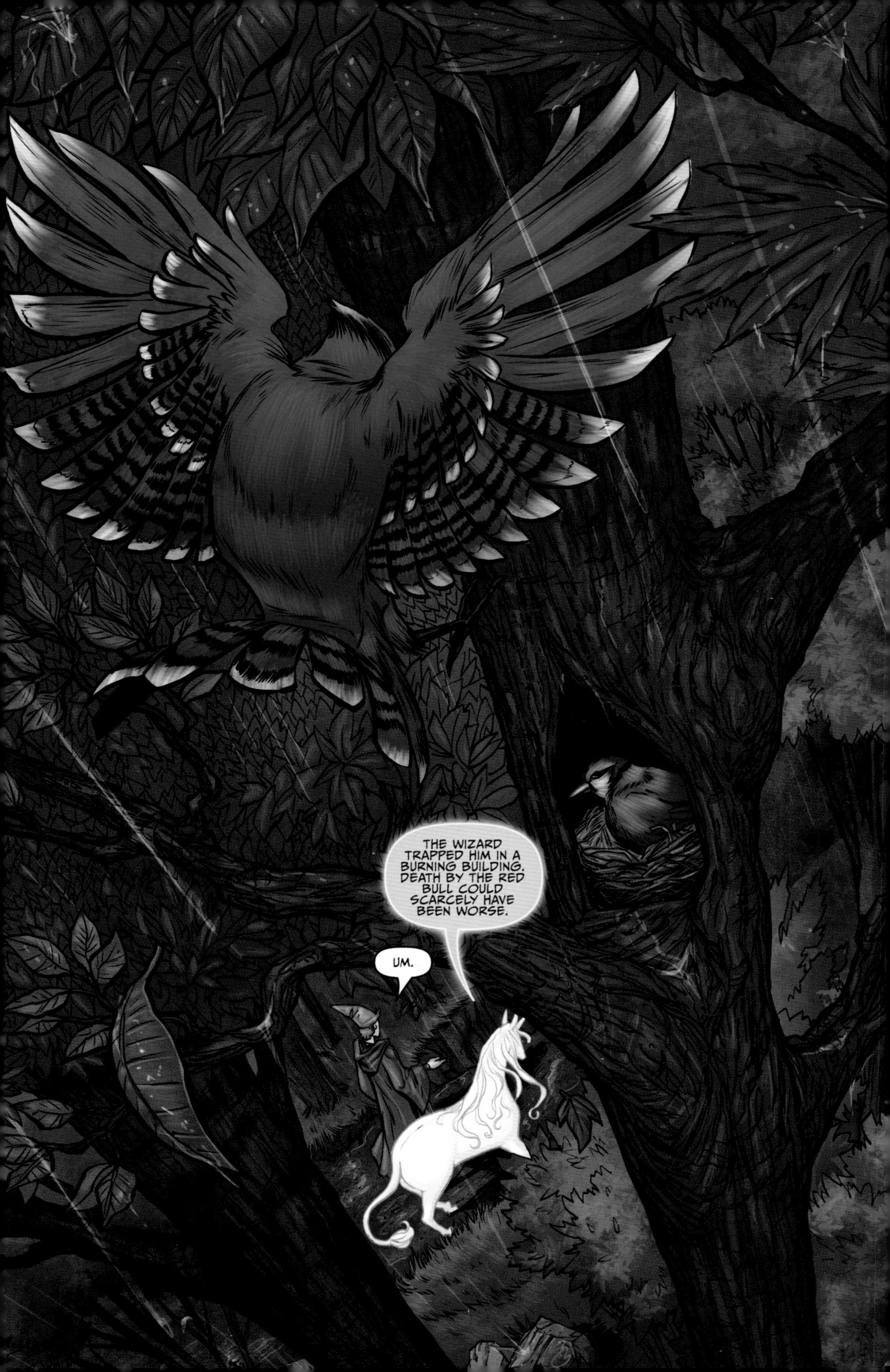
THE WIZARD TRAPPED HIM IN A BURNING BUILDING. DEATH BY THE RED BULL COULD SCARCELY HAVE BEEN WORSE.
UM.

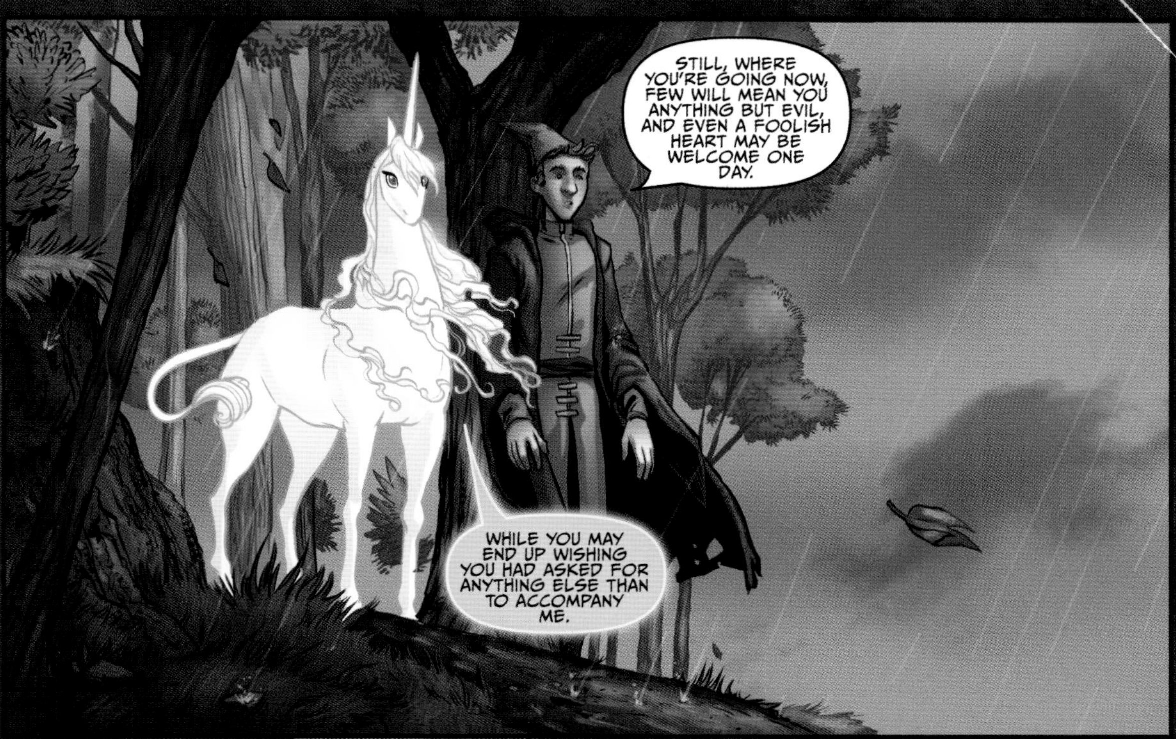
STILL, WHERE YOU'RE GOING NOW, FEW WILL MEAN YOU ANYTHING BUT EVIL, AND EVEN A FOOLISH HEART MAY BE WELCOME ONE DAY.
WHILE YOU MAY END UP WISHING YOU HAD ASKED FOR ANYTHING ELSE THAN TO ACCOMPANY ME.

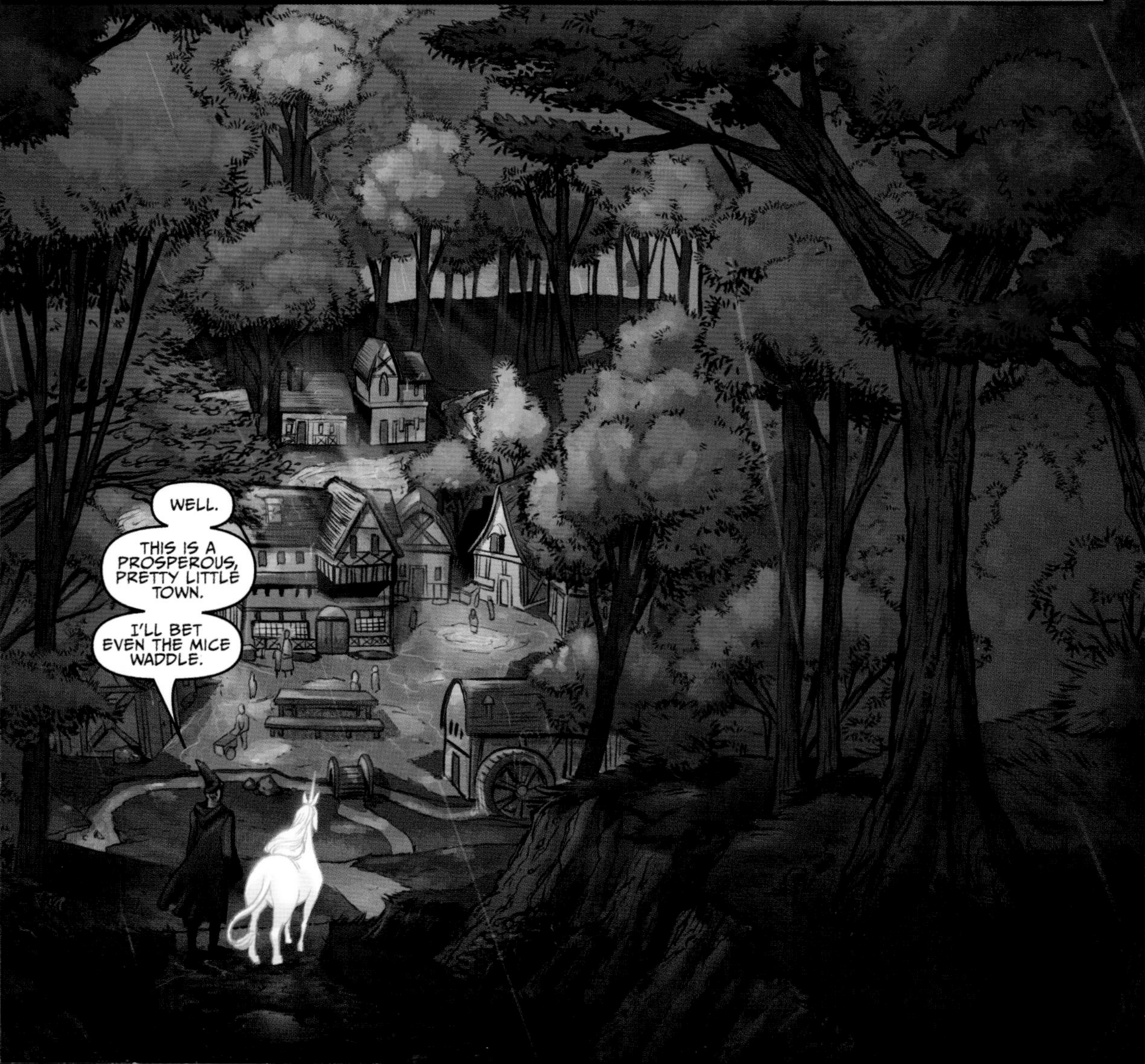
WELL.
THIS IS A PROSPEROUS, PRETTY LITTLE TOWN.
I'LL BET EVEN THE MICE WADDLE.

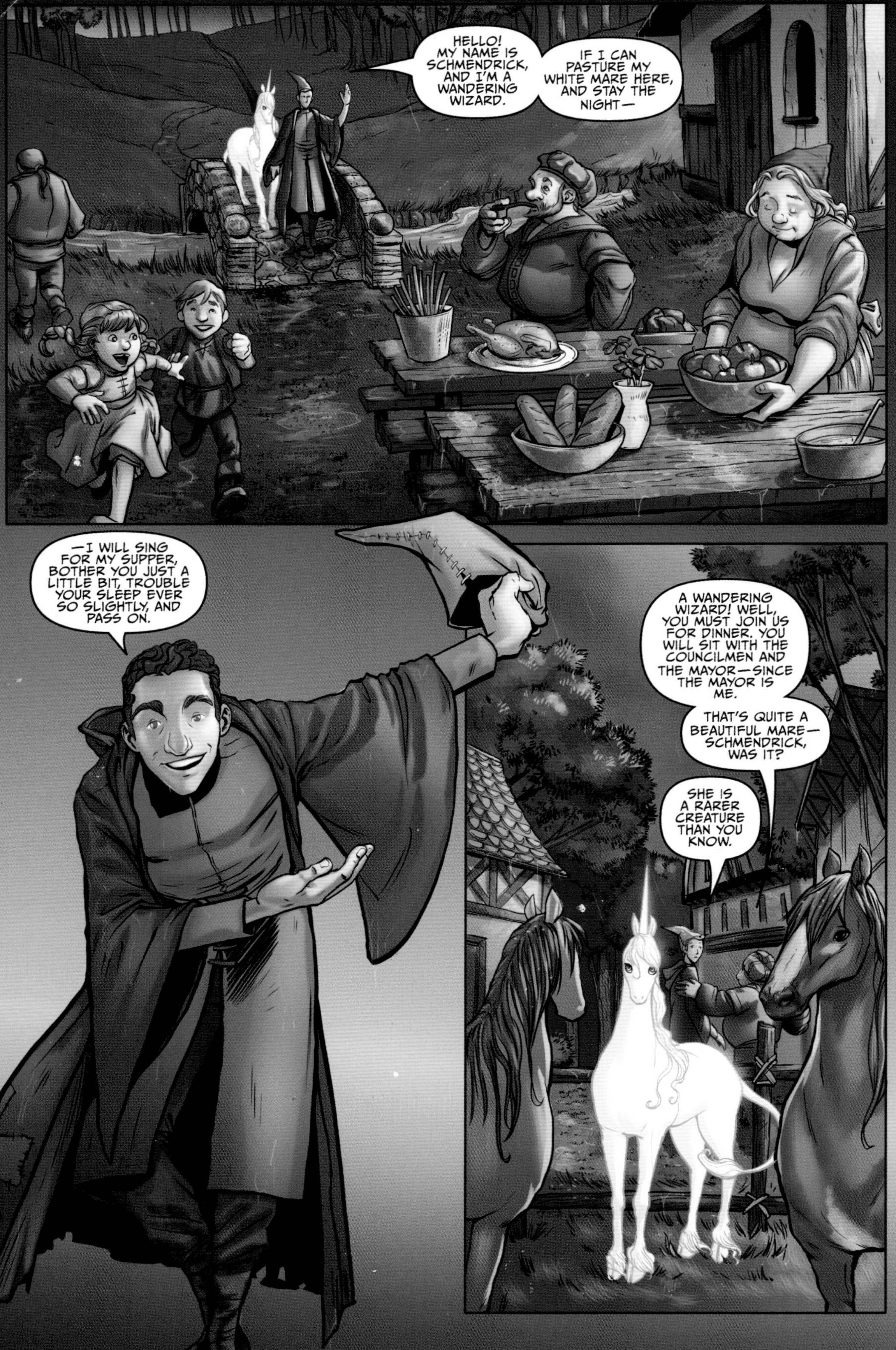
HELLO! MY NAME IS SCHMENDRICK, AND I'M A WANDERING WIZARD.
IF I CAN PASTURE MY WHITE MARE HERE, AND STAY THE NIGHT—
—I WILL SING FOR MY SUPPER, BOTHER YOU JUST A LITTLE BIT, TROUBLE YOUR SLEEP EVER SO SLIGHTLY, AND PASS ON.
A WANDERING WIZARD! WELL, YOU MUST JOIN US FOR DINNER. YOU WILL SIT WITH THE COUNCILMEN AND THE MAYOR—SINCE THE MAYOR IS ME.
THAT'S QUITE A BEAUTIFUL MARE—SCHMENDRICK, WAS IT?
SHE IS A RARER CREATURE THAN YOU KNOW.

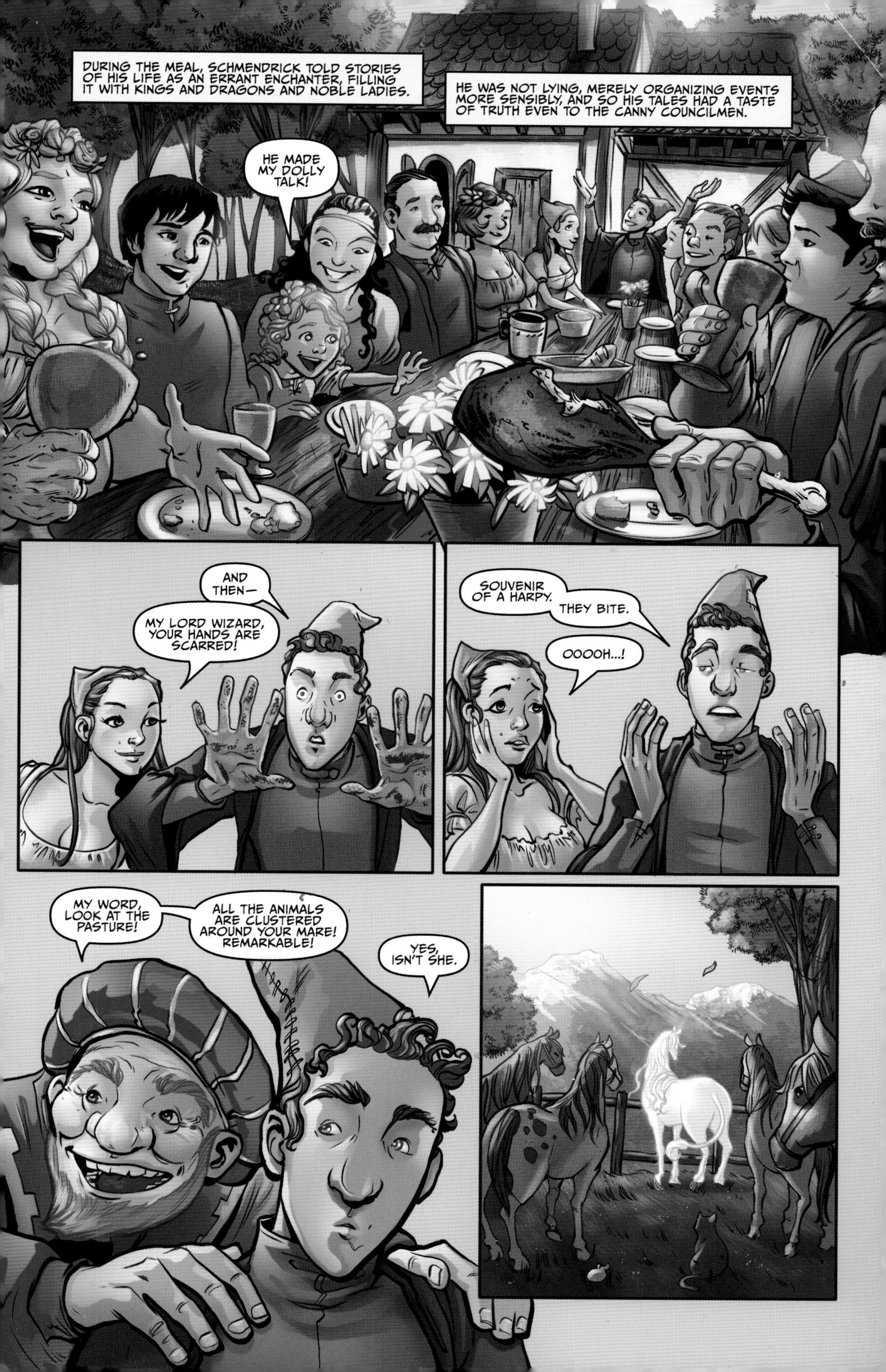
DURING THE MEAL, SCHMENDRICK TOLD STORIES OF HIS LIFE AS AN ERRANT ENCHANTER, FILLING IT WITH KINGS AND DRAGONS AND NOBLE LADIES.
HE WAS NOT LYING, MERELY ORGANIZING EVENTS MORE SENSIBLY, AND SO HIS TALES HAD A TASTE OF TRUTH EVEN TO THE CANNY COUNCILMEN.
HE MADE MY DOLLY TALK!
AND THEN—
MY LORD WIZARD, YOUR HANDS ARE SCARRED!
SOUVENIR OF A HARPY.
THEY BITE.
OOOOH...!
MY WORD, LOOK AT THE PASTURE!
ALL THE ANIMALS ARE CLUSTERED AROUND YOUR MARE! REMARKABLE!
YES, ISN'T SHE.

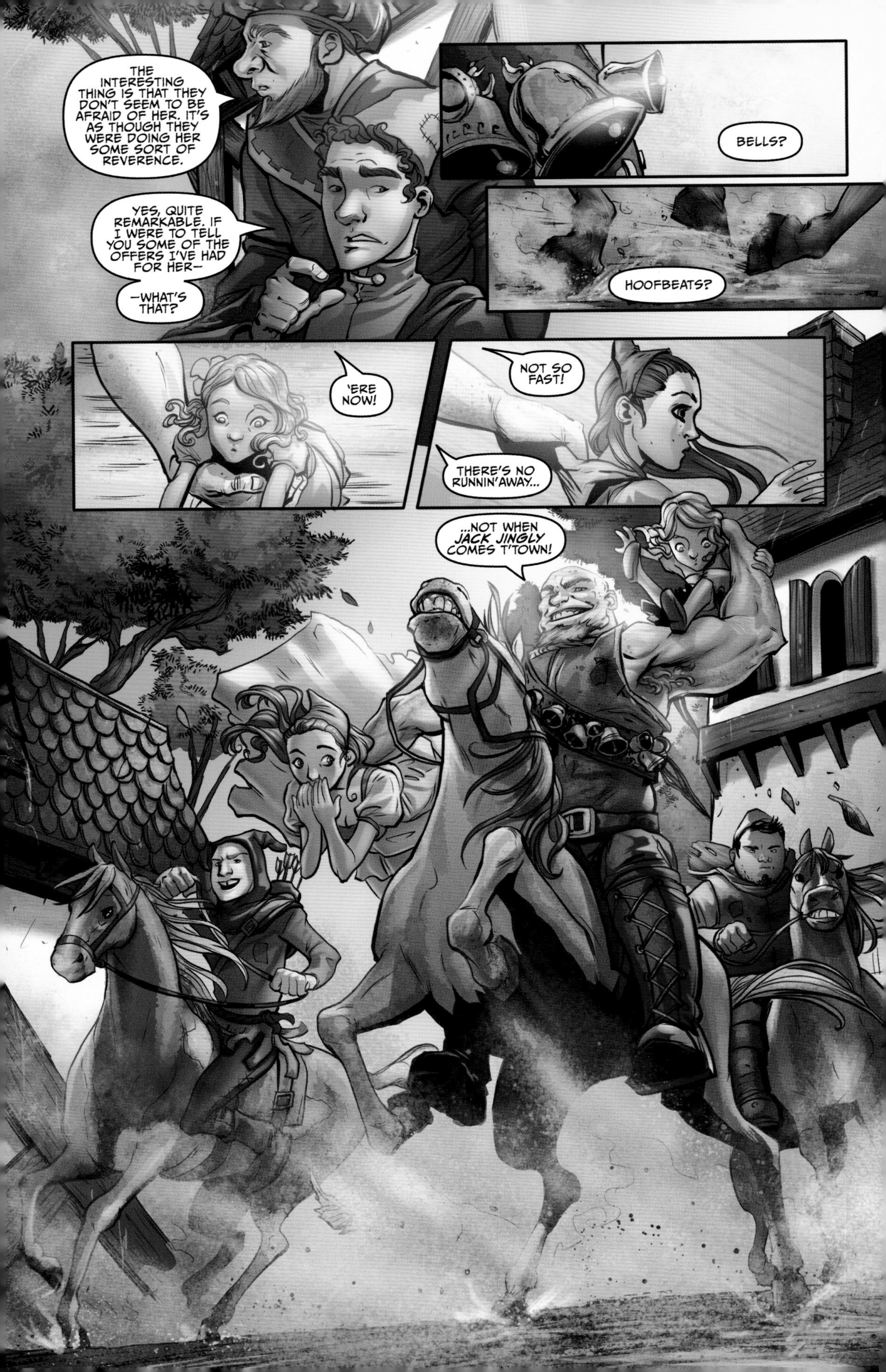
THE INTERESTING THING IS THAT THEY DON'T SEEM TO BE AFRAID OF HER. IT'S AS THOUGH THEY WERE DOING HER SOME SORT OF REVERENCE.
YES, QUITE REMARKABLE. IF I WERE TO TELL YOU SOME OF THE OFFERS I'VE HAD FOR HER--
--WHAT'S THAT?
BELLS?
HOOFBEATS?
'ERE NOW!
NOT SO FAST!
THERE'S NO RUNNIN'AWAY...
...NOT WHEN JACK JINGLY COMES T'TOWN!

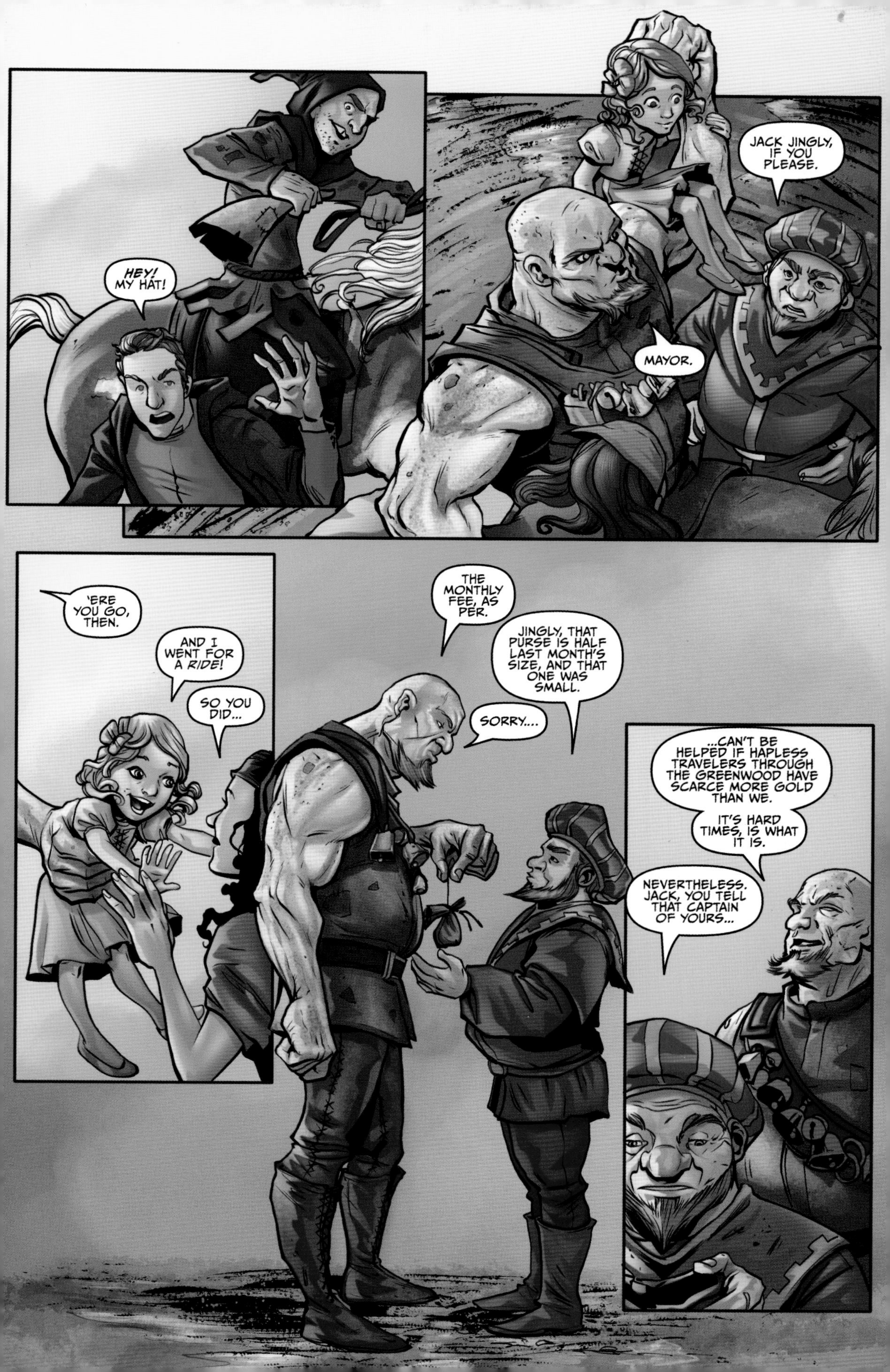
HEY! MY HAT!
JACK JINGLY, IF YOU PLEASE.
MAYOR.
'ERE YOU GO, THEN.
AND I WENT FOR A RIDE!
SO YOU DID...
THE MONTHLY FEE, AS PER.
SORRY....
JINGLY, THAT PURSE IS HALF LAST MONTH'S SIZE, AND THAT ONE WAS SMALL.
...CAN'T BE HELPED IF HAPLESS TRAVELERS THROUGH THE GREENWOOD HAVE SCARCE MORE GOLD THAN WE.
IT'S HARD TIMES, IS WHAT IT IS.
NEVERTHELESS. JACK, YOU TELL THAT CAPTAIN OF YOURS...

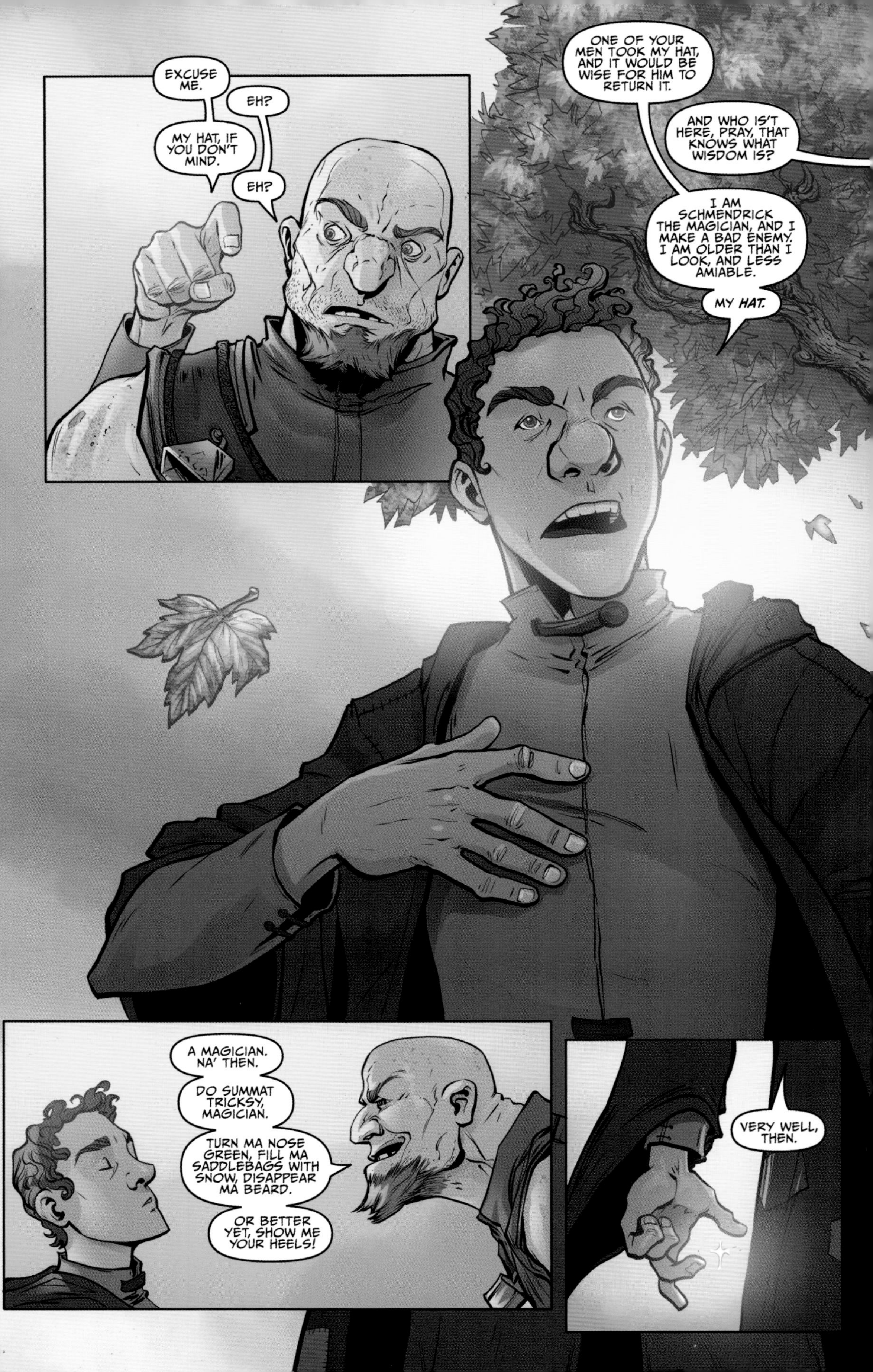
EXCUSE ME.
EH?
MY HAT, IF YOU DON'T MIND.
EH?
ONE OF YOUR MEN TOOK MY HAT, AND IT WOULD BE WISE FOR HIM TO RETURN IT.
AND WHO IS'T HERE, PRAY, THAT KNOWS WHAT WISDOM IS?
I AM SCHMENDRICK THE MAGICIAN, AND I MAKE A BAD ENEMY. I AM OLDER THAN I LOOK, AND LESS AMIABLE.
MY *HAT.*
A MAGICIAN. NA' THEN.
DO SUMMAT TRICKSY, MAGICIAN.
TURN MA NOSE GREEN, FILL MA SADDLEBAGS WITH SNOW, DISAPPEAR MA BEARD.
OR BETTER YET, SHOW ME YOUR HEELS!
VERY WELL, THEN.

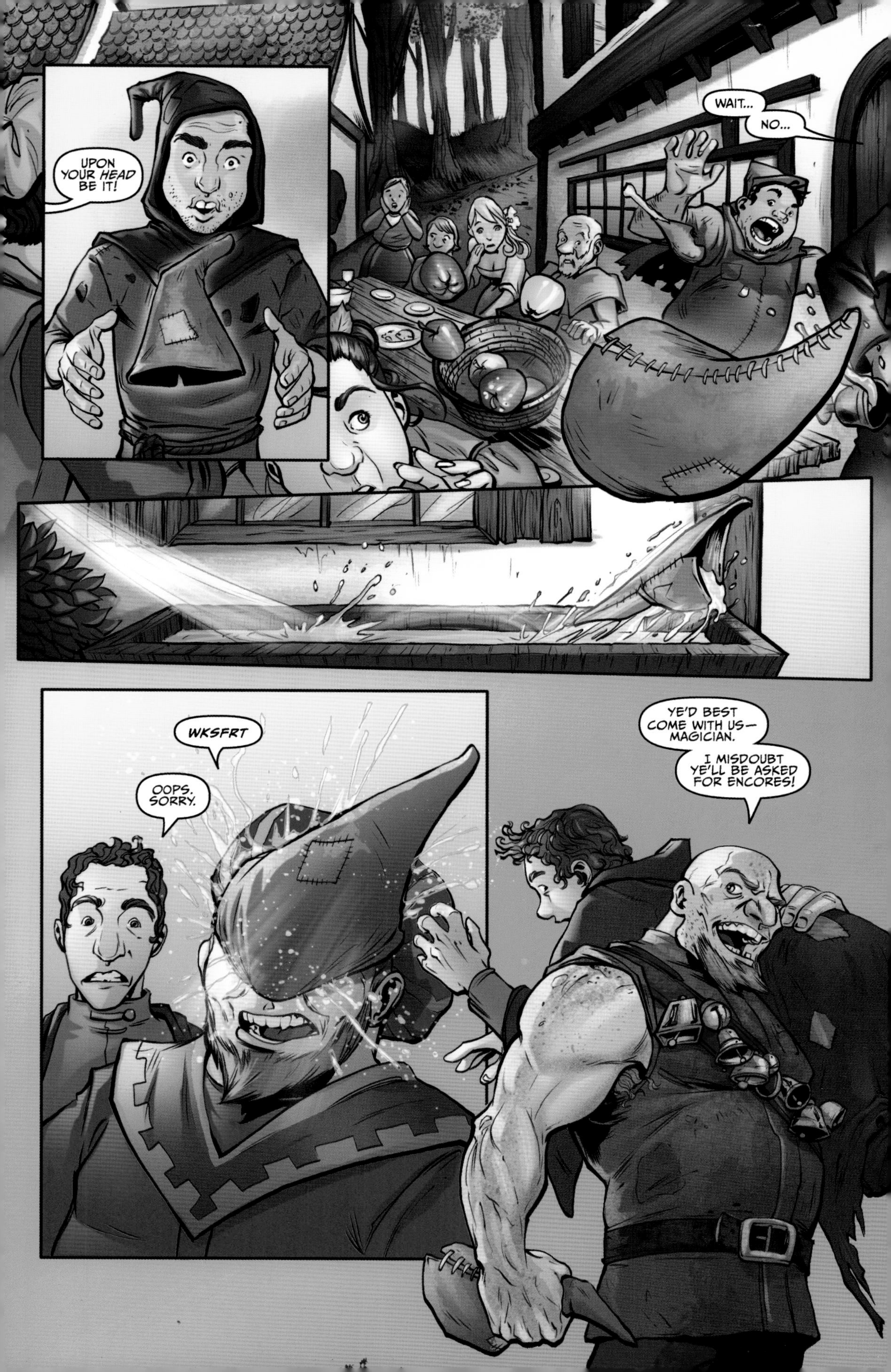
UPON YOUR *HEAD* BE IT!
WAIT...
NO...
WKSFRT
OOPS. SORRY.
YE'D BEST COME WITH US— MAGICIAN.
I MISDOUBT YE'LL BE ASKED FOR ENCORES!

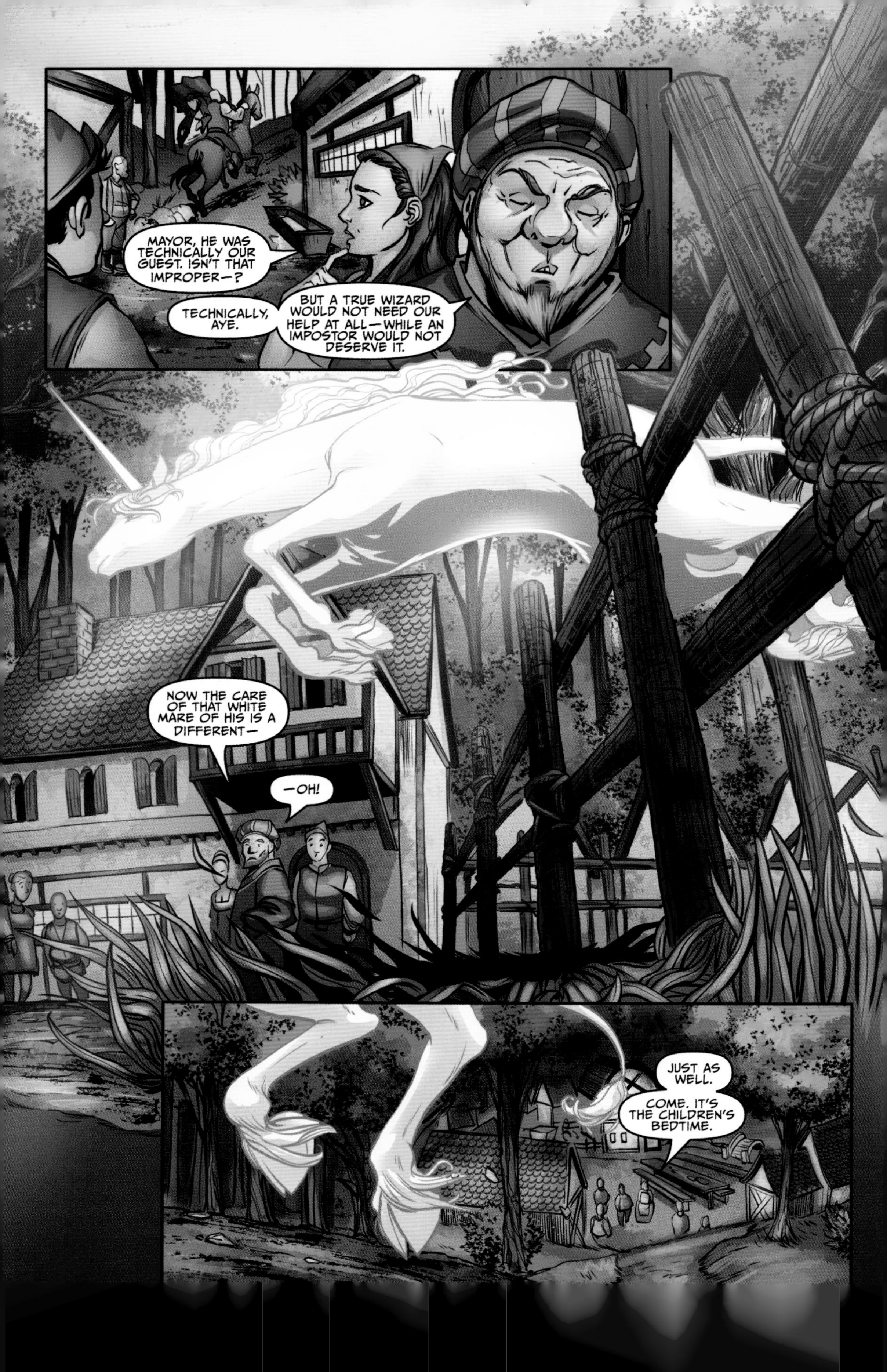
MAYOR, HE WAS TECHNICALLY OUR GUEST. ISN'T THAT IMPROPER—?
TECHNICALLY, AYE.
BUT A TRUE WIZARD WOULD NOT NEED OUR HELP AT ALL—WHILE AN IMPOSTOR WOULD NOT DESERVE IT.
NOW THE CARE OF THAT WHITE MARE OF HIS IS A DIFFERENT—
—OH!
JUST AS WELL.
COME. IT'S THE CHILDREN'S BEDTIME.

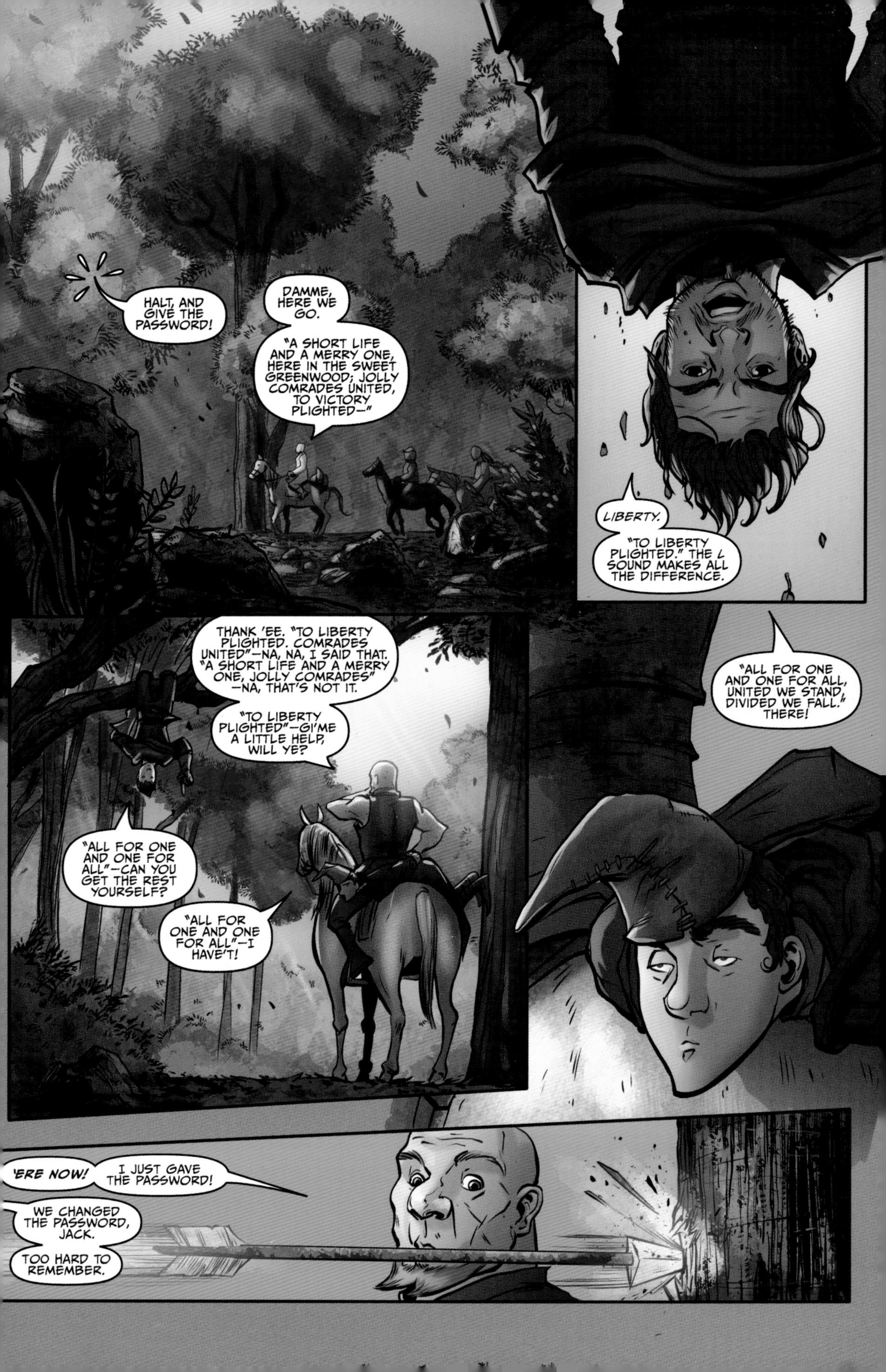
HALT, AND GIVE THE PASSWORD!
DAMME, HERE WE GO.
"A SHORT LIFE AND A MERRY ONE, HERE IN THE SWEET GREENWOOD; JOLLY COMRADES UNITED, TO VICTORY PLIGHTED--"
LIBERTY.
"TO LIBERTY PLIGHTED." THE L SOUND MAKES ALL THE DIFFERENCE.
THANK 'EE. "TO LIBERTY PLIGHTED. COMRADES UNITED"--NA, NA, I SAID THAT. "A SHORT LIFE AND A MERRY ONE, JOLLY COMRADES"--NA, THAT'S NOT IT.
"TO LIBERTY PLIGHTED"--GI'ME A LITTLE HELP, WILL YE?
"ALL FOR ONE AND ONE FOR ALL"--CAN YOU GET THE REST YOURSELF?
"ALL FOR ONE AND ONE FOR ALL"--I HAVE'T!
"ALL FOR ONE AND ONE FOR ALL, UNITED WE STAND, DIVIDED WE FALL." THERE!
'ERE NOW!
I JUST GAVE THE PASSWORD!
WE CHANGED THE PASSWORD, JACK.
TOO HARD TO REMEMBER.

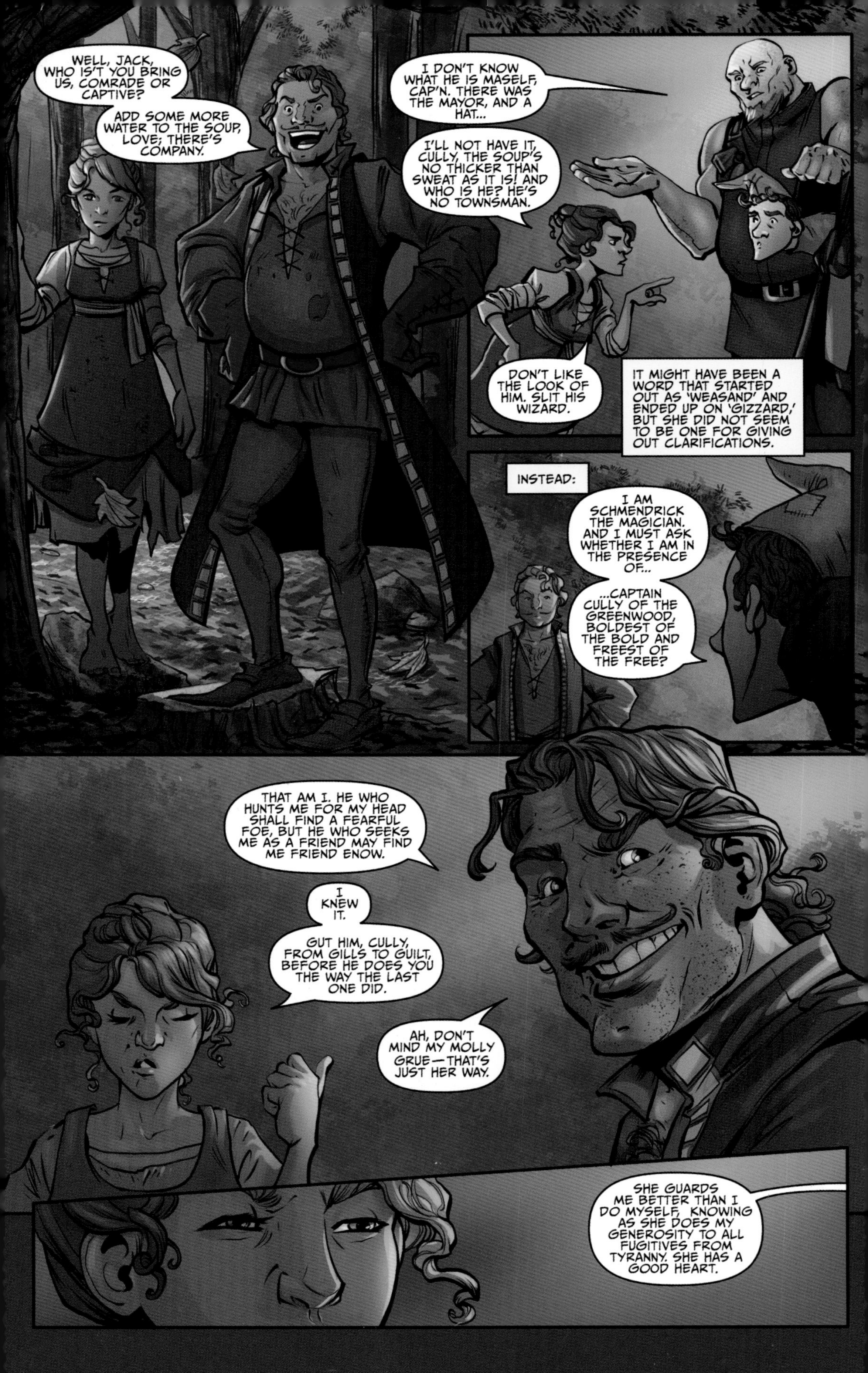
WELL, JACK, WHO IS'T YOU BRING US, COMRADE OR CAPTIVE?
ADD SOME MORE WATER TO THE SOUP, LOVE; THERE'S COMPANY.
I DON'T KNOW WHAT HE IS MASELF, CAP'N. THERE WAS THE MAYOR, AND A HAT...
I'LL NOT HAVE IT, CULLY, THE SOUP'S NO THICKER THAN SWEAT AS IT IS! AND WHO IS HE? HE'S NO TOWNSMAN.
DON'T LIKE THE LOOK OF HIM. SLIT HIS WIZARD.
IT MIGHT HAVE BEEN A WORD THAT STARTED OUT AS 'WEASAND' AND ENDED UP ON 'GIZZARD,' BUT SHE DID NOT SEEM TO BE ONE FOR GIVING OUT CLARIFICATIONS.
INSTEAD:
I AM SCHMENDRICK THE MAGICIAN. AND I MUST ASK WHETHER I AM IN THE PRESENCE OF...
...CAPTAIN CULLY OF THE GREENWOOD, BOLDEST OF THE BOLD AND FREEST OF THE FREE?
THAT AM I. HE WHO HUNTS ME FOR MY HEAD SHALL FIND A FEARFUL FOE, BUT HE WHO SEEKS ME AS A FRIEND MAY FIND ME FRIEND ENOW.
I KNEW IT.
GUT HIM, CULLY, FROM GILLS TO GUILT, BEFORE HE DOES YOU THE WAY THE LAST ONE DID.
AH, DON'T MIND MY MOLLY GRUE—THAT'S JUST HER WAY.
SHE GUARDS ME BETTER THAN I DO MYSELF, KNOWING AS SHE DOES MY GENEROSITY TO ALL FUGITIVES FROM TYRANNY. SHE HAS A GOOD HEART.

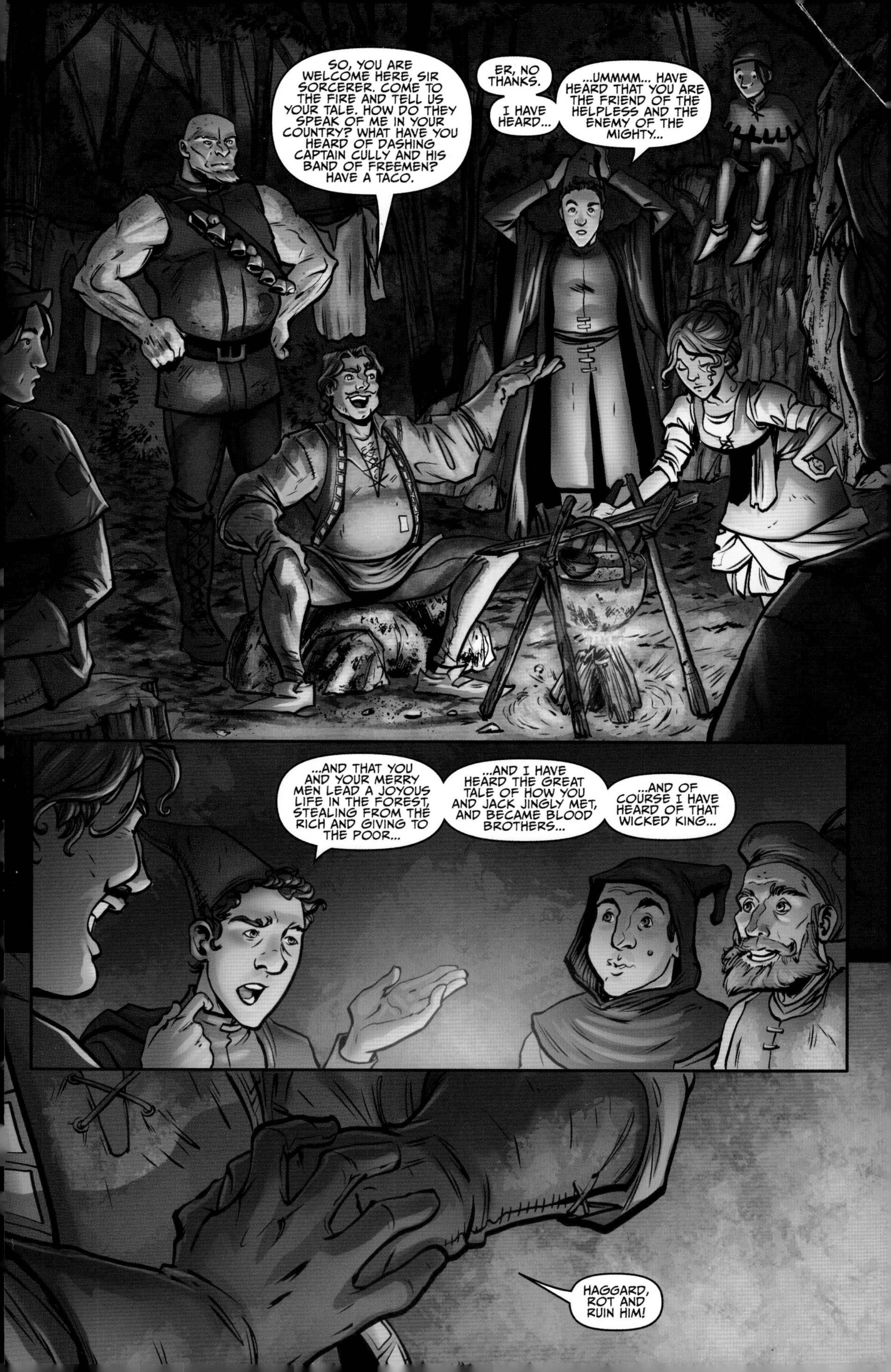
SO, YOU ARE WELCOME HERE, SIR SORCERER. COME TO THE FIRE AND TELL US YOUR TALE. HOW DO THEY SPEAK OF ME IN YOUR COUNTRY? WHAT HAVE YOU HEARD OF DASHING CAPTAIN CULLY AND HIS BAND OF FREEMEN? HAVE A TACO.
ER, NO THANKS.
I HAVE HEARD...
...UMMMM... HAVE HEARD THAT YOU ARE THE FRIEND OF THE HELPLESS AND THE ENEMY OF THE MIGHTY...
...AND THAT YOU AND YOUR MERRY MEN LEAD A JOYOUS LIFE IN THE FOREST, STEALING FROM THE RICH AND GIVING TO THE POOR...
...AND I HAVE HEARD THE GREAT TALE OF HOW YOU AND JACK JINGLY MET, AND BECAME BLOOD BROTHERS...
...AND OF COURSE I HAVE HEARD OF THAT WICKED KING...
HAGGARD, ROT AND RUIN HIM!

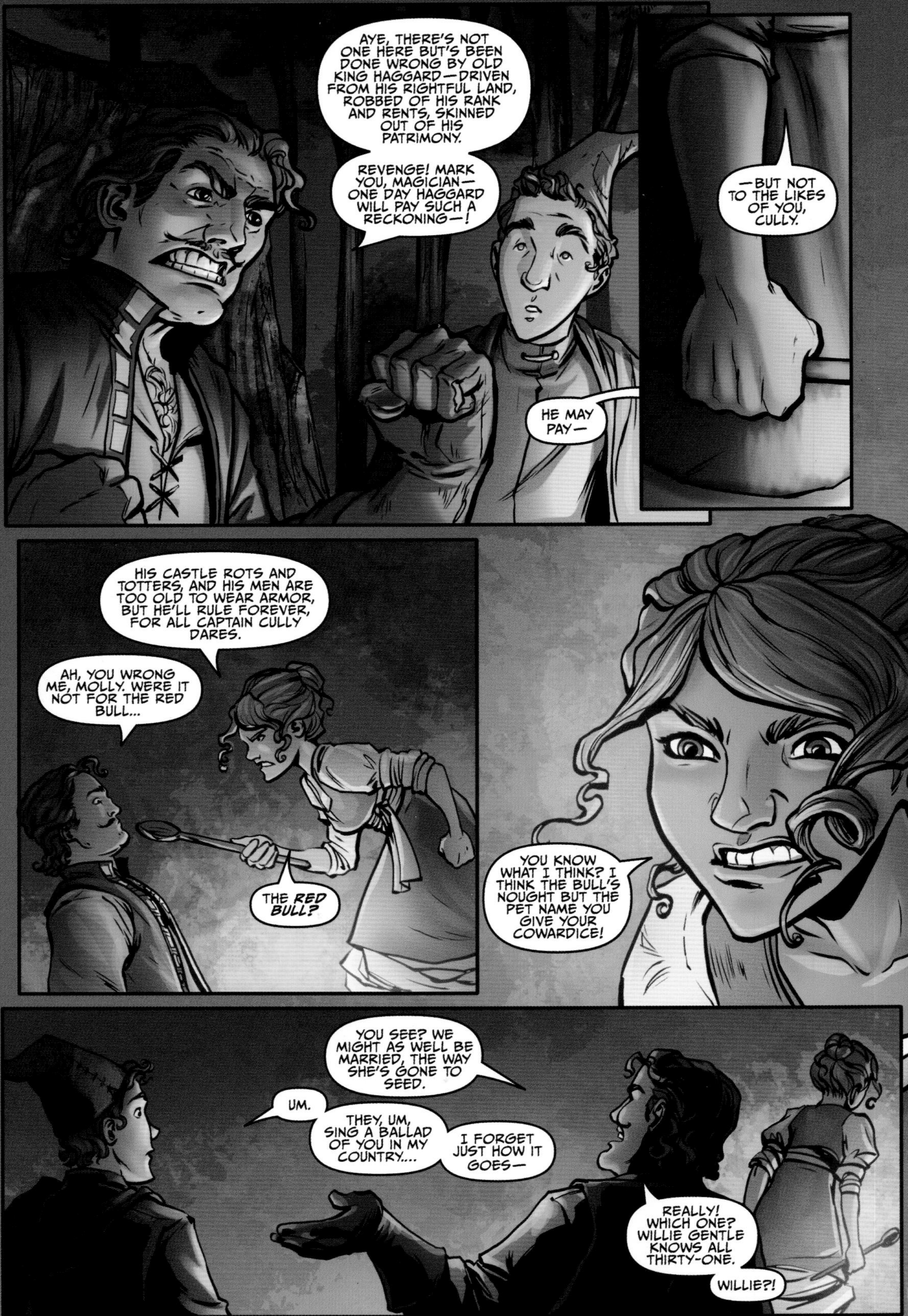
AYE, THERE'S NOT ONE HERE BUT'S BEEN DONE WRONG BY OLD KING HAGGARD—DRIVEN FROM HIS RIGHTFUL LAND, ROBBED OF HIS RANK AND RENTS, SKINNED OUT OF HIS PATRIMONY.
REVENGE! MARK YOU, MAGICIAN—ONE DAY HAGGARD WILL PAY SUCH A RECKONING—!
HE MAY PAY—
—BUT NOT TO THE LIKES OF YOU, CULLY.
HIS CASTLE ROTS AND TOTTERS, AND HIS MEN ARE TOO OLD TO WEAR ARMOR, BUT HE'LL RULE FOREVER, FOR ALL CAPTAIN CULLY DARES.
AH, YOU WRONG ME, MOLLY. WERE IT NOT FOR THE RED BULL...
THE *RED BULL?*
YOU KNOW WHAT I THINK? I THINK THE BULL'S NOUGHT BUT THE PET NAME YOU GIVE YOUR COWARDICE!
YOU SEE? WE MIGHT AS WELL BE MARRIED, THE WAY SHE'S GONE TO SEED.
UM.
THEY, UM, SING A BALLAD OF YOU IN MY COUNTRY....
I FORGET JUST HOW IT GOES—
REALLY! WHICH ONE? WILLIE GENTLE KNOWS ALL THIRTY-ONE.
WILLIE?!

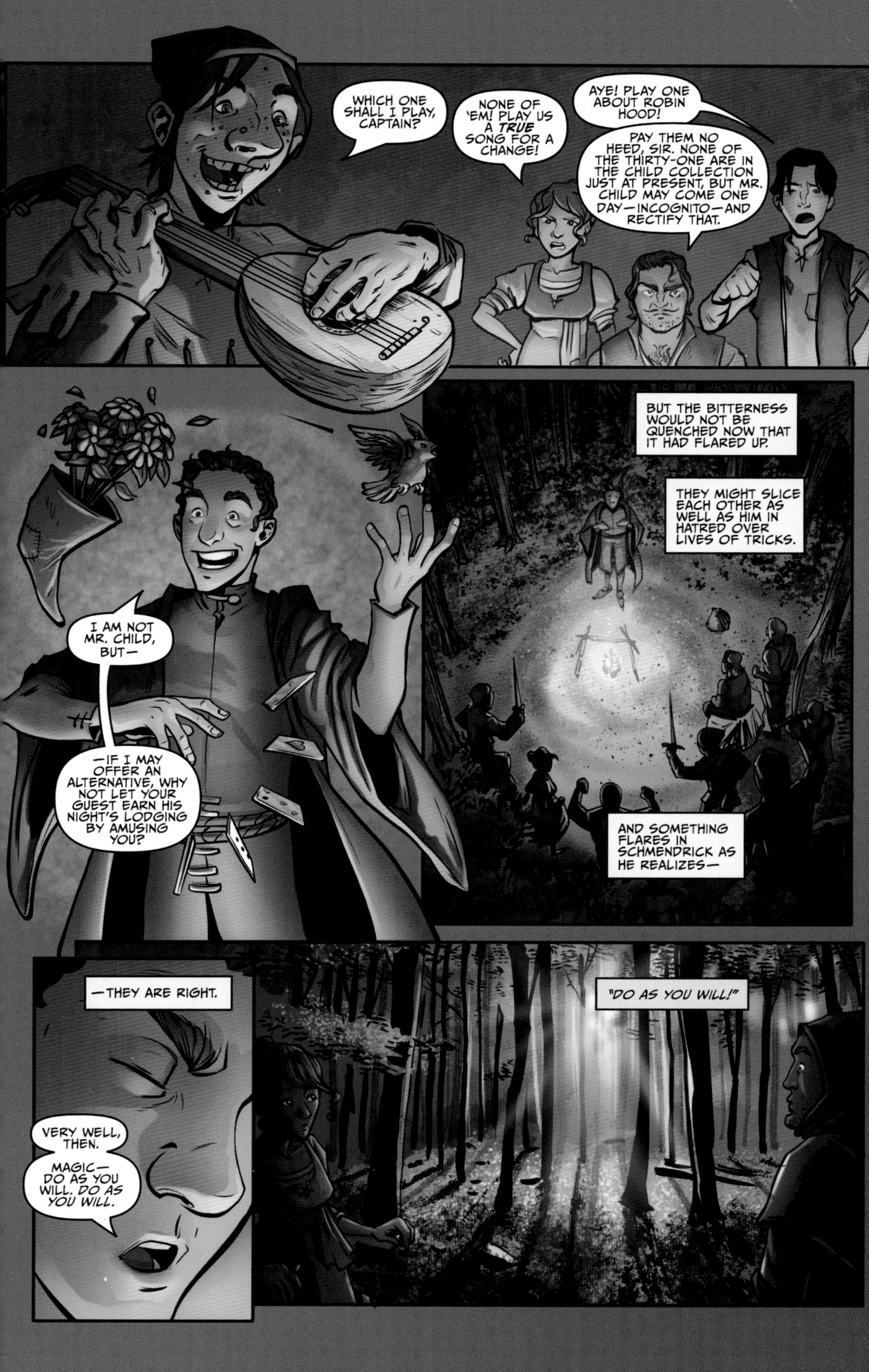
WHICH ONE SHALL I PLAY, CAPTAIN?
NONE OF 'EM! PLAY US A *TRUE* SONG FOR A CHANGE!
AYE! PLAY ONE ABOUT ROBIN HOOD!
PAY THEM NO HEED, SIR. NONE OF THE THIRTY-ONE ARE IN THE CHILD COLLECTION JUST AT PRESENT, BUT MR. CHILD MAY COME ONE DAY—INCOGNITO—AND RECTIFY THAT.
I AM NOT MR. CHILD, BUT—
—IF I MAY OFFER AN ALTERNATIVE, WHY NOT LET YOUR GUEST EARN HIS NIGHT'S LODGING BY AMUSING YOU?
BUT THE BITTERNESS WOULD NOT BE QUENCHED NOW THAT IT HAD FLARED UP.
THEY MIGHT SLICE EACH OTHER AS WELL AS HIM IN HATRED OVER LIVES OF TRICKS.
AND SOMETHING FLARES IN SCHMENDRICK AS HE REALIZES—
—THEY ARE RIGHT.
VERY WELL, THEN.
MAGIC—DO AS YOU WILL. *DO AS YOU WILL.*
"DO AS YOU WILL!"

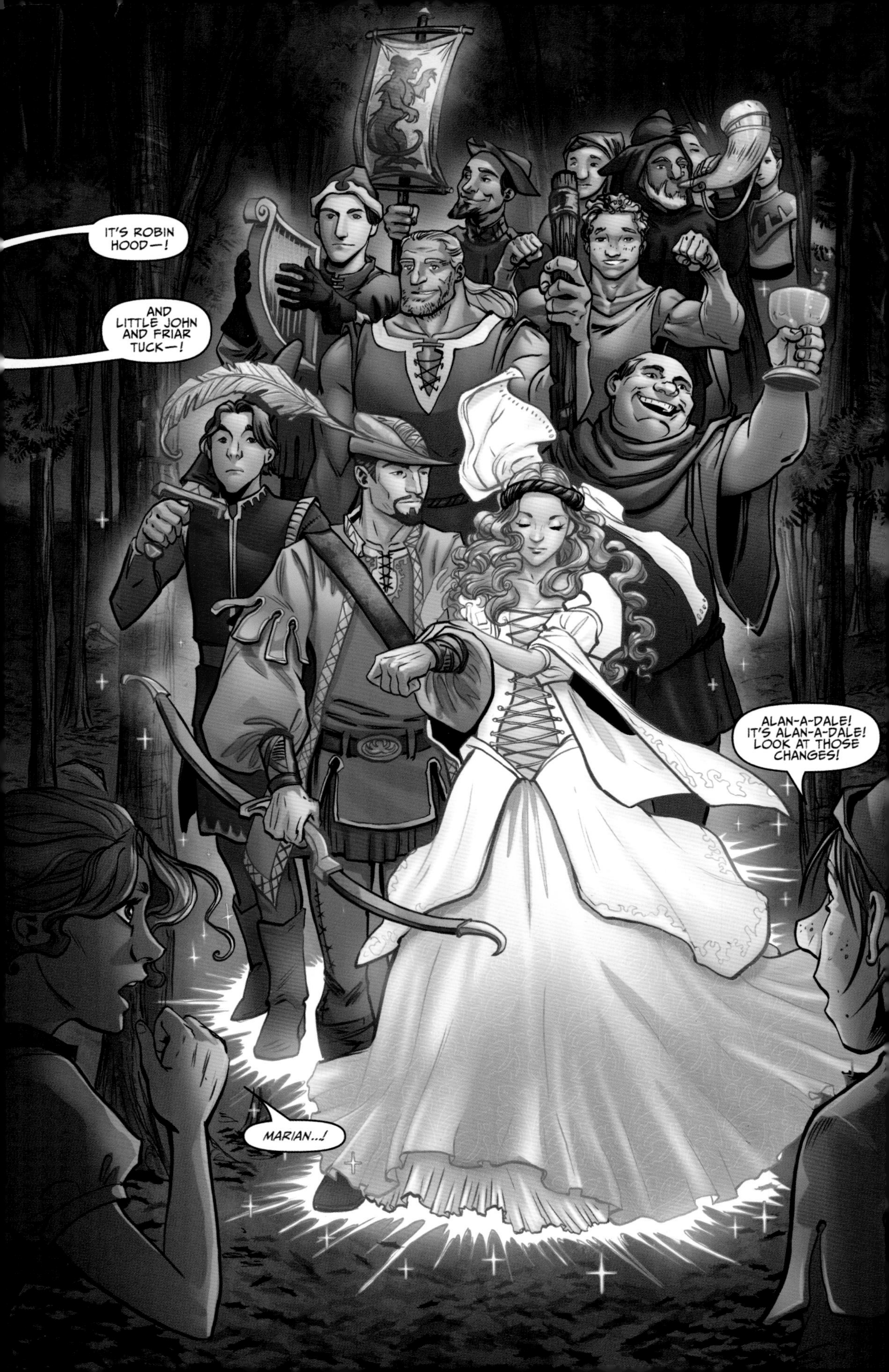
IT'S ROBIN HOOD—!
AND LITTLE JOHN AND FRIAR TUCK—!
ALAN-A-DALE! IT'S ALAN-A-DALE! LOOK AT THOSE CHANGES!
MARIAN...!

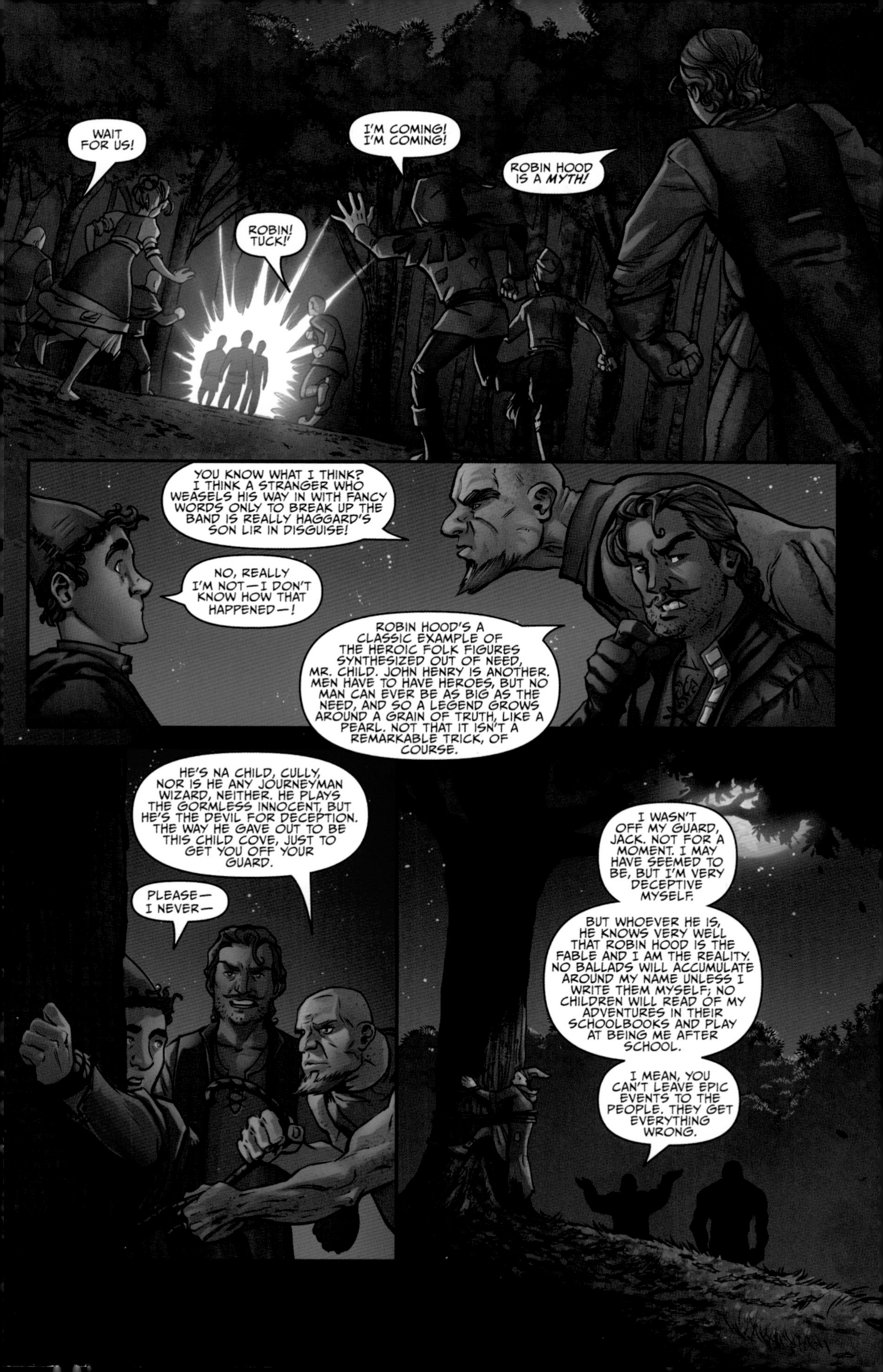
WAIT FOR US!
ROBIN! TUCK!'
I'M COMING! I'M COMING!
ROBIN HOOD IS A *MYTH!*
YOU KNOW WHAT I THINK? I THINK A STRANGER WHO WEASELS HIS WAY IN WITH FANCY WORDS ONLY TO BREAK UP THE BAND IS REALLY HAGGARD'S SON LIR IN DISGUISE!
NO, REALLY I'M NOT—I DON'T KNOW HOW THAT HAPPENED—!
ROBIN HOOD'S A CLASSIC EXAMPLE OF THE HEROIC FOLK FIGURES SYNTHESIZED OUT OF NEED, MR. CHILD. JOHN HENRY IS ANOTHER. MEN HAVE TO HAVE HEROES, BUT NO MAN CAN EVER BE AS BIG AS THE NEED, AND SO A LEGEND GROWS AROUND A GRAIN OF TRUTH, LIKE A PEARL. NOT THAT IT ISN'T A REMARKABLE TRICK, OF COURSE.
HE'S NA CHILD, CULLY, NOR IS HE ANY JOURNEYMAN WIZARD, NEITHER. HE PLAYS THE GORMLESS INNOCENT, BUT HE'S THE DEVIL FOR DECEPTION. THE WAY HE GAVE OUT TO BE THIS CHILD COVE, JUST TO GET YOU OFF YOUR GUARD.
PLEASE— I NEVER—
I WASN'T OFF MY GUARD, JACK. NOT FOR A MOMENT. I MAY HAVE SEEMED TO BE, BUT I'M VERY DECEPTIVE MYSELF.
BUT WHOEVER HE IS, HE KNOWS VERY WELL THAT ROBIN HOOD IS THE FABLE AND I AM THE REALITY. NO BALLADS WILL ACCUMULATE AROUND MY NAME UNLESS I WRITE THEM MYSELF; NO CHILDREN WILL READ OF MY ADVENTURES IN THEIR SCHOOLBOOKS AND PLAY AT BEING ME AFTER SCHOOL.
I MEAN, YOU CAN'T LEAVE EPIC EVENTS TO THE PEOPLE. THEY GET EVERYTHING WRONG.

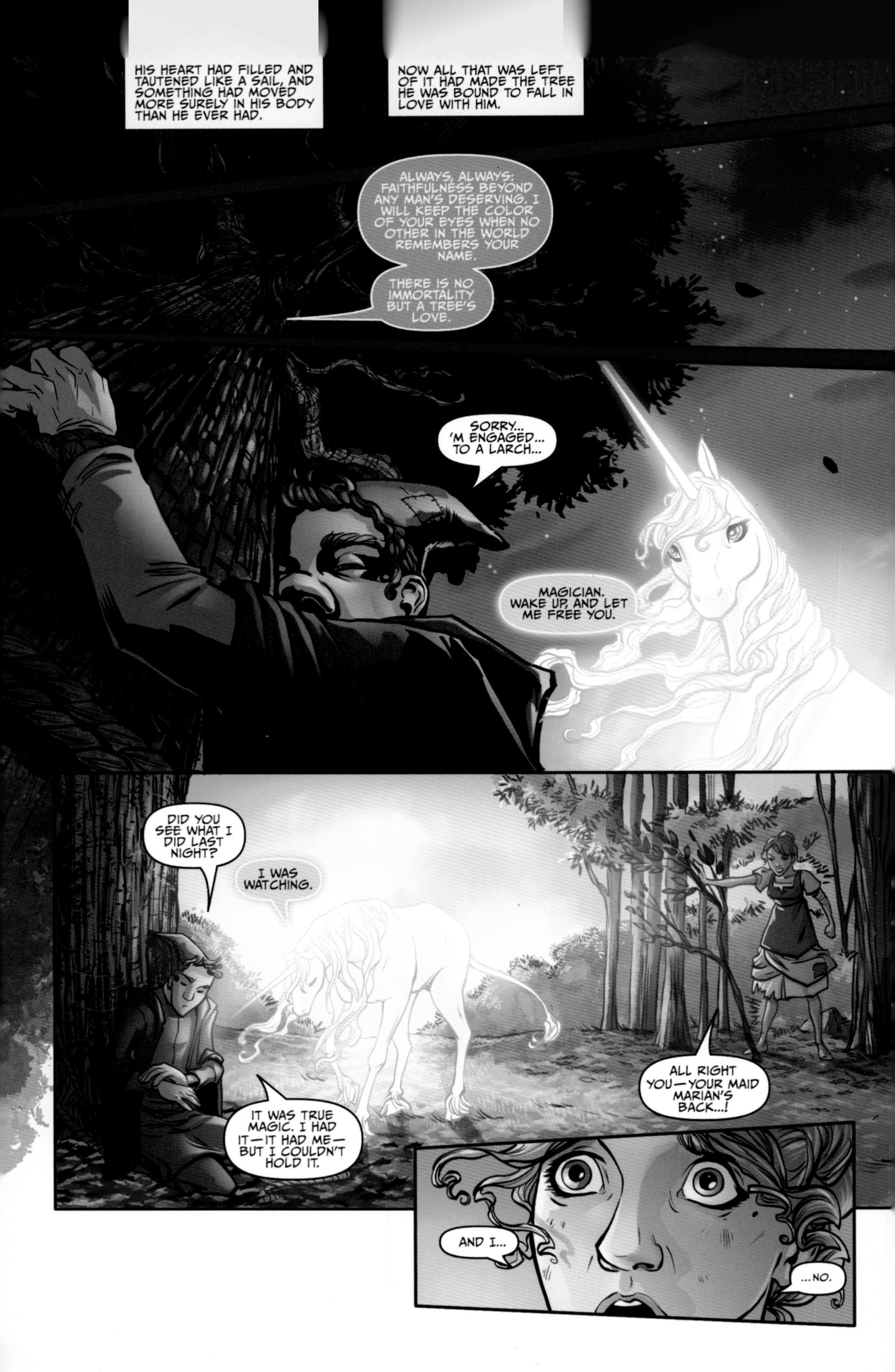
HIS HEART HAD FILLED AND TAUTENED LIKE A SAIL, AND SOMETHING HAD MOVED MORE SURELY IN HIS BODY THAN HE EVER HAD.
NOW ALL THAT WAS LEFT OF IT HAD MADE THE TREE HE WAS BOUND TO FALL IN LOVE WITH HIM.
ALWAYS, ALWAYS: FAITHFULNESS BEYOND ANY MAN'S DESERVING. I WILL KEEP THE COLOR OF YOUR EYES WHEN NO OTHER IN THE WORLD REMEMBERS YOUR NAME.
THERE IS NO IMMORTALITY BUT A TREE'S LOVE.
SORRY... 'M ENGAGED... TO A LARCH...
MAGICIAN. WAKE UP, AND LET ME FREE YOU.
DID YOU SEE WHAT I DID LAST NIGHT?
I WAS WATCHING.
IT WAS TRUE MAGIC. I HAD IT—IT HAD ME—BUT I COULDN'T HOLD IT.
ALL RIGHT YOU—YOUR MAID MARIAN'S BACK...!
AND I...
...NO.

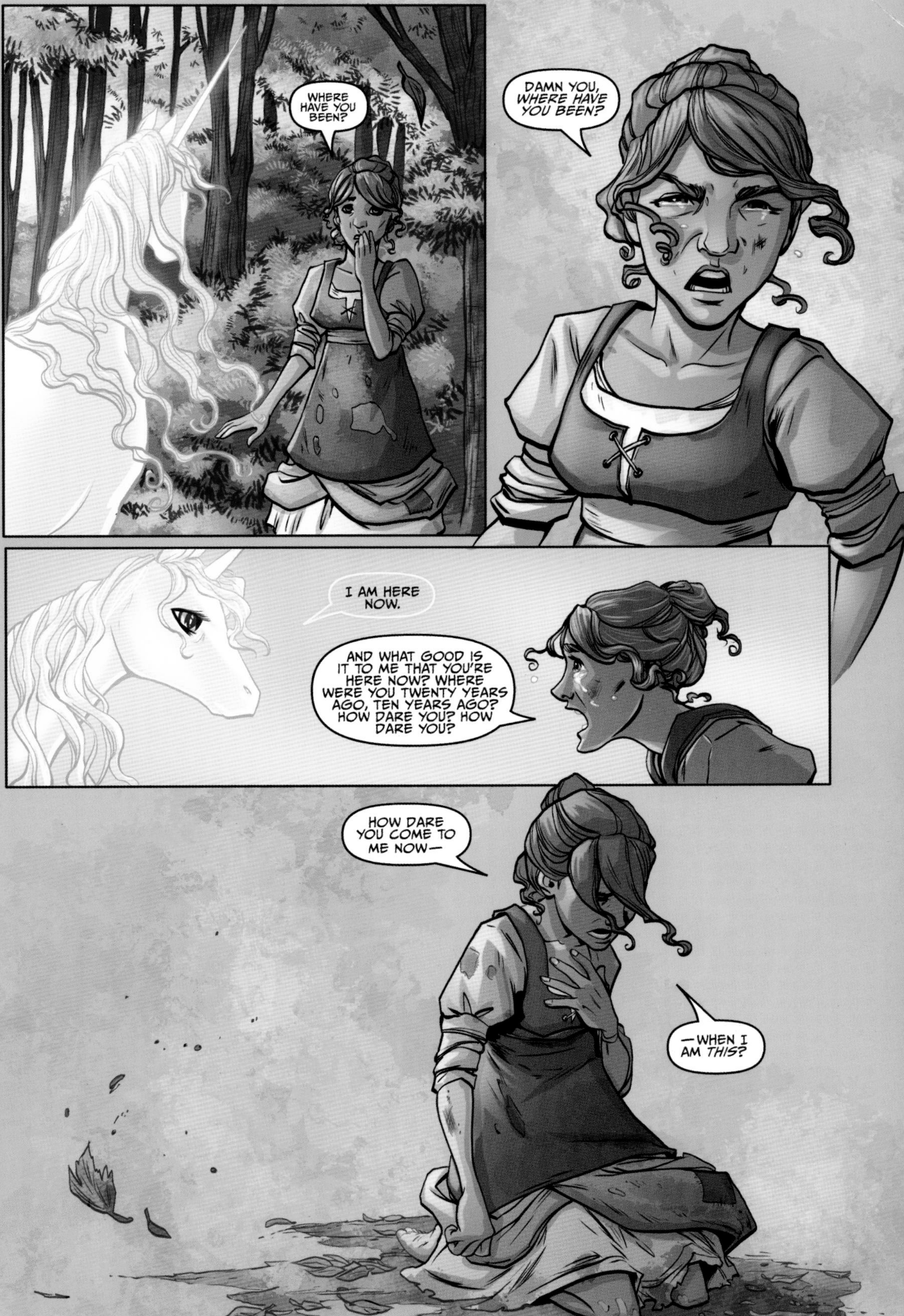
WHERE HAVE YOU BEEN?
DAMN YOU, *WHERE HAVE YOU BEEN?*
I AM HERE NOW.
AND WHAT GOOD IS IT TO ME THAT YOU'RE HERE NOW? WHERE WERE YOU TWENTY YEARS AGO, TEN YEARS AGO? HOW DARE YOU? HOW DARE YOU?
HOW DARE YOU COME TO ME NOW—
—WHEN I AM *THIS?*

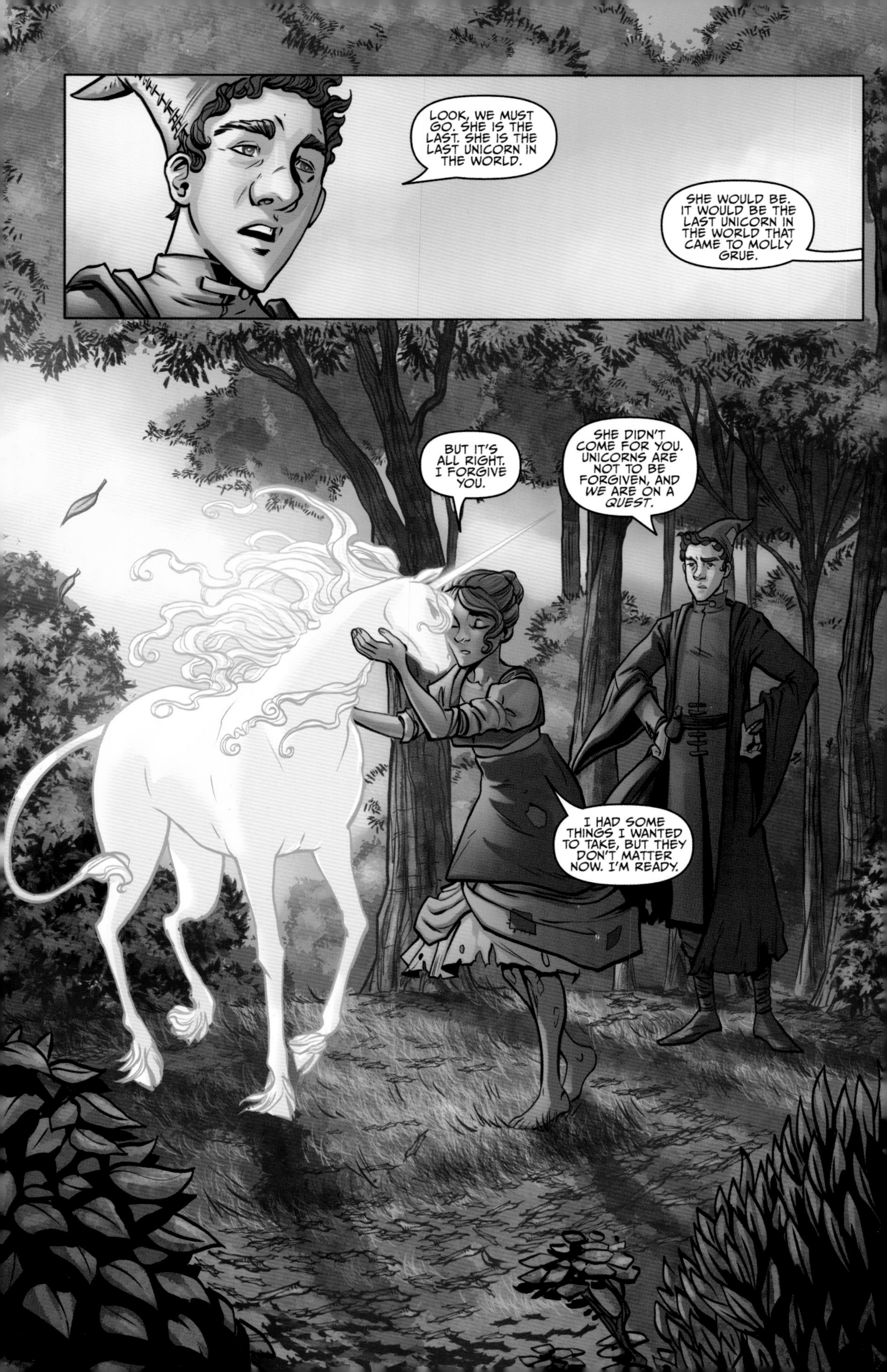
LOOK, WE MUST GO. SHE IS THE LAST. SHE IS THE LAST UNICORN IN THE WORLD.
SHE WOULD BE. IT WOULD BE THE LAST UNICORN IN THE WORLD THAT CAME TO MOLLY GRUE.
BUT IT'S ALL RIGHT. I FORGIVE YOU.
SHE DIDN'T COME FOR YOU. UNICORNS ARE NOT TO BE FORGIVEN, AND WE ARE ON A *QUEST*.
I HAD SOME THINGS I WANTED TO TAKE, BUT THEY DON'T MATTER NOW. I'M READY.

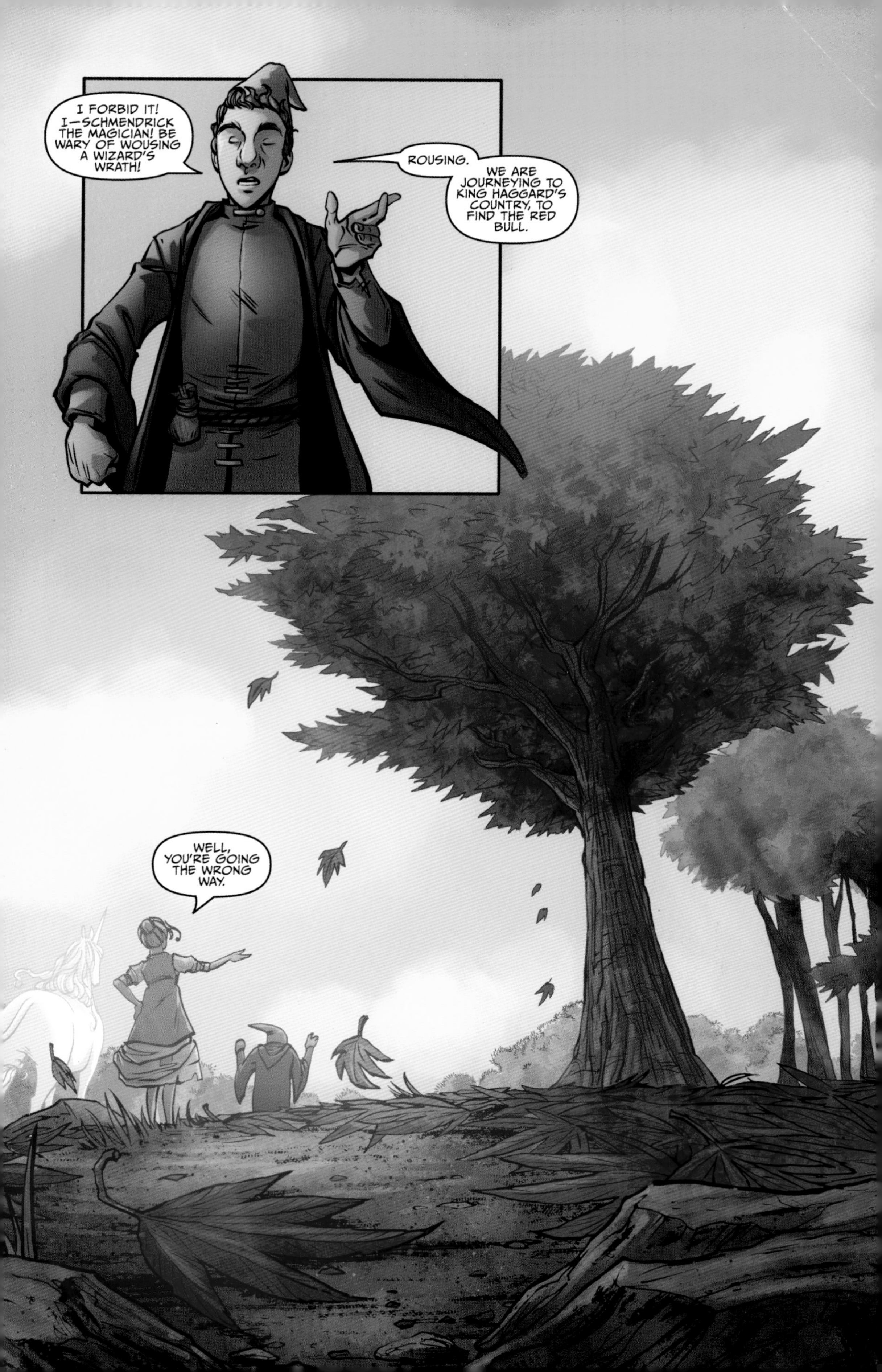
I FORBID IT! I—SCHMENDRICK THE MAGICIAN! BE WARY OF WOUSING A WIZARD'S WRATH!
ROUSING.
WE ARE JOURNEYING TO KING HAGGARD'S COUNTRY, TO FIND THE RED BULL.
WELL, YOU'RE GOING THE WRONG WAY.

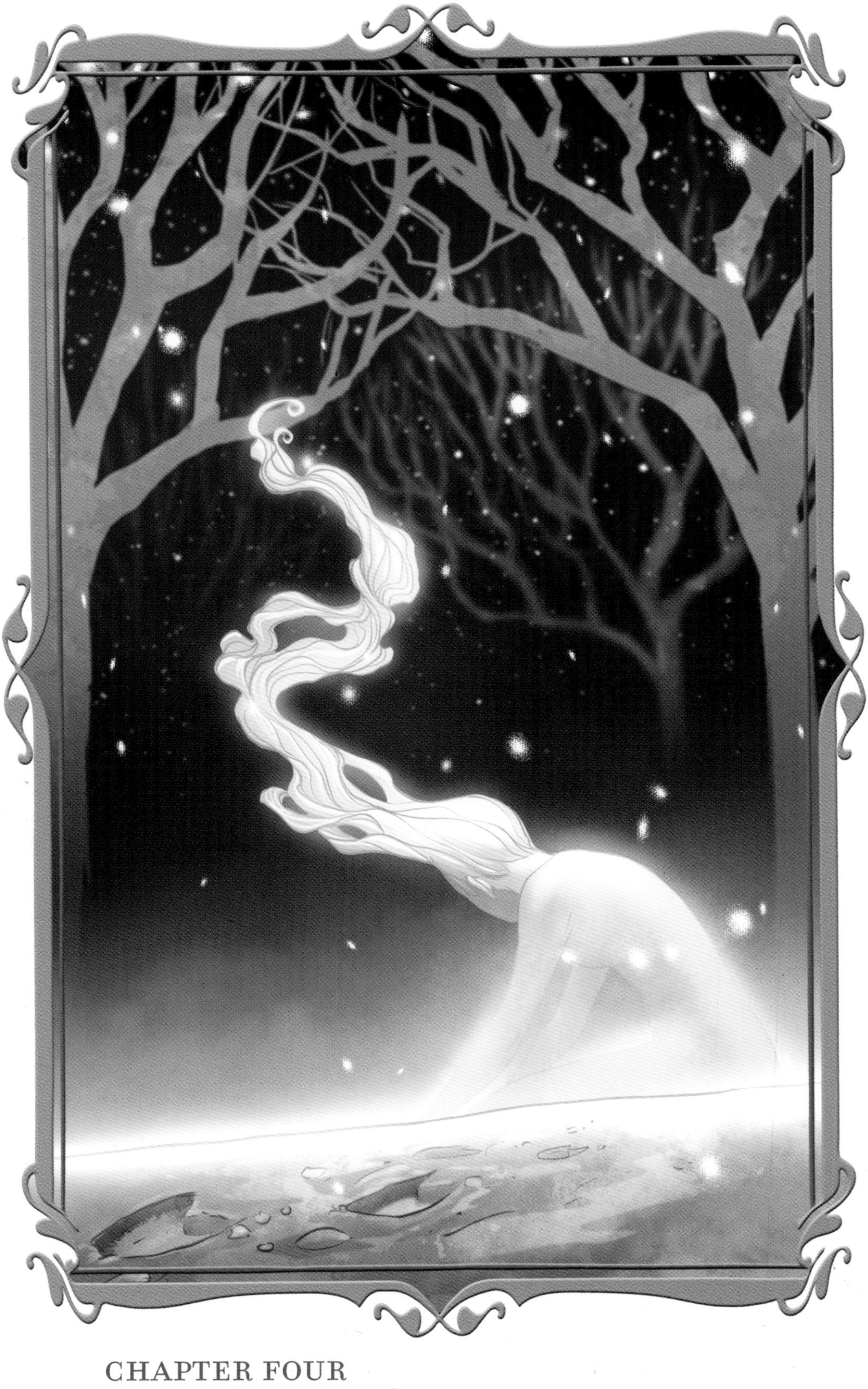

CHAPTER FOUR

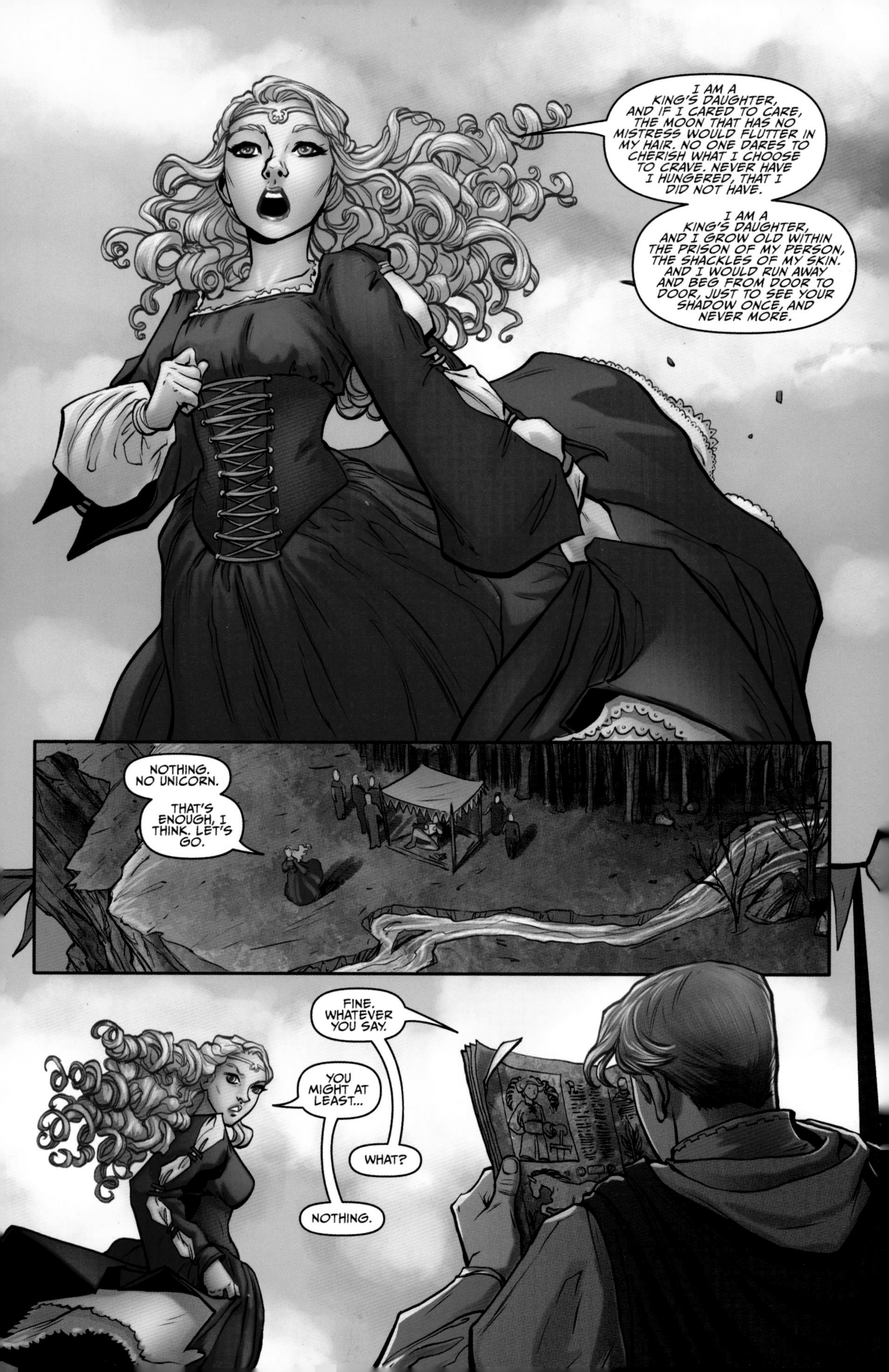
I AM A KING'S DAUGHTER, AND IF I CARED TO CARE, THE MOON THAT HAS NO MISTRESS WOULD FLUTTER IN MY HAIR. NO ONE DARES TO CHERISH WHAT I CHOOSE TO CRAVE. NEVER HAVE I HUNGERED, THAT I DID NOT HAVE.
I AM A KING'S DAUGHTER, AND I GROW OLD WITHIN THE PRISON OF MY PERSON, THE SHACKLES OF MY SKIN. AND I WOULD RUN AWAY AND BEG FROM DOOR TO DOOR, JUST TO SEE YOUR SHADOW ONCE, AND NEVER MORE.
NOTHING. NO UNICORN.
THAT'S ENOUGH, I THINK. LET'S GO.
FINE. WHATEVER YOU SAY.
YOU MIGHT AT LEAST...
WHAT?
NOTHING.

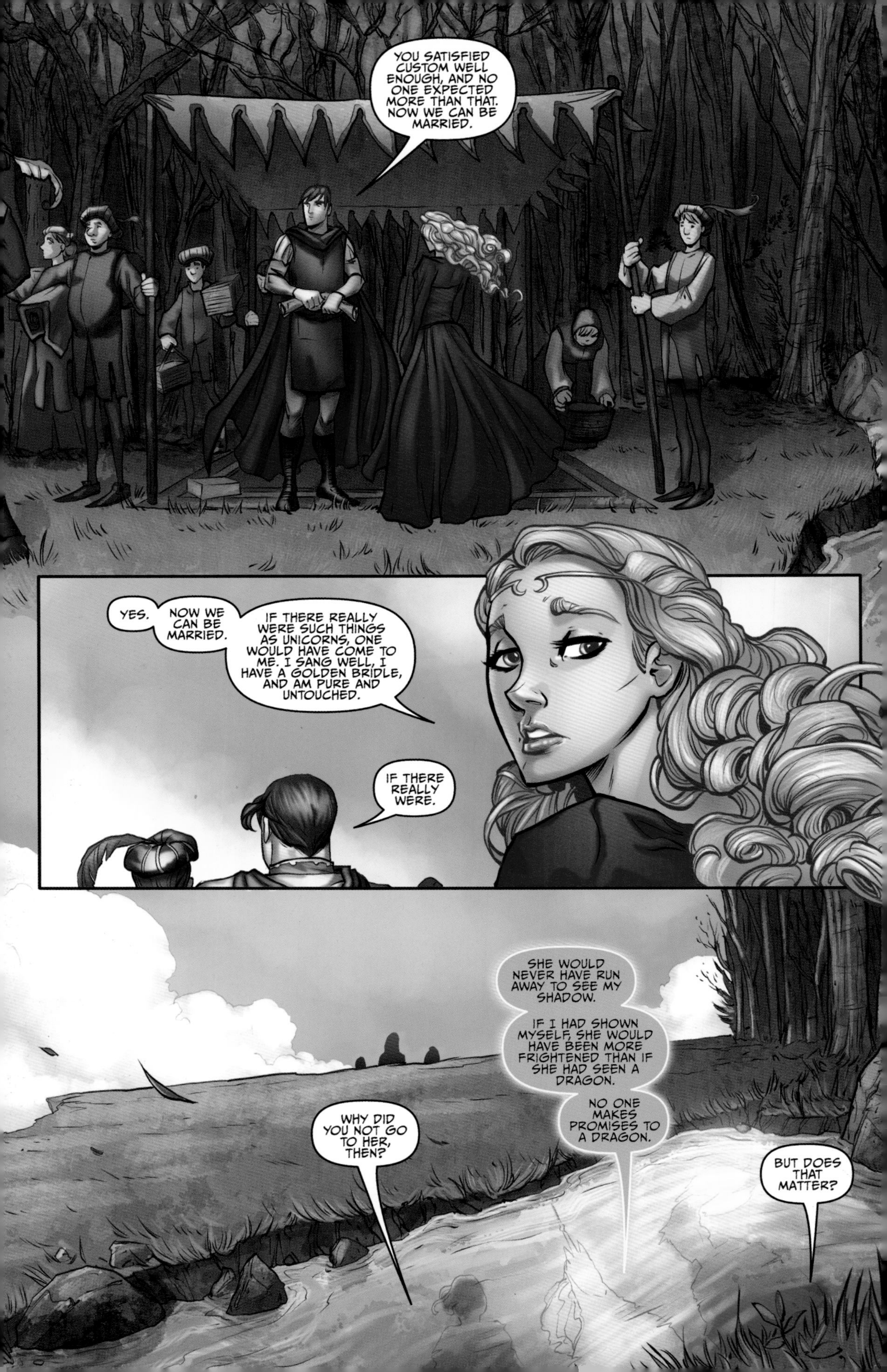
YOU SATISFIED CUSTOM WELL ENOUGH, AND NO ONE EXPECTED MORE THAN THAT. NOW WE CAN BE MARRIED.
YES.
NOW WE CAN BE MARRIED.
IF THERE REALLY WERE SUCH THINGS AS UNICORNS, ONE WOULD HAVE COME TO ME. I SANG WELL, I HAVE A GOLDEN BRIDLE, AND AM PURE AND UNTOUCHED.
IF THERE REALLY WERE.
SHE WOULD NEVER HAVE RUN AWAY TO SEE MY SHADOW.
IF I HAD SHOWN MYSELF, SHE WOULD HAVE BEEN MORE FRIGHTENED THAN IF SHE HAD SEEN A DRAGON.
NO ONE MAKES PROMISES TO A DRAGON.
WHY DID YOU NOT GO TO HER, THEN?
BUT DOES THAT MATTER?

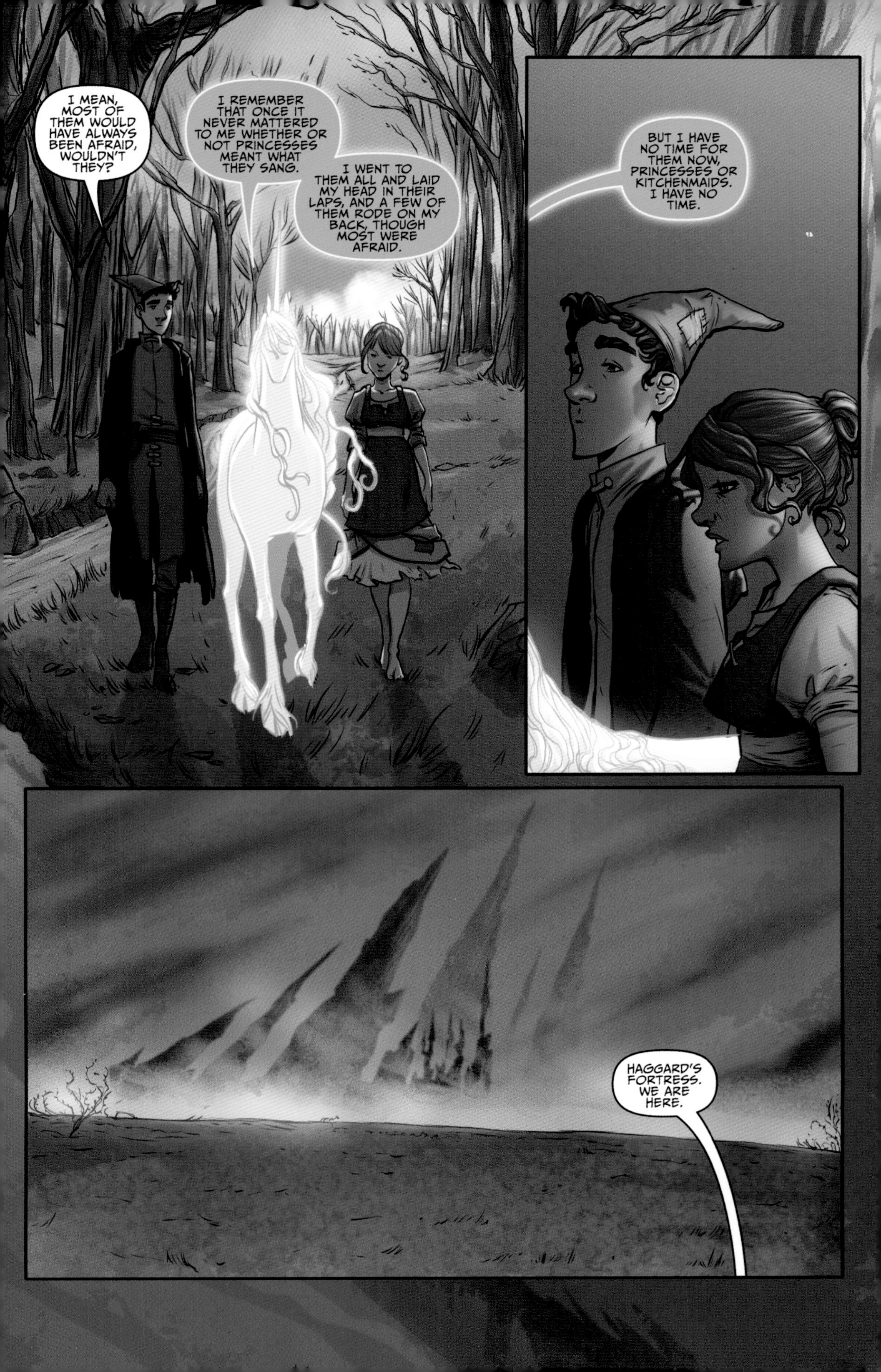
I MEAN, MOST OF THEM WOULD HAVE ALWAYS BEEN AFRAID, WOULDN'T THEY?
I REMEMBER THAT ONCE IT NEVER MATTERED TO ME WHETHER OR NOT PRINCESSES MEANT WHAT THEY SANG.
I WENT TO THEM ALL AND LAID MY HEAD IN THEIR LAPS, AND A FEW OF THEM RODE ON MY BACK, THOUGH MOST WERE AFRAID.
BUT I HAVE NO TIME FOR THEM NOW, PRINCESSES OR KITCHENMAIDS. I HAVE NO TIME.
HAGGARD'S FORTRESS. WE ARE HERE.

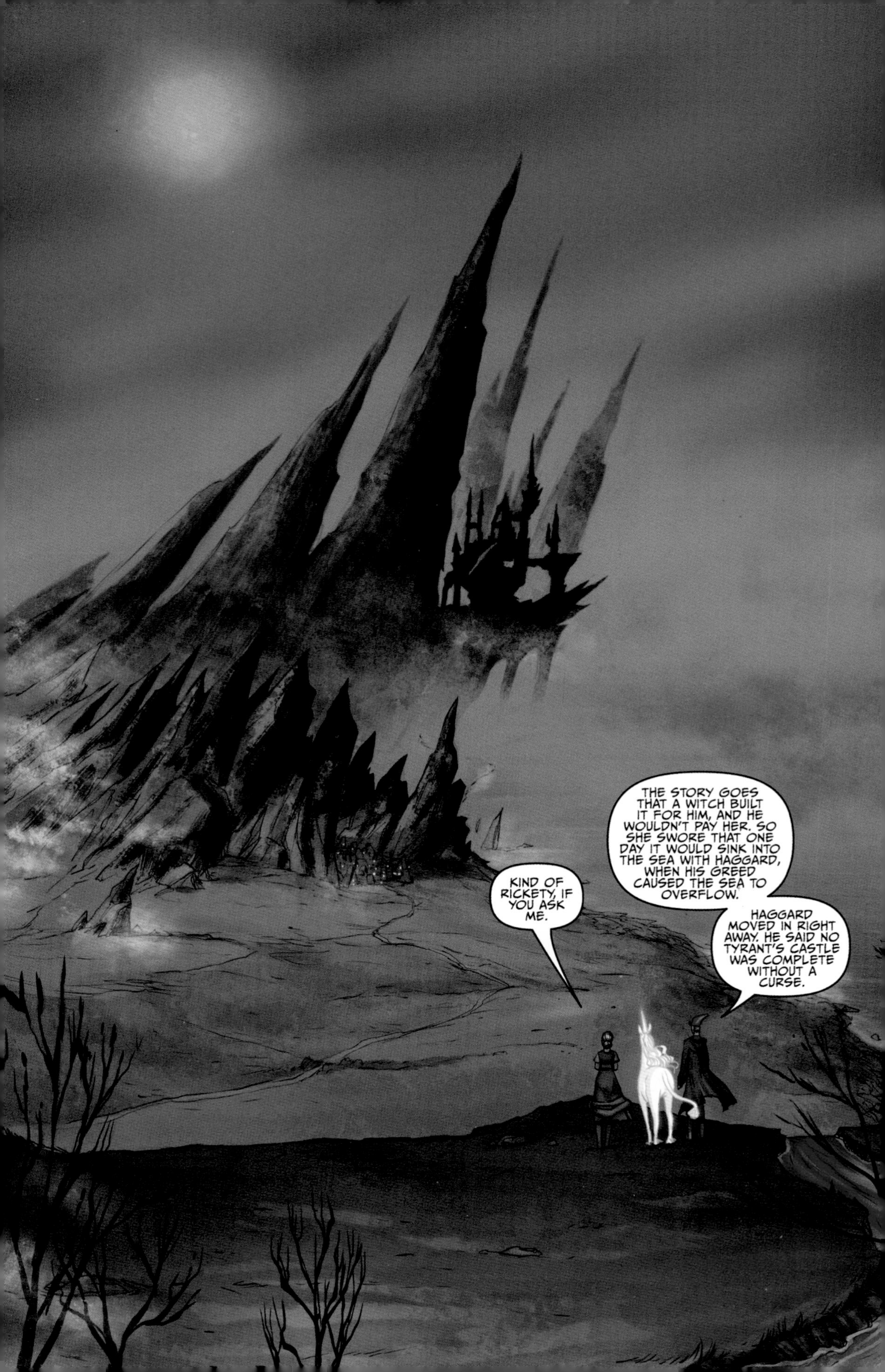
KIND OF RICKETY, IF YOU ASK ME.
THE STORY GOES THAT A WITCH BUILT IT FOR HIM, AND HE WOULDN'T PAY HER. SO SHE SWORE THAT ONE DAY IT WOULD SINK INTO THE SEA WITH HAGGARD, WHEN HIS GREED CAUSED THE SEA TO OVERFLOW.
HAGGARD MOVED IN RIGHT AWAY. HE SAID NO TYRANT'S CASTLE WAS COMPLETE WITHOUT A CURSE.

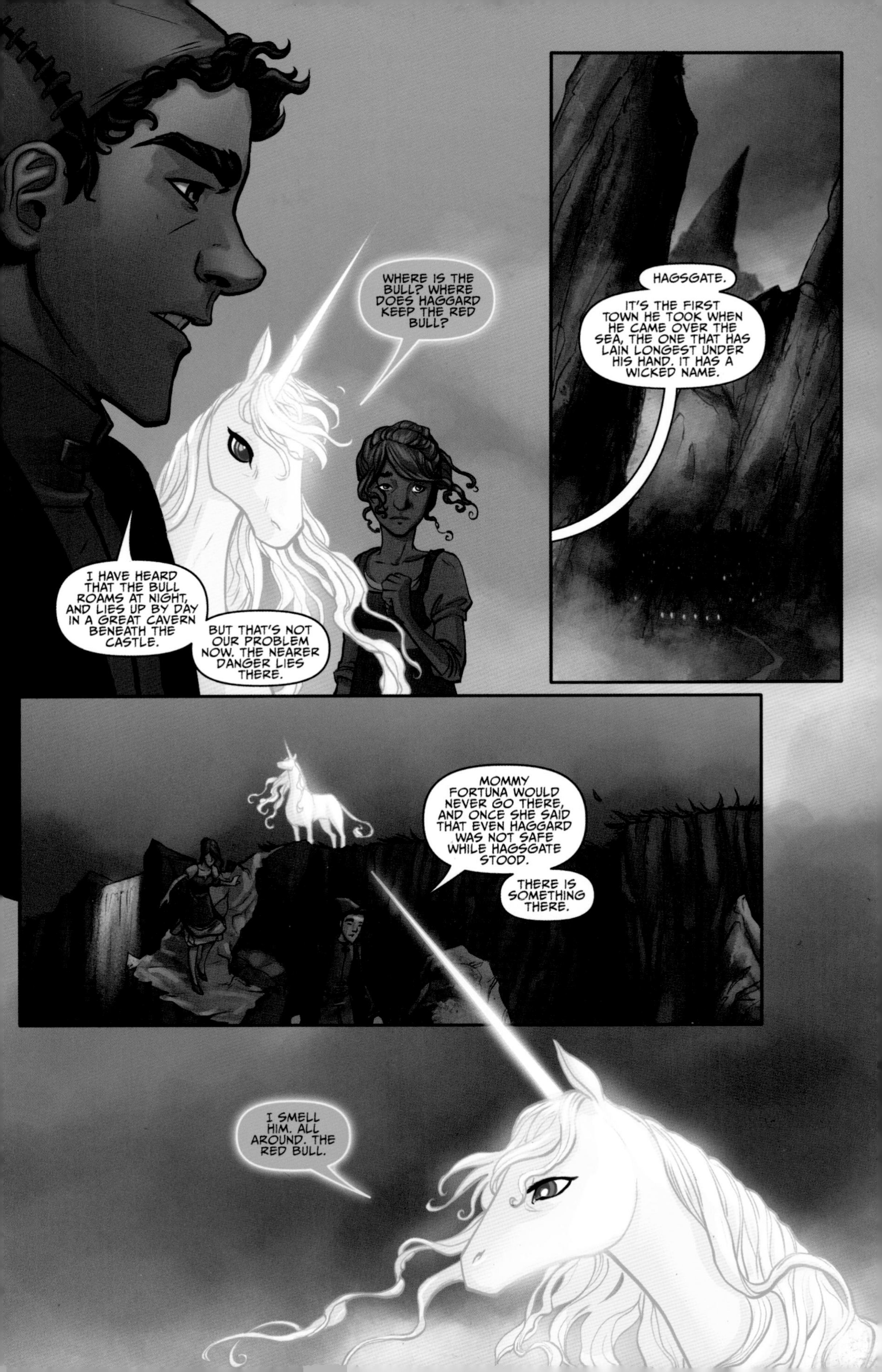
WHERE IS THE BULL? WHERE DOES HAGGARD KEEP THE RED BULL?
I HAVE HEARD THAT THE BULL ROAMS AT NIGHT, AND LIES UP BY DAY IN A GREAT CAVERN BENEATH THE CASTLE.
BUT THAT'S NOT OUR PROBLEM NOW. THE NEARER DANGER LIES THERE.
HAGSGATE.
IT'S THE FIRST TOWN HE TOOK WHEN HE CAME OVER THE SEA, THE ONE THAT HAS LAIN LONGEST UNDER HIS HAND. IT HAS A WICKED NAME.
MOMMY FORTUNA WOULD NEVER GO THERE, AND ONCE SHE SAID THAT EVEN HAGGARD WAS NOT SAFE WHILE HAGSGATE STOOD.
THERE IS SOMETHING THERE.
I SMELL HIM. ALL AROUND. THE RED BULL.

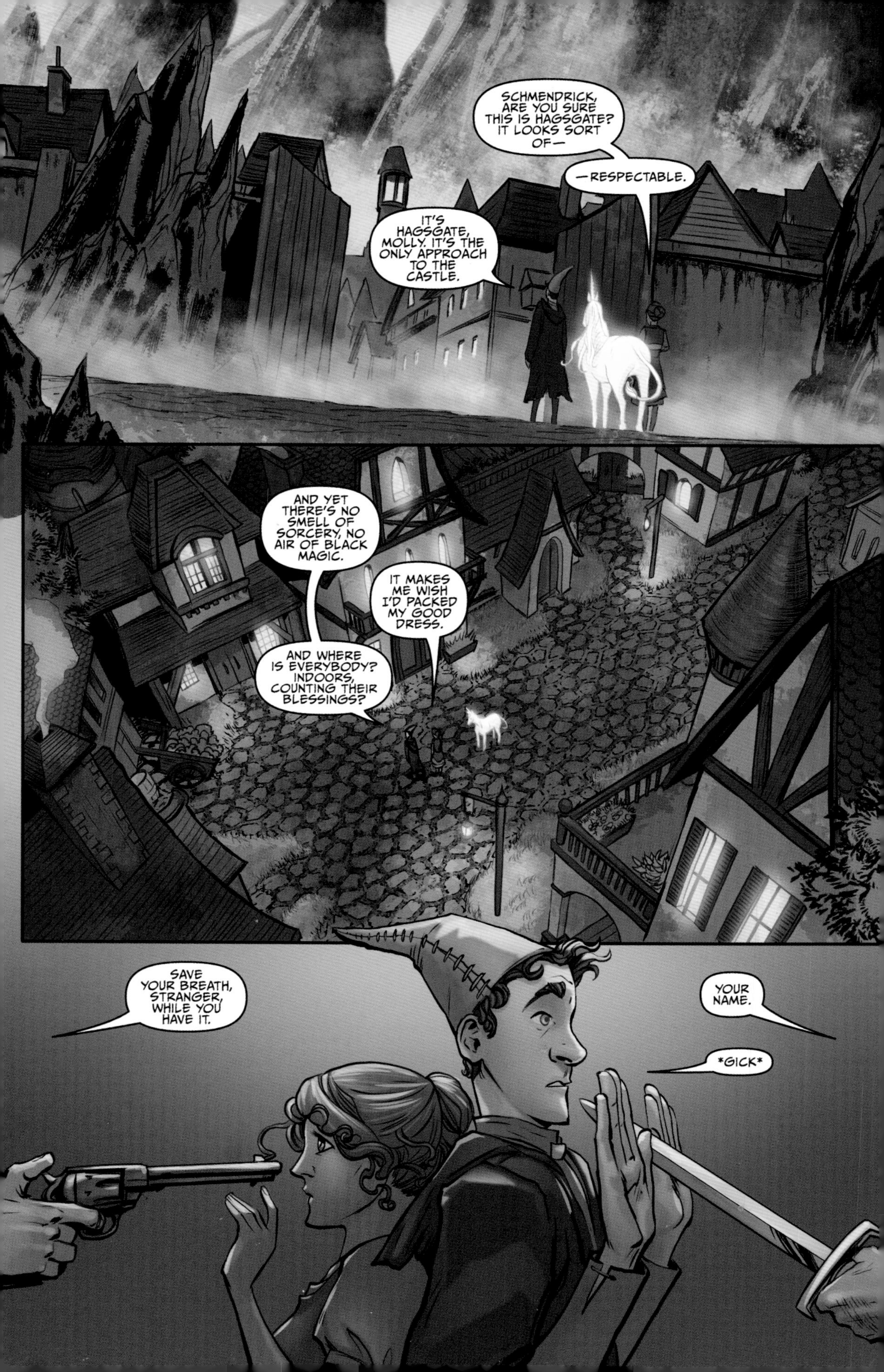
SCHMENDRICK, ARE YOU SURE THIS IS HAGSGATE? IT LOOKS SORT OF—
—RESPECTABLE.
IT'S HAGSGATE, MOLLY. IT'S THE ONLY APPROACH TO THE CASTLE.
AND YET THERE'S NO SMELL OF SORCERY, NO AIR OF BLACK MAGIC.
IT MAKES ME WISH I'D PACKED MY GOOD DRESS.
AND WHERE IS EVERYBODY? INDOORS, COUNTING THEIR BLESSINGS?
SAVE YOUR BREATH, STRANGER, WHILE YOU HAVE IT.
YOUR NAME.
GICK

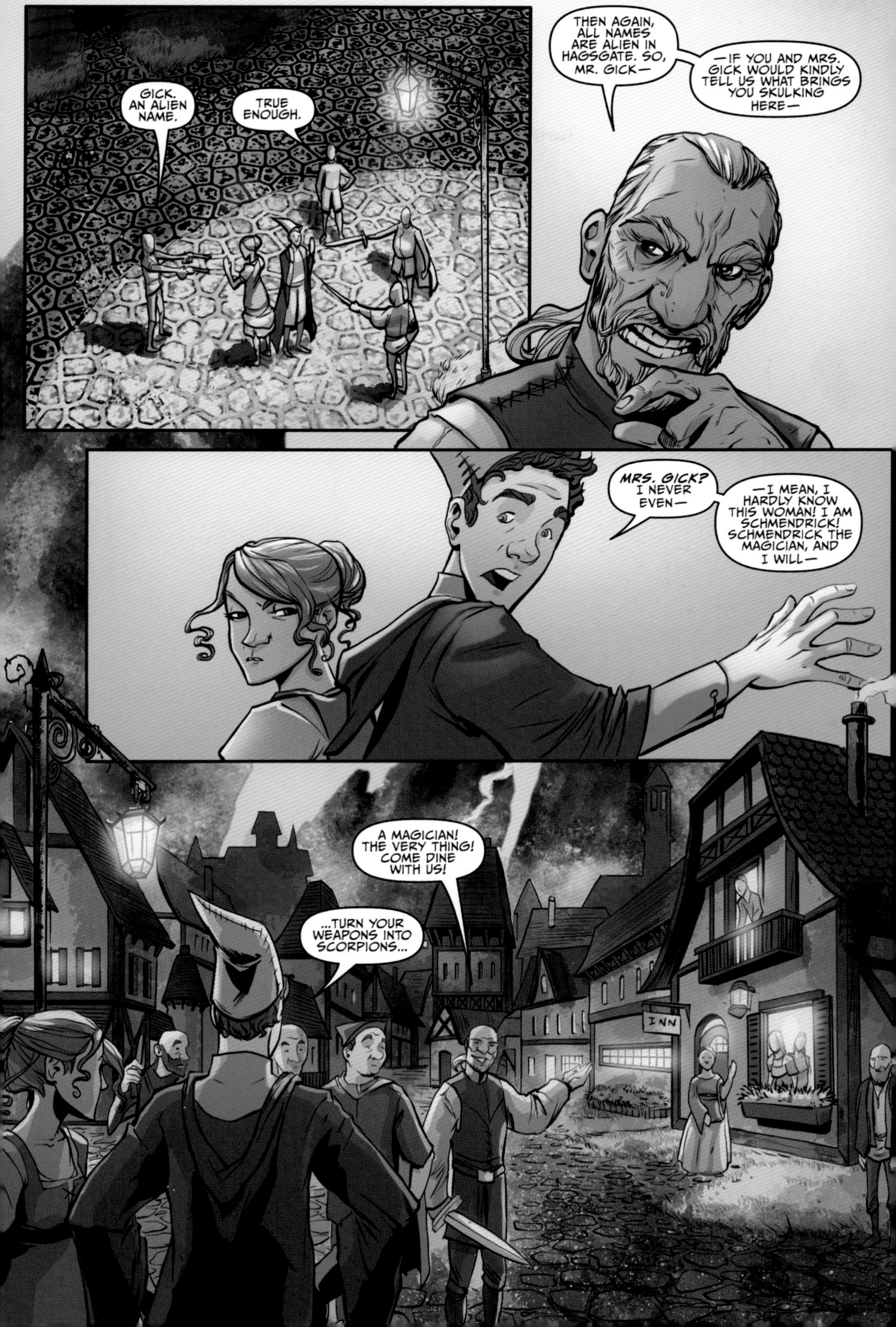
GICK. AN ALIEN NAME.
TRUE ENOUGH.
THEN AGAIN, ALL NAMES ARE ALIEN IN HAGSGATE. SO, MR. GICK—
—IF YOU AND MRS. GICK WOULD KINDLY TELL US WHAT BRINGS YOU SKULKING HERE—
MRS. GICK? I NEVER EVEN—
—I MEAN, I HARDLY KNOW THIS WOMAN! I AM SCHMENDRICK! SCHMENDRICK THE MAGICIAN, AND I WILL—
...TURN YOUR WEAPONS INTO SCORPIONS...
A MAGICIAN! THE VERY THING! COME DINE WITH US!
INN

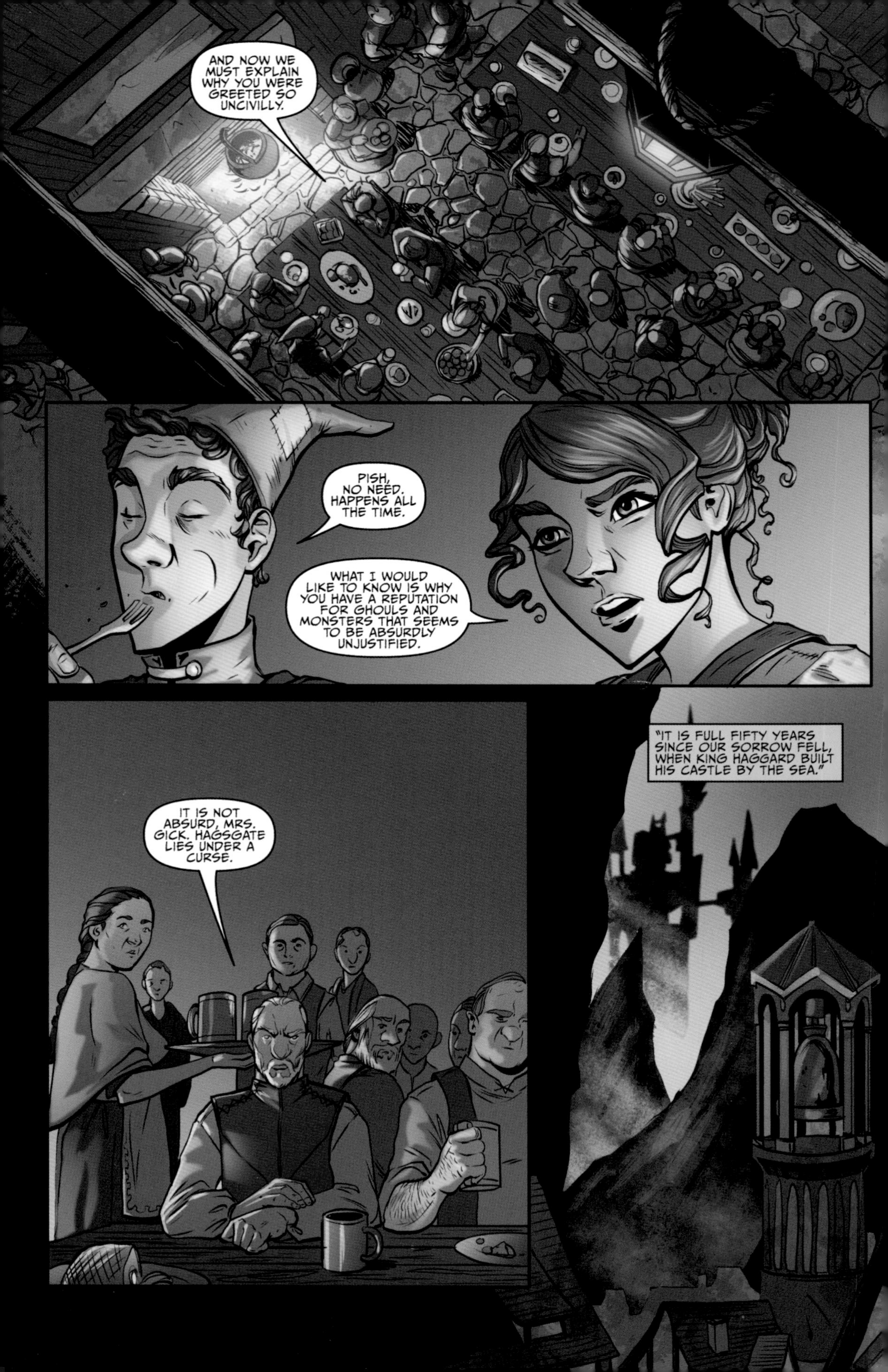
AND NOW WE MUST EXPLAIN WHY YOU WERE GREETED SO UNCIVILLY.
PISH, NO NEED. HAPPENS ALL THE TIME.
WHAT I WOULD LIKE TO KNOW IS WHY YOU HAVE A REPUTATION FOR GHOULS AND MONSTERS THAT SEEMS TO BE ABSURDLY UNJUSTIFIED.
IT IS NOT ABSURD, MRS. GICK. HAGSGATE LIES UNDER A CURSE.
"IT IS FULL FIFTY YEARS SINCE OUR SORROW FELL, WHEN KING HAGGARD BUILT HIS CASTLE BY THE SEA."

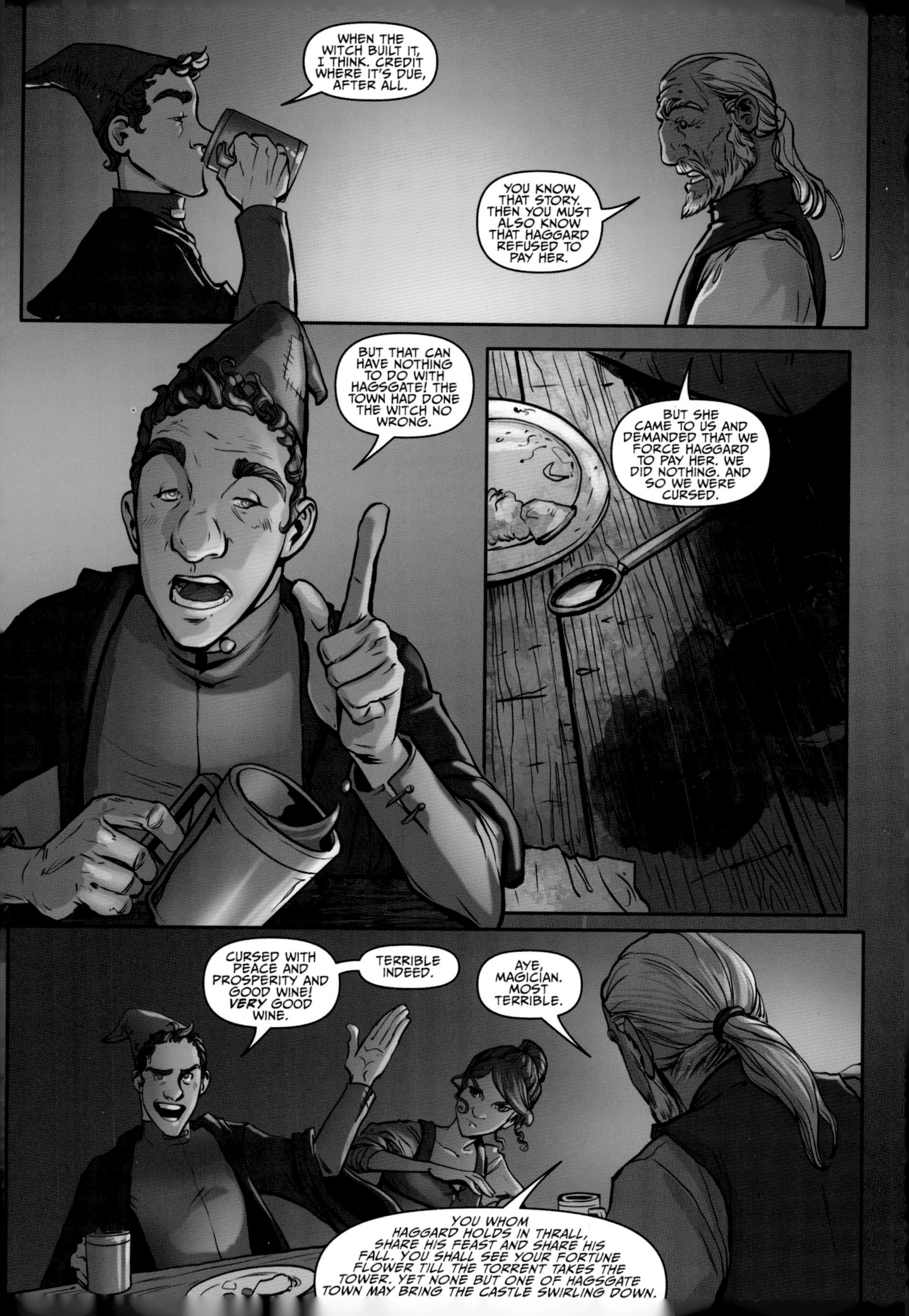
WHEN THE WITCH BUILT IT, I THINK. CREDIT WHERE IT'S DUE, AFTER ALL.
YOU KNOW THAT STORY. THEN YOU MUST ALSO KNOW THAT HAGGARD REFUSED TO PAY HER.
BUT THAT CAN HAVE NOTHING TO DO WITH HAGSGATE! THE TOWN HAD DONE THE WITCH NO WRONG.
BUT SHE CAME TO US AND DEMANDED THAT WE FORCE HAGGARD TO PAY HER. WE DID NOTHING. AND SO WE WERE CURSED.
CURSED WITH PEACE AND PROSPERITY AND GOOD WINE! VERY GOOD WINE.
TERRIBLE INDEED.
AYE, MAGICIAN. MOST TERRIBLE.
YOU WHOM HAGGARD HOLDS IN THRALL, SHARE HIS FEAST AND SHARE HIS FALL. YOU SHALL SEE YOUR FORTUNE FLOWER TILL THE TORRENT TAKES THE TOWER. YET NONE BUT ONE OF HAGSGATE TOWN MAY BRING THE CASTLE SWIRLING DOWN.

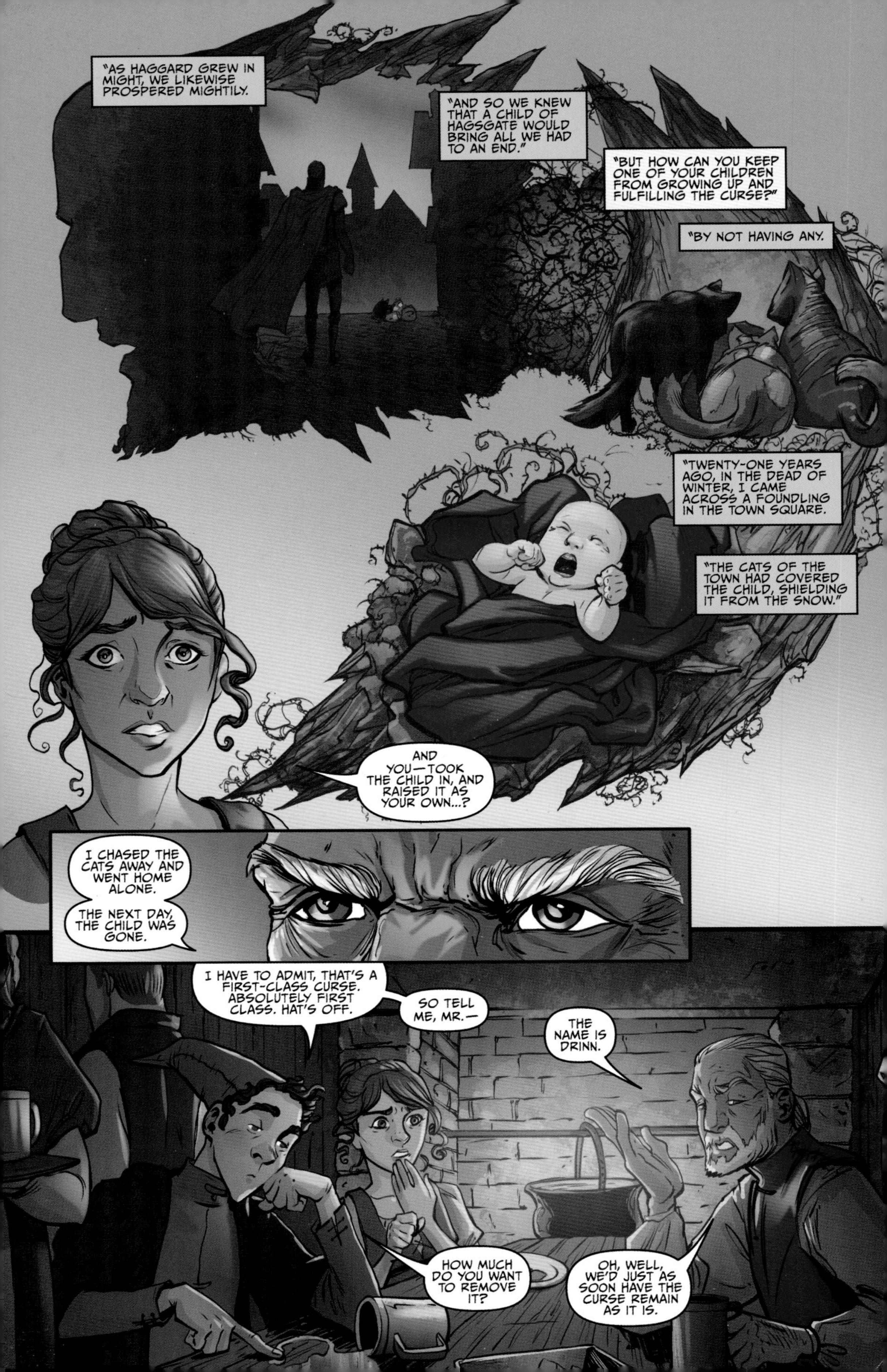
"AS HAGGARD GREW IN MIGHT, WE LIKEWISE PROSPERED MIGHTILY.
"AND SO WE KNEW THAT A CHILD OF HAGSGATE WOULD BRING ALL WE HAD TO AN END."
"BUT HOW CAN YOU KEEP ONE OF YOUR CHILDREN FROM GROWING UP AND FULFILLING THE CURSE?"
"BY NOT HAVING ANY.
"TWENTY-ONE YEARS AGO, IN THE DEAD OF WINTER, I CAME ACROSS A FOUNDLING IN THE TOWN SQUARE.
"THE CATS OF THE TOWN HAD COVERED THE CHILD, SHIELDING IT FROM THE SNOW."
AND YOU—TOOK THE CHILD IN, AND RAISED IT AS YOUR OWN...?
I CHASED THE CATS AWAY AND WENT HOME ALONE.
THE NEXT DAY, THE CHILD WAS GONE.
I HAVE TO ADMIT, THAT'S A FIRST-CLASS CURSE. ABSOLUTELY FIRST CLASS. HAT'S OFF.
SO TELL ME, MR.—
THE NAME IS DRINN.
HOW MUCH DO YOU WANT TO REMOVE IT?
OH, WELL, WE'D JUST AS SOON HAVE THE CURSE REMAIN AS IT IS.

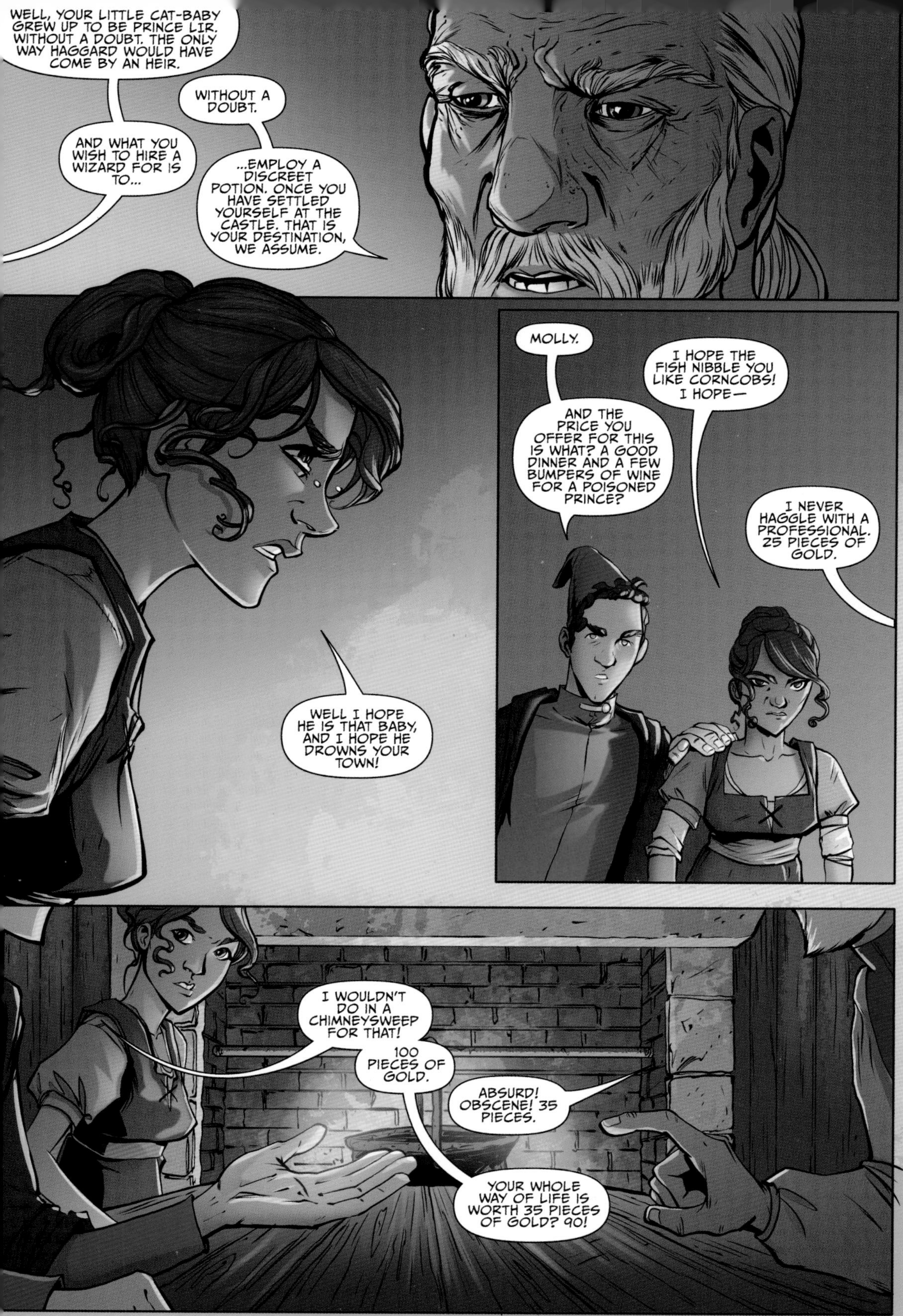
WELL, YOUR LITTLE CAT-BABY GREW UP TO BE PRINCE LIR. WITHOUT A DOUBT. THE ONLY WAY HAGGARD WOULD HAVE COME BY AN HEIR.
WITHOUT A DOUBT.
AND WHAT YOU WISH TO HIRE A WIZARD FOR IS TO...
...EMPLOY A DISCREET POTION. ONCE YOU HAVE SETTLED YOURSELF AT THE CASTLE. THAT IS YOUR DESTINATION, WE ASSUME.
WELL I HOPE HE IS THAT BABY, AND I HOPE HE DROWNS YOUR TOWN!
MOLLY.
I HOPE THE FISH NIBBLE YOU LIKE CORNCOBS! I HOPE—
AND THE PRICE YOU OFFER FOR THIS IS WHAT? A GOOD DINNER AND A FEW BUMPERS OF WINE FOR A POISONED PRINCE?
I NEVER HAGGLE WITH A PROFESSIONAL. 25 PIECES OF GOLD.
I WOULDN'T DO IN A CHIMNEYSWEEP FOR THAT!
100 PIECES OF GOLD.
ABSURD! OBSCENE! 35 PIECES.
YOUR WHOLE WAY OF LIFE IS WORTH 35 PIECES OF GOLD? 90!

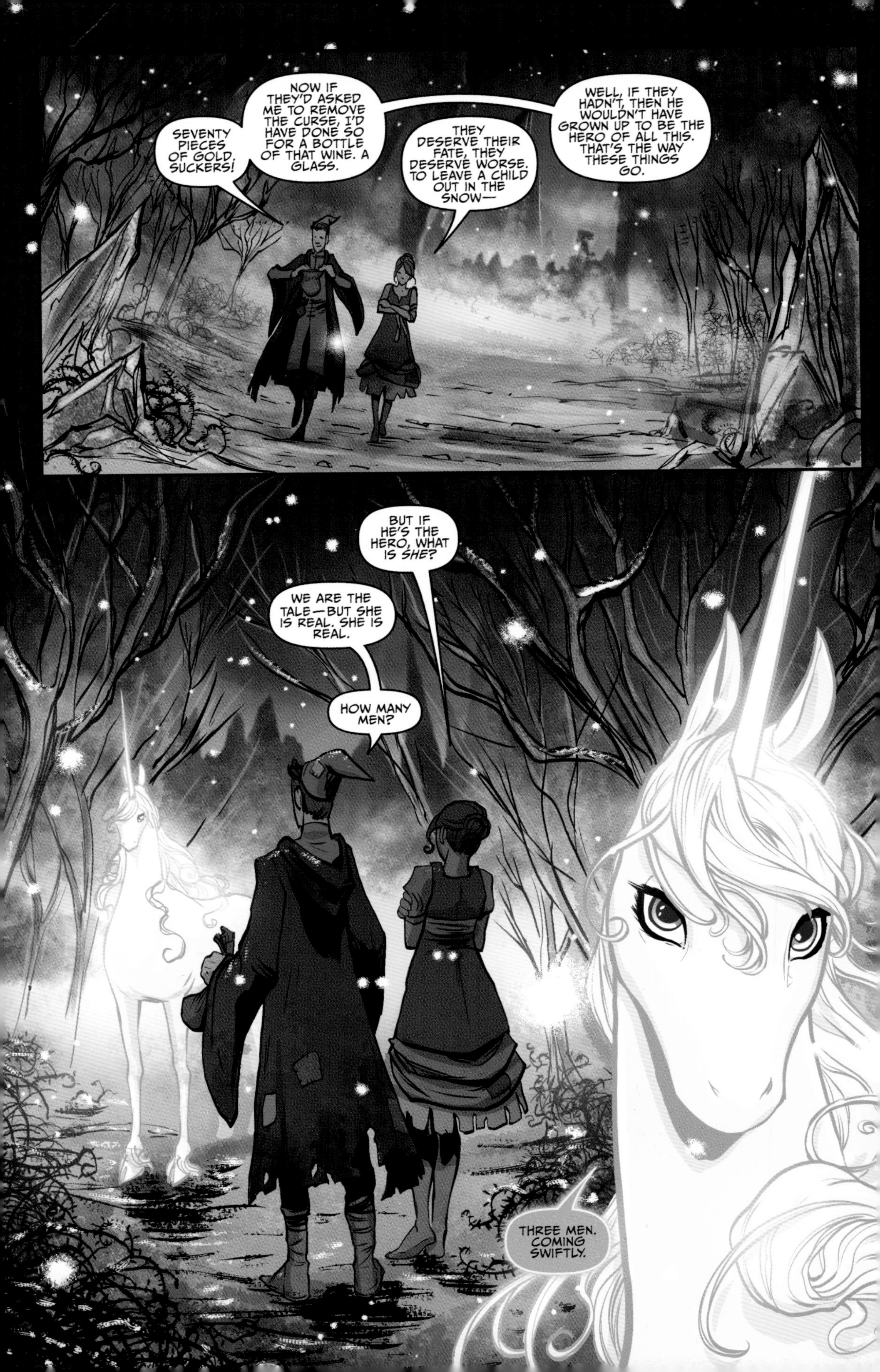
SEVENTY PIECES OF GOLD. SUCKERS!
NOW IF THEY'D ASKED ME TO REMOVE THE CURSE, I'D HAVE DONE SO FOR A BOTTLE OF THAT WINE. A GLASS.
THEY DESERVE THEIR FATE, THEY DESERVE WORSE. TO LEAVE A CHILD OUT IN THE SNOW—
WELL, IF THEY HADN'T, THEN HE WOULDN'T HAVE GROWN UP TO BE THE HERO OF ALL THIS. THAT'S THE WAY THESE THINGS GO.
BUT IF HE'S THE HERO, WHAT IS SHE?
WE ARE THE TALE—BUT SHE IS REAL. SHE IS REAL.
HOW MANY MEN?
THREE MEN. COMING SWIFTLY.

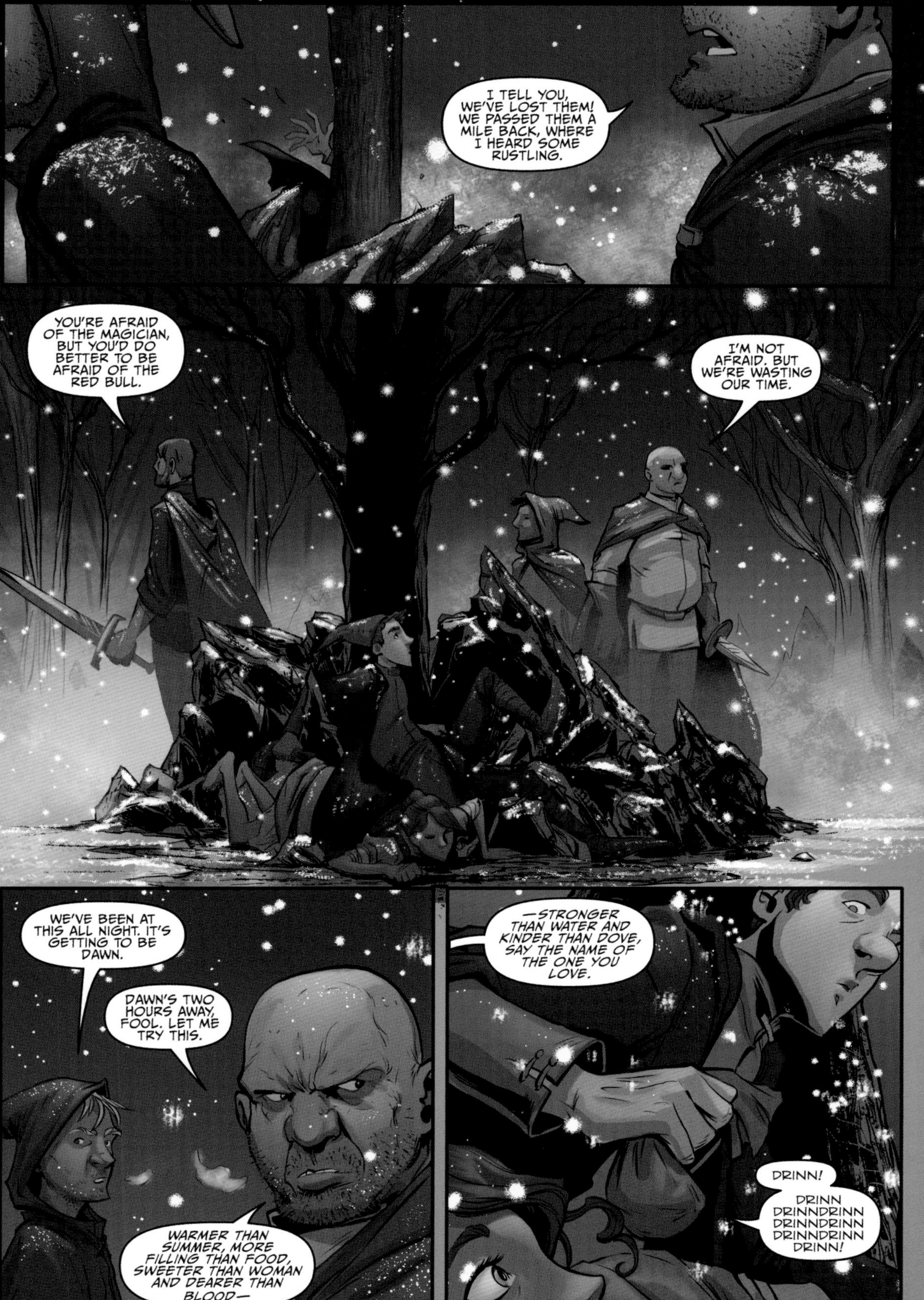
I TELL YOU, WE'VE LOST THEM! WE PASSED THEM A MILE BACK, WHERE I HEARD SOME RUSTLING.
YOU'RE AFRAID OF THE MAGICIAN, BUT YOU'D DO BETTER TO BE AFRAID OF THE RED BULL.
I'M NOT AFRAID. BUT WE'RE WASTING OUR TIME.
WE'VE BEEN AT THIS ALL NIGHT. IT'S GETTING TO BE DAWN.
DAWN'S TWO HOURS AWAY, FOOL. LET ME TRY THIS.
WARMER THAN SUMMER, MORE FILLING THAN FOOD, SWEETER THAN WOMAN AND DEARER THAN BLOOD—
—STRONGER THAN WATER AND KINDER THAN DOVE, SAY THE NAME OF THE ONE YOU LOVE.
DRINN!
DRINN DRINNDRINN DRINNDRINN DRINNDRINN DRINN!

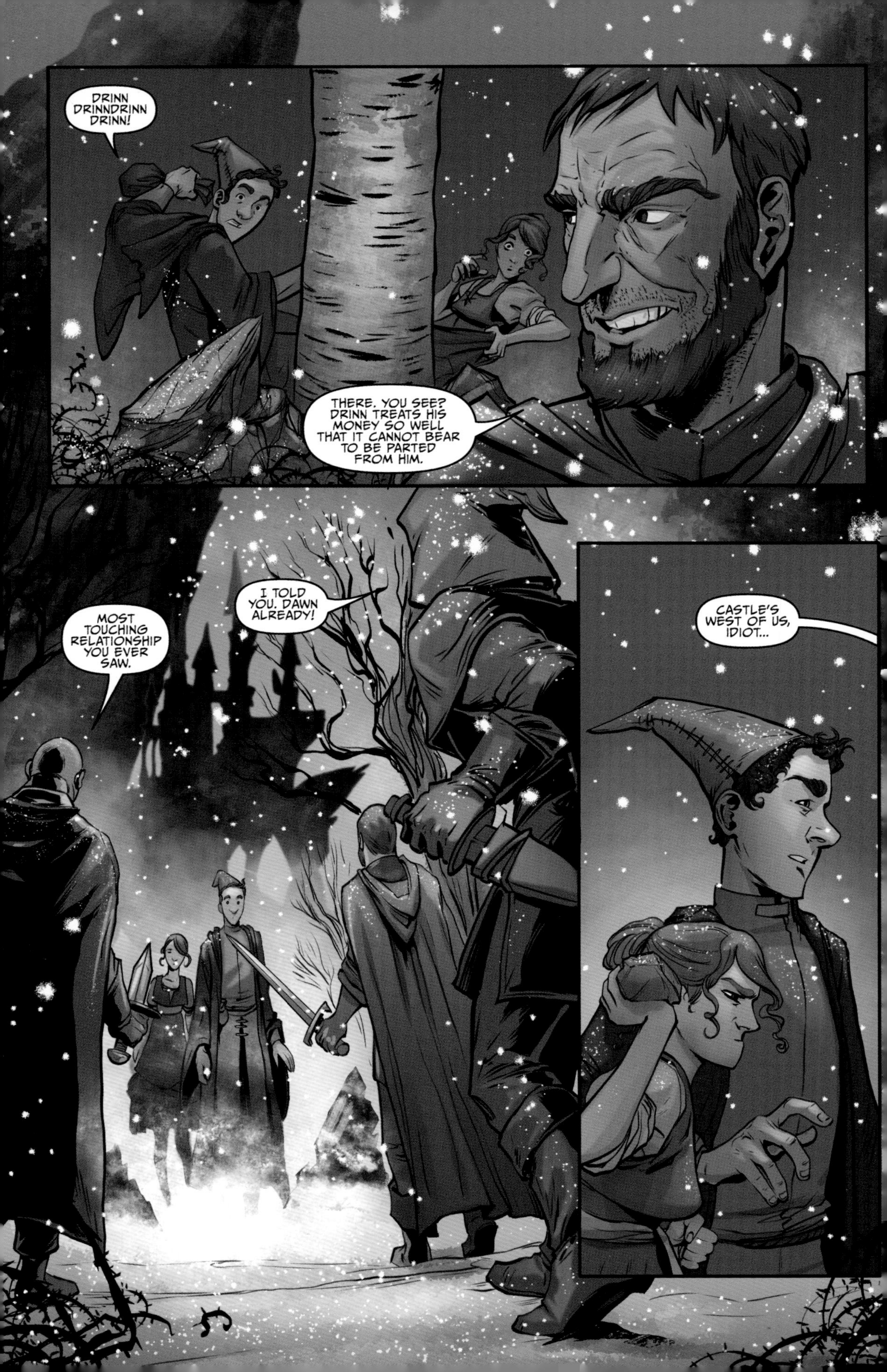
DRINN DRINNDRINN DRINN!
THERE. YOU SEE? DRINN TREATS HIS MONEY SO WELL THAT IT CANNOT BEAR TO BE PARTED FROM HIM.
MOST TOUCHING RELATIONSHIP YOU EVER SAW.
I TOLD YOU. DAWN ALREADY!
CASTLE'S WEST OF US, IDIOT...

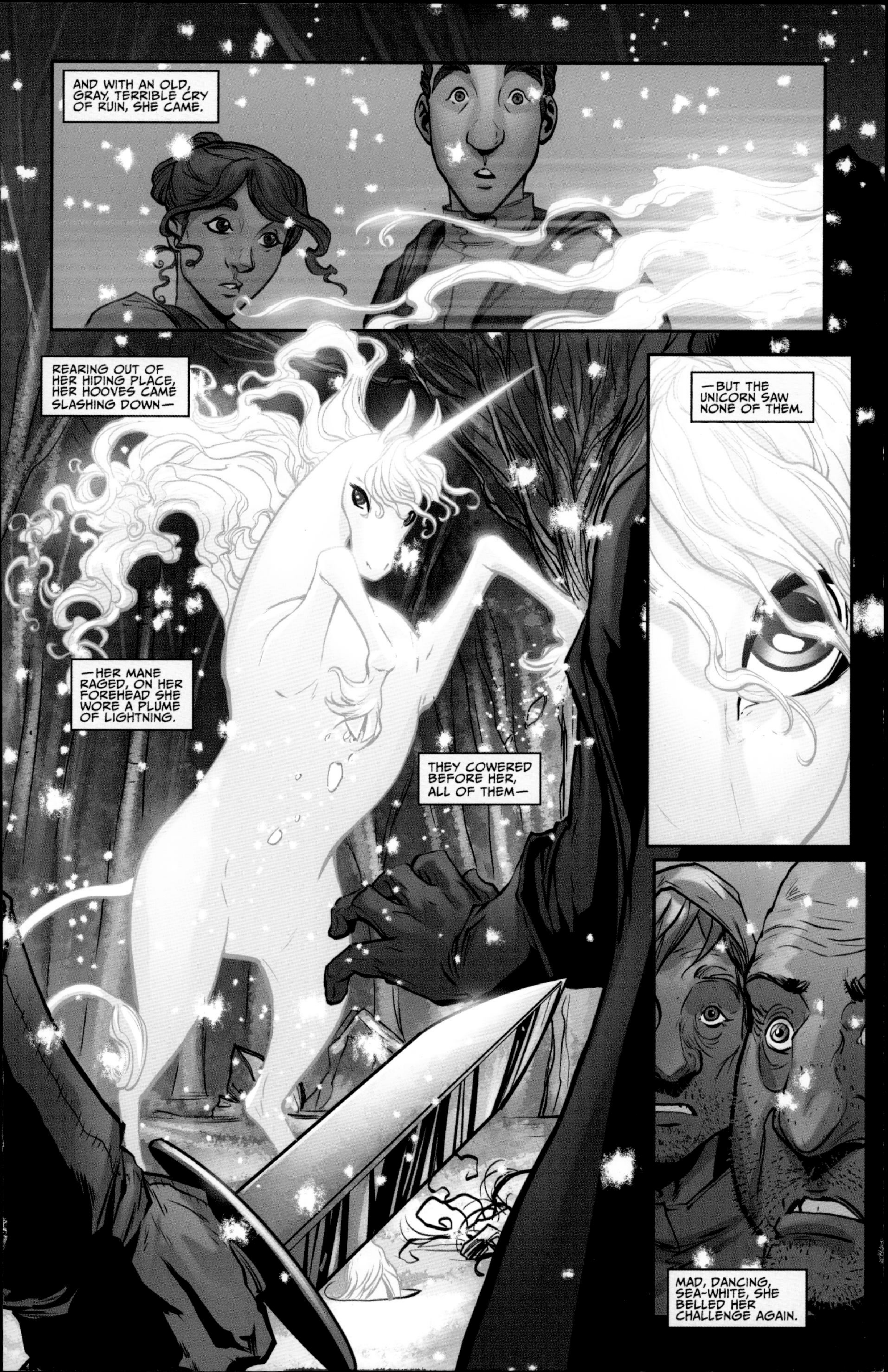
AND WITH AN OLD, GRAY, TERRIBLE CRY OF RUIN, SHE CAME.
REARING OUT OF HER HIDING PLACE, HER HOOVES CAME SLASHING DOWN—
—HER MANE RAGED, ON HER FOREHEAD SHE WORE A PLUME OF LIGHTNING.
THEY COWERED BEFORE HER, ALL OF THEM—
—BUT THE UNICORN SAW NONE OF THEM.
MAD, DANCING, SEA-WHITE, SHE BELLED HER CHALLENGE AGAIN.

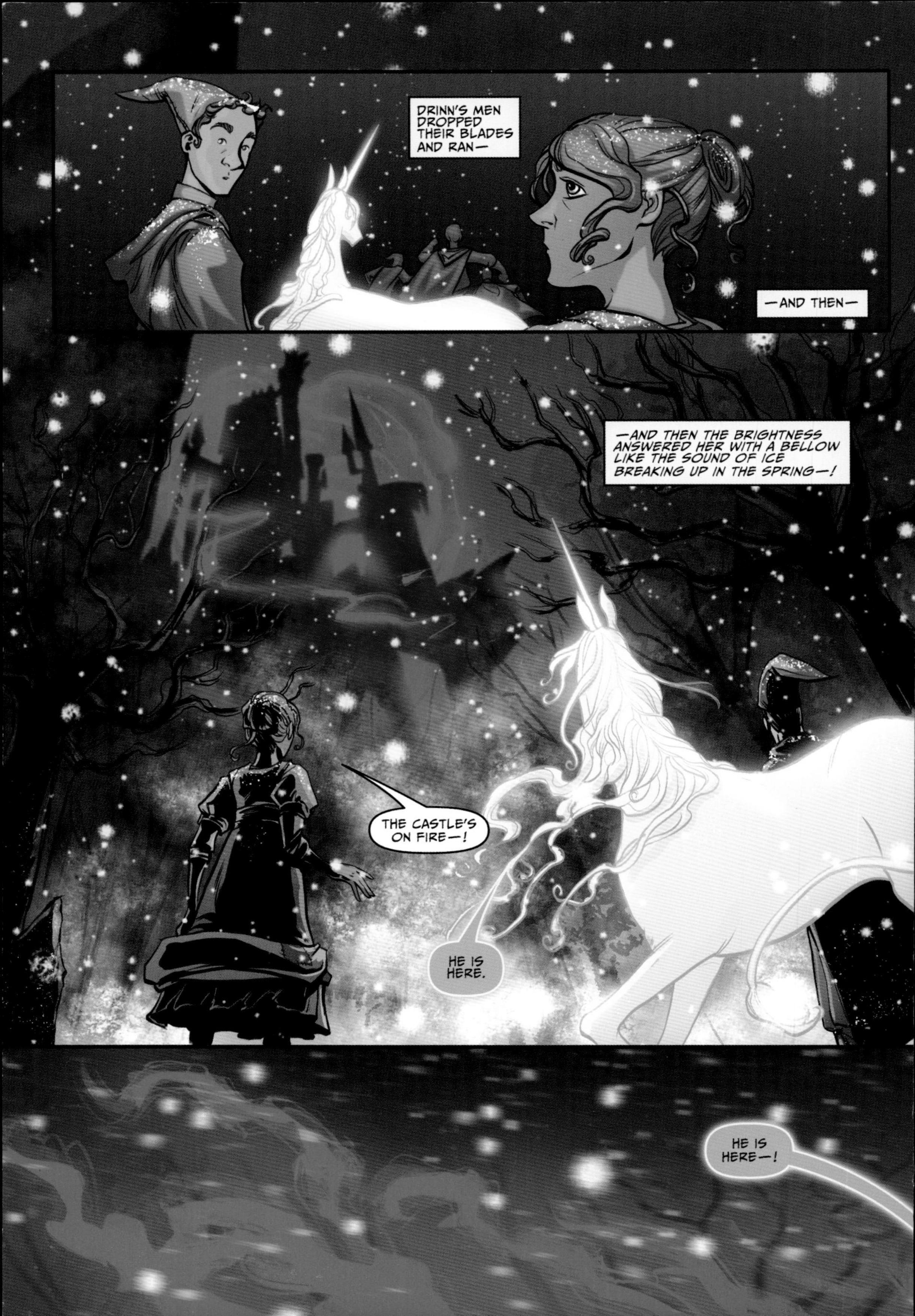
DRINN'S MEN DROPPED THEIR BLADES AND RAN—
—AND THEN—
—AND THEN THE BRIGHTNESS ANSWERED HER WITH A BELLOW LIKE THE SOUND OF ICE BREAKING UP IN THE SPRING—!
THE CASTLE'S ON FIRE—!
HE IS HERE.
HE IS HERE—!

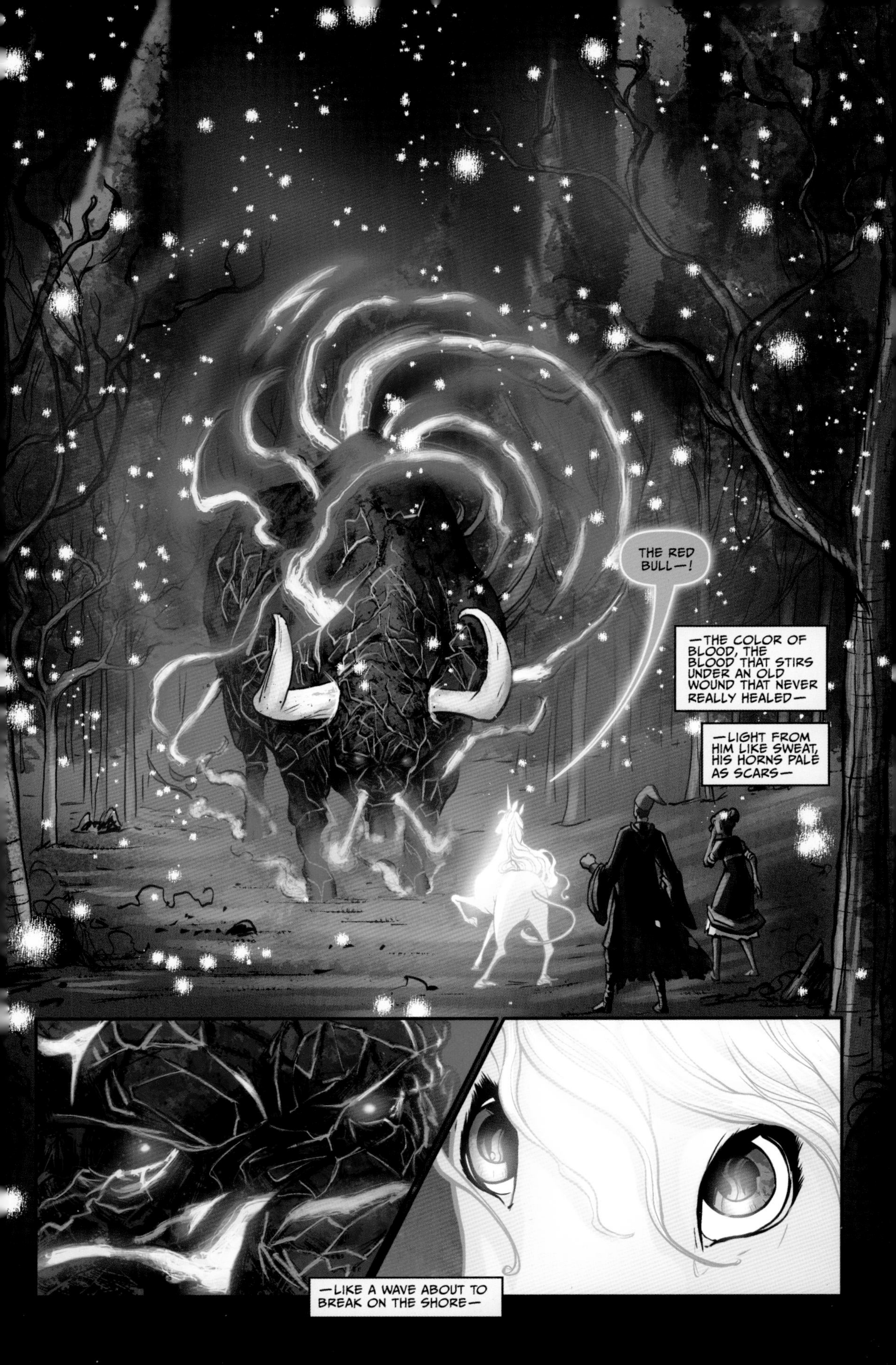
THE RED BULL—!
—THE COLOR OF BLOOD, THE BLOOD THAT STIRS UNDER AN OLD WOUND THAT NEVER REALLY HEALED—
—LIGHT FROM HIM LIKE SWEAT, HIS HORNS PALE AS SCARS—
—LIKE A WAVE ABOUT TO BREAK ON THE SHORE—

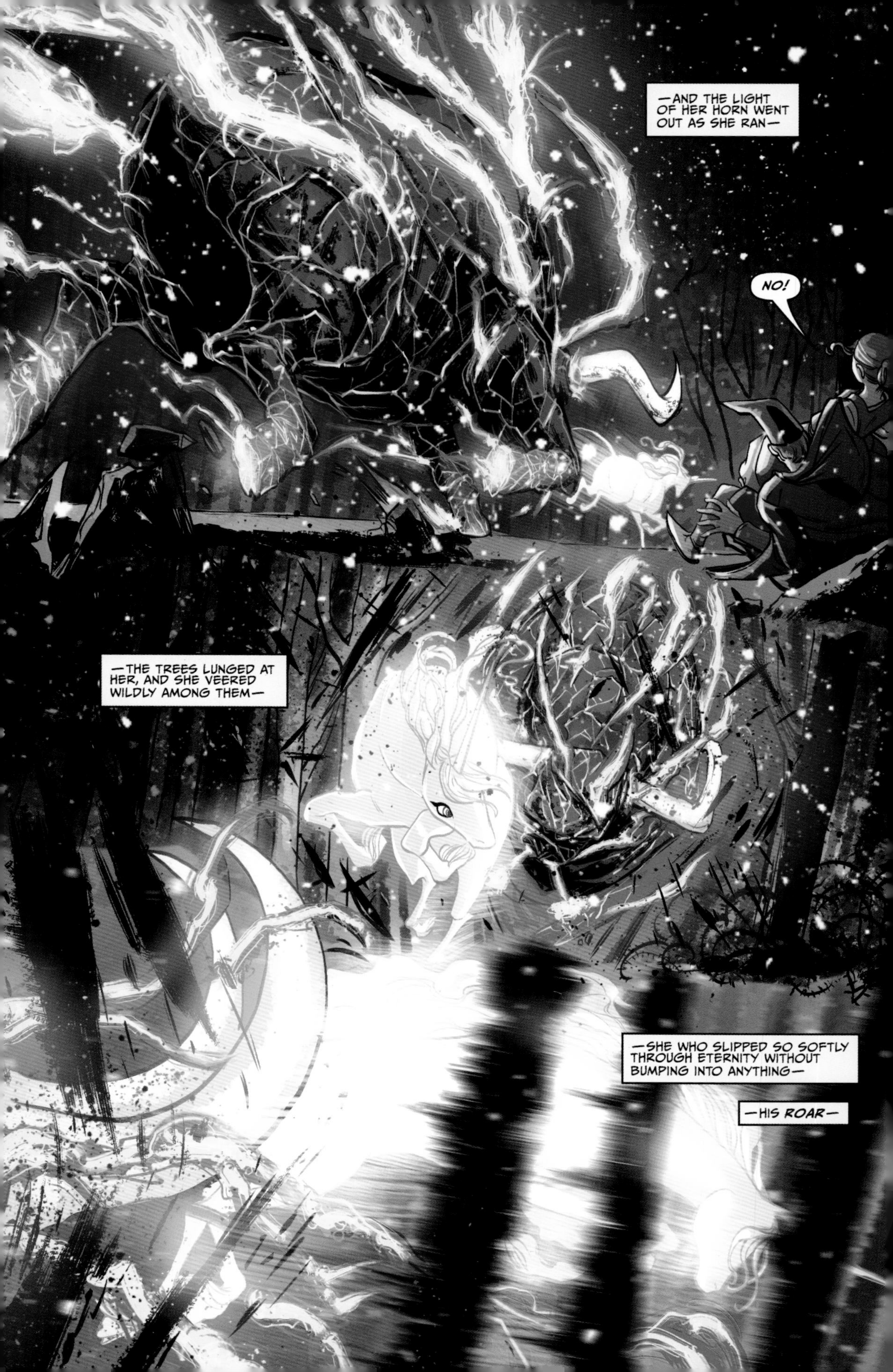
—AND THE LIGHT OF HER HORN WENT OUT AS SHE RAN—
NO!
—THE TREES LUNGED AT HER, AND SHE VEERED WILDLY AMONG THEM—
—SHE WHO SLIPPED SO SOFTLY THROUGH ETERNITY WITHOUT BUMPING INTO ANYTHING—
—HIS ROAR—

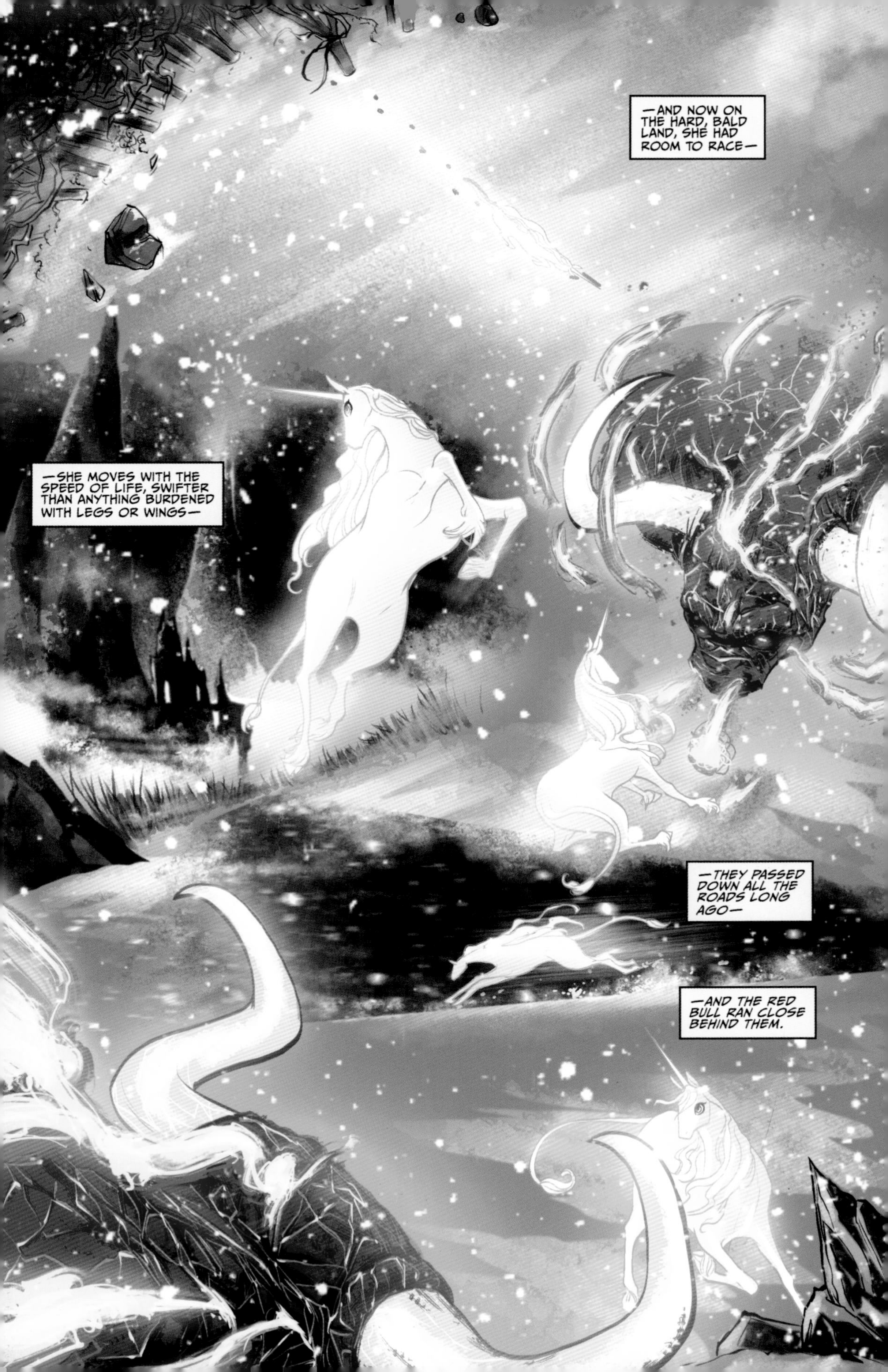
—AND NOW ON THE HARD, BALD LAND, SHE HAD ROOM TO RACE—
—SHE MOVES WITH THE SPEED OF LIFE, SWIFTER THAN ANYTHING BURDENED WITH LEGS OR WINGS—
—THEY PASSED DOWN ALL THE ROADS LONG AGO—
—AND THE RED BULL RAN CLOSE BEHIND THEM.

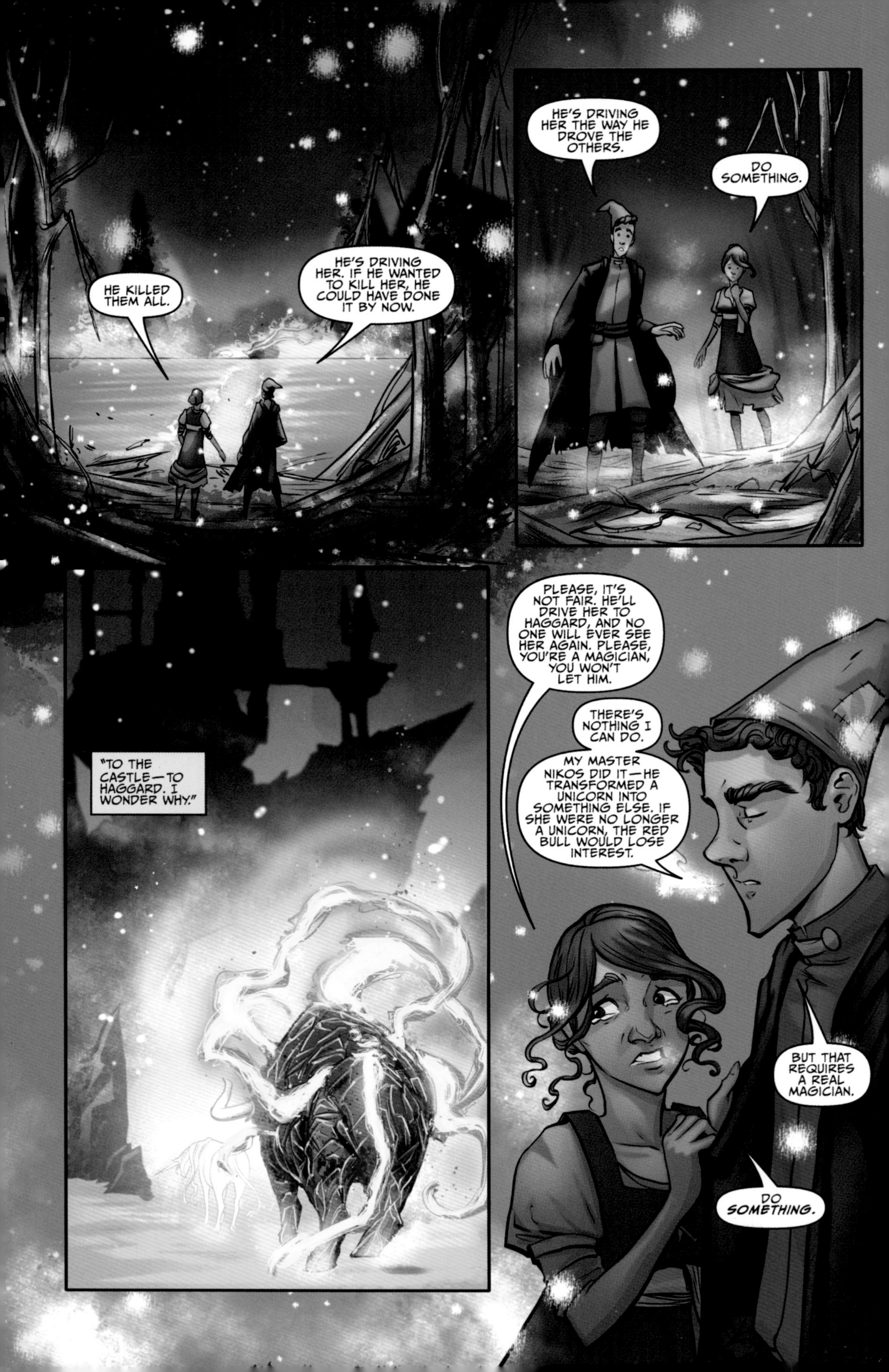
HE KILLED THEM ALL.
HE'S DRIVING HER. IF HE WANTED TO KILL HER, HE COULD HAVE DONE IT BY NOW.
HE'S DRIVING HER THE WAY HE DROVE THE OTHERS.
DO SOMETHING.
"TO THE CASTLE—TO HAGGARD. I WONDER WHY."
PLEASE, IT'S NOT FAIR. HE'LL DRIVE HER TO HAGGARD, AND NO ONE WILL EVER SEE HER AGAIN. PLEASE, YOU'RE A MAGICIAN, YOU WON'T LET HIM.
THERE'S NOTHING I CAN DO.
MY MASTER NIKOS DID IT—HE TRANSFORMED A UNICORN INTO SOMETHING ELSE. IF SHE WERE NO LONGER A UNICORN, THE RED BULL WOULD LOSE INTEREST.
BUT THAT REQUIRES A REAL MAGICIAN.
DO *SOMETHING.*

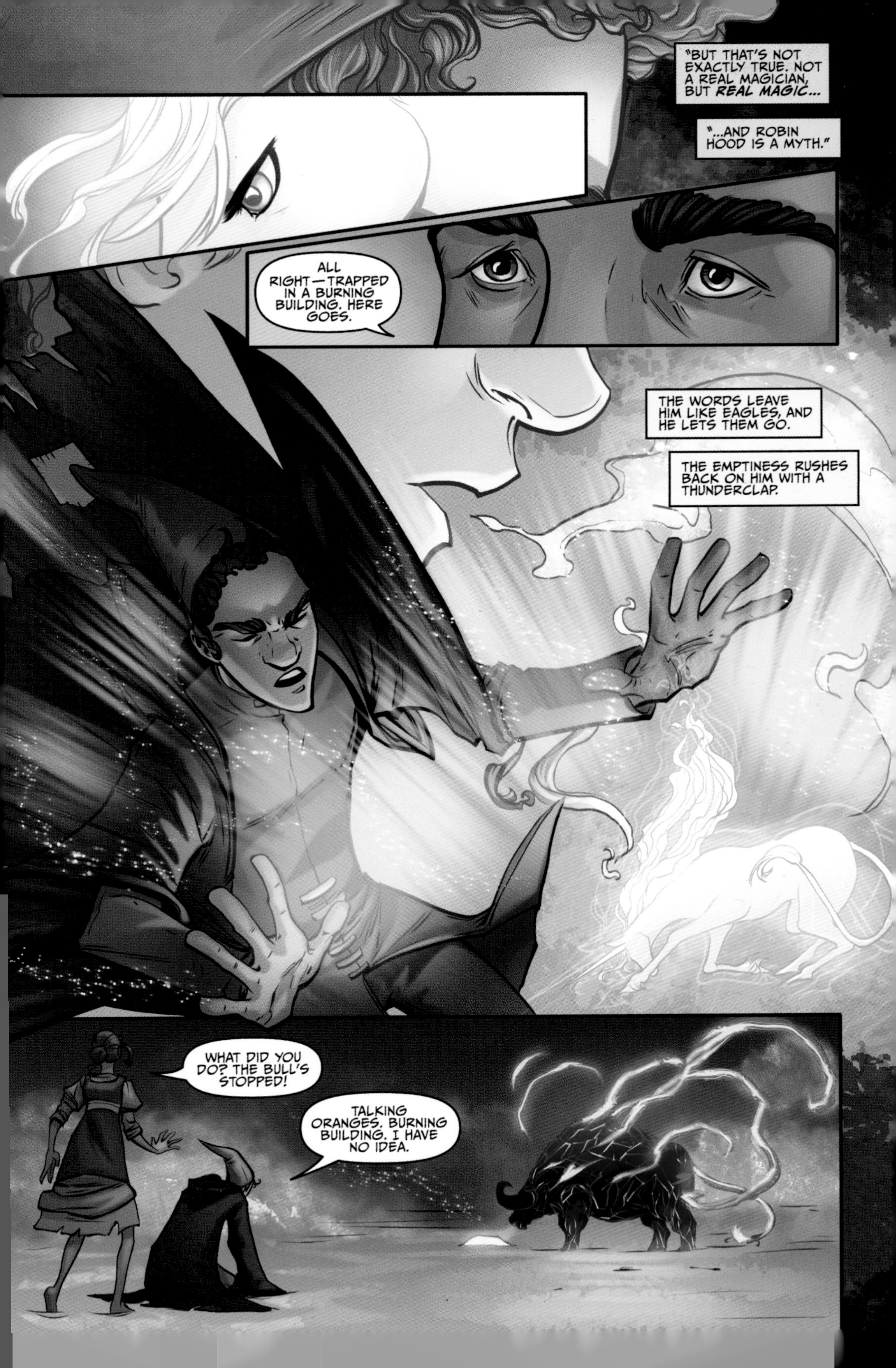
"BUT THAT'S NOT EXACTLY TRUE. NOT A REAL MAGICIAN, BUT REAL MAGIC...
"...AND ROBIN HOOD IS A MYTH."
ALL RIGHT—TRAPPED IN A BURNING BUILDING. HERE GOES.
THE WORDS LEAVE HIM LIKE EAGLES, AND HE LETS THEM GO.
THE EMPTINESS RUSHES BACK ON HIM WITH A THUNDERCLAP.
WHAT DID YOU DO? THE BULL'S STOPPED!
TALKING ORANGES. BURNING BUILDING. I HAVE NO IDEA.

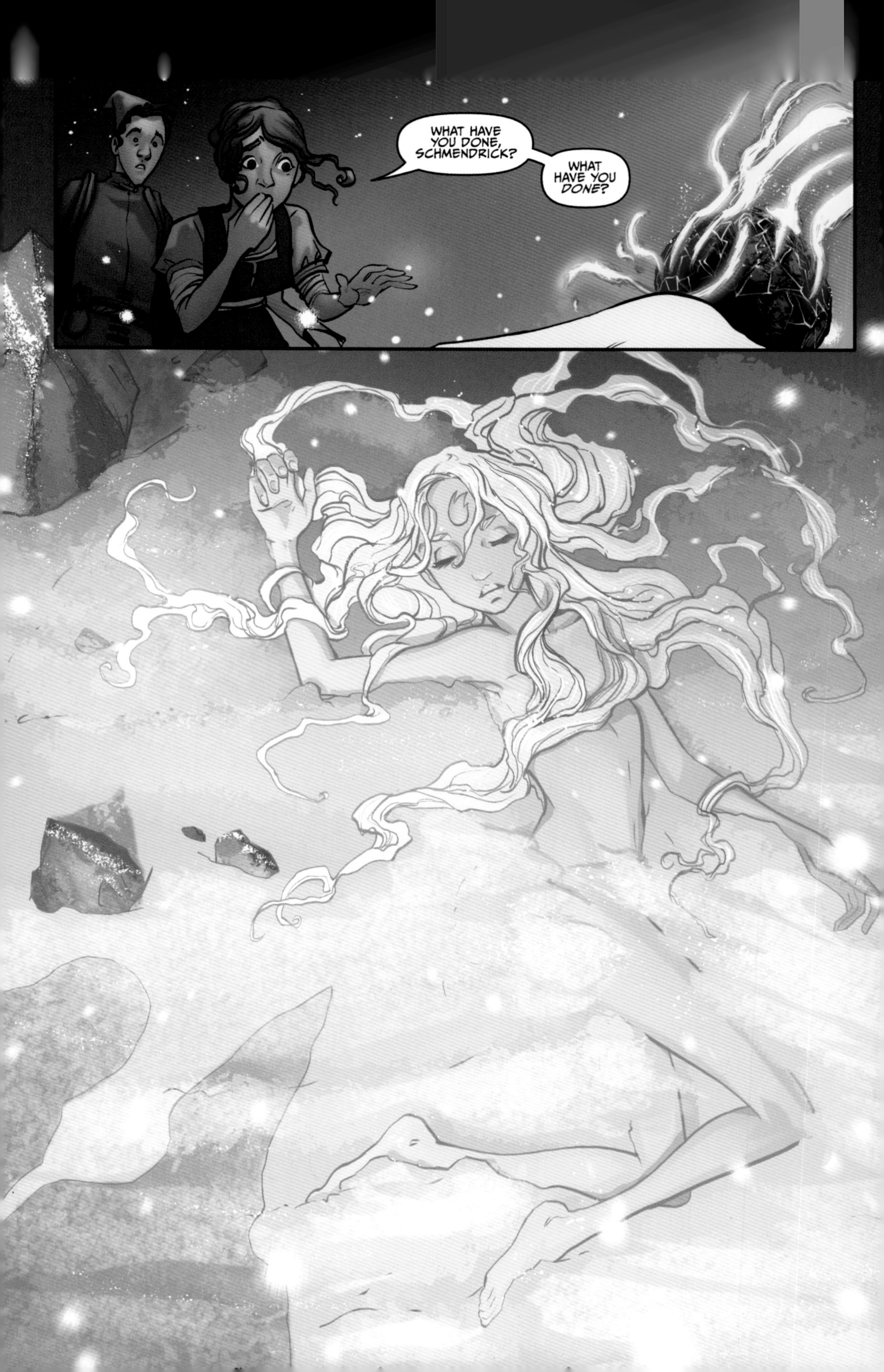
WHAT HAVE YOU DONE, SCHMENDRICK?
WHAT HAVE YOU DONE?

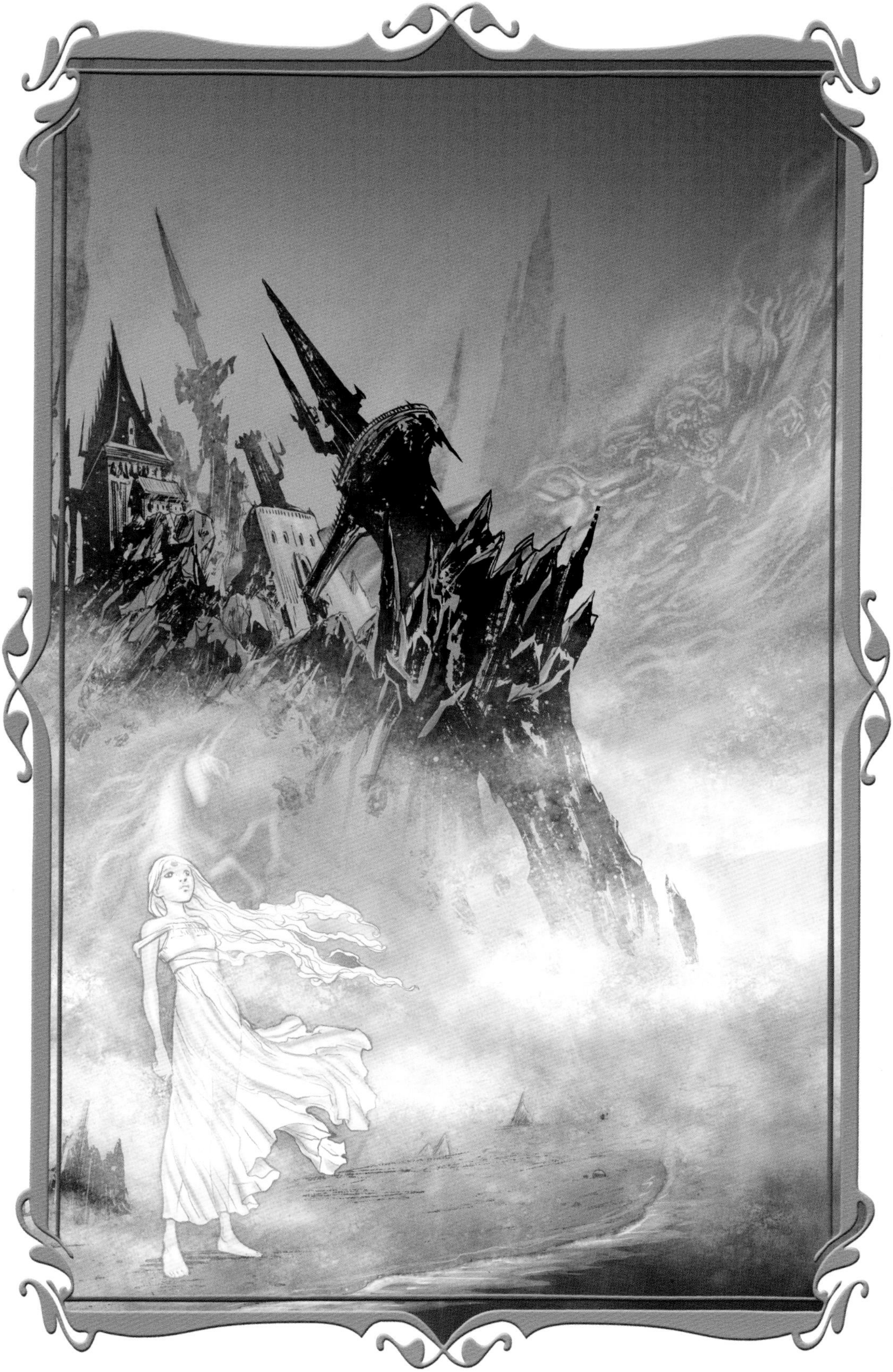

CHAPTER FIVE

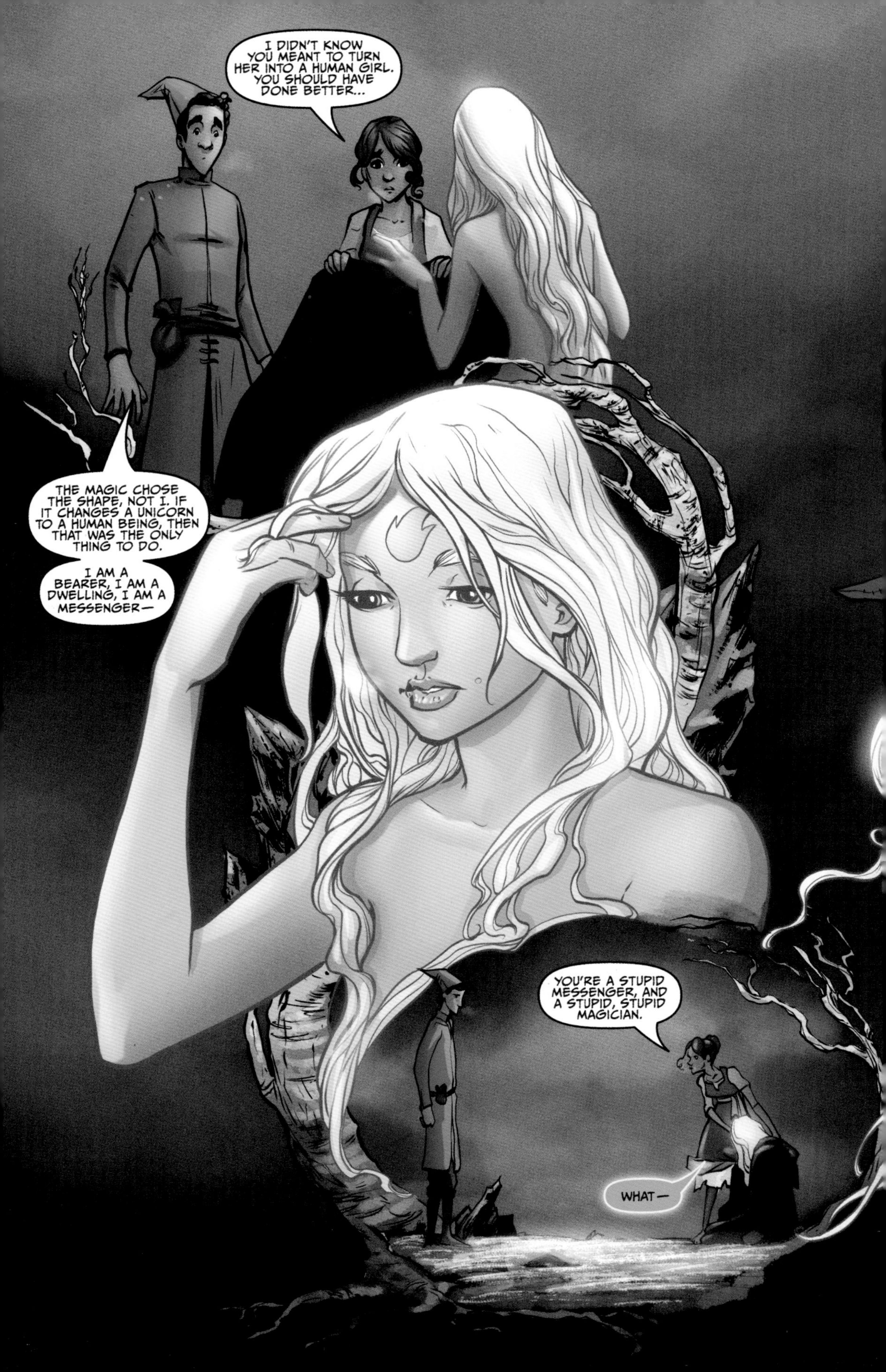
I DIDN'T KNOW YOU MEANT TO TURN HER INTO A HUMAN GIRL. YOU SHOULD HAVE DONE BETTER...
THE MAGIC CHOSE THE SHAPE, NOT I. IF IT CHANGES A UNICORN TO A HUMAN BEING, THEN THAT WAS THE ONLY THING TO DO.
I AM A BEARER, I AM A DWELLING, I AM A MESSENGER—
YOU'RE A STUPID MESSENGER, AND A STUPID, STUPID MAGICIAN.
WHAT—

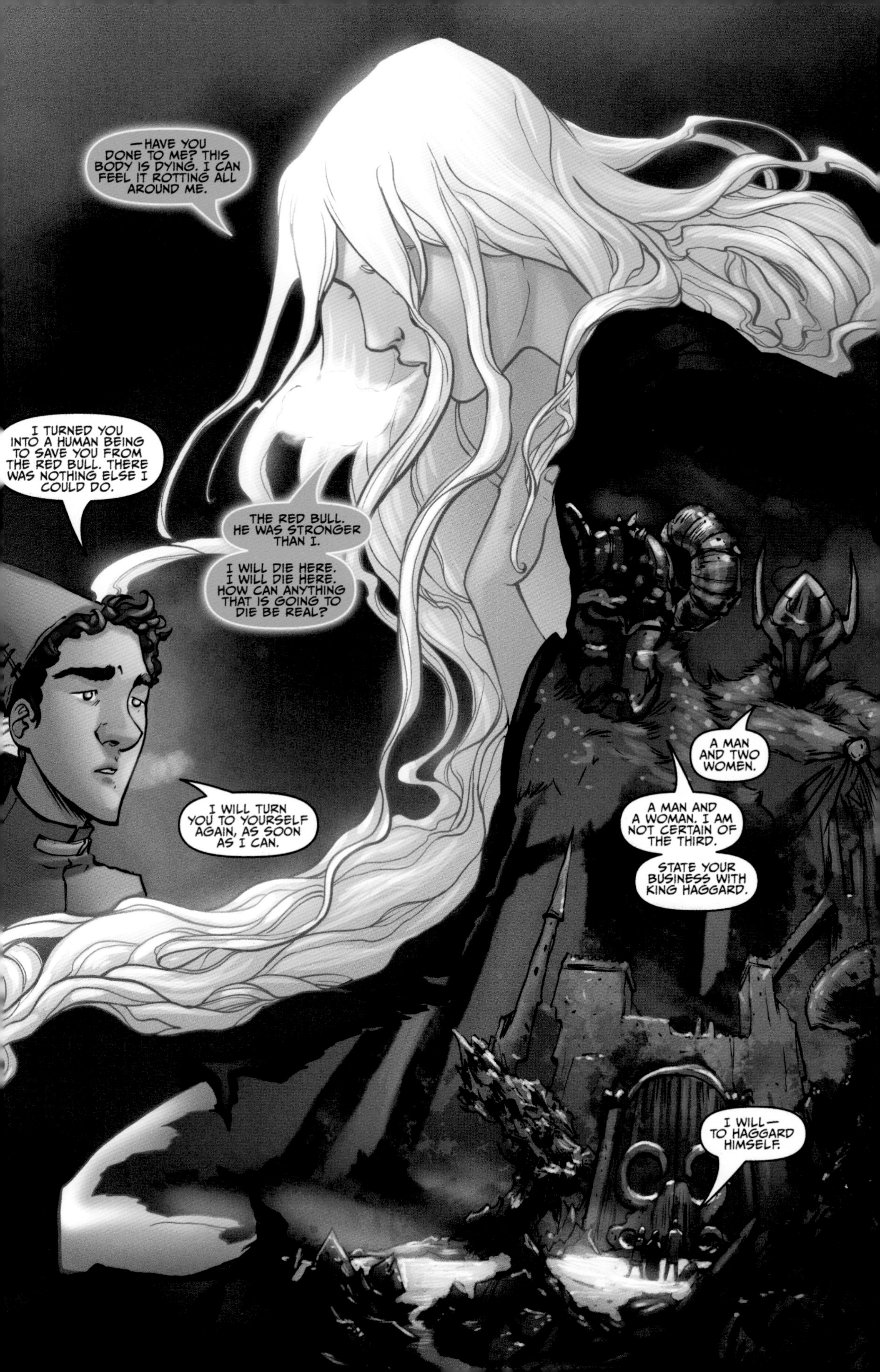
—HAVE YOU DONE TO ME? THIS BODY IS DYING. I CAN FEEL IT ROTTING ALL AROUND ME.
I TURNED YOU INTO A HUMAN BEING TO SAVE YOU FROM THE RED BULL. THERE WAS NOTHING ELSE I COULD DO.
THE RED BULL. HE WAS STRONGER THAN I.
I WILL DIE HERE. I WILL DIE HERE. HOW CAN ANYTHING THAT IS GOING TO DIE BE REAL?
I WILL TURN YOU TO YOURSELF AGAIN, AS SOON AS I CAN.
A MAN AND TWO WOMEN.
A MAN AND A WOMAN. I AM NOT CERTAIN OF THE THIRD.
STATE YOUR BUSINESS WITH KING HAGGARD.
I WILL— TO HAGGARD HIMSELF.

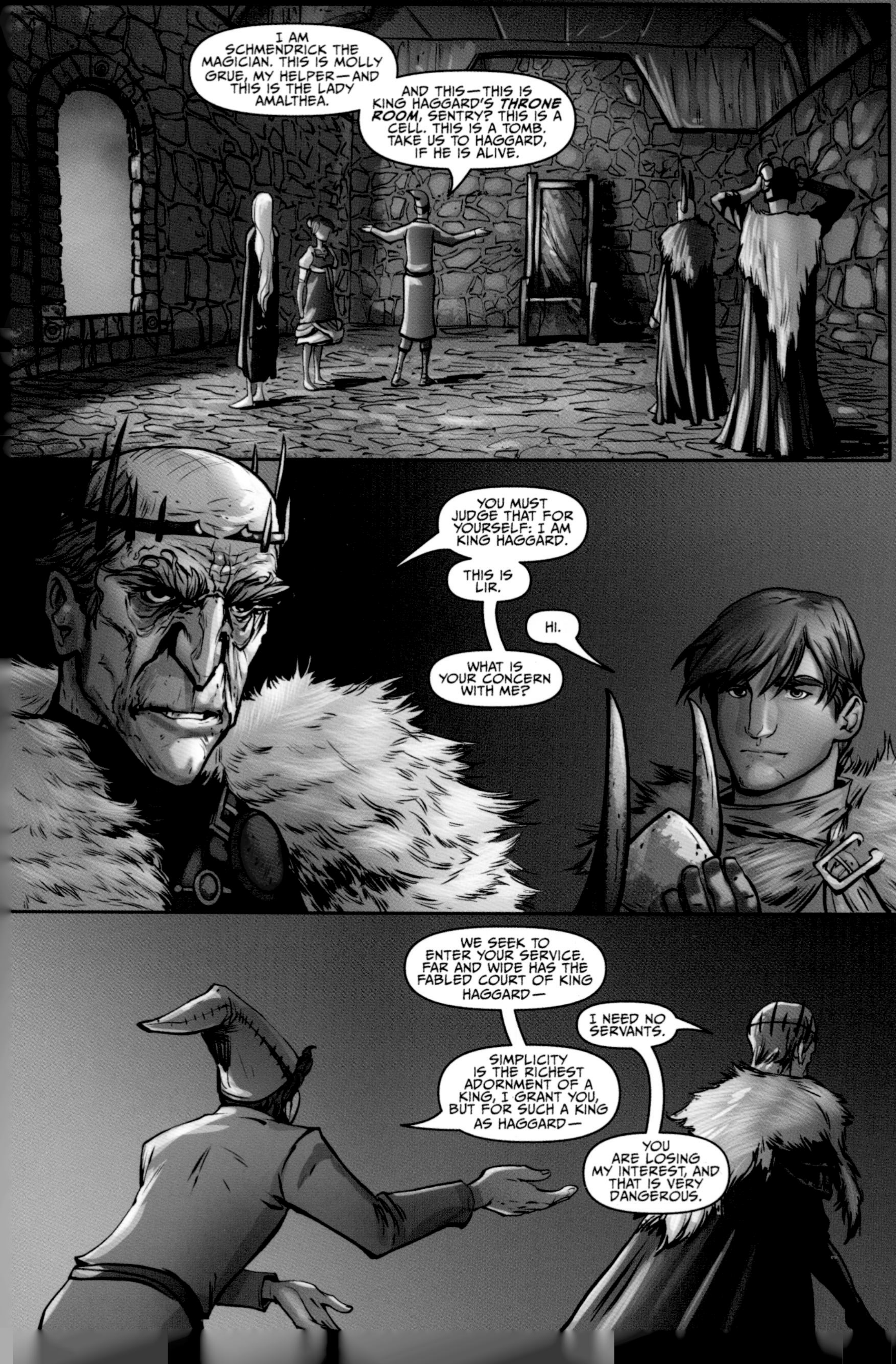
I AM SCHMENDRICK THE MAGICIAN. THIS IS MOLLY GRUE, MY HELPER—AND THIS IS THE LADY AMALTHEA.
AND THIS—THIS IS KING HAGGARD'S ***THRONE ROOM***, SENTRY? THIS IS A CELL. THIS IS A TOMB. TAKE US TO HAGGARD, IF HE IS ALIVE.
YOU MUST JUDGE THAT FOR YOURSELF: I AM KING HAGGARD.
THIS IS LIR.
HI.
WHAT IS YOUR CONCERN WITH ME?
WE SEEK TO ENTER YOUR SERVICE. FAR AND WIDE HAS THE FABLED COURT OF KING HAGGARD—
I NEED NO SERVANTS.
SIMPLICITY IS THE RICHEST ADORNMENT OF A KING, I GRANT YOU, BUT FOR SUCH A KING AS HAGGARD—
YOU ARE LOSING MY INTEREST, AND THAT IS VERY DANGEROUS.

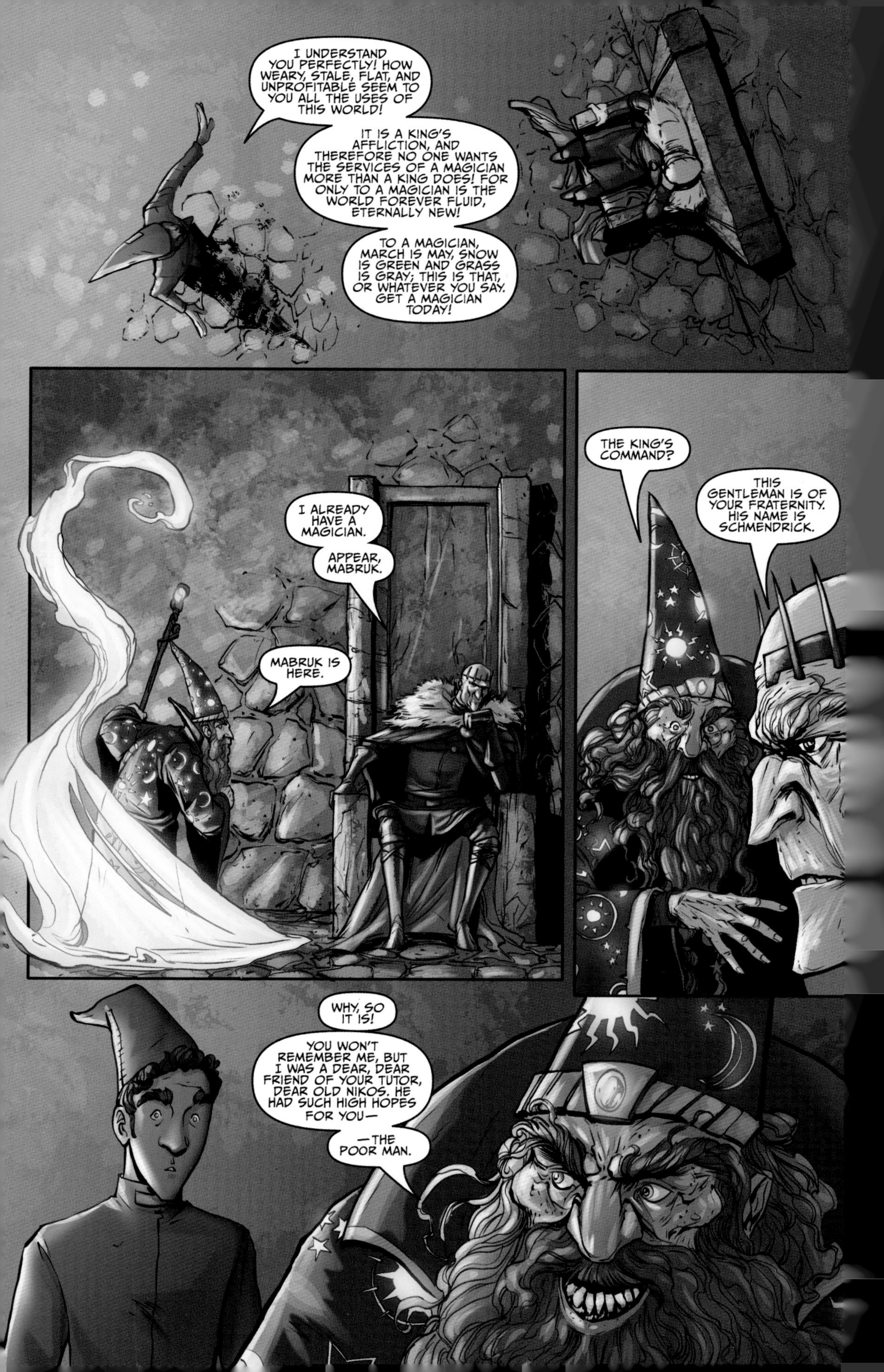
I UNDERSTAND YOU PERFECTLY! HOW WEARY, STALE, FLAT, AND UNPROFITABLE SEEM TO YOU ALL THE USES OF THIS WORLD!
IT IS A KING'S AFFLICTION, AND THEREFORE NO ONE WANTS THE SERVICES OF A MAGICIAN MORE THAN A KING DOES! FOR ONLY TO A MAGICIAN IS THE WORLD FOREVER FLUID, ETERNALLY NEW!
TO A MAGICIAN, MARCH IS MAY, SNOW IS GREEN AND GRASS IS GRAY; THIS IS THAT, OR WHATEVER YOU SAY. GET A MAGICIAN TODAY!
I ALREADY HAVE A MAGICIAN.
APPEAR, MABRUK.
MABRUK IS HERE.
THE KING'S COMMAND?
THIS GENTLEMAN IS OF YOUR FRATERNITY. HIS NAME IS SCHMENDRICK.
WHY, SO IT IS!
YOU WON'T REMEMBER ME, BUT I WAS A DEAR, DEAR FRIEND OF YOUR TUTOR, DEAR OLD NIKOS. HE HAD SUCH HIGH HOPES FOR YOU—
—THE POOR MAN.

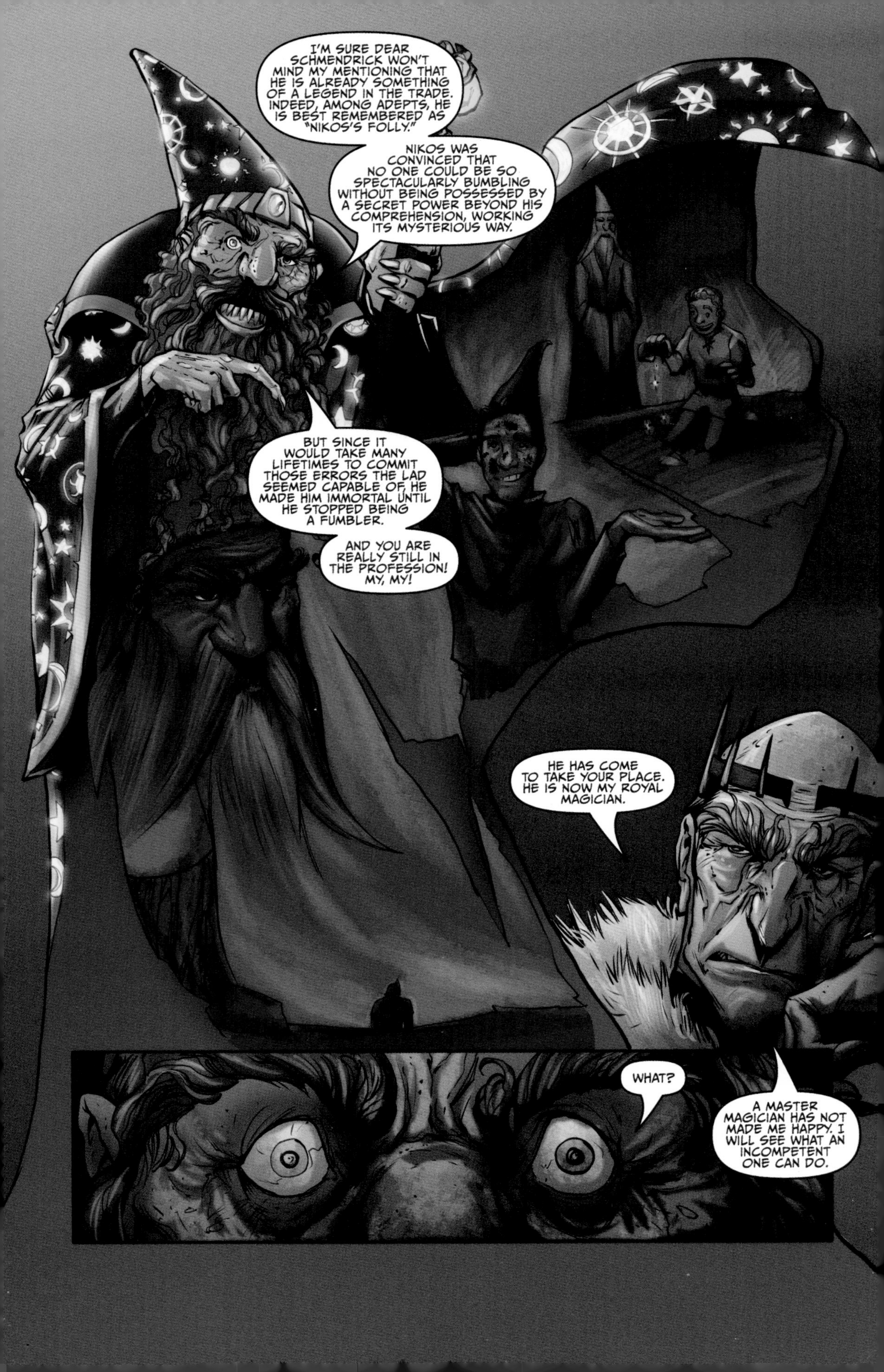
I'M SURE DEAR SCHMENDRICK WON'T MIND MY MENTIONING THAT HE IS ALREADY SOMETHING OF A LEGEND IN THE TRADE. INDEED, AMONG ADEPTS, HE IS BEST REMEMBERED AS "NIKOS'S FOLLY."
NIKOS WAS CONVINCED THAT NO ONE COULD BE SO SPECTACULARLY BUMBLING WITHOUT BEING POSSESSED BY A SECRET POWER BEYOND HIS COMPREHENSION, WORKING ITS MYSTERIOUS WAY.
BUT SINCE IT WOULD TAKE MANY LIFETIMES TO COMMIT THOSE ERRORS THE LAD SEEMED CAPABLE OF, HE MADE HIM IMMORTAL UNTIL HE STOPPED BEING A FUMBLER.
AND YOU ARE REALLY STILL IN THE PROFESSION! MY, MY!
HE HAS COME TO TAKE YOUR PLACE. HE IS NOW MY ROYAL MAGICIAN.
WHAT?
A MASTER MAGICIAN HAS NOT MADE ME HAPPY. I WILL SEE WHAT AN INCOMPETENT ONE CAN DO.

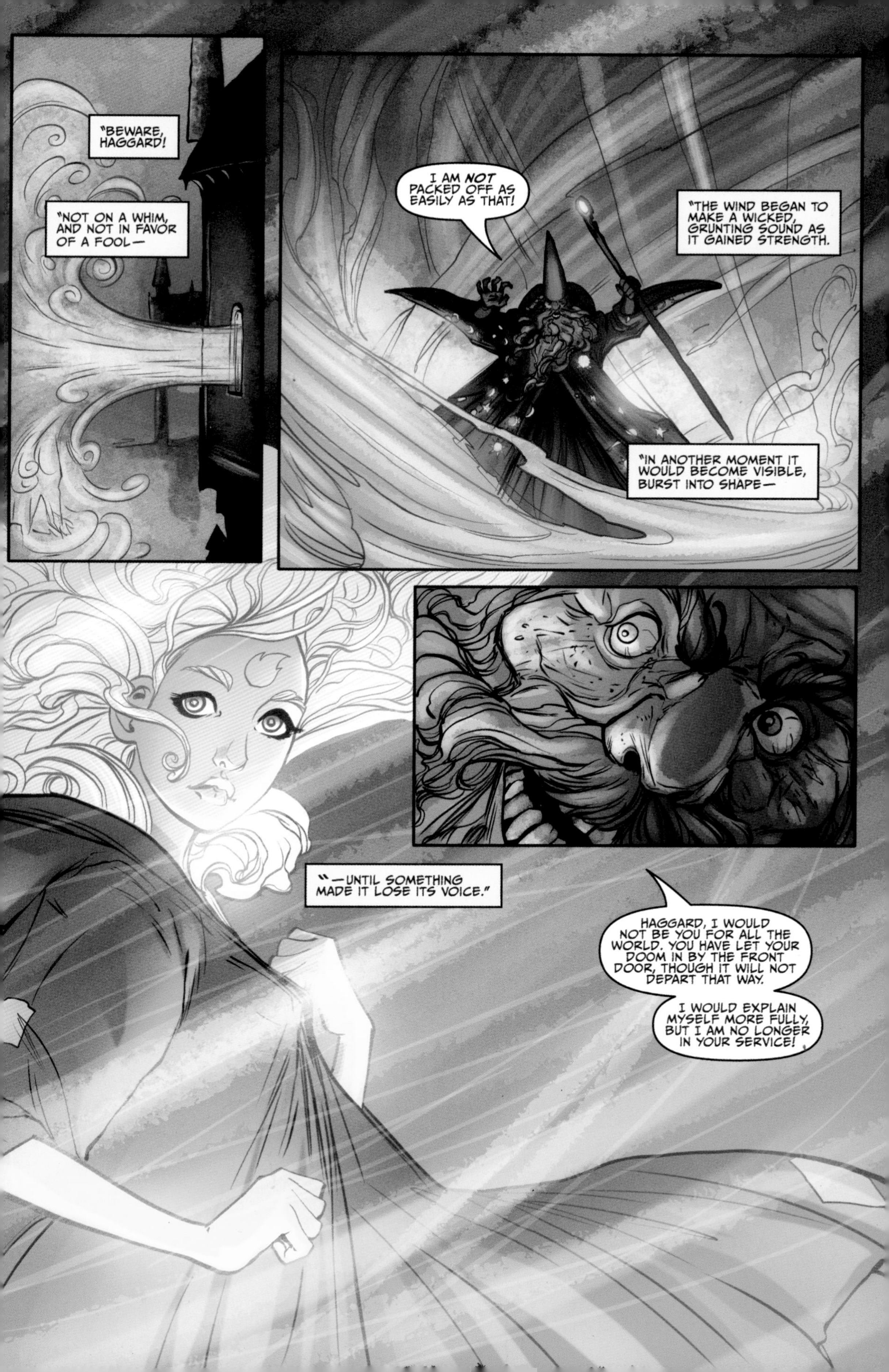
"BEWARE, HAGGARD!
"NOT ON A WHIM, AND NOT IN FAVOR OF A FOOL—
I AM ***NOT*** PACKED OFF AS EASILY AS THAT!
"THE WIND BEGAN TO MAKE A WICKED, GRUNTING SOUND AS IT GAINED STRENGTH.
"IN ANOTHER MOMENT IT WOULD BECOME VISIBLE, BURST INTO SHAPE—
"—UNTIL SOMETHING MADE IT LOSE ITS VOICE."
HAGGARD, I WOULD NOT BE YOU FOR ALL THE WORLD. YOU HAVE LET YOUR DOOM IN BY THE FRONT DOOR, THOUGH IT WILL NOT DEPART THAT WAY.
I WOULD EXPLAIN MYSELF MORE FULLY, BUT I AM NO LONGER IN YOUR SERVICE!

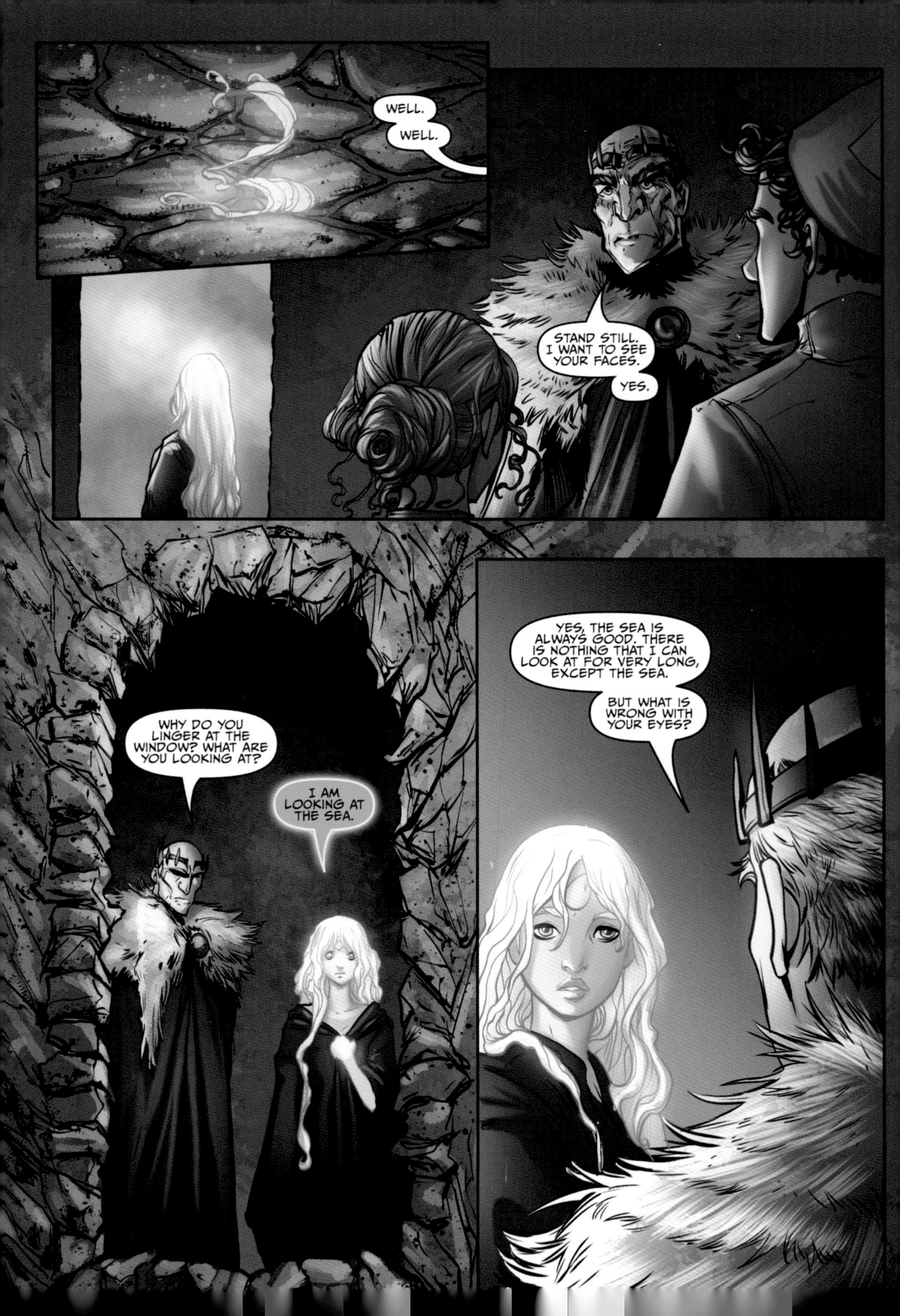
WELL.
WELL.
STAND STILL. I WANT TO SEE YOUR FACES.
YES.
WHY DO YOU LINGER AT THE WINDOW? WHAT ARE YOU LOOKING AT?
I AM LOOKING AT THE SEA.
YES, THE SEA IS ALWAYS GOOD. THERE IS NOTHING THAT I CAN LOOK AT FOR VERY LONG, EXCEPT THE SEA.
BUT WHAT IS WRONG WITH YOUR EYES?

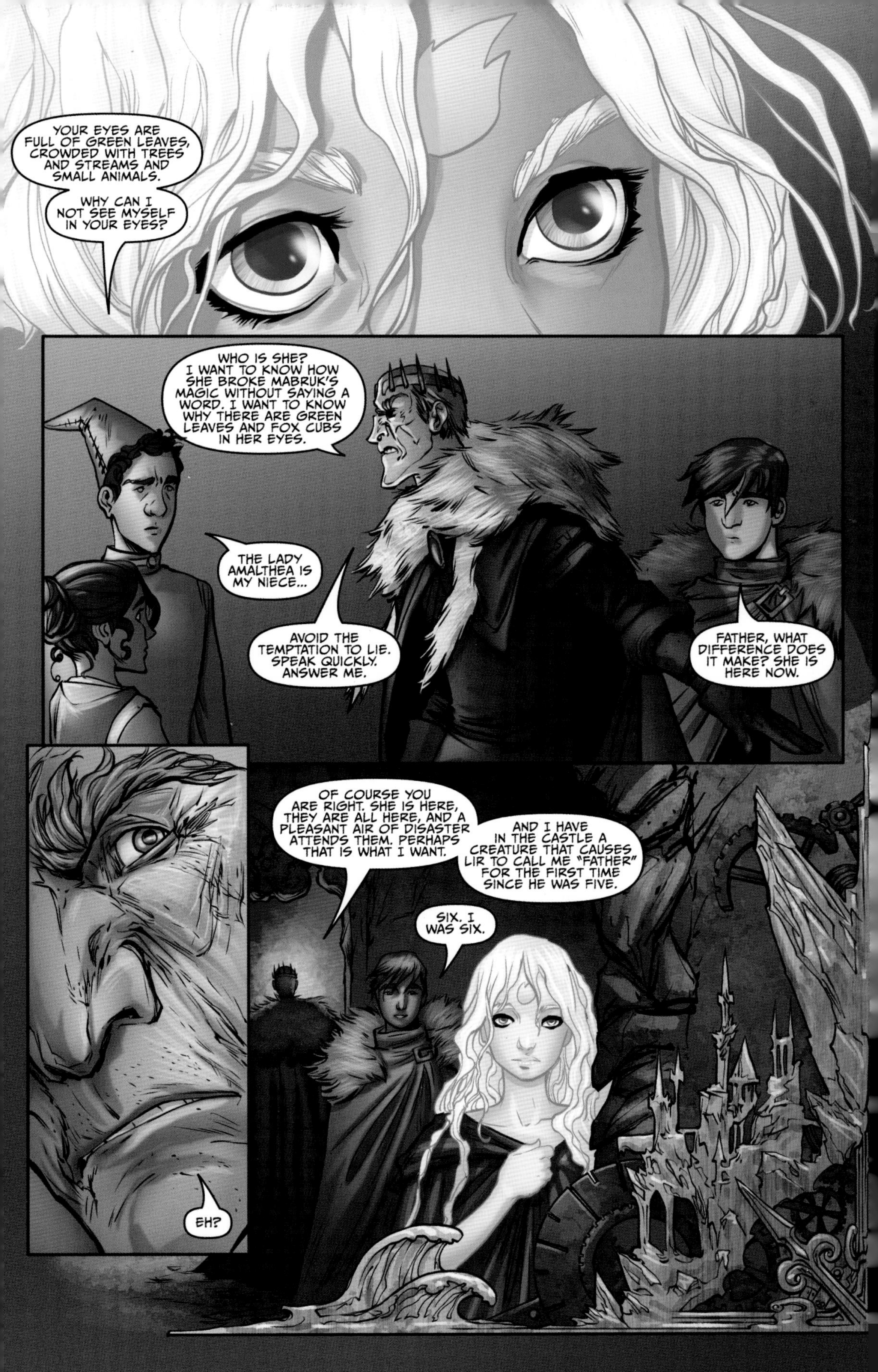
YOUR EYES ARE FULL OF GREEN LEAVES, CROWDED WITH TREES AND STREAMS AND SMALL ANIMALS.
WHY CAN I NOT SEE MYSELF IN YOUR EYES?
WHO IS SHE? I WANT TO KNOW HOW SHE BROKE MABRUK'S MAGIC WITHOUT SAYING A WORD. I WANT TO KNOW WHY THERE ARE GREEN LEAVES AND FOX CUBS IN HER EYES.
THE LADY AMALTHEA IS MY NIECE...
AVOID THE TEMPTATION TO LIE. SPEAK QUICKLY. ANSWER ME.
FATHER, WHAT DIFFERENCE DOES IT MAKE? SHE IS HERE NOW.
EH?
OF COURSE YOU ARE RIGHT. SHE IS HERE, THEY ARE ALL HERE, AND A PLEASANT AIR OF DISASTER ATTENDS THEM. PERHAPS THAT IS WHAT I WANT.
AND I HAVE IN THE CASTLE A CREATURE THAT CAUSES LIR TO CALL ME "FATHER" FOR THE FIRST TIME SINCE HE WAS FIVE.
SIX. I WAS SIX.

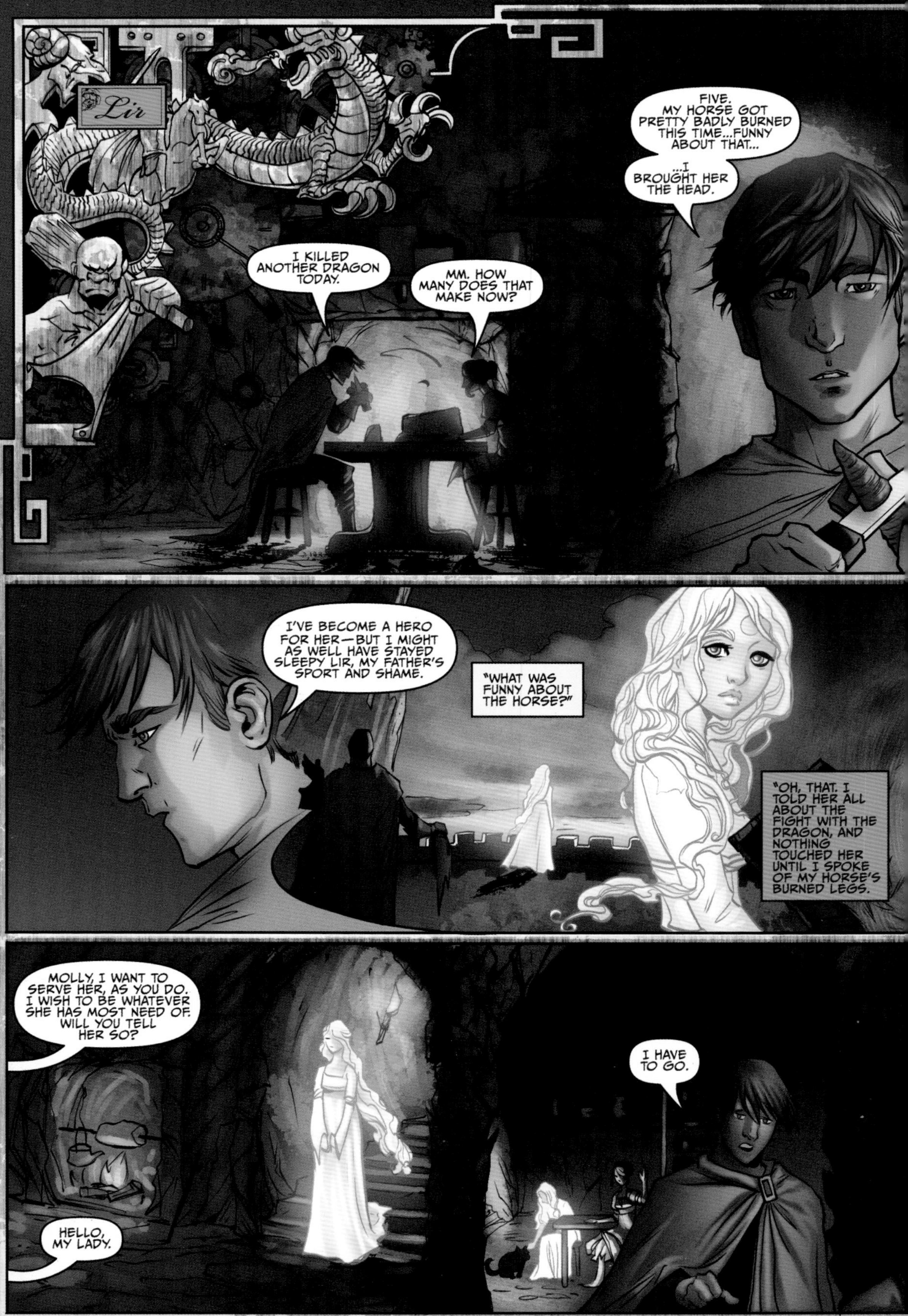
Lir
I KILLED ANOTHER DRAGON TODAY.
MM. HOW MANY DOES THAT MAKE NOW?
FIVE. MY HORSE GOT PRETTY BADLY BURNED THIS TIME...FUNNY ABOUT THAT...
...I BROUGHT HER THE HEAD.
I'VE BECOME A HERO FOR HER—BUT I MIGHT AS WELL HAVE STAYED SLEEPY LIR, MY FATHER'S SPORT AND SHAME.
"WHAT WAS FUNNY ABOUT THE HORSE?"
"OH, THAT. I TOLD HER ALL ABOUT THE FIGHT WITH THE DRAGON, AND NOTHING TOUCHED HER UNTIL I SPOKE OF MY HORSE'S BURNED LEGS.
MOLLY, I WANT TO SERVE HER, AS YOU DO. I WISH TO BE WHATEVER SHE HAS MOST NEED OF. WILL YOU TELL HER SO?
HELLO, MY LADY.
I HAVE TO GO.

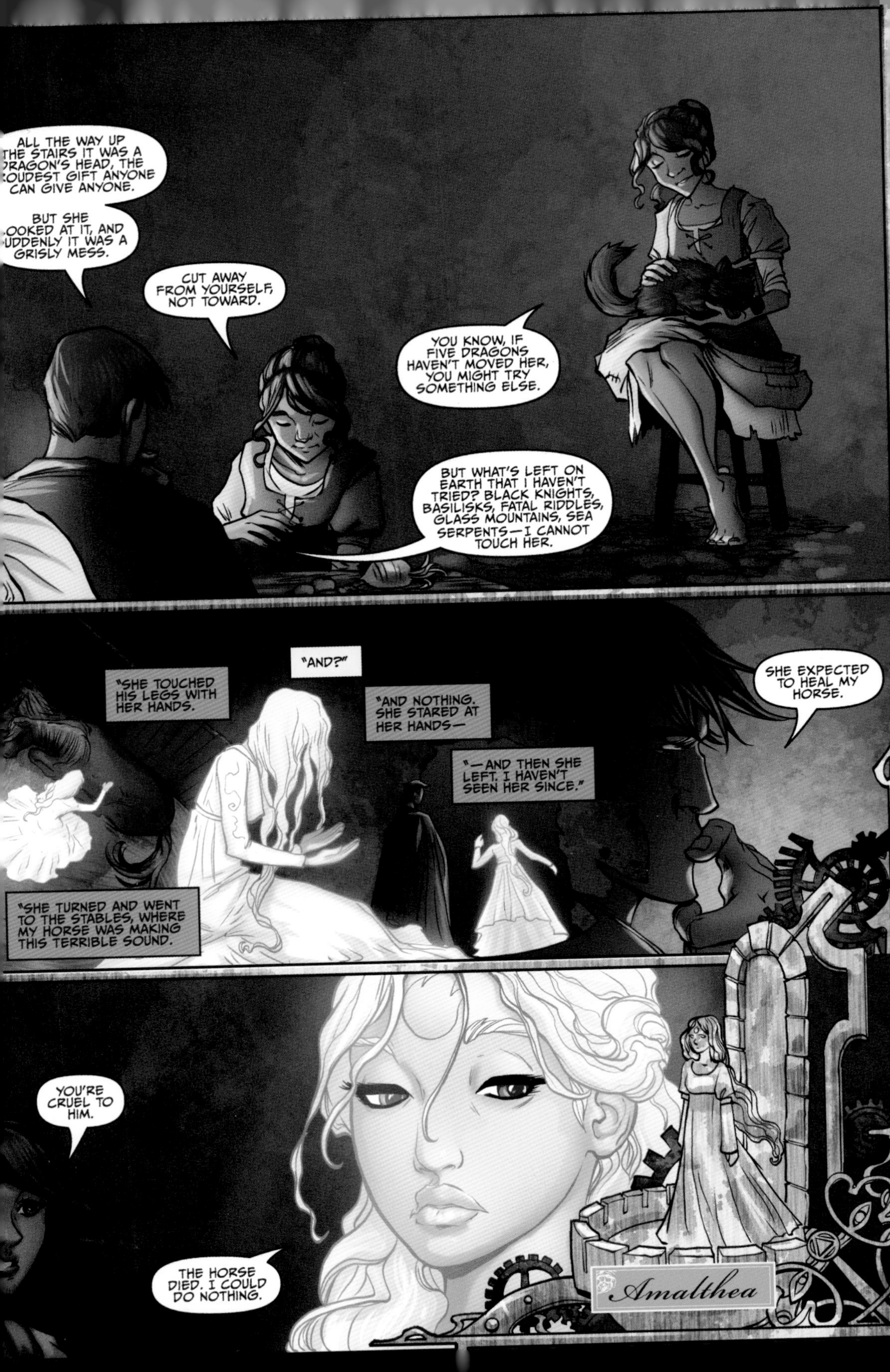
ALL THE WAY UP THE STAIRS IT WAS A RAGON'S HEAD, THE ROUDEST GIFT ANYONE CAN GIVE ANYONE.
BUT SHE OOKED AT IT, AND UDDENLY IT WAS A GRISLY MESS.
CUT AWAY FROM YOURSELF, NOT TOWARD.
YOU KNOW, IF FIVE DRAGONS HAVEN'T MOVED HER, YOU MIGHT TRY SOMETHING ELSE.
BUT WHAT'S LEFT ON EARTH THAT I HAVEN'T TRIED? BLACK KNIGHTS, BASILISKS, FATAL RIDDLES, GLASS MOUNTAINS, SEA SERPENTS—I CANNOT TOUCH HER.
"SHE TOUCHED HIS LEGS WITH HER HANDS.
"AND?"
"AND NOTHING. SHE STARED AT HER HANDS—
"—AND THEN SHE LEFT. I HAVEN'T SEEN HER SINCE."
SHE EXPECTED TO HEAL MY HORSE.
"SHE TURNED AND WENT TO THE STABLES, WHERE MY HORSE WAS MAKING THIS TERRIBLE SOUND.
YOU'RE CRUEL TO HIM.
THE HORSE DIED. I COULD DO NOTHING.
Amalthea

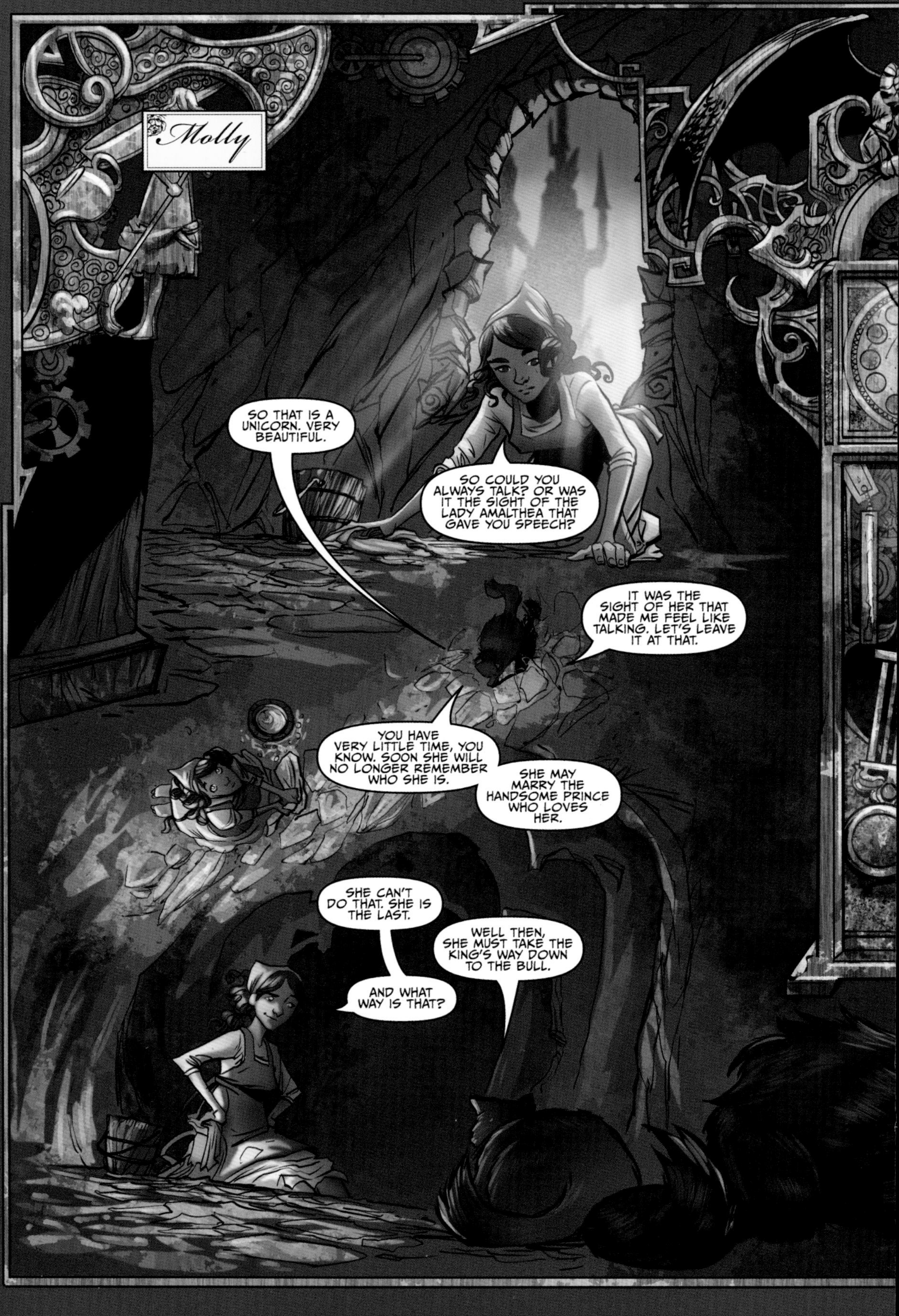
Molly
SO THAT IS A UNICORN. VERY BEAUTIFUL.
SO COULD YOU ALWAYS TALK? OR WAS IT THE SIGHT OF THE LADY AMALTHEA THAT GAVE YOU SPEECH?
IT WAS THE SIGHT OF HER THAT MADE ME FEEL LIKE TALKING. LET'S LEAVE IT AT THAT.
YOU HAVE VERY LITTLE TIME, YOU KNOW. SOON SHE WILL NO LONGER REMEMBER WHO SHE IS.
SHE MAY MARRY THE HANDSOME PRINCE WHO LOVES HER.
SHE CAN'T DO THAT. SHE IS THE LAST.
WELL THEN, SHE MUST TAKE THE KING'S WAY DOWN TO THE BULL.
AND WHAT WAY IS THAT?

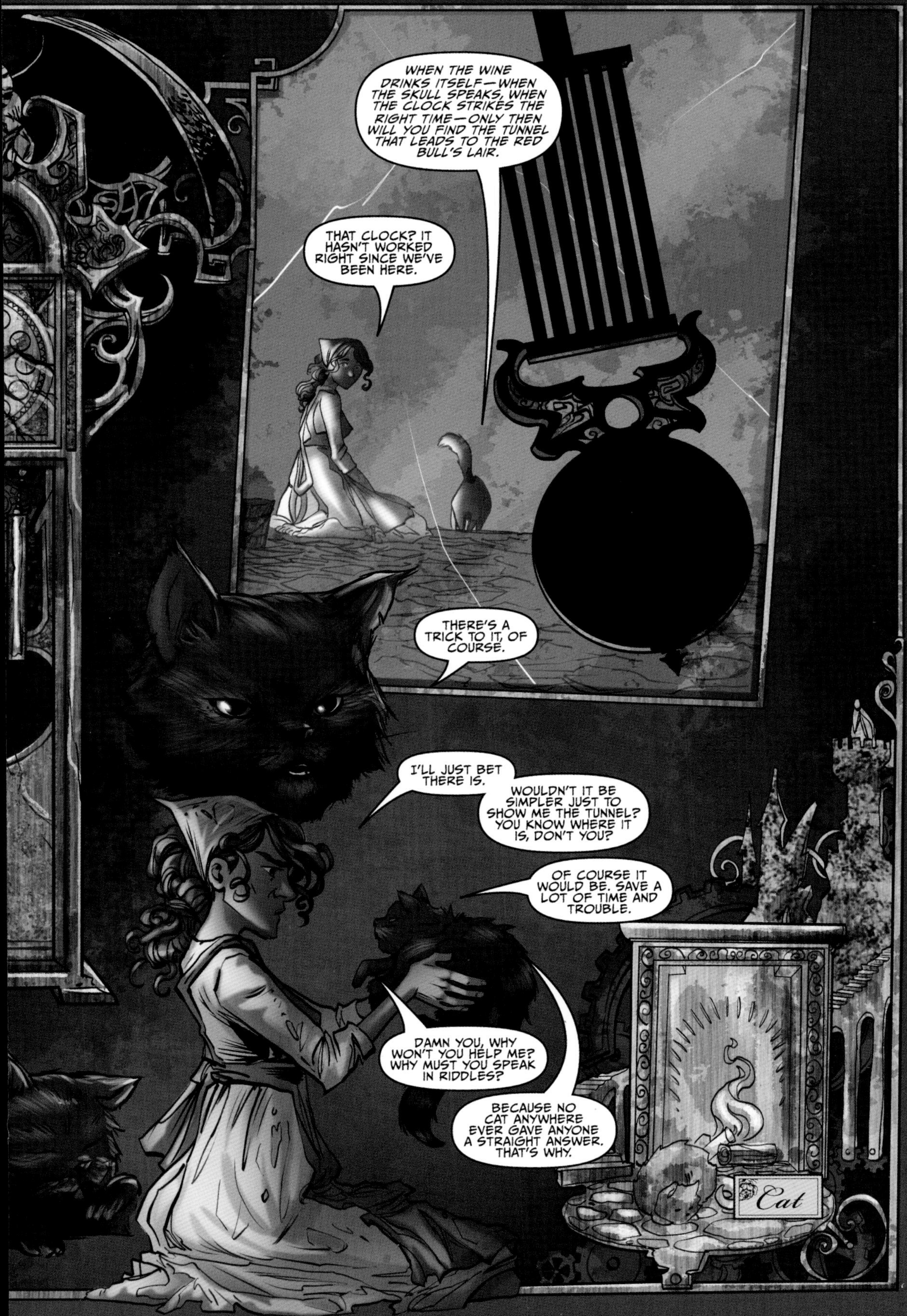
WHEN THE WINE DRINKS ITSELF—WHEN THE SKULL SPEAKS, WHEN THE CLOCK STRIKES THE RIGHT TIME—ONLY THEN WILL YOU FIND THE TUNNEL THAT LEADS TO THE RED BULL'S LAIR.
THAT CLOCK? IT HASN'T WORKED RIGHT SINCE WE'VE BEEN HERE.
THERE'S A TRICK TO IT, OF COURSE.
I'LL JUST BET THERE IS.
WOULDN'T IT BE SIMPLER JUST TO SHOW ME THE TUNNEL? YOU KNOW WHERE IT IS, DON'T YOU?
OF COURSE IT WOULD BE. SAVE A LOT OF TIME AND TROUBLE.
DAMN YOU, WHY WON'T YOU HELP ME? WHY MUST YOU SPEAK IN RIDDLES?
BECAUSE NO CAT ANYWHERE EVER GAVE ANYONE A STRAIGHT ANSWER. THAT'S WHY.
Cat

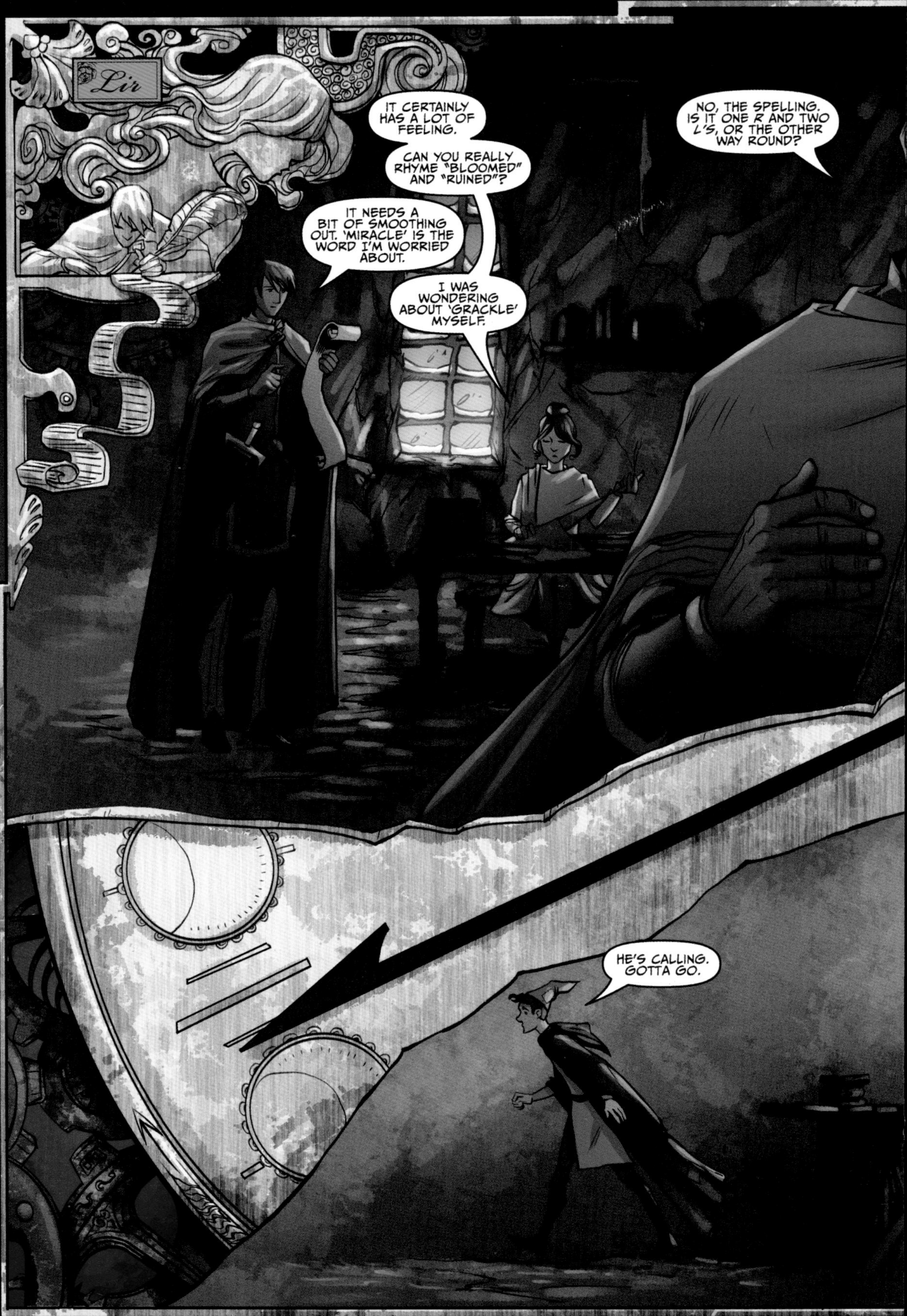
Lir
IT CERTAINLY HAS A LOT OF FEELING.
CAN YOU REALLY RHYME "BLOOMED" AND "RUINED"?
IT NEEDS A BIT OF SMOOTHING OUT. 'MIRACLE' IS THE WORD I'M WORRIED ABOUT.
I WAS WONDERING ABOUT 'GRACKLE' MYSELF.
NO, THE SPELLING. IS IT ONE *R* AND TWO *L'S*, OR THE OTHER WAY ROUND?
HE'S CALLING. GOTTA GO.

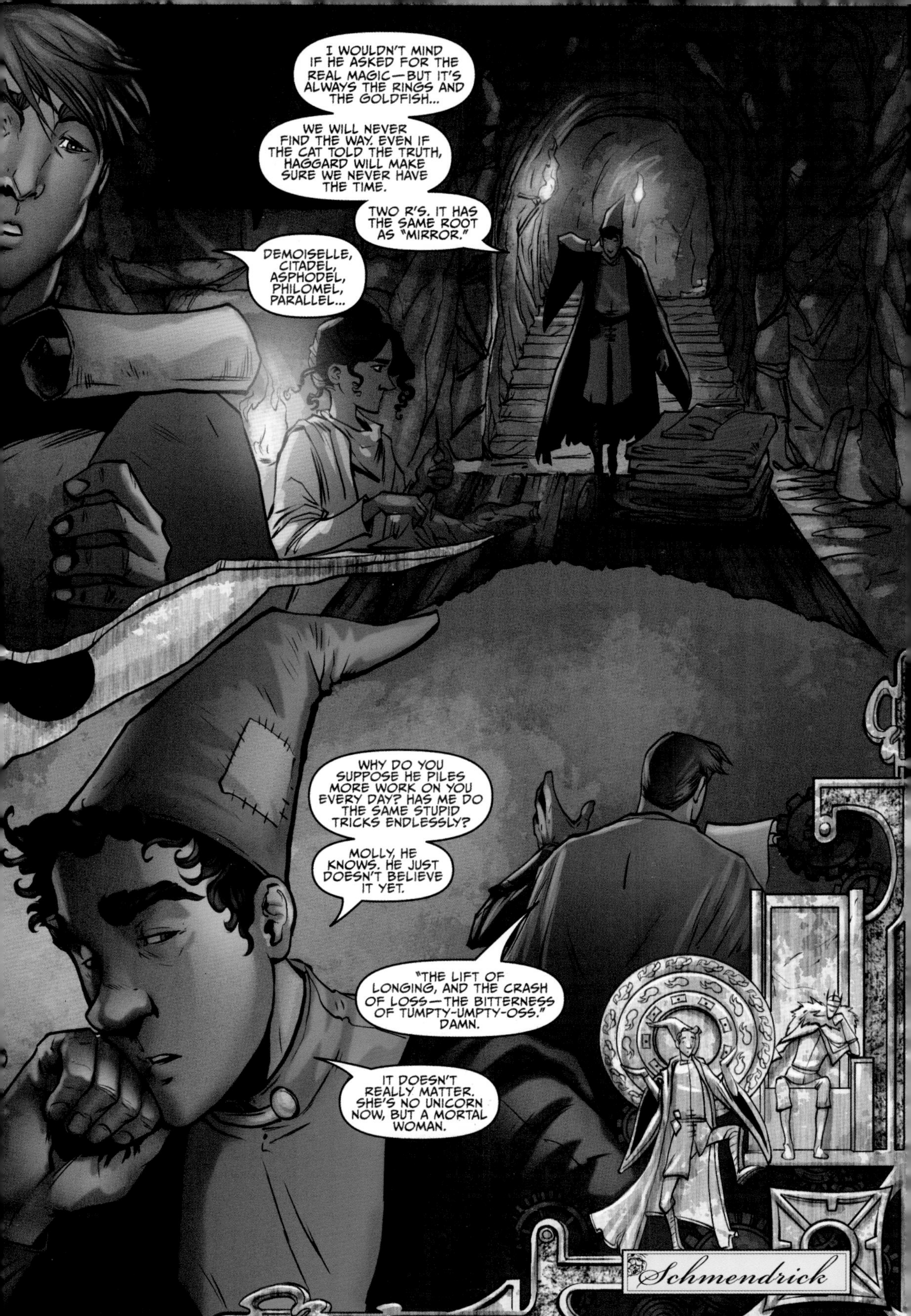
I WOULDN'T MIND IF HE ASKED FOR THE REAL MAGIC—BUT IT'S ALWAYS THE RINGS AND THE GOLDFISH...
WE WILL NEVER FIND THE WAY. EVEN IF THE CAT TOLD THE TRUTH, HAGGARD WILL MAKE SURE WE NEVER HAVE THE TIME.
TWO R'S. IT HAS THE SAME ROOT AS "MIRROR."
DEMOISELLE, CITADEL, ASPHODEL, PHILOMEL, PARALLEL...
WHY DO YOU SUPPOSE HE PILES MORE WORK ON YOU EVERY DAY? HAS ME DO THE SAME STUPID TRICKS ENDLESSLY?
MOLLY, HE KNOWS. HE JUST DOESN'T BELIEVE IT YET.
"THE LIFT OF LONGING, AND THE CRASH OF LOSS—THE BITTERNESS OF TUMPTY-UMPTY-OSS." DAMN.
IT DOESN'T REALLY MATTER. SHE'S NO UNICORN NOW, BUT A MORTAL WOMAN.
Schmendrick

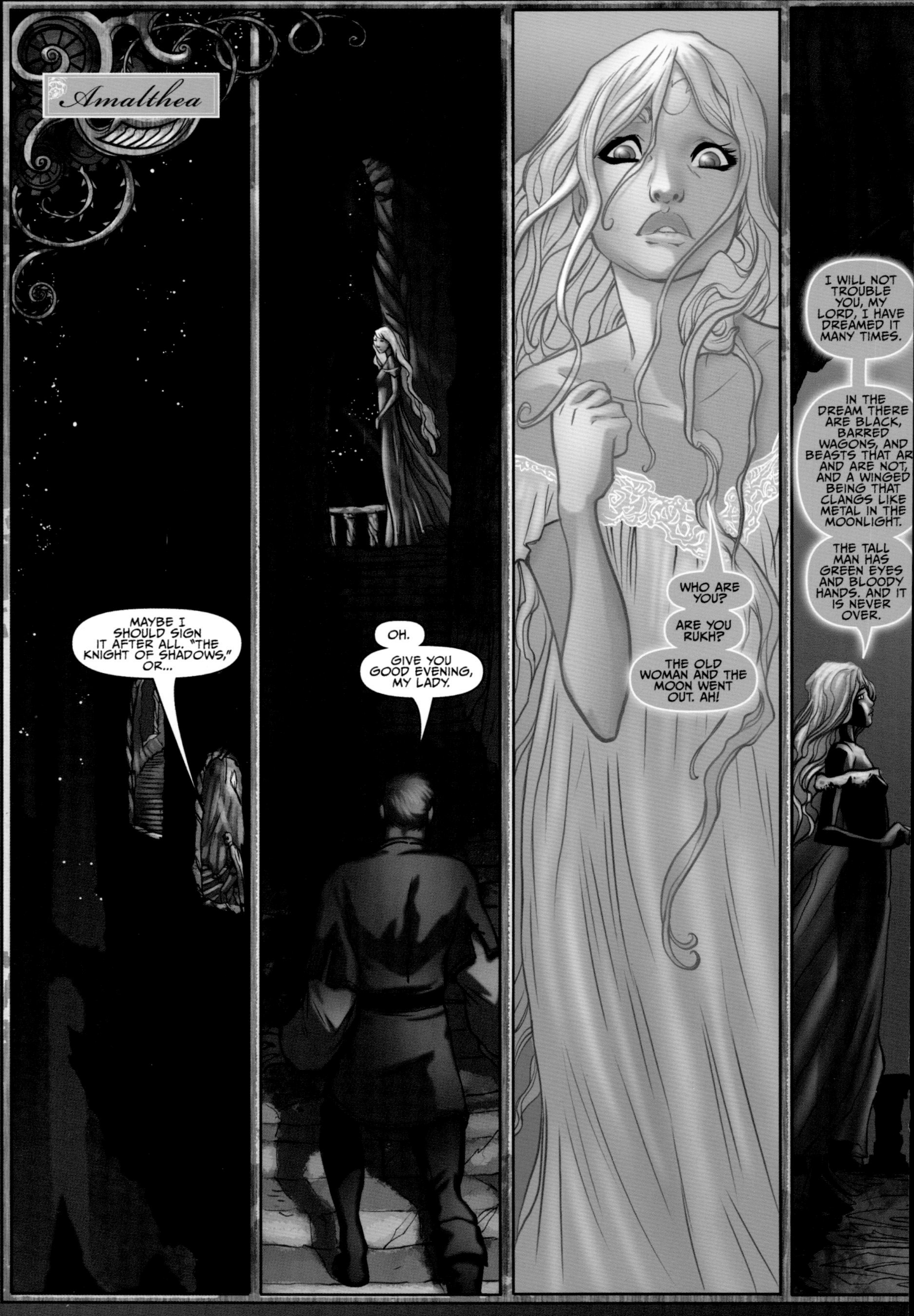
Amalthea
MAYBE I SHOULD SIGN IT AFTER ALL. "THE KNIGHT OF SHADOWS," OR...
OH.
GIVE YOU GOOD EVENING, MY LADY.
WHO ARE YOU?
ARE YOU RUKH?
THE OLD WOMAN AND THE MOON WENT OUT. AH!
I WILL NOT TROUBLE YOU, MY LORD, I HAVE DREAMED IT MANY TIMES.
IN THE DREAM THERE ARE BLACK, BARRED WAGONS, AND BEASTS THAT AR AND ARE NOT, AND A WINGED BEING THAT CLANGS LIKE METAL IN THE MOONLIGHT.
THE TALL MAN HAS GREEN EYES AND BLOODY HANDS. AND IT IS NEVER OVER.

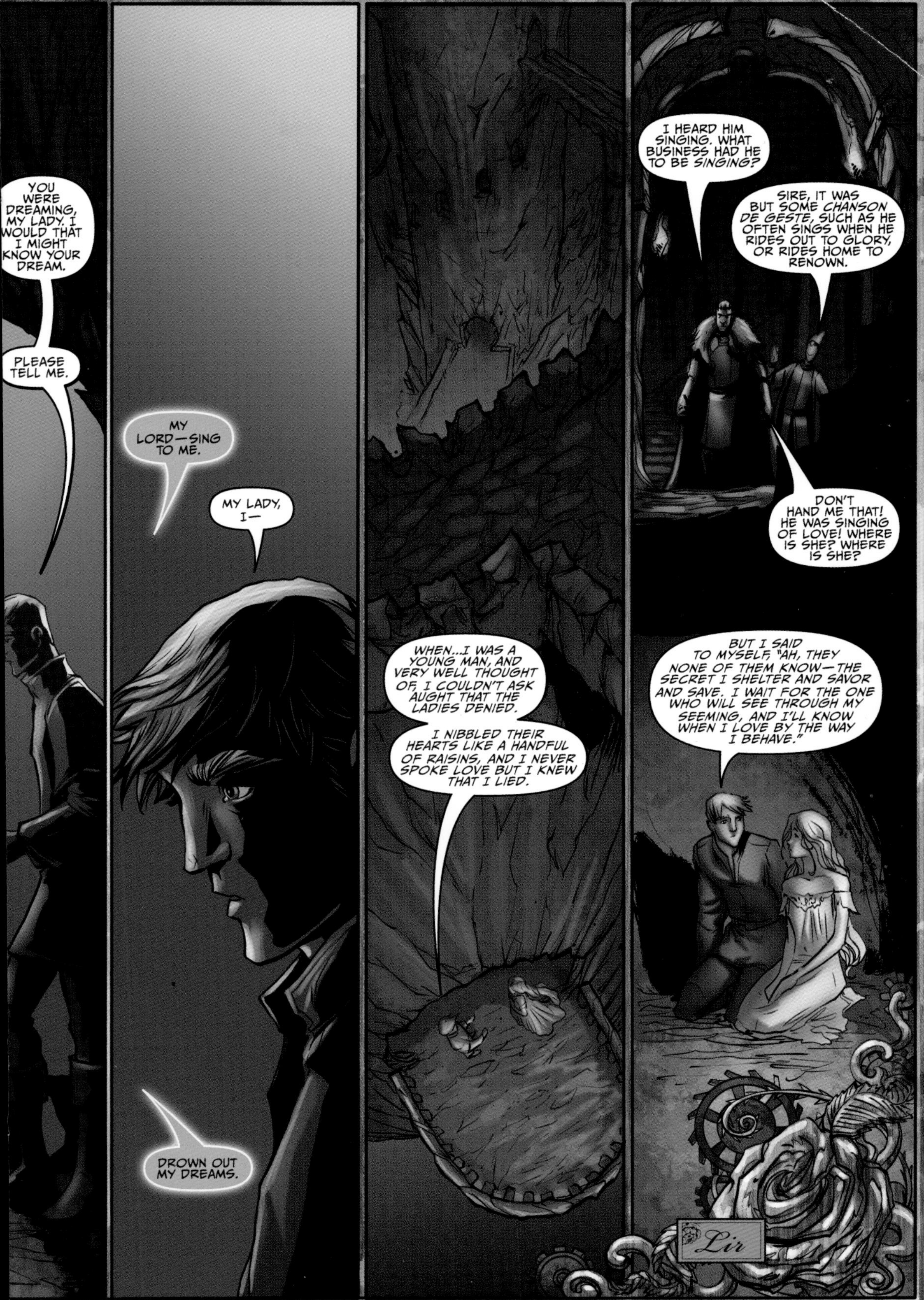
YOU WERE DREAMING, MY LADY. I WOULD THAT I MIGHT KNOW YOUR DREAM.
PLEASE TELL ME.
MY LORD—SING TO ME.
MY LADY, I—
DROWN OUT MY DREAMS.
WHEN...I WAS A YOUNG MAN, AND VERY WELL THOUGHT OF, I COULDN'T ASK AUGHT THAT THE LADIES DENIED.
I NIBBLED THEIR HEARTS LIKE A HANDFUL OF RAISINS, AND I NEVER SPOKE LOVE BUT I KNEW THAT I LIED.
I HEARD HIM SINGING. WHAT BUSINESS HAD HE TO BE SINGING?
SIRE, IT WAS BUT SOME CHANSON DE GESTE, SUCH AS HE OFTEN SINGS WHEN HE RIDES OUT TO GLORY, OR RIDES HOME TO RENOWN.
DON'T HAND ME THAT! HE WAS SINGING OF LOVE! WHERE IS SHE? WHERE IS SHE?
BUT I SAID TO MYSELF, "AH, THEY NONE OF THEM KNOW—THE SECRET I SHELTER AND SAVOR AND SAVE. I WAIT FOR THE ONE WHO WILL SEE THROUGH MY SEEMING, AND I'LL KNOW WHEN I LOVE BY THE WAY I BEHAVE."
Lir

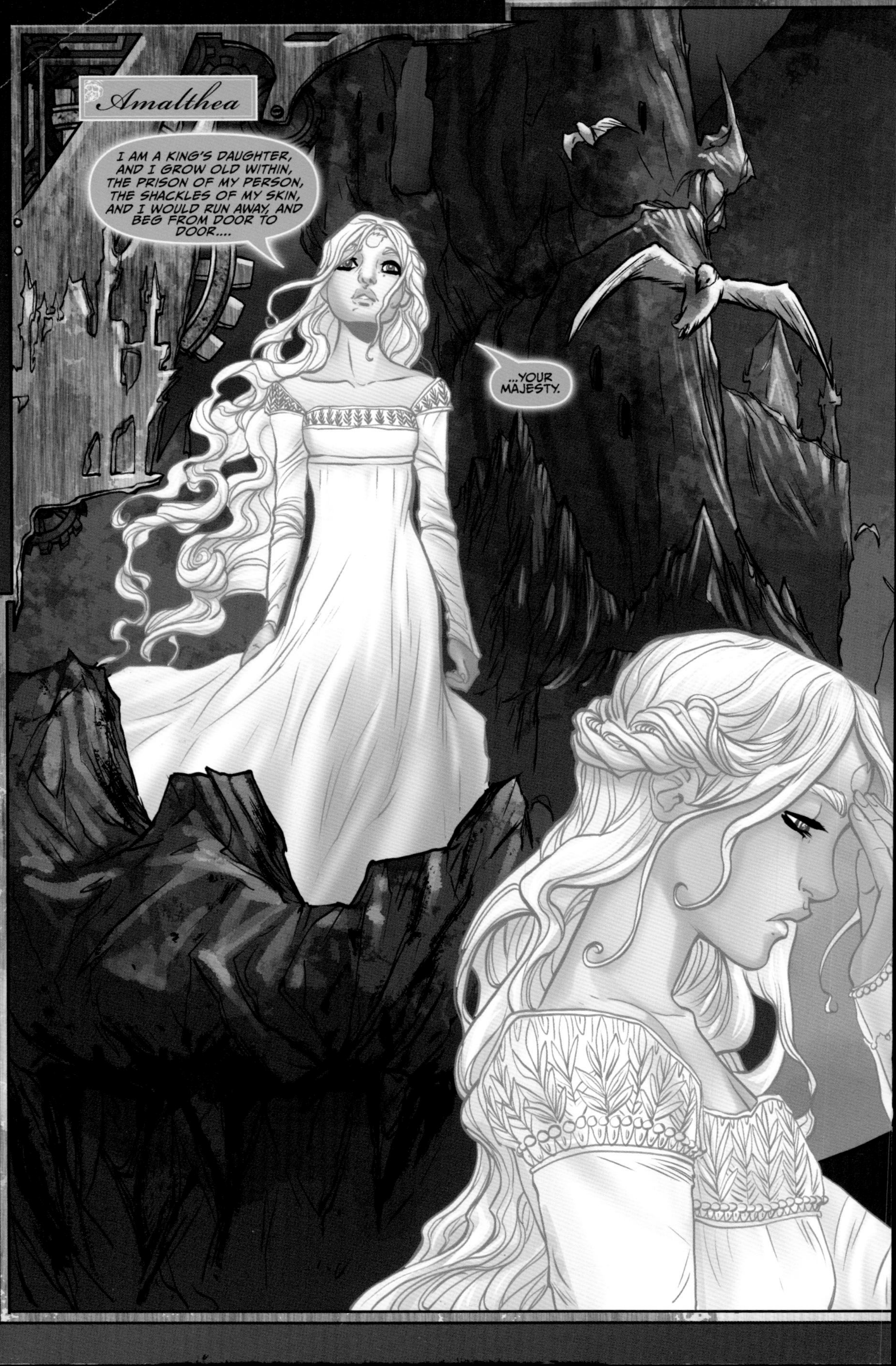
Amalthea
I AM A KING'S DAUGHTER, AND I GROW OLD WITHIN, THE PRISON OF MY PERSON, THE SHACKLES OF MY SKIN, AND I WOULD RUN AWAY, AND BEG FROM DOOR TO DOOR....
...YOUR MAJESTY.

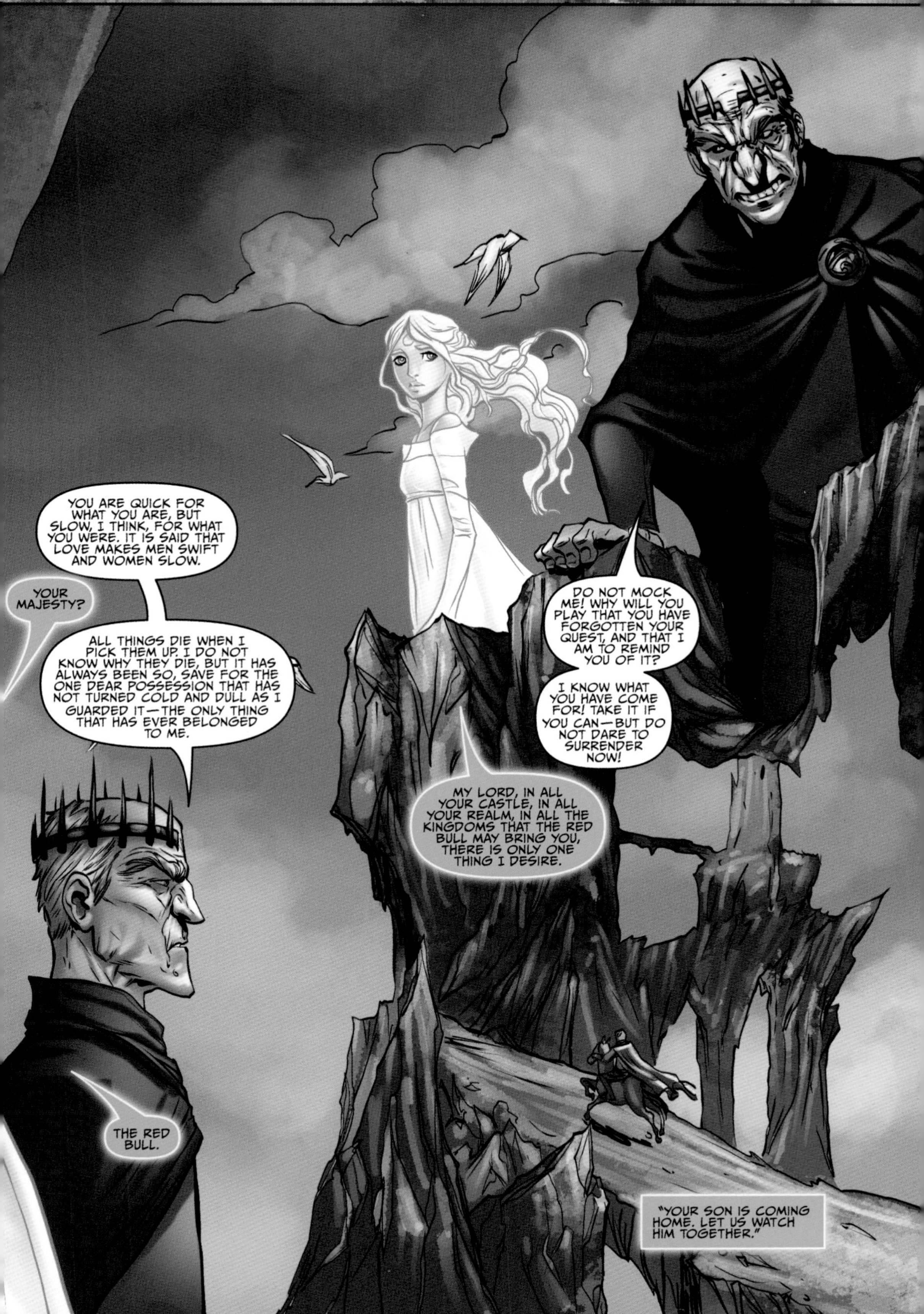

YOU ARE QUICK FOR WHAT YOU ARE, BUT SLOW, I THINK, FOR WHAT YOU WERE. IT IS SAID THAT LOVE MAKES MEN SWIFT AND WOMEN SLOW.
YOUR MAJESTY?
ALL THINGS DIE WHEN I PICK THEM UP. I DO NOT KNOW WHY THEY DIE, BUT IT HAS ALWAYS BEEN SO, SAVE FOR THE ONE DEAR POSSESSION THAT HAS NOT TURNED COLD AND DULL AS I GUARDED IT—THE ONLY THING THAT HAS EVER BELONGED TO ME.
DO NOT MOCK ME! WHY WILL YOU PLAY THAT YOU HAVE FORGOTTEN YOUR QUEST, AND THAT I AM TO REMIND YOU OF IT?
I KNOW WHAT YOU HAVE COME FOR! TAKE IT IF YOU CAN—BUT DO NOT DARE TO SURRENDER NOW!
MY LORD, IN ALL YOUR CASTLE, IN ALL YOUR REALM, IN ALL THE KINGDOMS THAT THE RED BULL MAY BRING YOU, THERE IS ONLY ONE THING I DESIRE.
THE RED BULL.
"YOUR SON IS COMING HOME. LET US WATCH HIM TOGETHER."

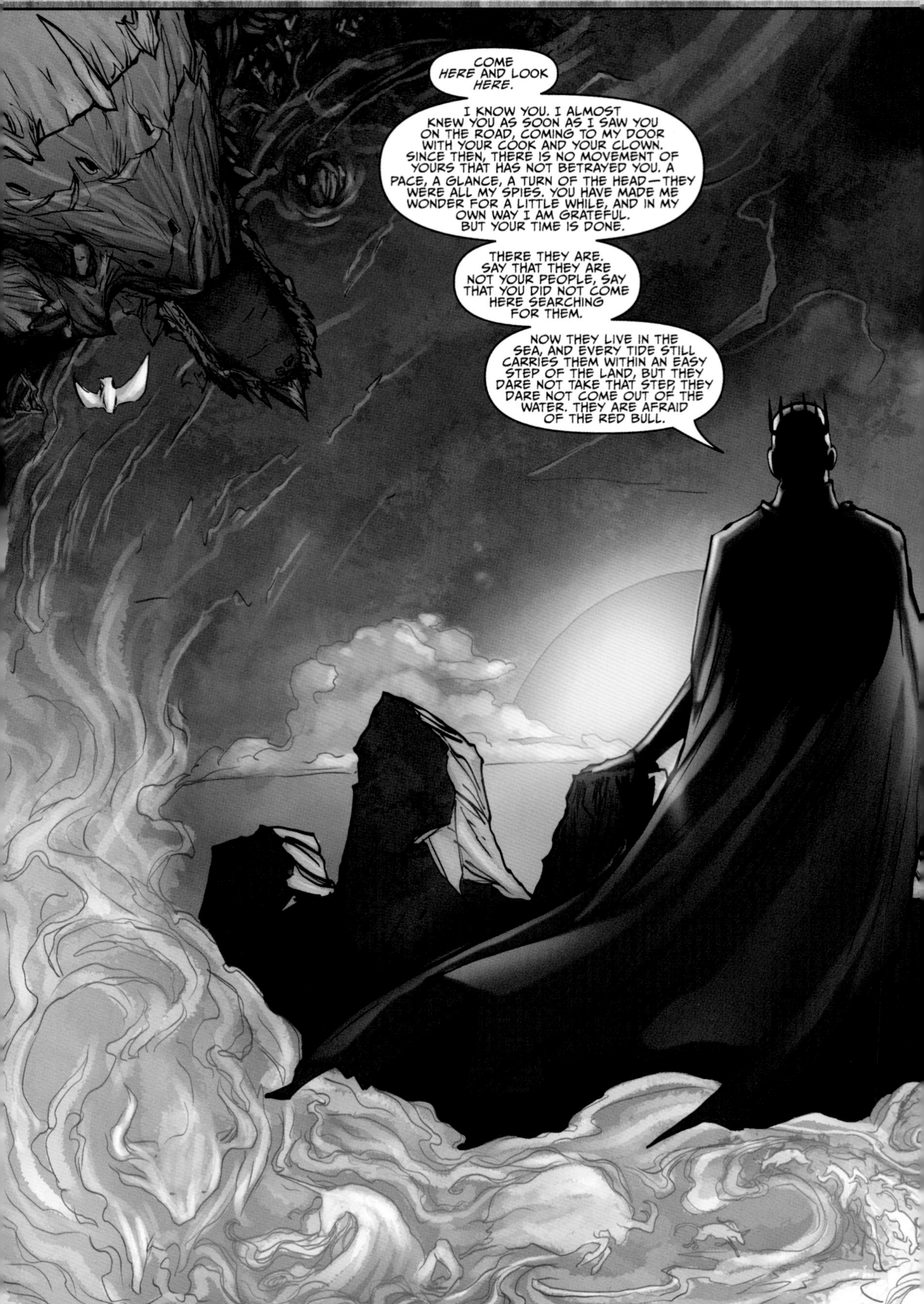
COME *HERE* AND LOOK *HERE*.
I KNOW YOU. I ALMOST KNEW YOU AS SOON AS I SAW YOU ON THE ROAD, COMING TO MY DOOR WITH YOUR COOK AND YOUR CLOWN. SINCE THEN, THERE IS NO MOVEMENT OF YOURS THAT HAS NOT BETRAYED YOU. A PACE, A GLANCE, A TURN OF THE HEAD—THEY WERE ALL MY SPIES. YOU HAVE MADE ME WONDER FOR A LITTLE WHILE, AND IN MY OWN WAY I AM GRATEFUL. BUT YOUR TIME IS DONE.
THERE THEY ARE. SAY THAT THEY ARE NOT YOUR PEOPLE, SAY THAT YOU DID NOT COME HERE SEARCHING FOR THEM.
NOW THEY LIVE IN THE SEA, AND EVERY TIDE STILL CARRIES THEM WITHIN AN EASY STEP OF THE LAND, BUT THEY DARE NOT TAKE THAT STEP, THEY DARE NOT COME OUT OF THE WATER. THEY ARE AFRAID OF THE RED BULL.

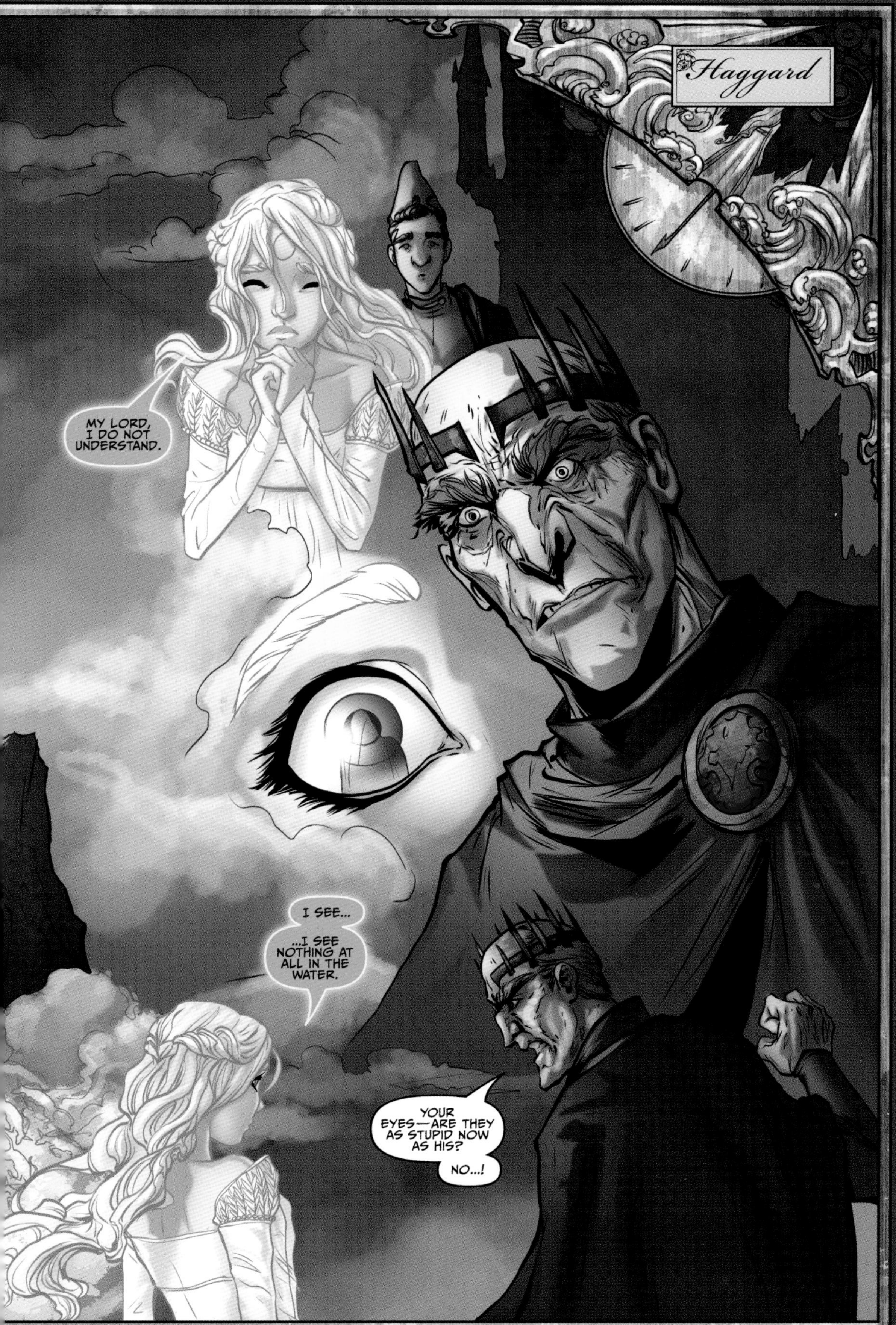
Haggard
MY LORD, I DO NOT UNDERSTAND.
I SEE...
...I SEE NOTHING AT ALL IN THE WATER.
YOUR EYES—ARE THEY AS STUPID NOW AS HIS?
NO...!

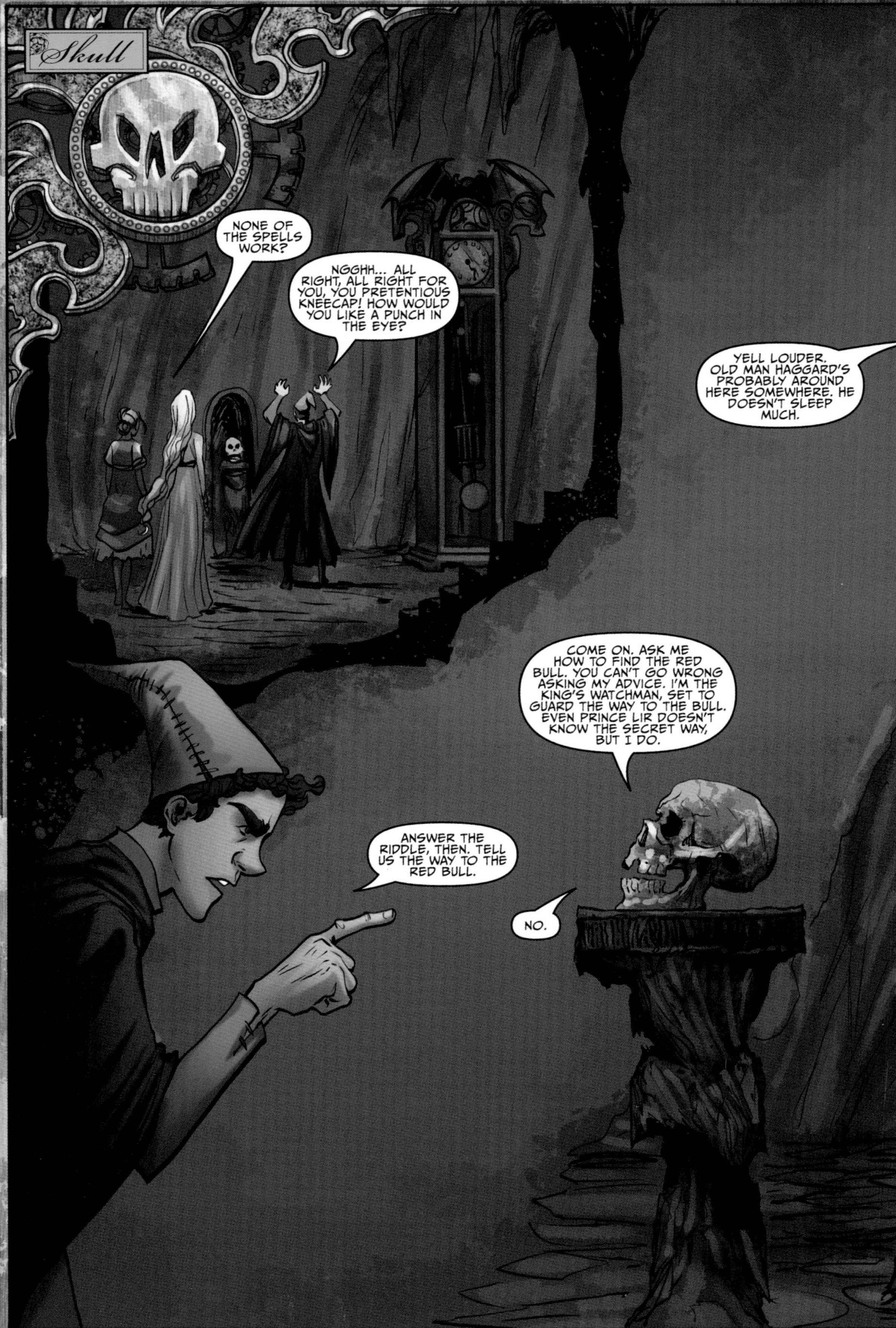
Skull
NONE OF THE SPELLS WORK?
NGGHH... ALL RIGHT, ALL RIGHT FOR YOU, YOU PRETENTIOUS KNEECAP! HOW WOULD YOU LIKE A PUNCH IN THE EYE?
YELL LOUDER. OLD MAN HAGGARD'S PROBABLY AROUND HERE SOMEWHERE. HE DOESN'T SLEEP MUCH.
COME ON. ASK ME HOW TO FIND THE RED BULL. YOU CAN'T GO WRONG ASKING MY ADVICE. I'M THE KING'S WATCHMAN, SET TO GUARD THE WAY TO THE BULL. EVEN PRINCE LIR DOESN'T KNOW THE SECRET WAY, BUT I DO.
ANSWER THE RIDDLE, THEN. TELL US THE WAY TO THE RED BULL.
NO.

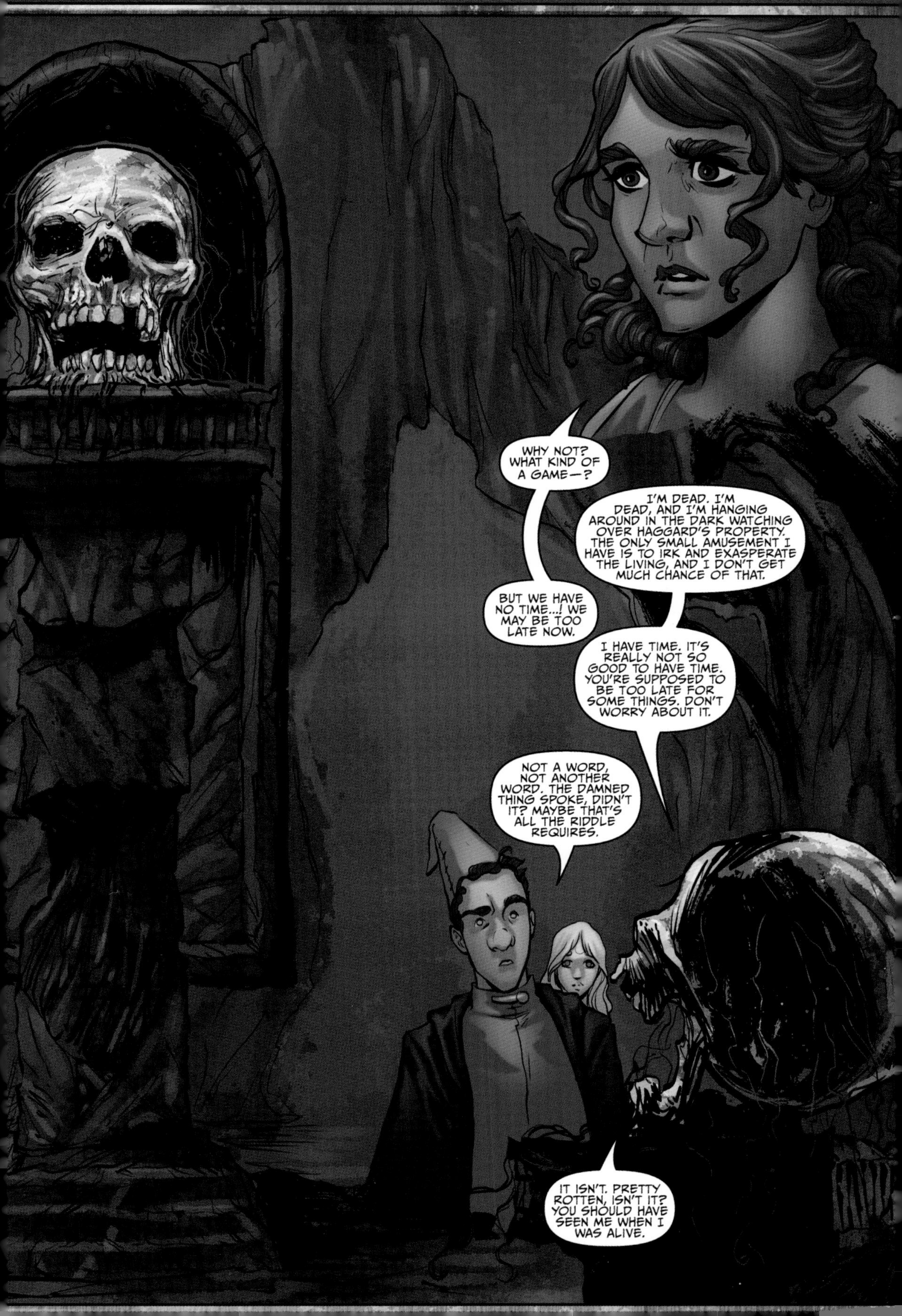
WHY NOT? WHAT KIND OF A GAME—?
I'M DEAD. I'M DEAD, AND I'M HANGING AROUND IN THE DARK WATCHING OVER HAGGARD'S PROPERTY. THE ONLY SMALL AMUSEMENT I HAVE IS TO IRK AND EXASPERATE THE LIVING, AND I DON'T GET MUCH CHANCE OF THAT.
BUT WE HAVE NO TIME...! WE MAY BE TOO LATE NOW.
I HAVE TIME. IT'S REALLY NOT SO GOOD TO HAVE TIME. YOU'RE SUPPOSED TO BE TOO LATE FOR SOME THINGS. DON'T WORRY ABOUT IT.
NOT A WORD, NOT ANOTHER WORD. THE DAMNED THING SPOKE, DIDN'T IT? MAYBE THAT'S ALL THE RIDDLE REQUIRES.
IT ISN'T. PRETTY ROTTEN, ISN'T IT? YOU SHOULD HAVE SEEN ME WHEN I WAS ALIVE.

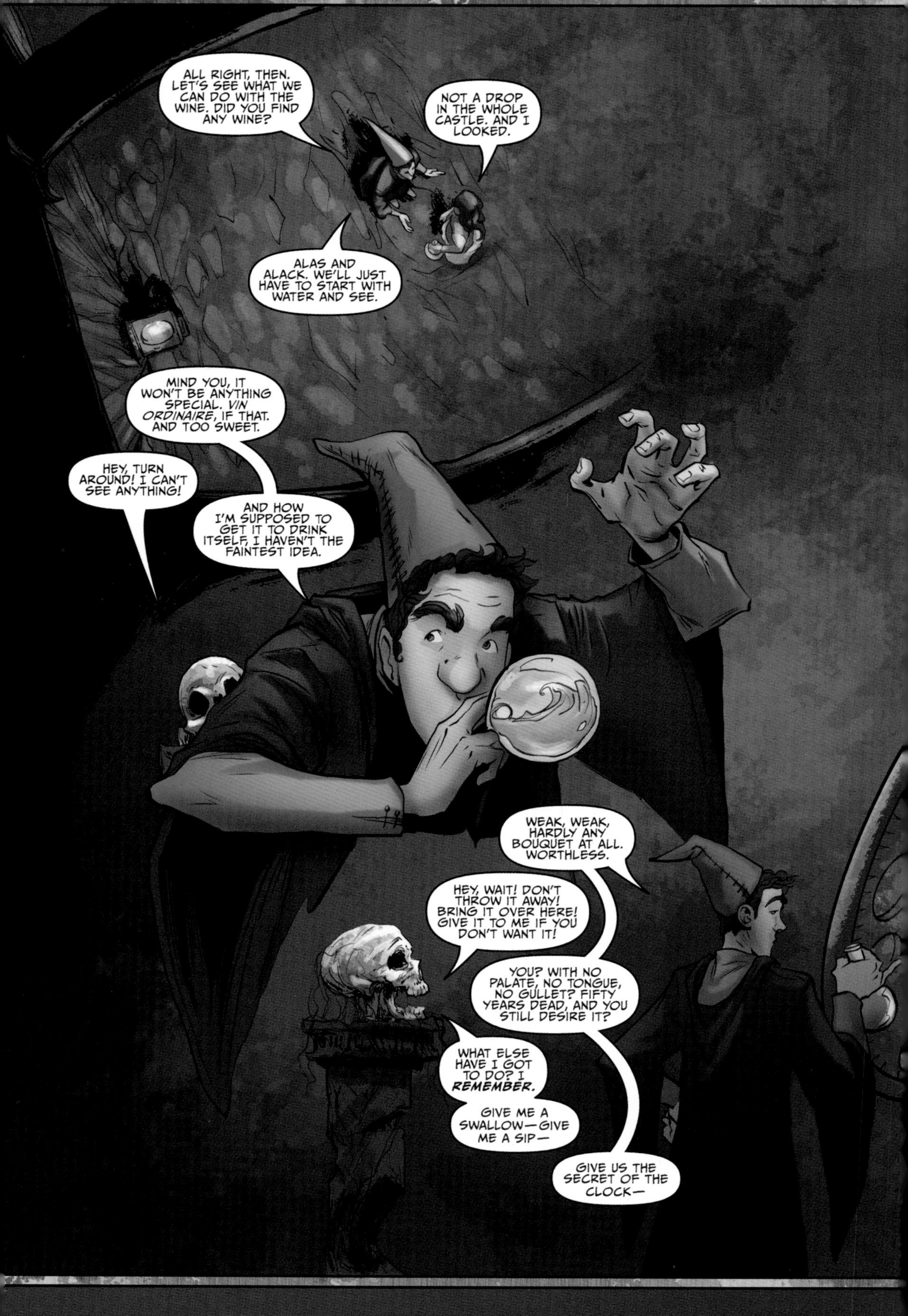

ALL RIGHT, THEN. LET'S SEE WHAT WE CAN DO WITH THE WINE. DID YOU FIND ANY WINE?
NOT A DROP IN THE WHOLE CASTLE. AND I LOOKED.
ALAS AND ALACK. WE'LL JUST HAVE TO START WITH WATER AND SEE.
MIND YOU, IT WON'T BE ANYTHING SPECIAL. *VIN ORDINAIRE*, IF THAT. AND TOO SWEET.
HEY, TURN AROUND! I CAN'T SEE ANYTHING!
AND HOW I'M SUPPOSED TO GET IT TO DRINK ITSELF, I HAVEN'T THE FAINTEST IDEA.
WEAK, WEAK, HARDLY ANY BOUQUET AT ALL. WORTHLESS.
HEY, WAIT! DON'T THROW IT AWAY! BRING IT OVER HERE! GIVE IT TO ME IF YOU DON'T WANT IT!
YOU? WITH NO PALATE, NO TONGUE, NO GULLET? FIFTY YEARS DEAD, AND YOU STILL DESIRE IT?
WHAT ELSE HAVE I GOT TO DO? I ***REMEMBER.***
GIVE ME A SWALLOW—GIVE ME A SIP—
GIVE US THE SECRET OF THE CLOCK—

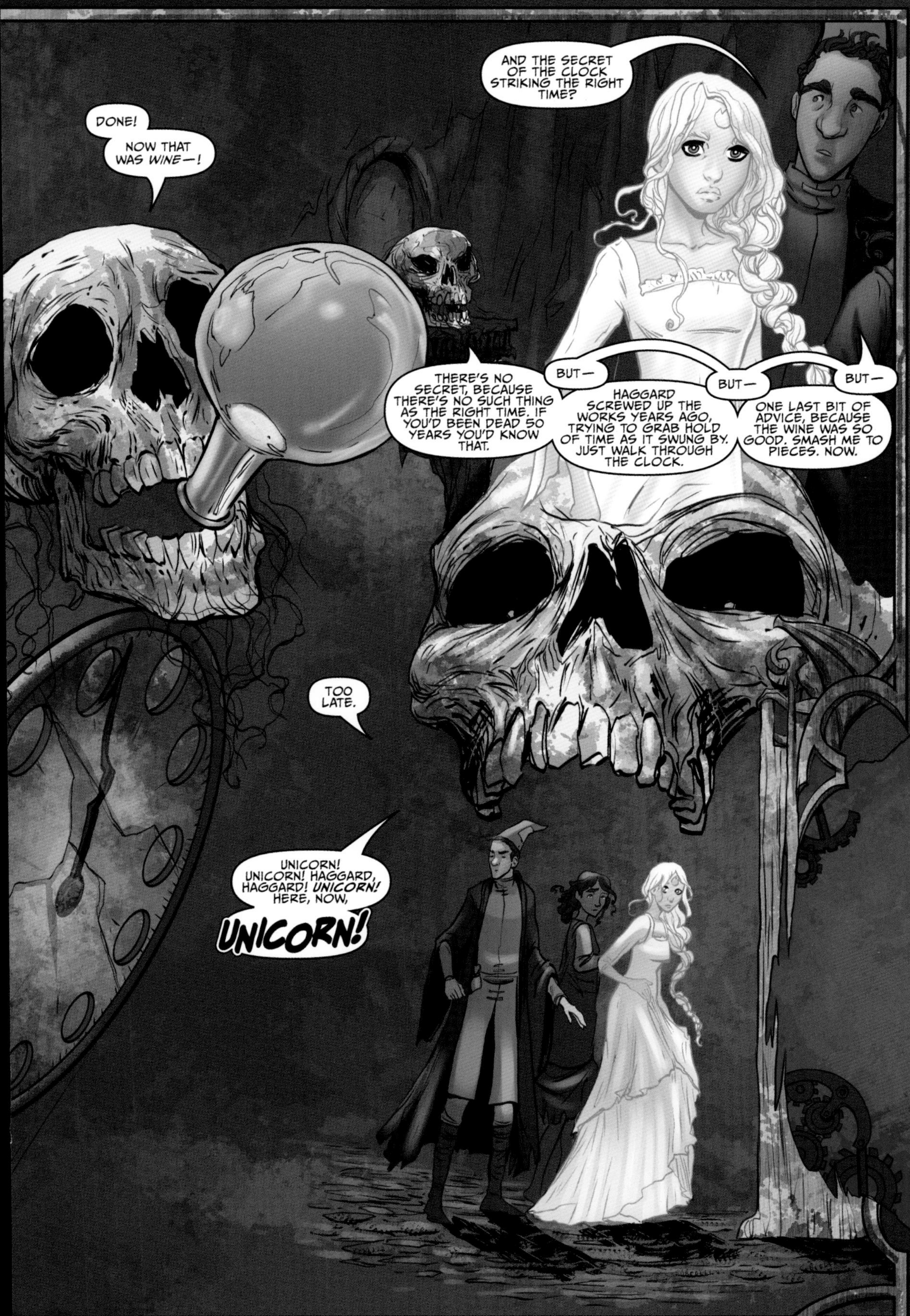
DONE!
NOW THAT WAS *WINE*—!
AND THE SECRET OF THE CLOCK STRIKING THE RIGHT TIME?
THERE'S NO SECRET, BECAUSE THERE'S NO SUCH THING AS THE RIGHT TIME. IF YOU'D BEEN DEAD 50 YEARS YOU'D KNOW THAT.
BUT—
HAGGARD SCREWED UP THE WORKS YEARS AGO, TRYING TO GRAB HOLD OF TIME AS IT SWUNG BY. JUST WALK THROUGH THE CLOCK.
BUT—
BUT—
ONE LAST BIT OF ADVICE, BECAUSE THE WINE WAS SO GOOD. SMASH ME TO PIECES. NOW.
TOO LATE.
UNICORN! UNICORN! HAGGARD, HAGGARD! *UNICORN!* HERE, NOW,
UNICORN!

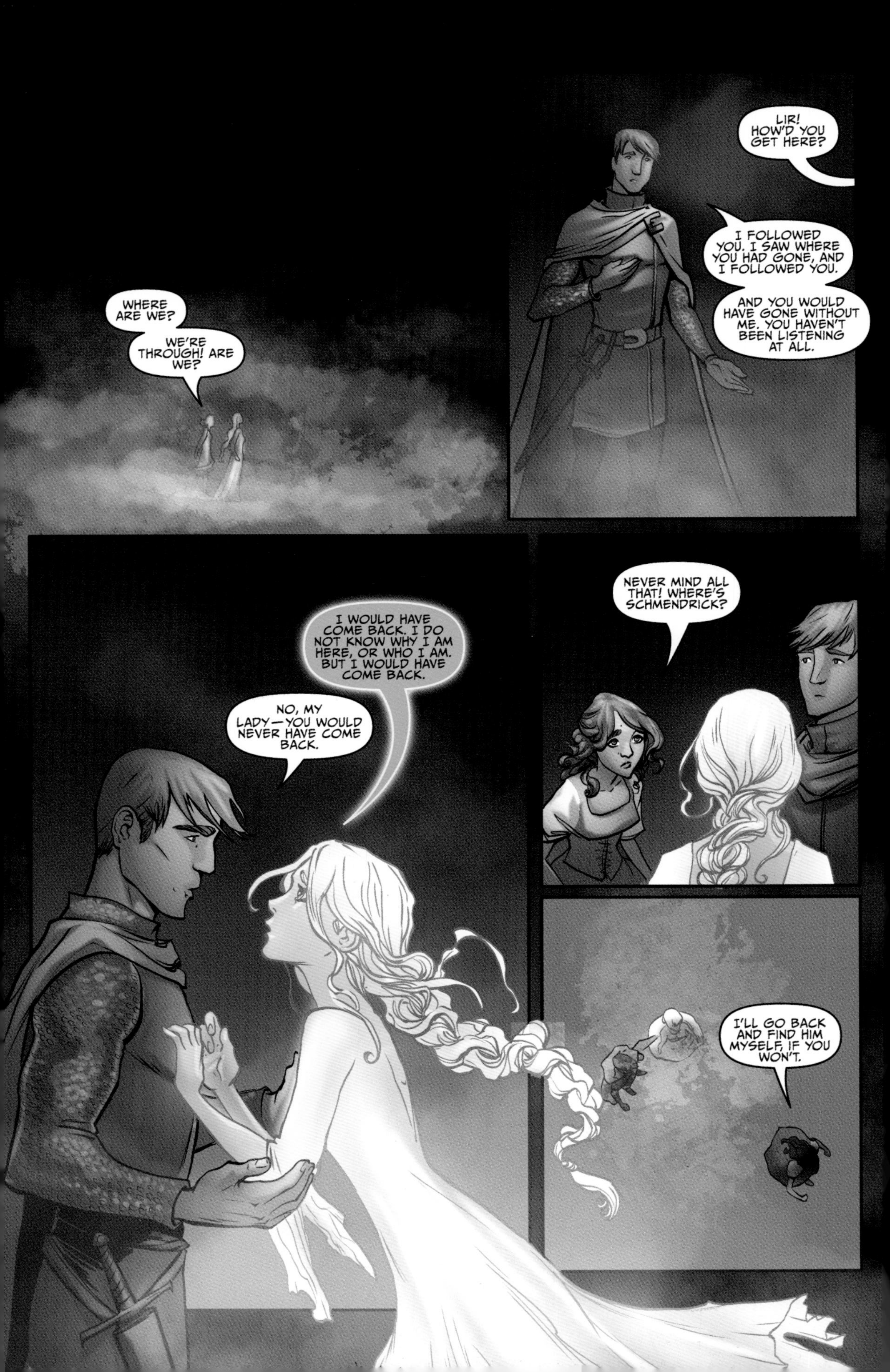
WHERE ARE WE?
WE'RE THROUGH! ARE WE?
LIR! HOW'D YOU GET HERE?
I FOLLOWED YOU. I SAW WHERE YOU HAD GONE, AND I FOLLOWED YOU.
AND YOU WOULD HAVE GONE WITHOUT ME. YOU HAVEN'T BEEN LISTENING AT ALL.
I WOULD HAVE COME BACK. I DO NOT KNOW WHY I AM HERE, OR WHO I AM. BUT I WOULD HAVE COME BACK.
NO, MY LADY—YOU WOULD NEVER HAVE COME BACK.
NEVER MIND ALL THAT! WHERE'S SCHMENDRICK?
I'LL GO BACK AND FIND HIM MYSELF, IF YOU WON'T.

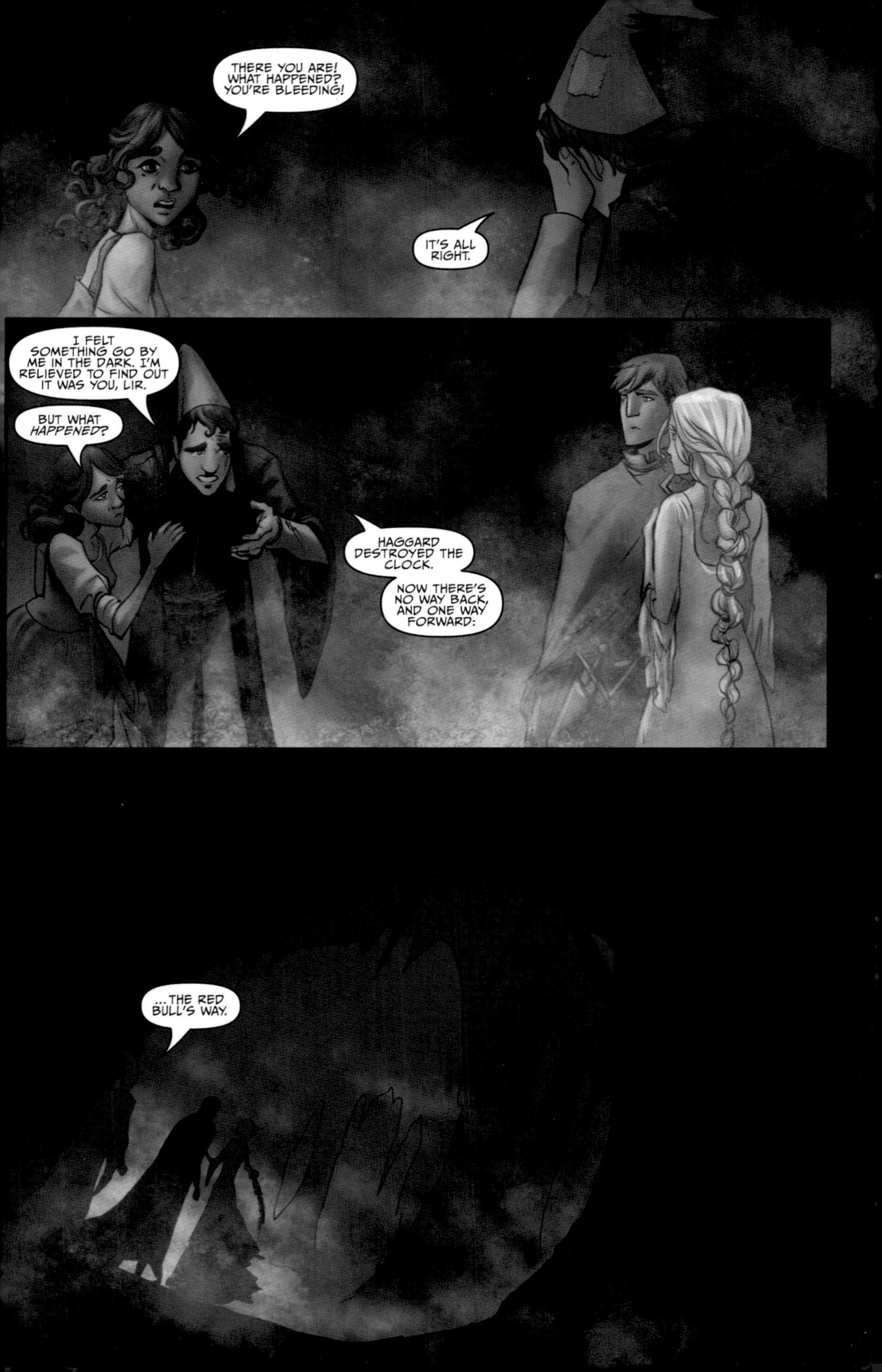
THERE YOU ARE! WHAT HAPPENED? YOU'RE BLEEDING!
IT'S ALL RIGHT.
I FELT SOMETHING GO BY ME IN THE DARK. I'M RELIEVED TO FIND OUT IT WAS YOU, LIR.
BUT WHAT *HAPPENED?*
HAGGARD DESTROYED THE CLOCK.
NOW THERE'S NO WAY BACK, AND ONE WAY FORWARD:
...THE RED BULL'S WAY.

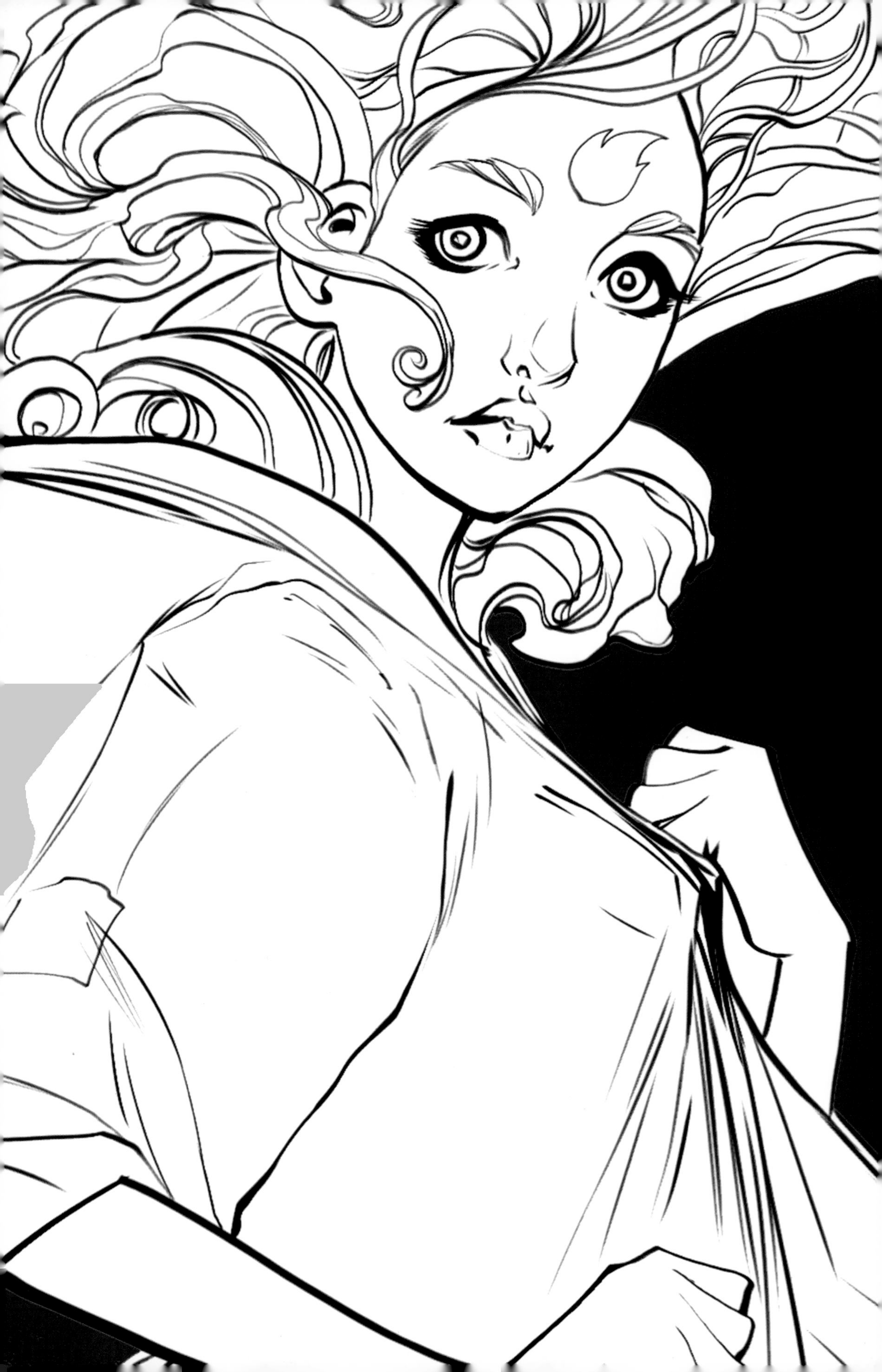

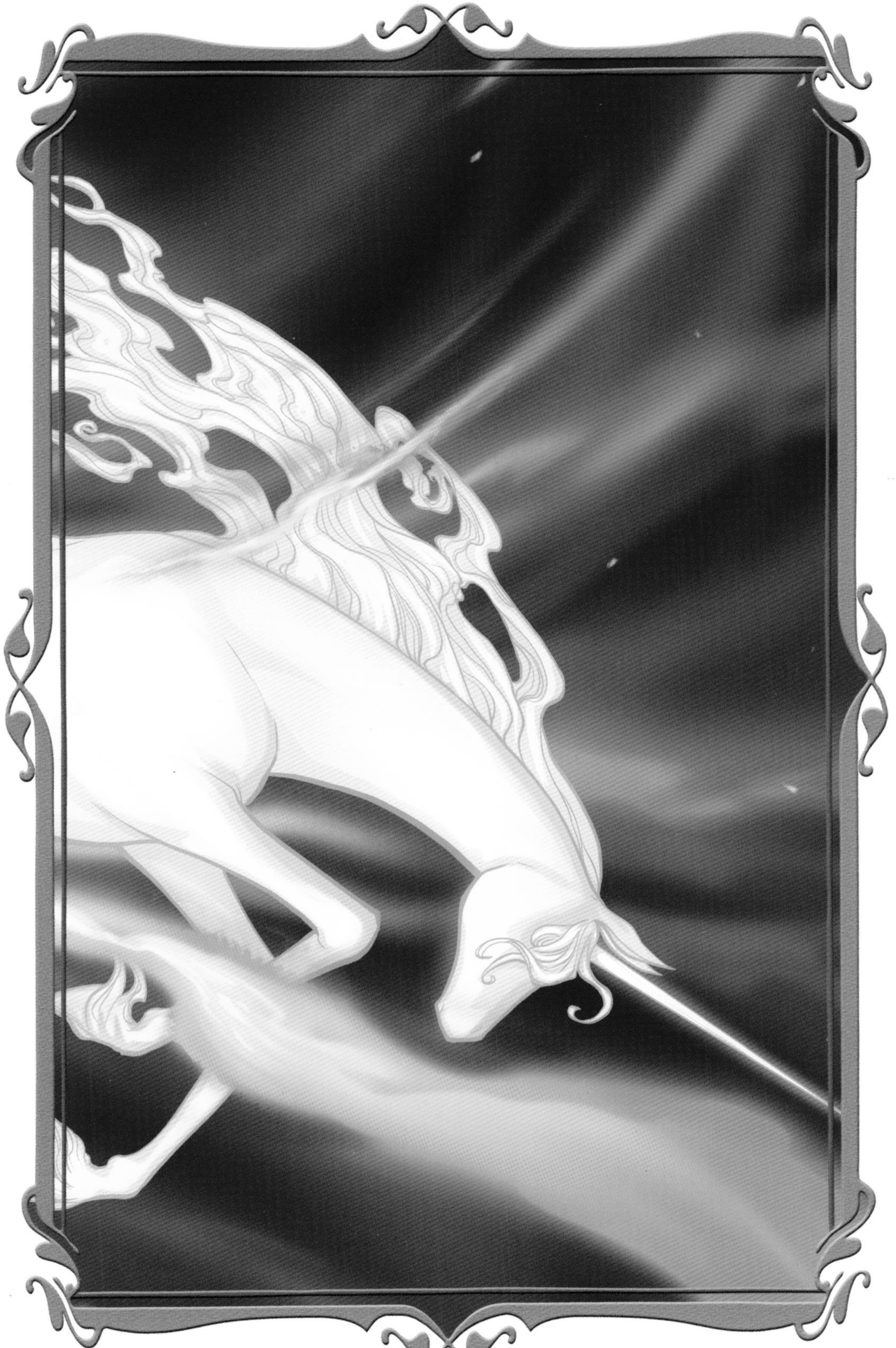

CHAPTER SIX

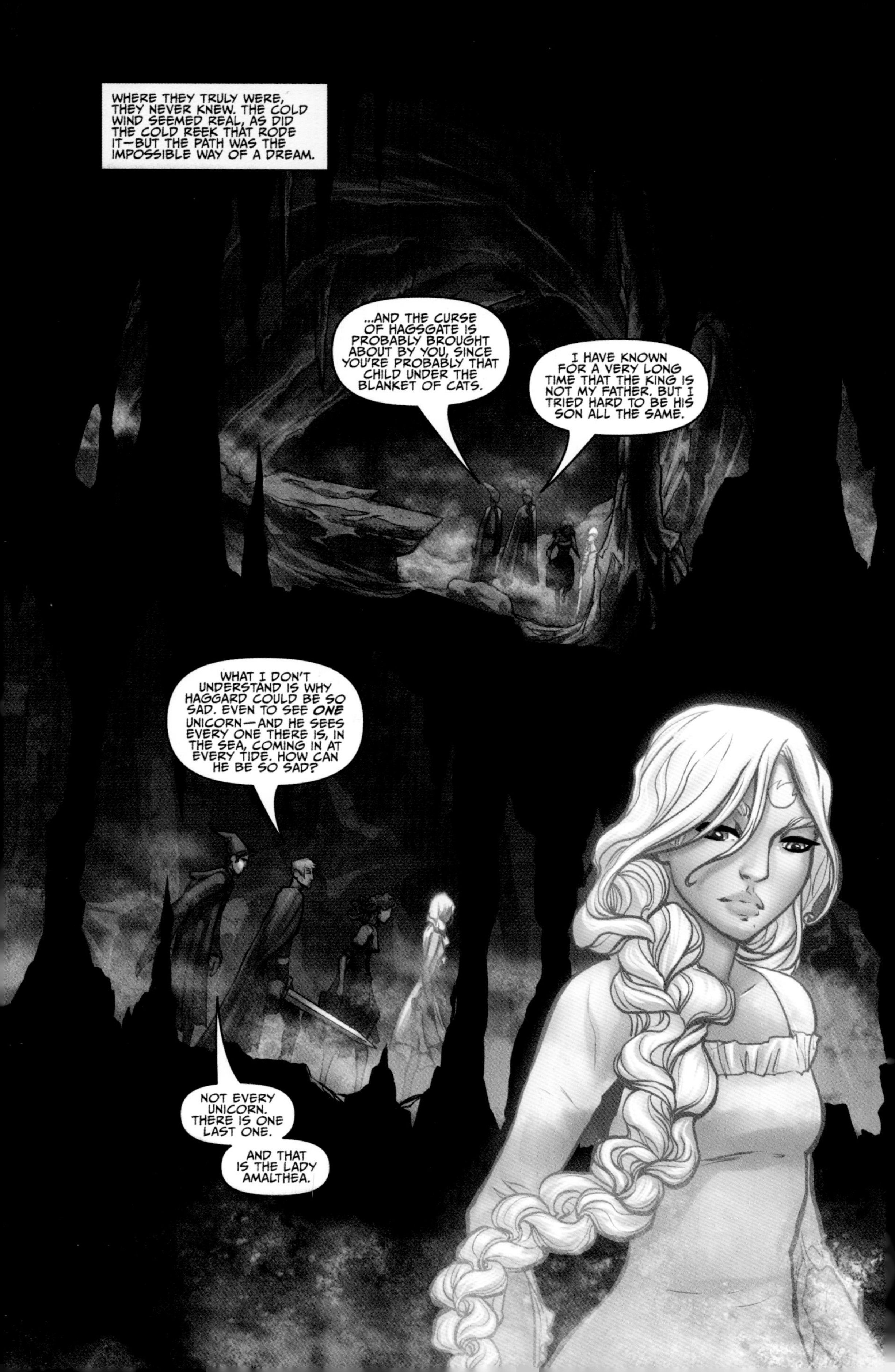
WHERE THEY TRULY WERE, THEY NEVER KNEW. THE COLD WIND SEEMED REAL, AS DID THE COLD REEK THAT RODE IT—BUT THE PATH WAS THE IMPOSSIBLE WAY OF A DREAM.
...AND THE CURSE OF HAGSGATE IS PROBABLY BROUGHT ABOUT BY YOU, SINCE YOU'RE PROBABLY THAT CHILD UNDER THE BLANKET OF CATS.
I HAVE KNOWN FOR A VERY LONG TIME THAT THE KING IS NOT MY FATHER. BUT I TRIED HARD TO BE HIS SON ALL THE SAME.
WHAT I DON'T UNDERSTAND IS WHY HAGGARD COULD BE SO SAD. EVEN TO SEE *ONE* UNICORN—AND HE SEES EVERY ONE THERE IS, IN THE SEA, COMING IN AT EVERY TIDE. HOW CAN HE BE SO SAD?
NOT EVERY UNICORN. THERE IS ONE LAST ONE.
AND THAT IS THE LADY AMALTHEA.

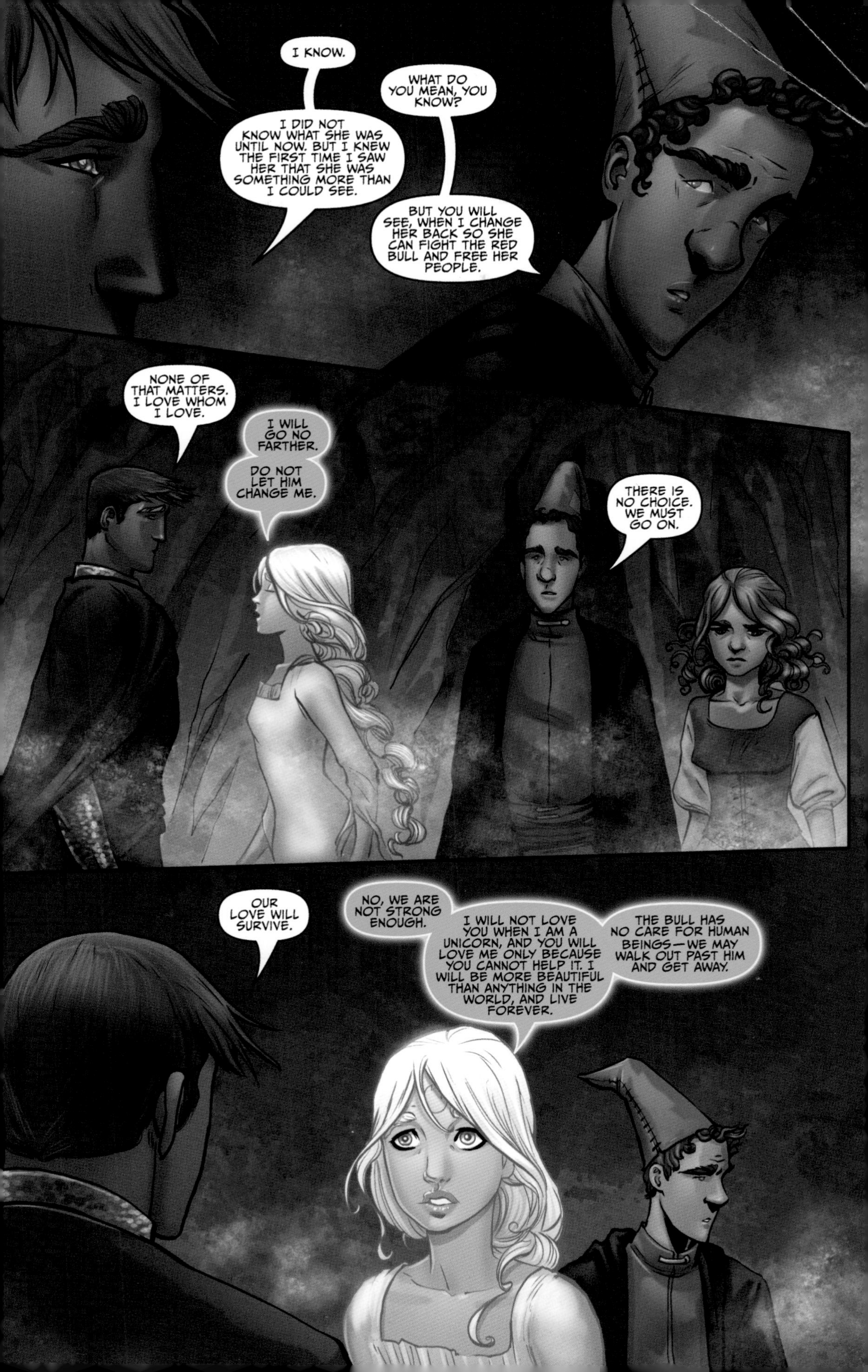
I KNOW.
I DID NOT KNOW WHAT SHE WAS UNTIL NOW. BUT I KNEW THE FIRST TIME I SAW HER THAT SHE WAS SOMETHING MORE THAN I COULD SEE.
WHAT DO YOU MEAN, YOU KNOW?
BUT YOU WILL SEE, WHEN I CHANGE HER BACK SO SHE CAN FIGHT THE RED BULL AND FREE HER PEOPLE.
NONE OF THAT MATTERS. I LOVE WHOM I LOVE.
I WILL GO NO FARTHER.
DO NOT LET HIM CHANGE ME.
THERE IS NO CHOICE. WE MUST GO ON.
OUR LOVE WILL SURVIVE.
NO, WE ARE NOT STRONG ENOUGH.
I WILL NOT LOVE YOU WHEN I AM A UNICORN, AND YOU WILL LOVE ME ONLY BECAUSE YOU CANNOT HELP IT. I WILL BE MORE BEAUTIFUL THAN ANYTHING IN THE WORLD, AND LIVE FOREVER.
THE BULL HAS NO CARE FOR HUMAN BEINGS—WE MAY WALK OUT PAST HIM AND GET AWAY.

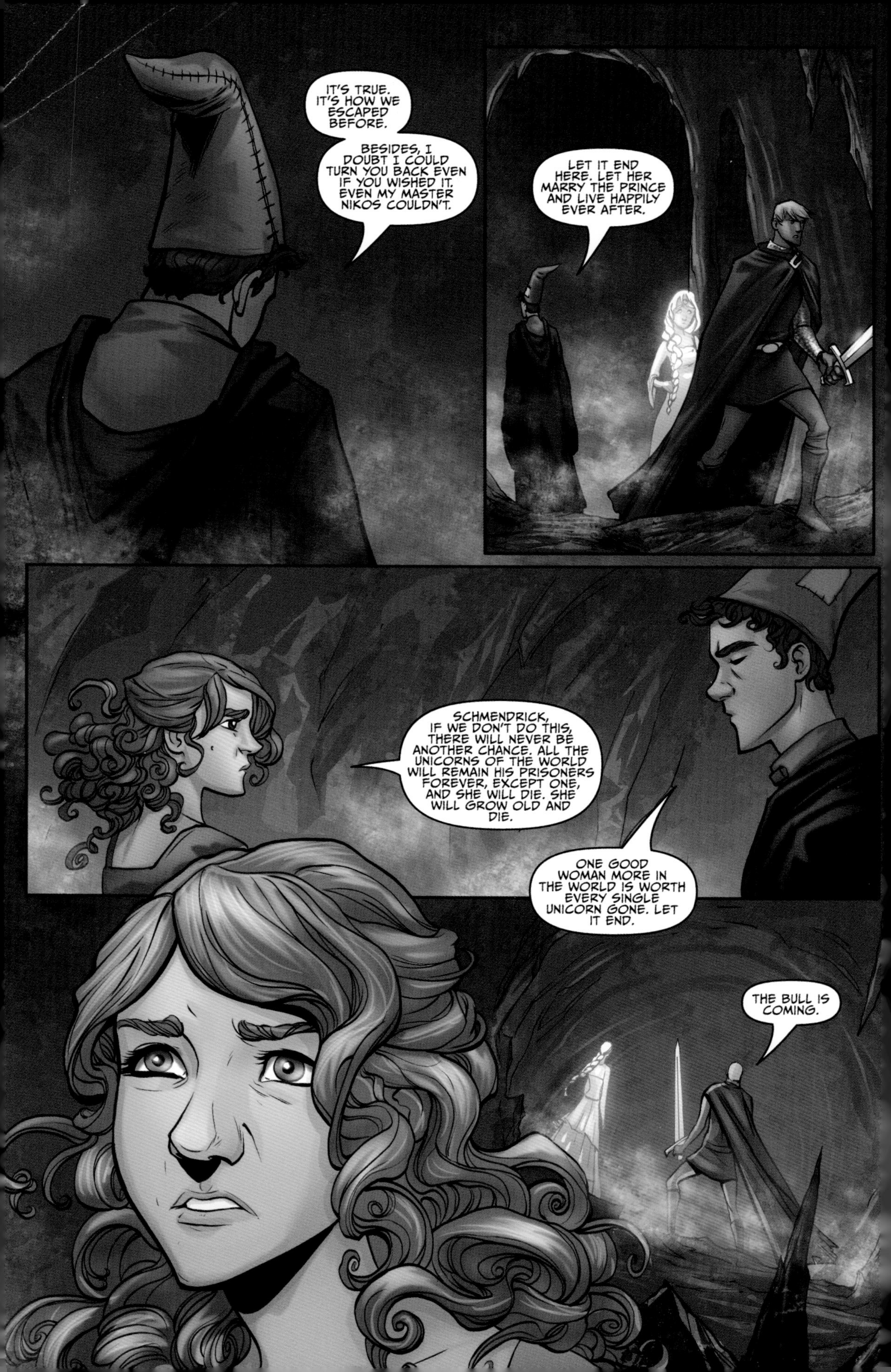
IT'S TRUE. IT'S HOW WE ESCAPED BEFORE.
BESIDES, I DOUBT I COULD TURN YOU BACK EVEN IF YOU WISHED IT. EVEN MY MASTER NIKOS COULDN'T.
LET IT END HERE. LET HER MARRY THE PRINCE AND LIVE HAPPILY EVER AFTER.
SCHMENDRICK, IF WE DON'T DO THIS, THERE WILL NEVER BE ANOTHER CHANCE. ALL THE UNICORNS OF THE WORLD WILL REMAIN HIS PRISONERS FOREVER, EXCEPT ONE, AND SHE WILL DIE. SHE WILL GROW OLD AND DIE.
ONE GOOD WOMAN MORE IN THE WORLD IS WORTH EVERY SINGLE UNICORN GONE. LET IT END.
THE BULL IS COMING.

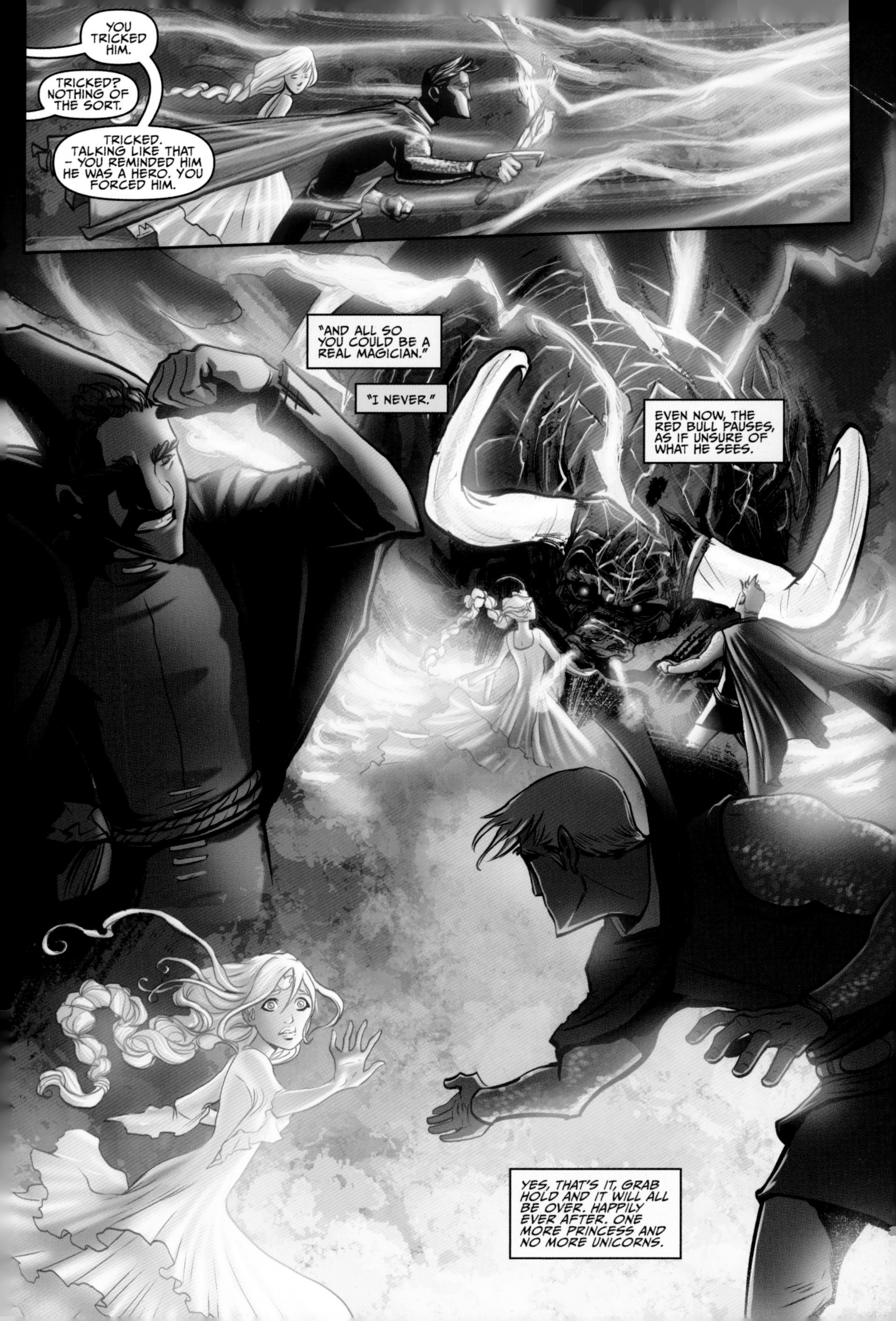
YOU TRICKED HIM.
TRICKED? NOTHING OF THE SORT.
TRICKED. TALKING LIKE THAT – YOU REMINDED HIM HE WAS A HERO. YOU FORCED HIM.
"AND ALL SO YOU COULD BE A REAL MAGICIAN."
"I NEVER."
EVEN NOW, THE RED BULL PAUSES, AS IF UNSURE OF WHAT HE SEES.
YES, THAT'S IT, GRAB HOLD AND IT WILL ALL BE OVER. HAPPILY EVER AFTER. ONE MORE PRINCESS AND NO MORE UNICORNS.

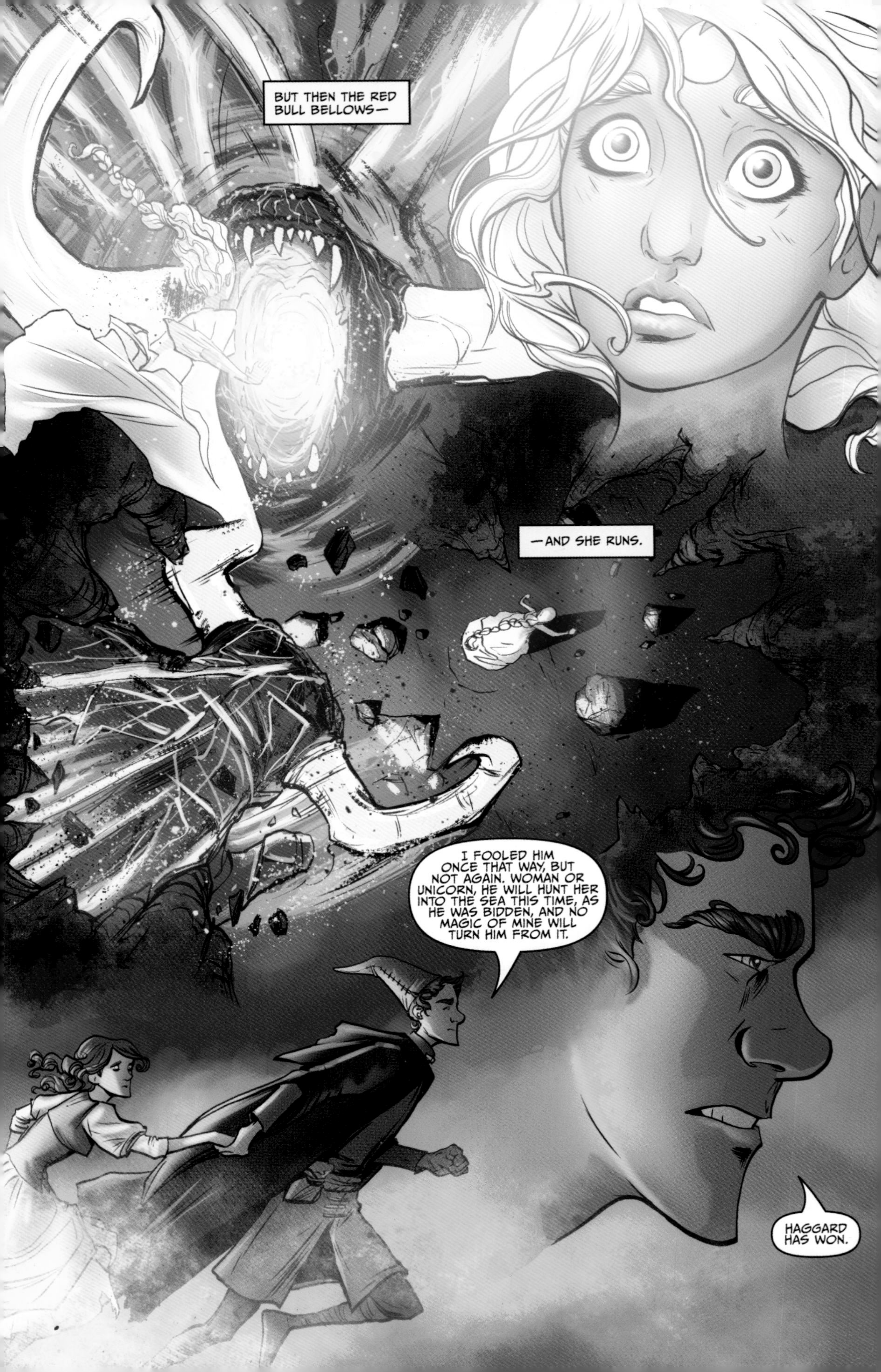
BUT THEN THE RED BULL BELLOWS—
—AND SHE RUNS.
I FOOLED HIM ONCE THAT WAY, BUT NOT AGAIN. WOMAN OR UNICORN, HE WILL HUNT HER INTO THE SEA THIS TIME, AS HE WAS BIDDEN, AND NO MAGIC OF MINE WILL TURN HIM FROM IT.
HAGGARD HAS WON.

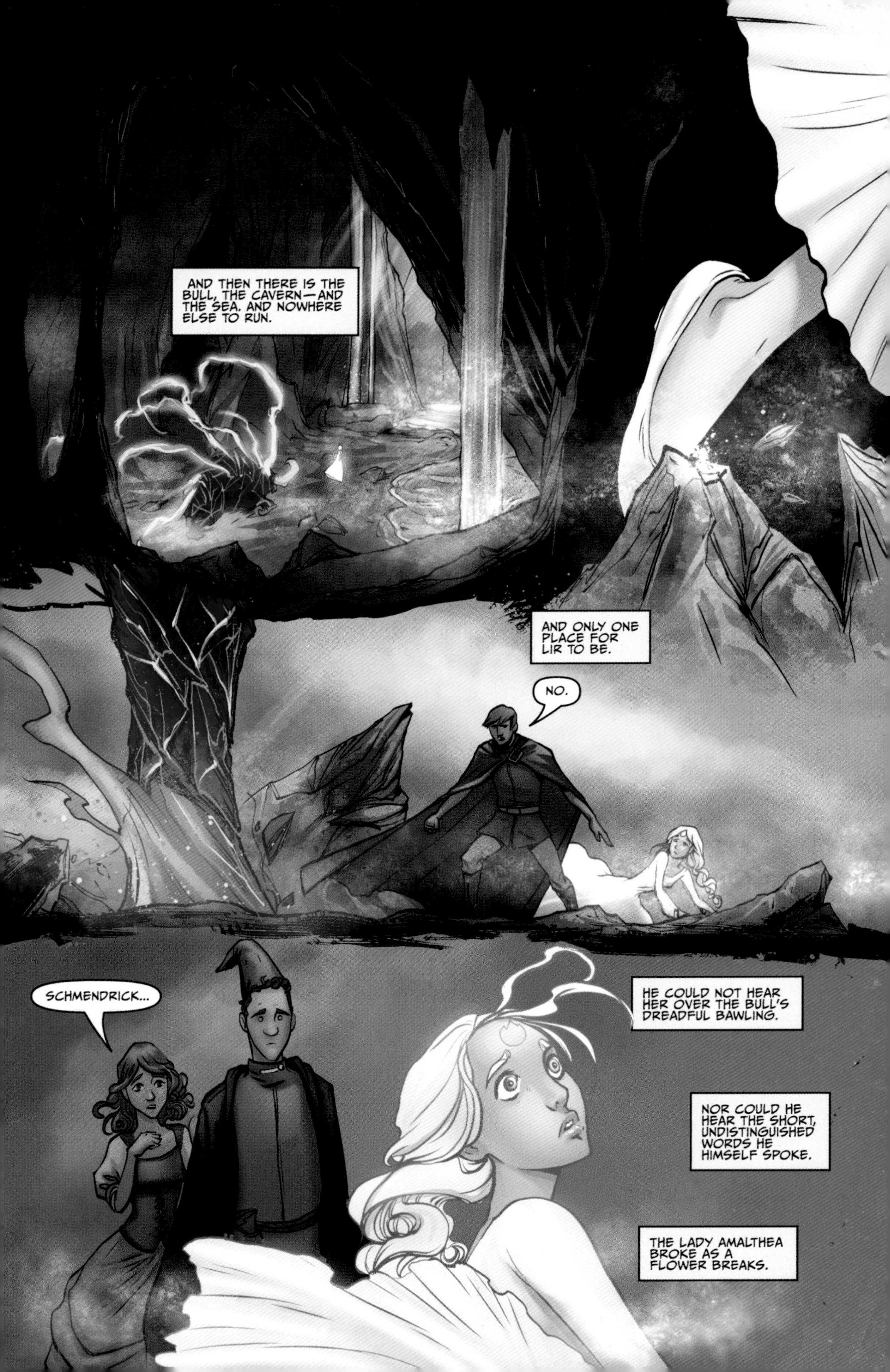

AND THEN THERE IS THE BULL, THE CAVERN—AND THE SEA. AND NOWHERE ELSE TO RUN.
AND ONLY ONE PLACE FOR LIR TO BE.
NO.
SCHMENDRICK...
HE COULD NOT HEAR HER OVER THE BULL'S DREADFUL BAWLING.
NOR COULD HE HEAR THE SHORT, UNDISTINGUISHED WORDS HE HIMSELF SPOKE.
THE LADY AMALTHEA BROKE AS A FLOWER BREAKS.

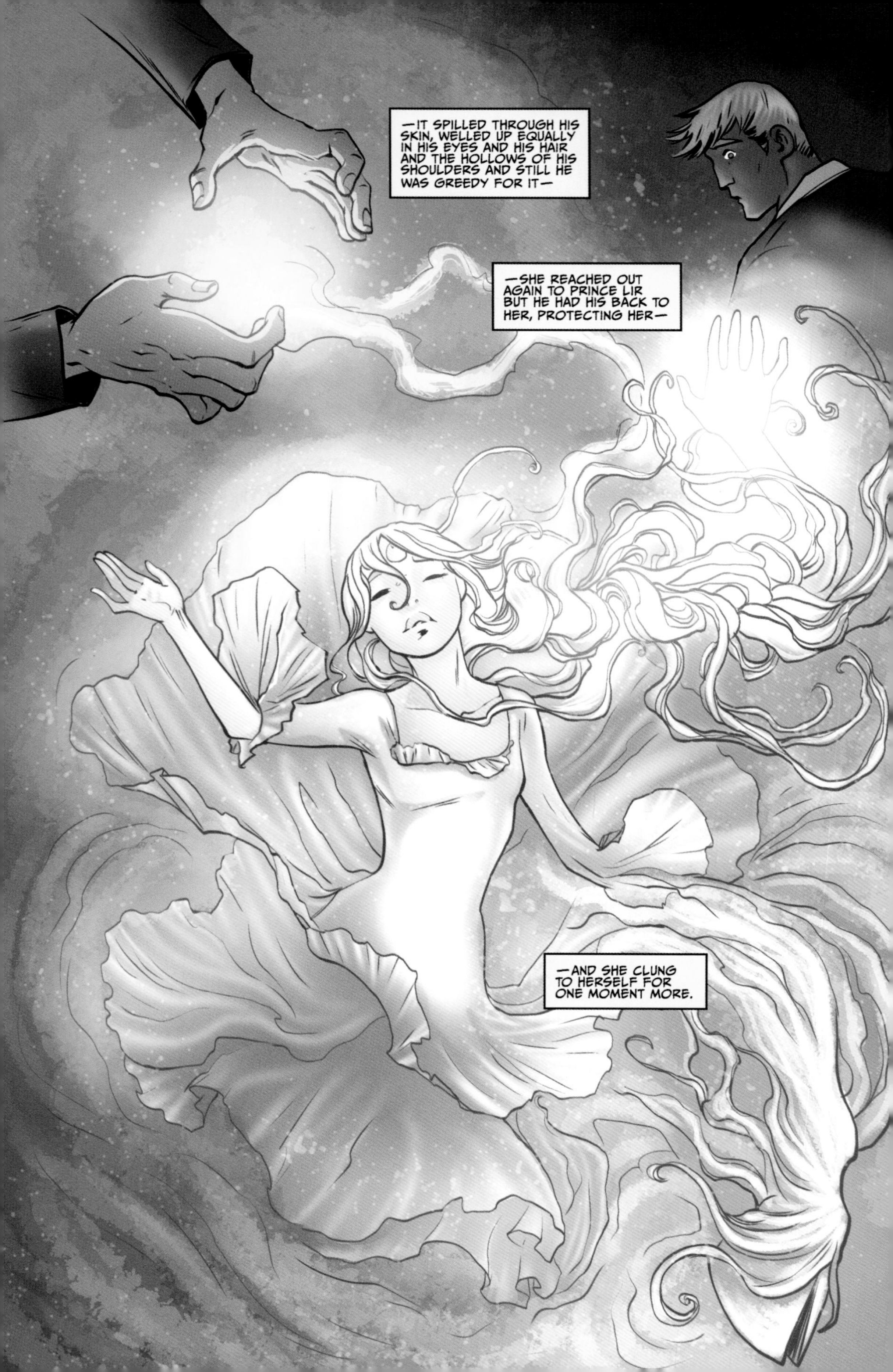
—IT SPILLED THROUGH HIS SKIN, WELLED UP EQUALLY IN HIS EYES AND HIS HAIR AND THE HOLLOWS OF HIS SHOULDERS AND STILL HE WAS GREEDY FOR IT—
—SHE REACHED OUT AGAIN TO PRINCE LIR BUT HE HAD HIS BACK TO HER, PROTECTING HER—
—AND SHE CLUNG TO HERSELF FOR ONE MOMENT MORE.

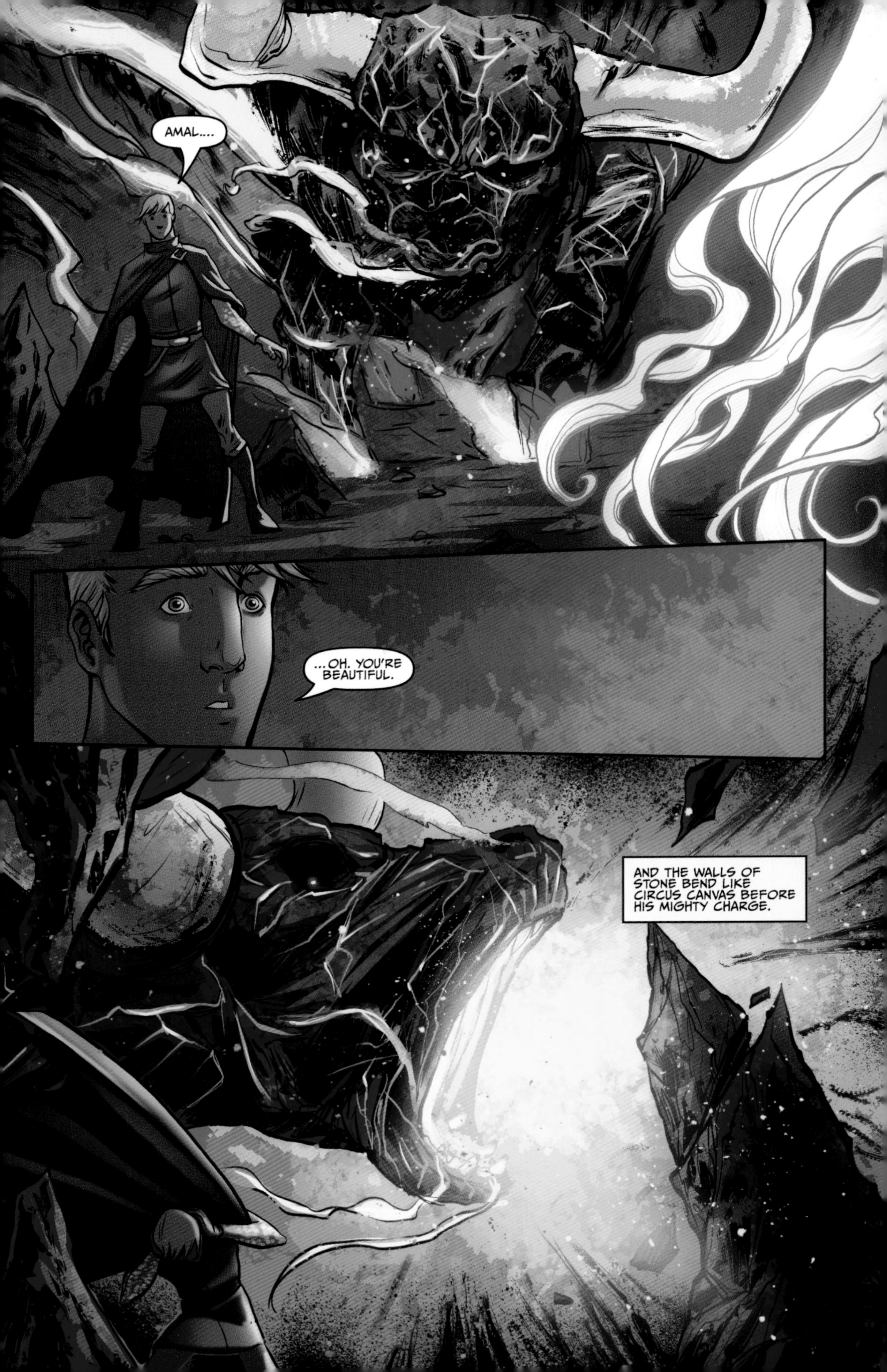
AMAL....
...OH. YOU'RE BEAUTIFUL.
AND THE WALLS OF STONE BEND LIKE CIRCUS CANVAS BEFORE HIS MIGHTY CHARGE.

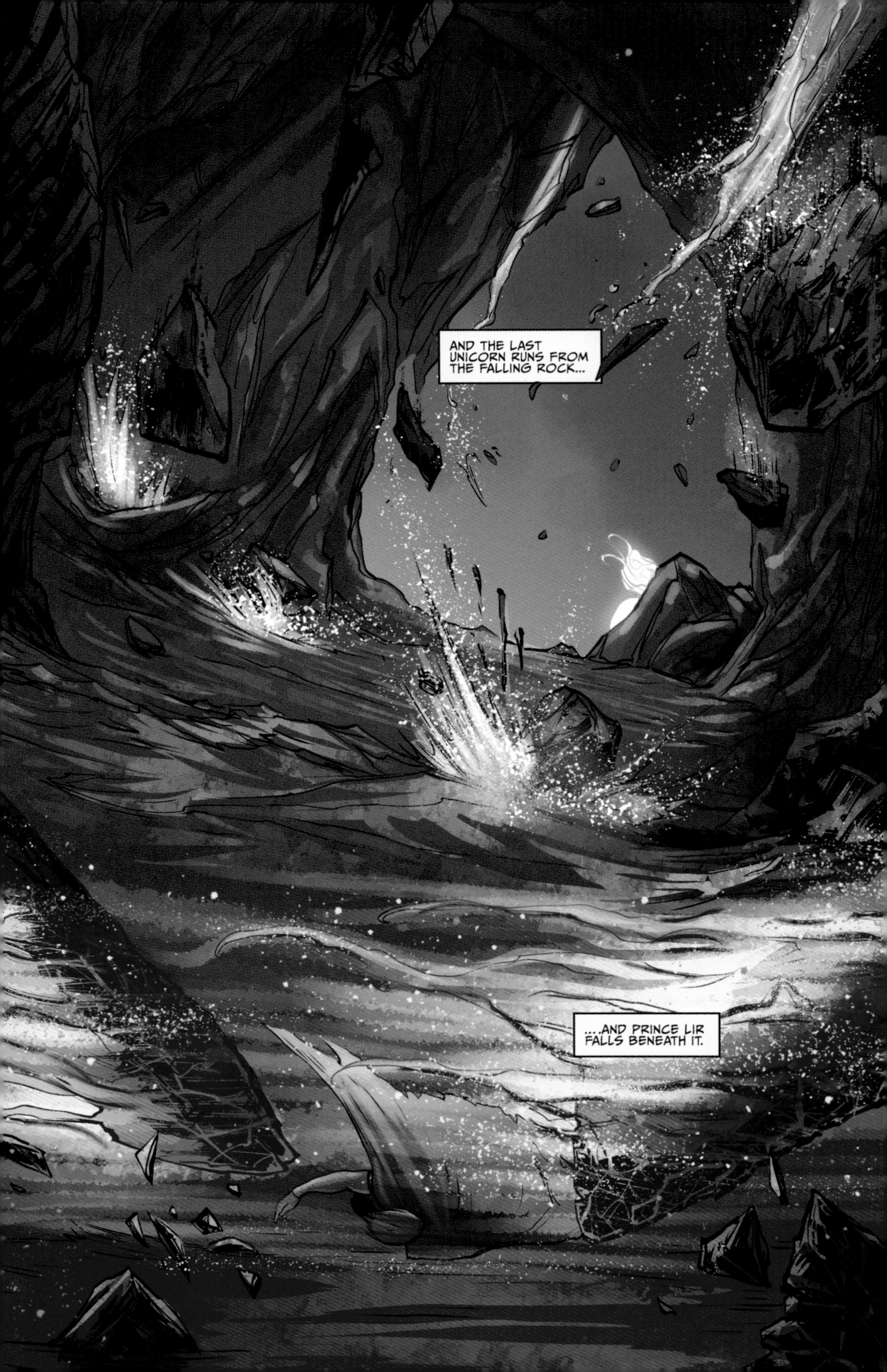
AND THE LAST UNICORN RUNS FROM THE FALLING ROCK...
...AND PRINCE LIR FALLS BENEATH IT.

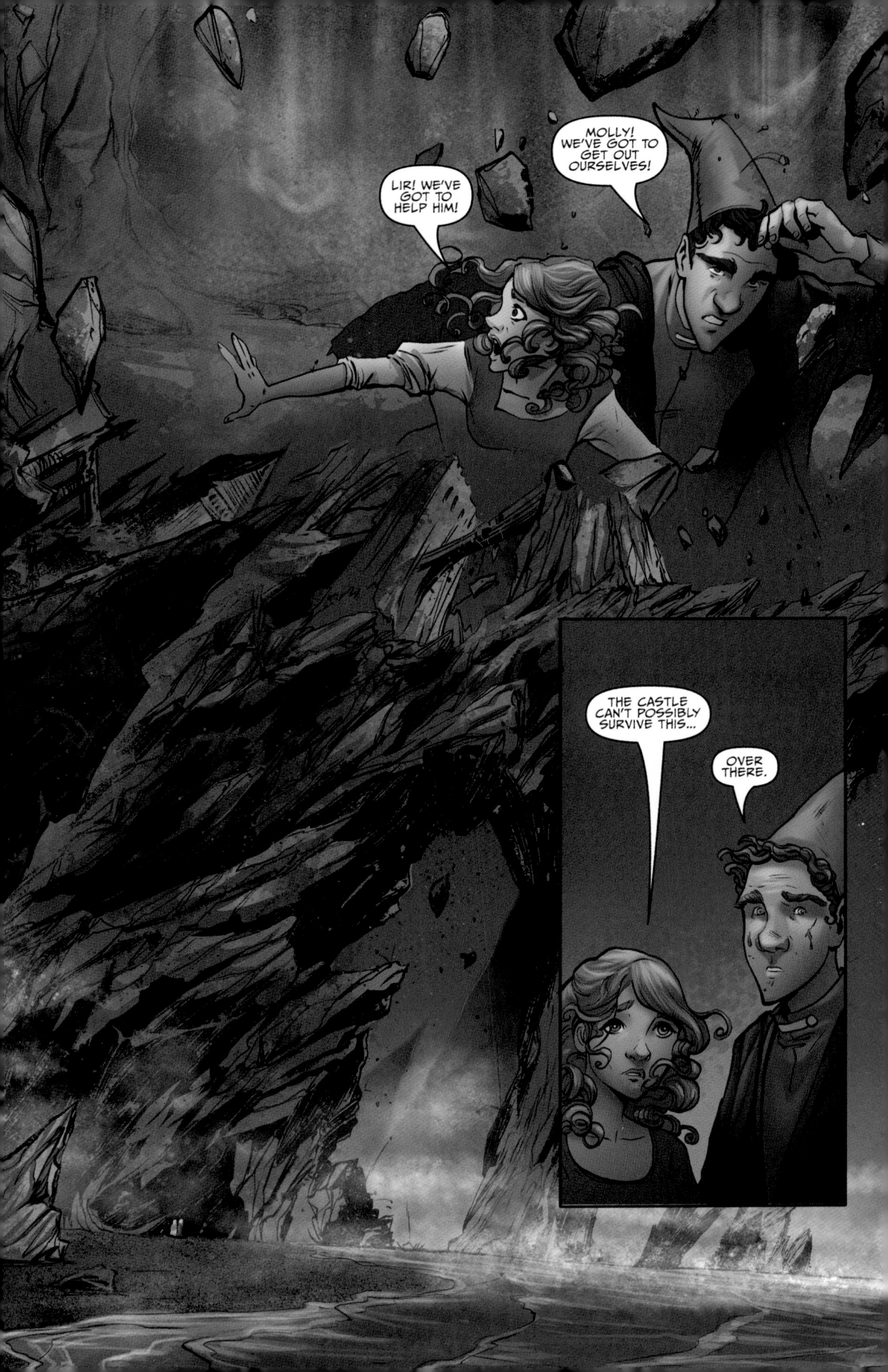
LIR! WE'VE GOT TO HELP HIM!
MOLLY! WE'VE GOT TO GET OUT OURSELVES!
THE CASTLE CAN'T POSSIBLY SURVIVE THIS...
OVER THERE.

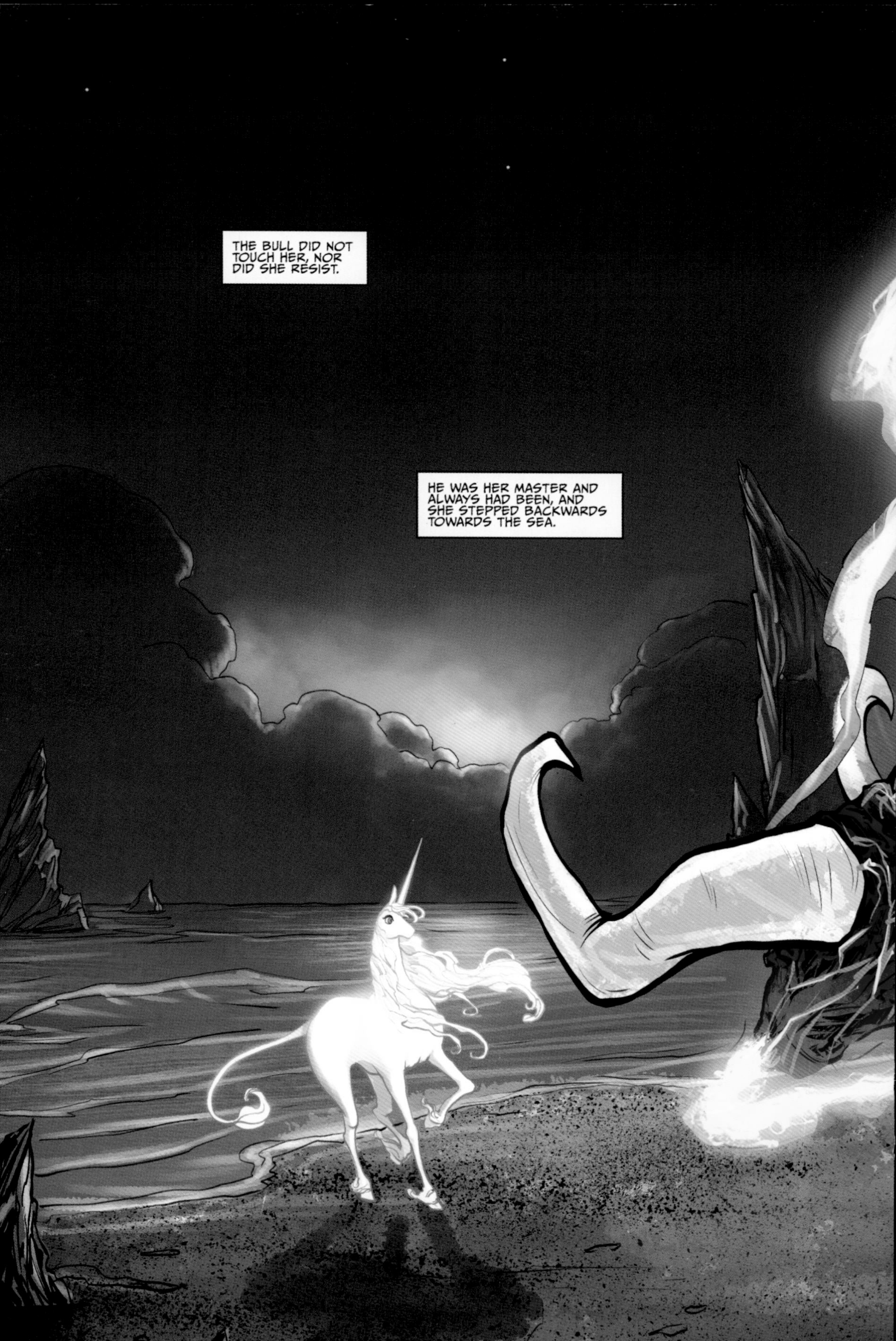
THE BULL DID NOT TOUCH HER, NOR DID SHE RESIST.
HE WAS HER MASTER AND ALWAYS HAD BEEN, AND SHE STEPPED BACKWARDS TOWARDS THE SEA.

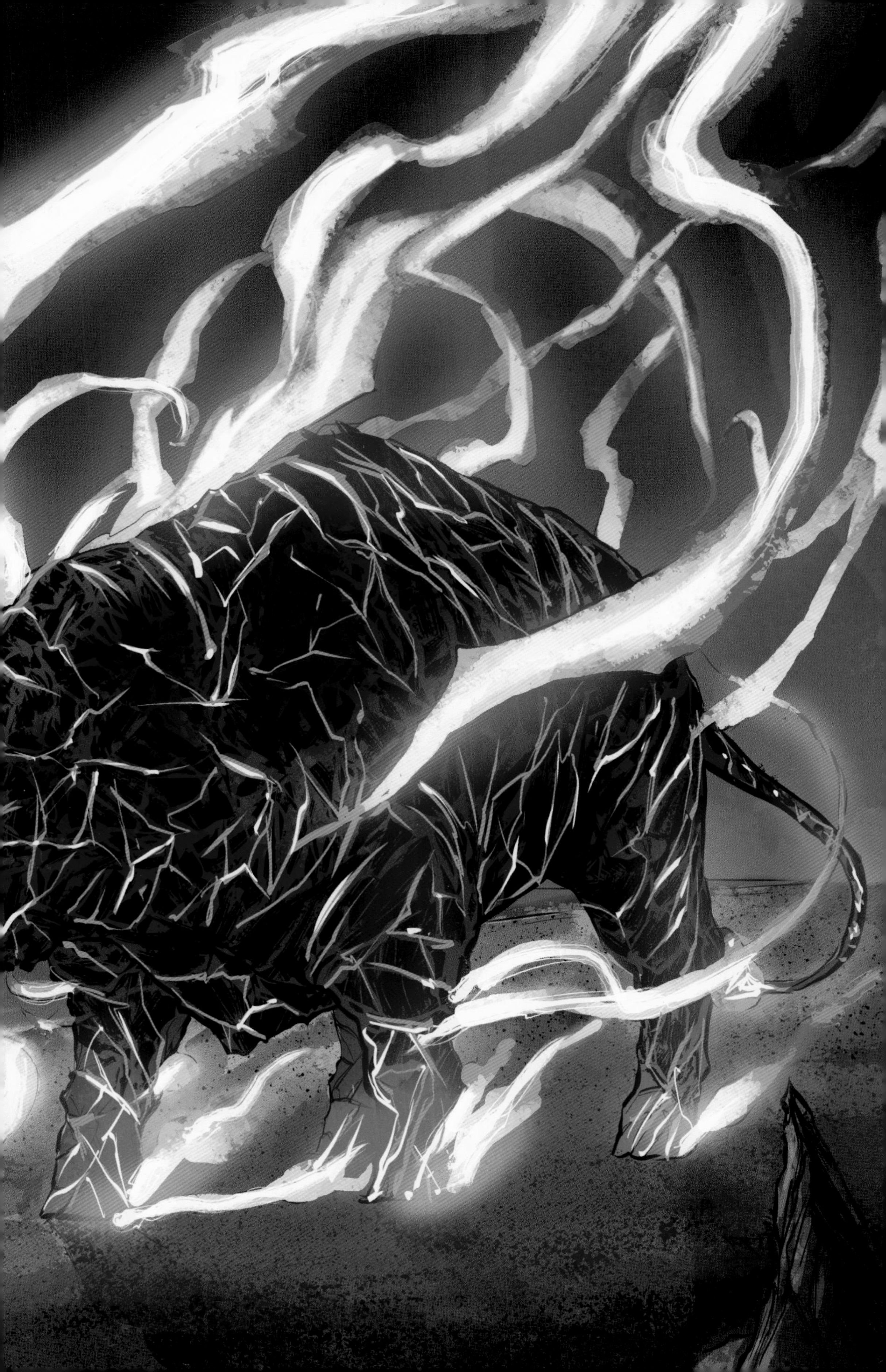

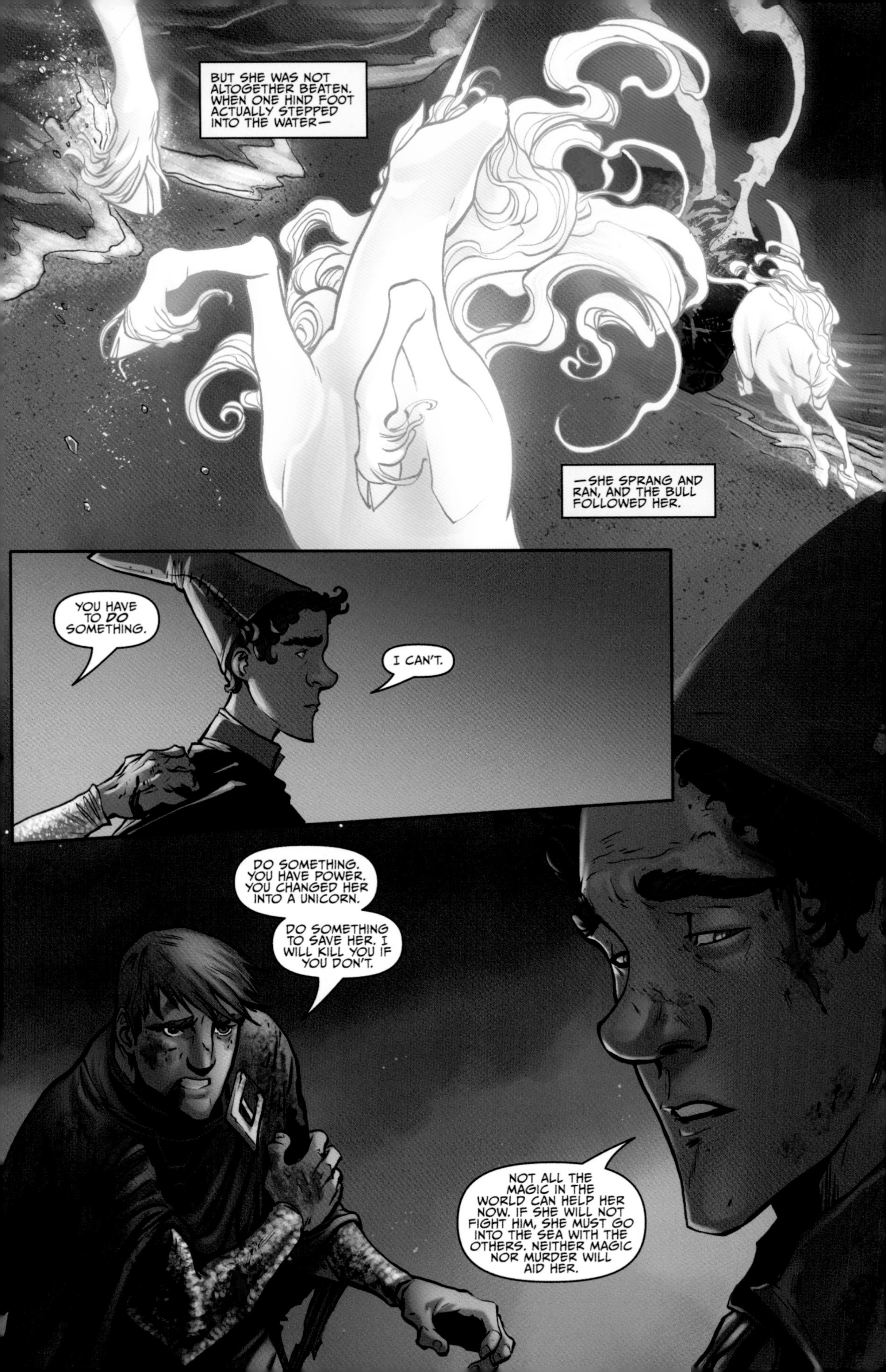
BUT SHE WAS NOT ALTOGETHER BEATEN. WHEN ONE HIND FOOT ACTUALLY STEPPED INTO THE WATER—
—SHE SPRANG AND RAN, AND THE BULL FOLLOWED HER.
YOU HAVE TO DO SOMETHING.
I CAN'T.
DO SOMETHING. YOU HAVE POWER. YOU CHANGED HER INTO A UNICORN.
DO SOMETHING TO SAVE HER. I WILL KILL YOU IF YOU DON'T.
NOT ALL THE MAGIC IN THE WORLD CAN HELP HER NOW. IF SHE WILL NOT FIGHT HIM, SHE MUST GO INTO THE SEA WITH THE OTHERS. NEITHER MAGIC NOR MURDER WILL AID HER.

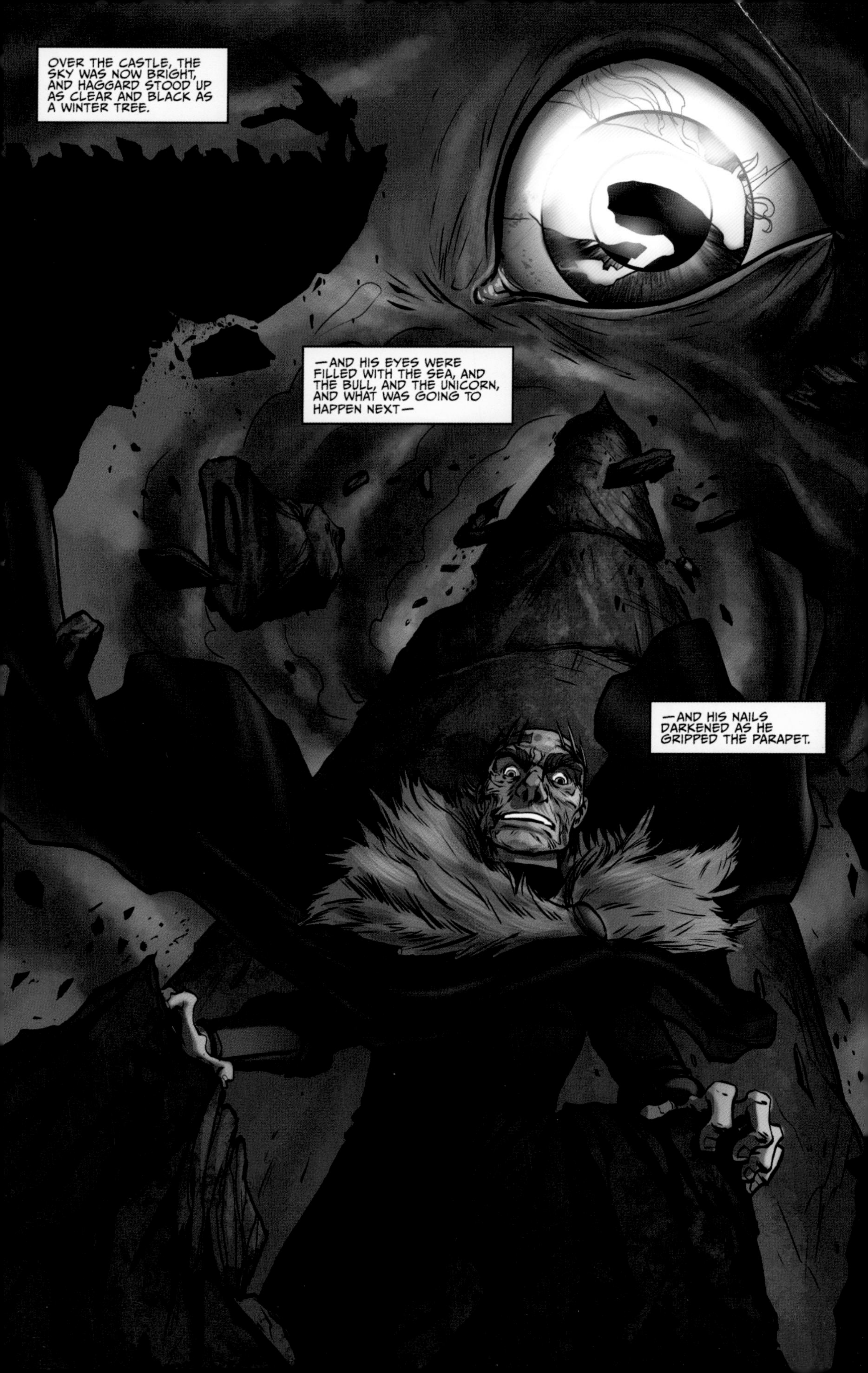
OVER THE CASTLE, THE SKY WAS NOW BRIGHT, AND HAGGARD STOOD UP AS CLEAR AND BLACK AS A WINTER TREE.
—AND HIS EYES WERE FILLED WITH THE SEA, AND THE BULL, AND THE UNICORN, AND WHAT WAS GOING TO HAPPEN NEXT—
—AND HIS NAILS DARKENED AS HE GRIPPED THE PARAPET.

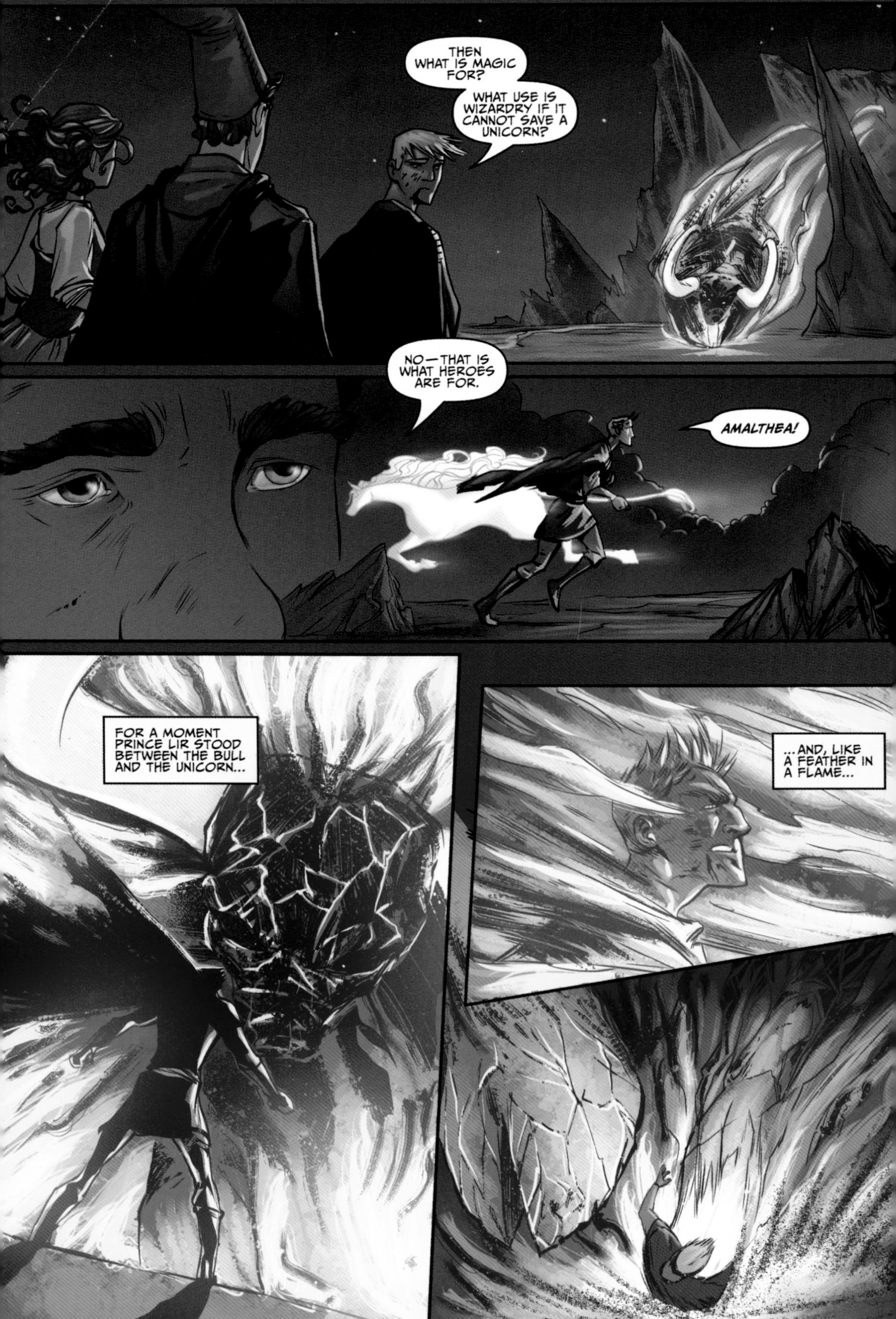
THEN WHAT IS MAGIC FOR?
WHAT USE IS WIZARDRY IF IT CANNOT SAVE A UNICORN?
NO—THAT IS WHAT HEROES ARE FOR.
AMALTHEA!
FOR A MOMENT PRINCE LIR STOOD BETWEEN THE BULL AND THE UNICORN...
...AND, LIKE A FEATHER IN A FLAME...

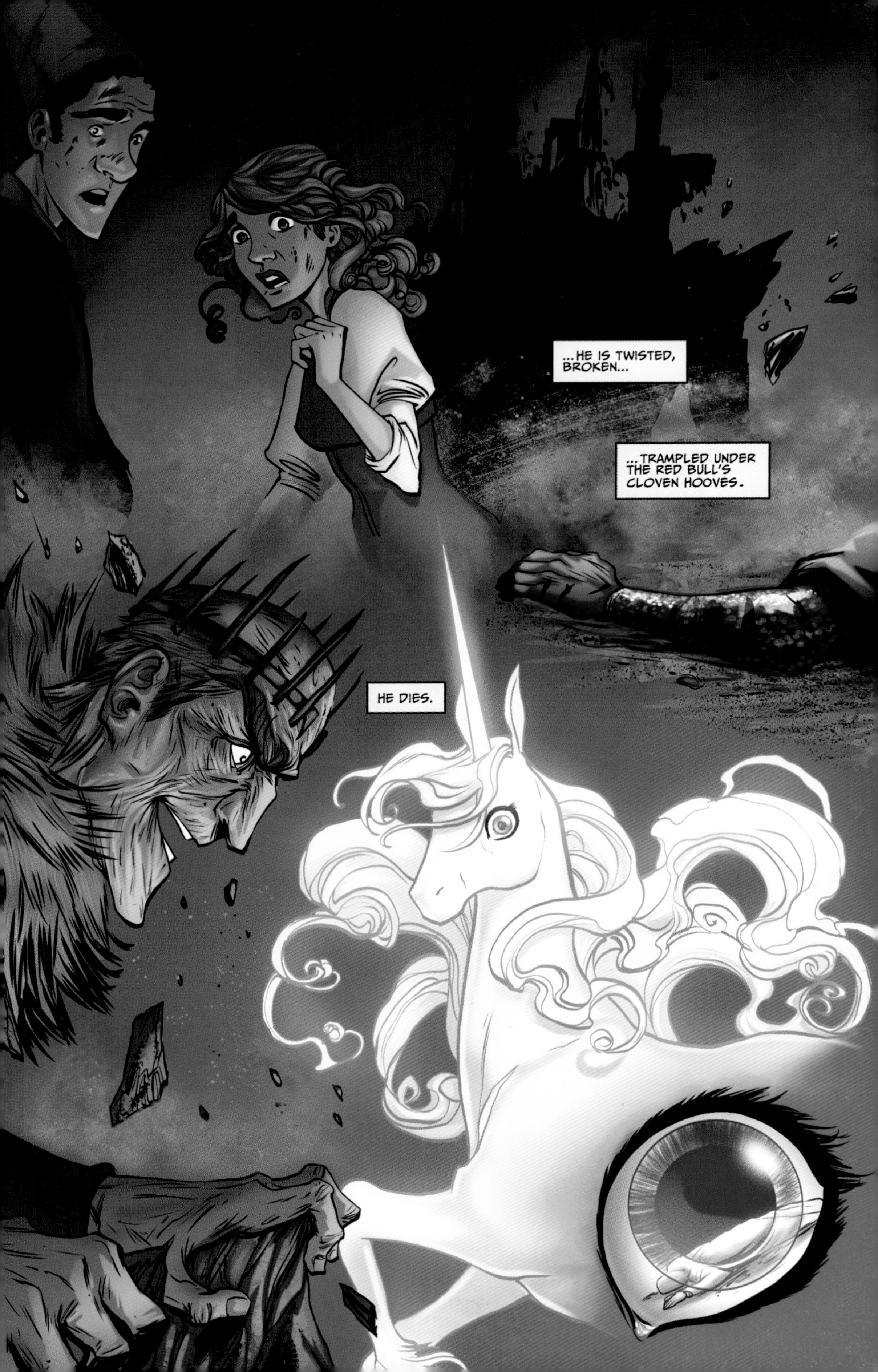
...HE IS TWISTED, BROKEN...
...TRAMPLED UNDER THE RED BULL'S CLOVEN HOOVES.
HE DIES.

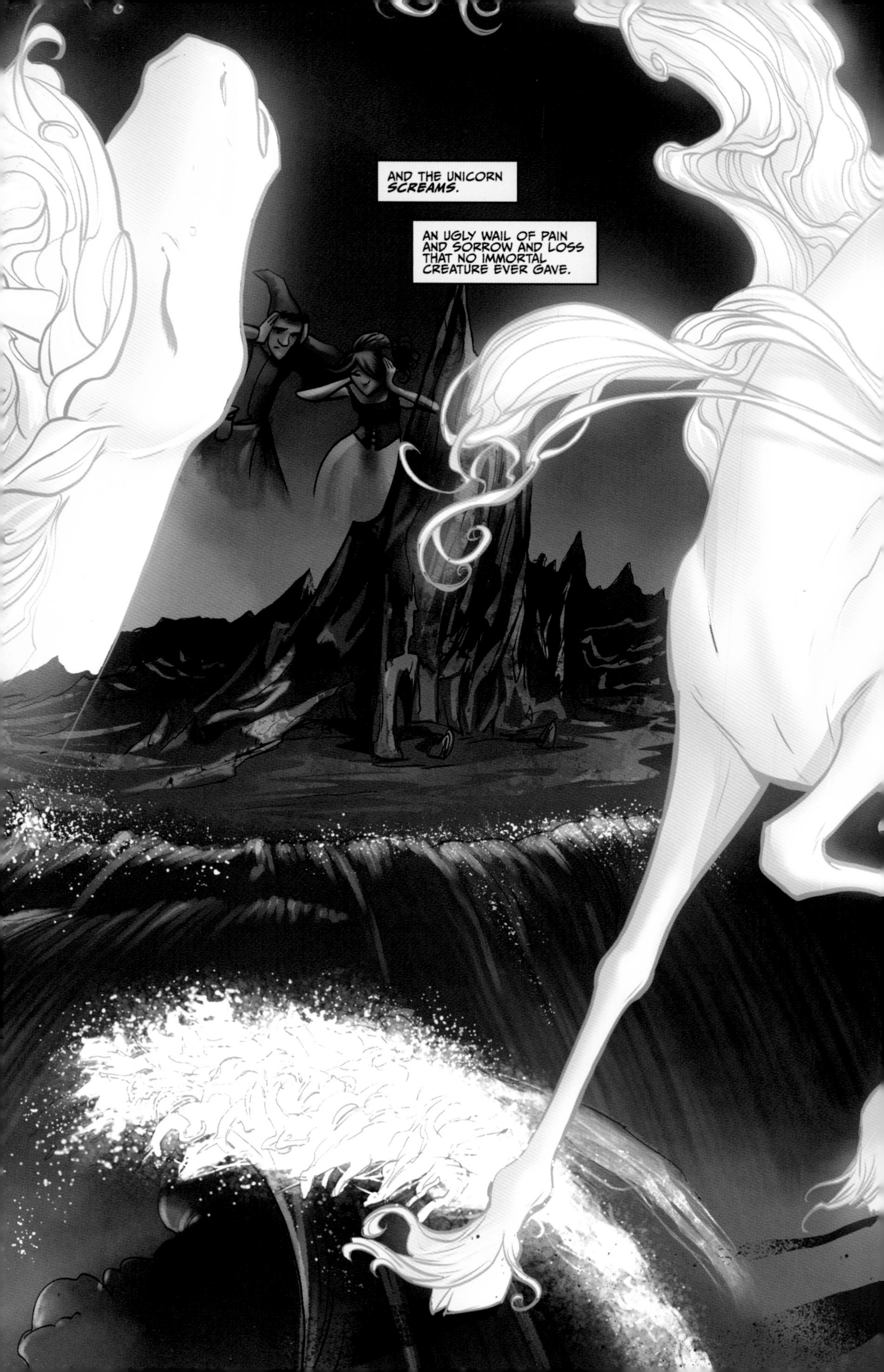
AND THE UNICORN *SCREAMS.*
AN UGLY WAIL OF PAIN AND SORROW AND LOSS THAT NO IMMORTAL CREATURE EVER GAVE.

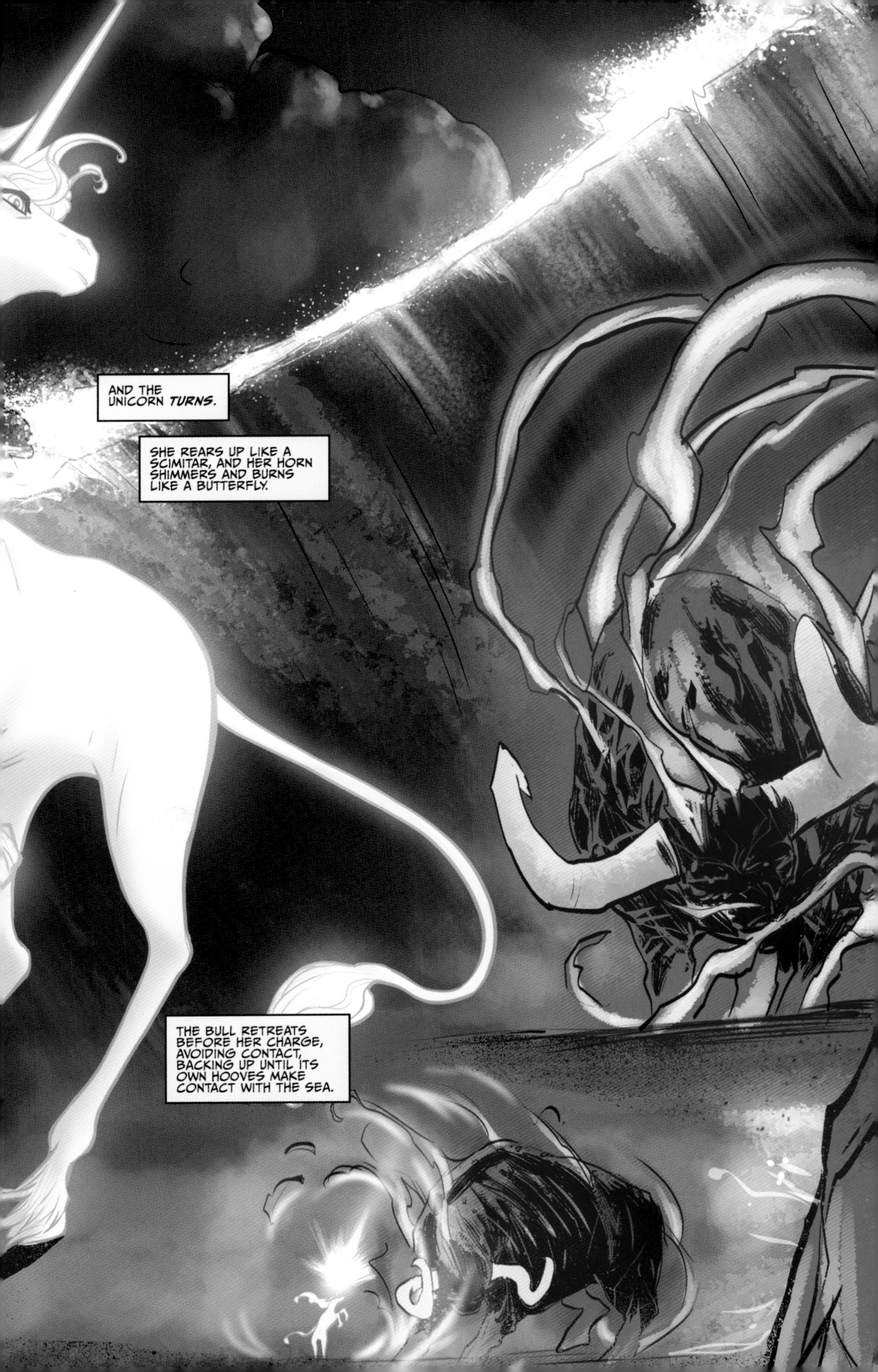
AND THE UNICORN *TURNS*.
SHE REARS UP LIKE A SCIMITAR, AND HER HORN SHIMMERS AND BURNS LIKE A BUTTERFLY.
THE BULL RETREATS BEFORE HER CHARGE, AVOIDING CONTACT, BACKING UP UNTIL ITS OWN HOOVES MAKE CONTACT WITH THE SEA.

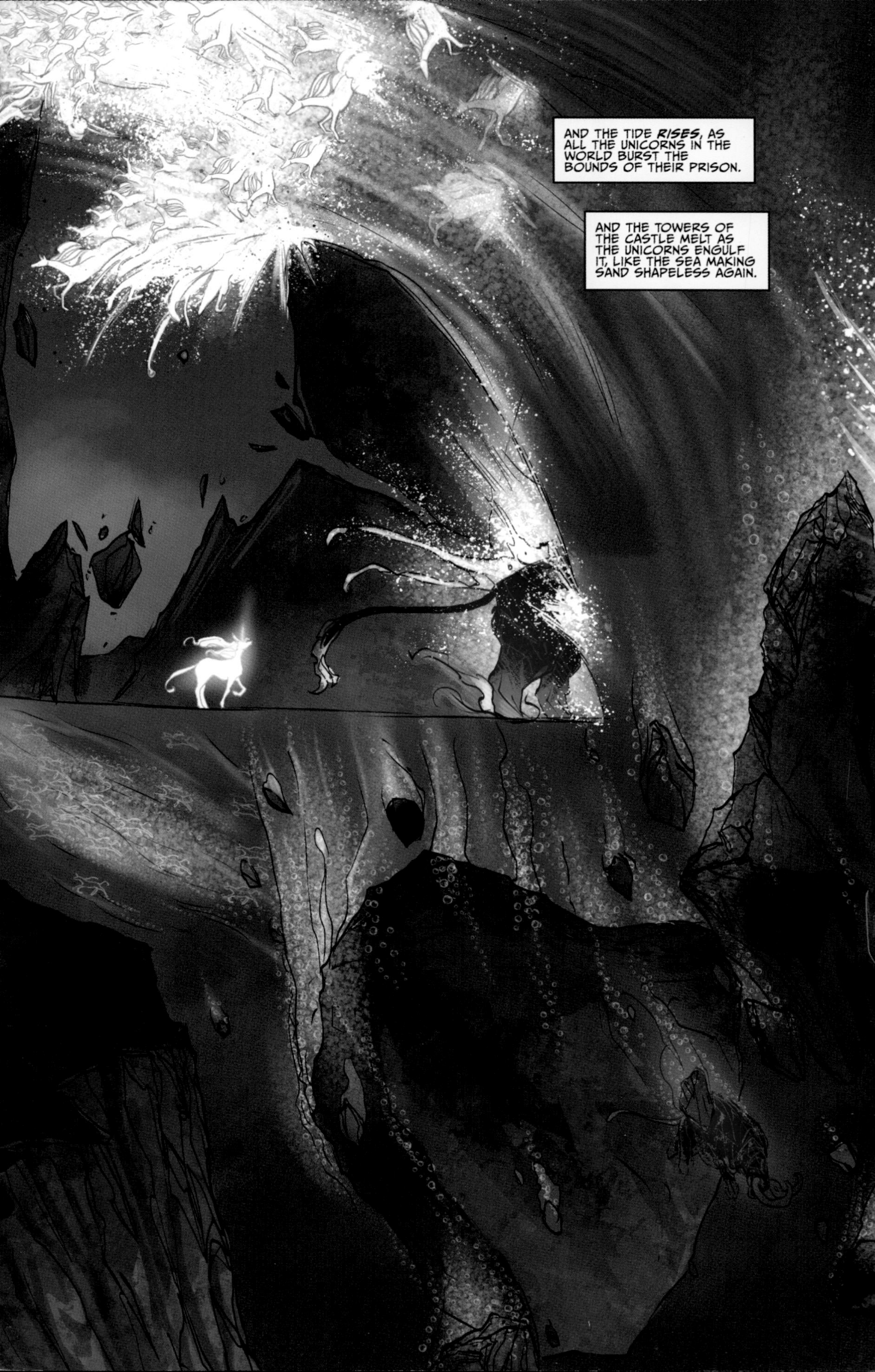
AND THE TIDE *RISES*, AS ALL THE UNICORNS IN THE WORLD BURST THE BOUNDS OF THEIR PRISON.
AND THE TOWERS OF THE CASTLE MELT AS THE UNICORNS ENGULF IT, LIKE THE SEA MAKING SAND SHAPELESS AGAIN.

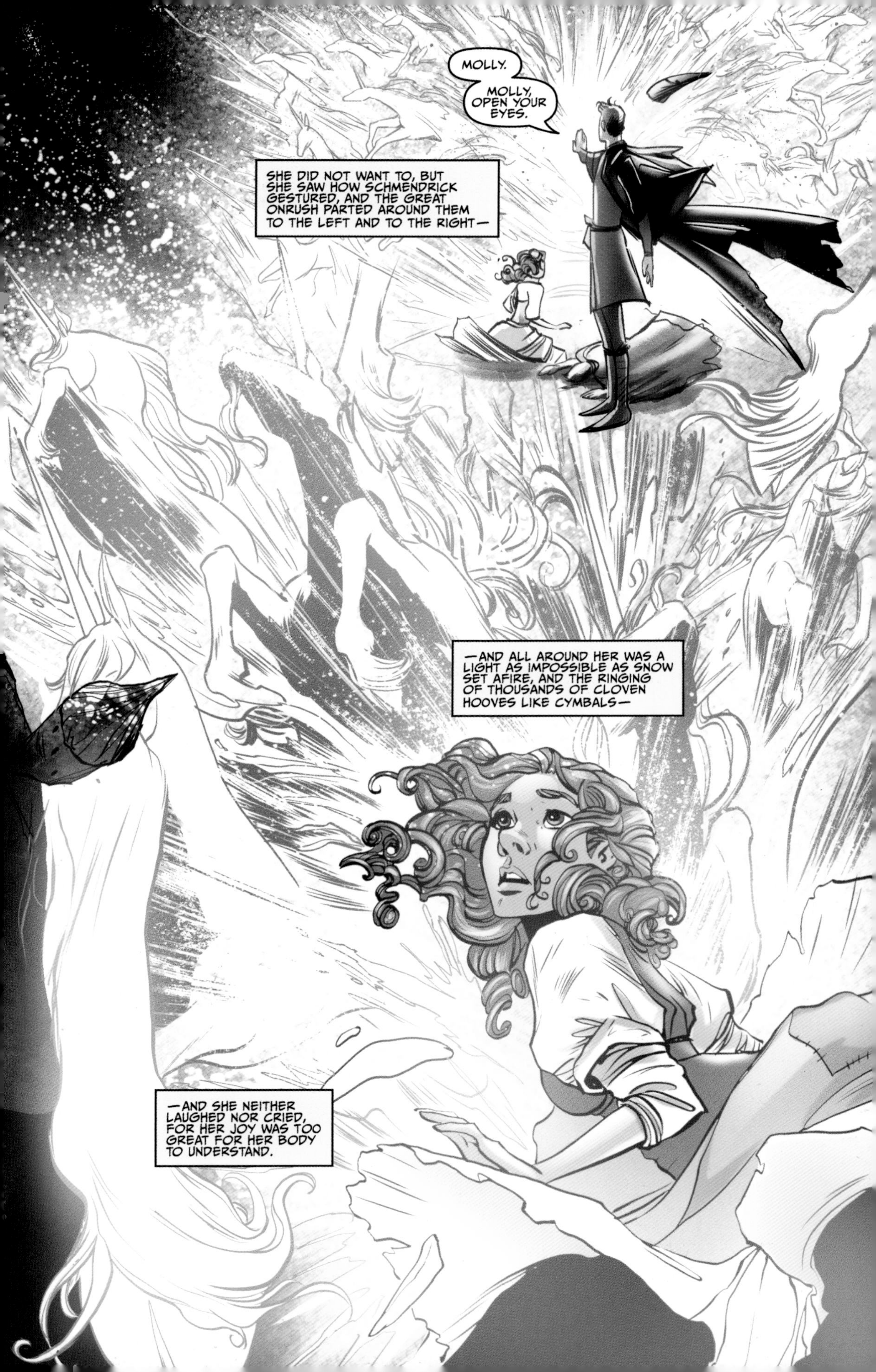
MOLLY.
MOLLY, OPEN YOUR EYES.
SHE DID NOT WANT TO, BUT SHE SAW HOW SCHMENDRICK GESTURED, AND THE GREAT ONRUSH PARTED AROUND THEM TO THE LEFT AND TO THE RIGHT—
—AND ALL AROUND HER WAS A LIGHT AS IMPOSSIBLE AS SNOW SET AFIRE, AND THE RINGING OF THOUSANDS OF CLOVEN HOOVES LIKE CYMBALS—
—AND SHE NEITHER LAUGHED NOR CRIED, FOR HER JOY WAS TOO GREAT FOR HER BODY TO UNDERSTAND.

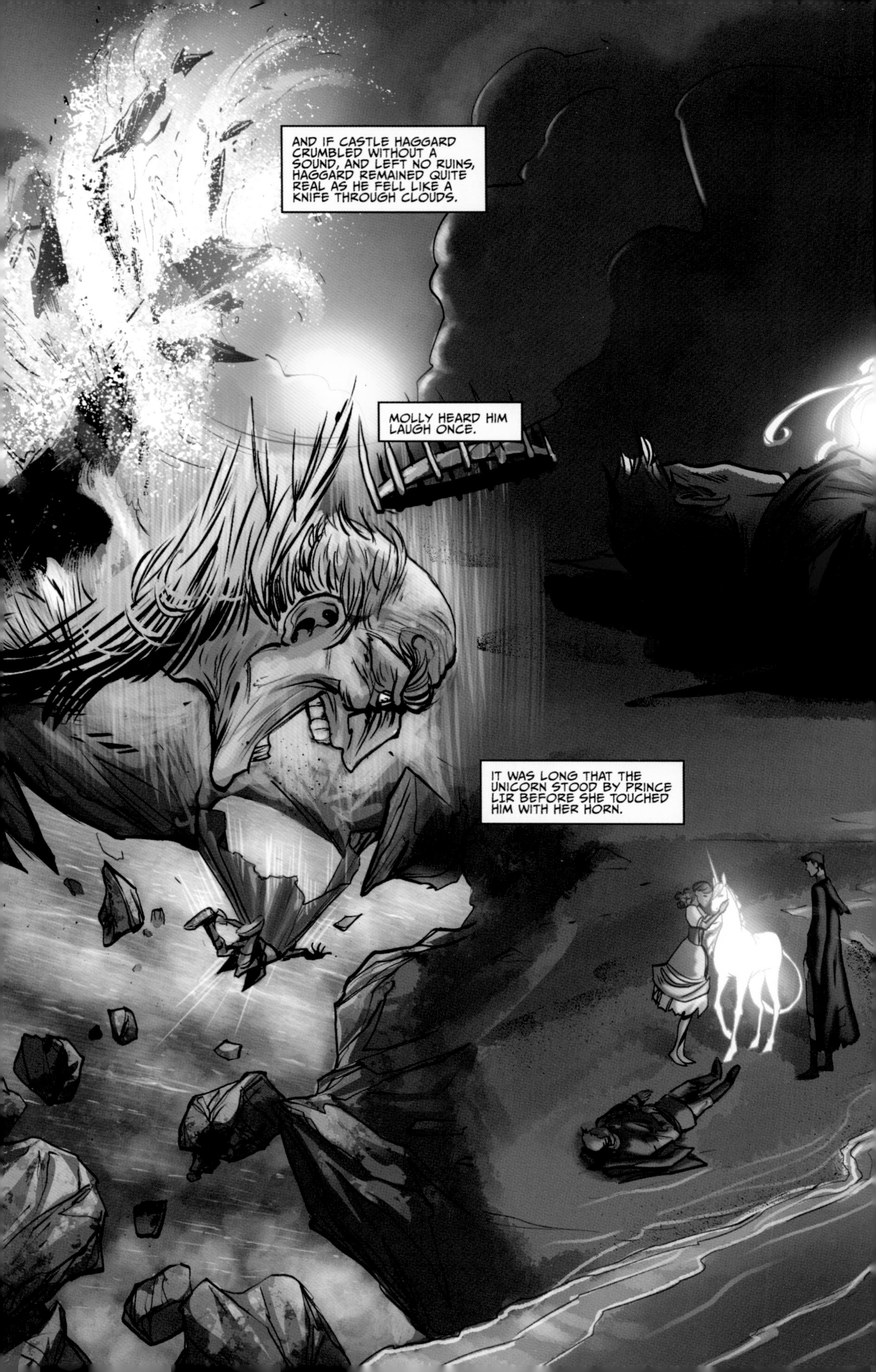
AND IF CASTLE HAGGARD CRUMBLED WITHOUT A SOUND, AND LEFT NO RUINS, HAGGARD REMAINED QUITE REAL AS HE FELL LIKE A KNIFE THROUGH CLOUDS.
MOLLY HEARD HIM LAUGH ONCE.
IT WAS LONG THAT THE UNICORN STOOD BY PRINCE LIR BEFORE SHE TOUCHED HIM WITH HER HORN.

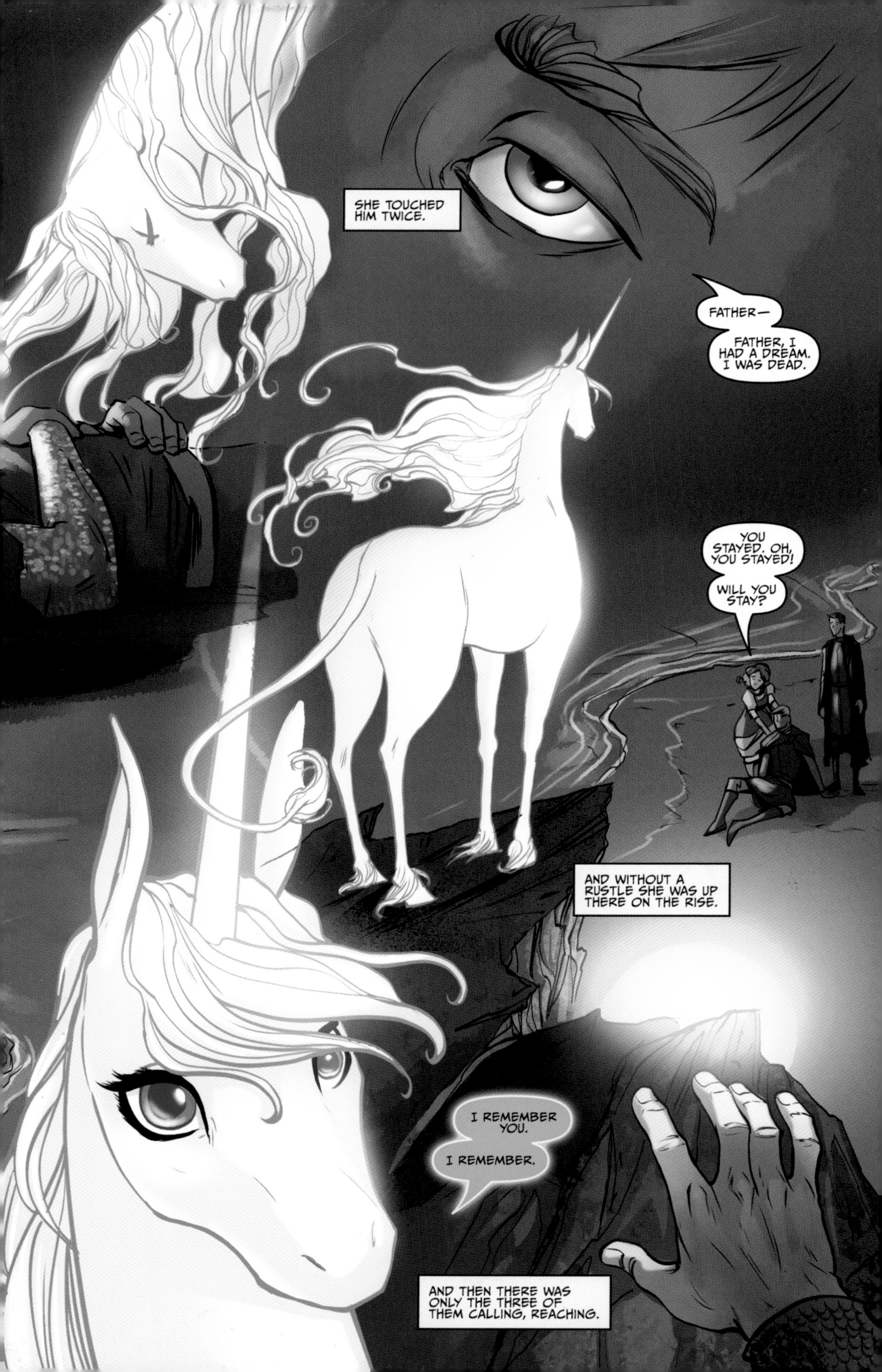
SHE TOUCHED HIM TWICE.
FATHER—
FATHER, I HAD A DREAM. I WAS DEAD.
YOU STAYED. OH, YOU STAYED!
WILL YOU STAY?
AND WITHOUT A RUSTLE SHE WAS UP THERE ON THE RISE.
I REMEMBER YOU.
I REMEMBER.
AND THEN THERE WAS ONLY THE THREE OF THEM CALLING, REACHING.

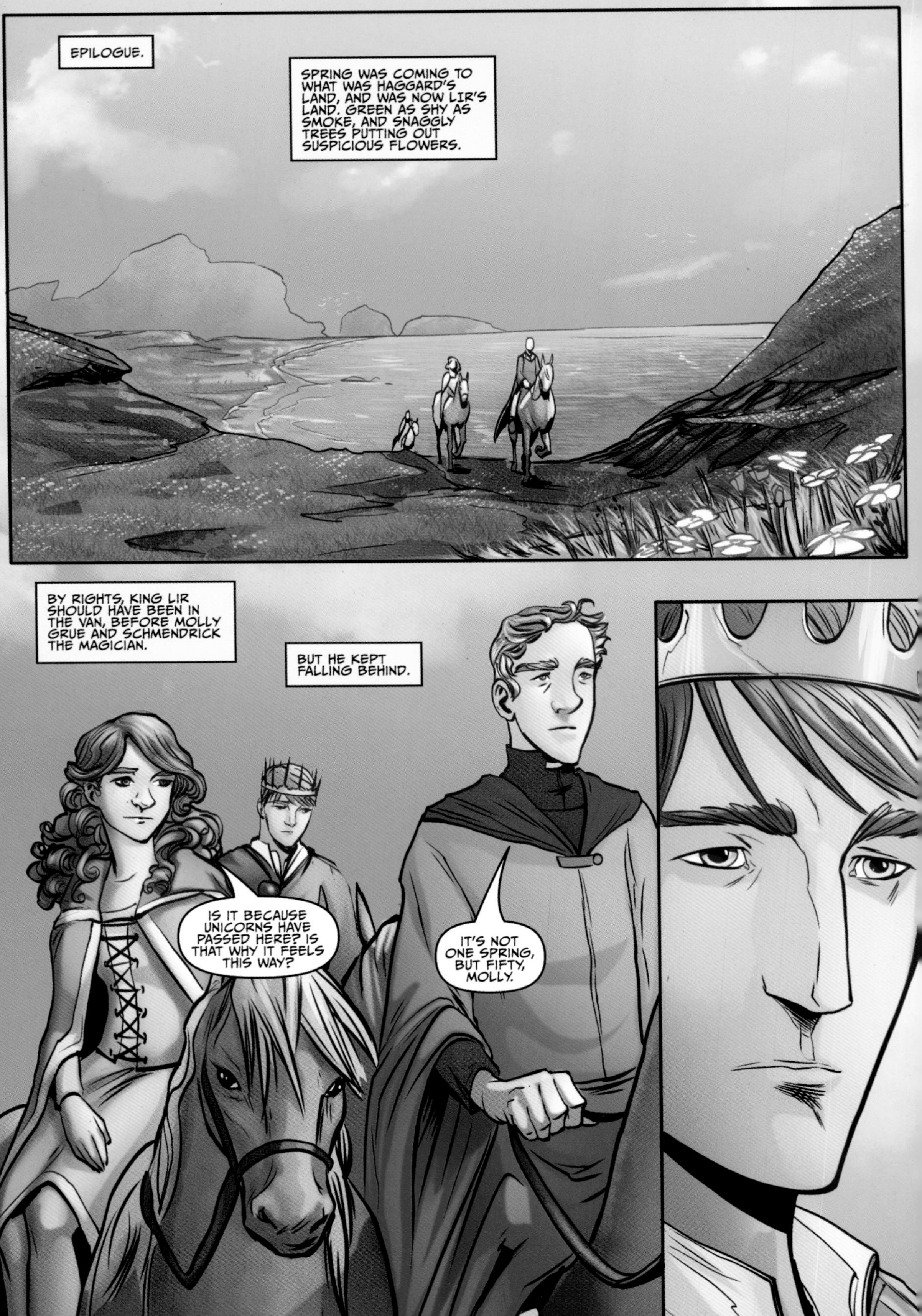

EPILOGUE.
SPRING WAS COMING TO WHAT WAS HAGGARD'S LAND, AND WAS NOW LIR'S LAND. GREEN AS SHY AS SMOKE, AND SNAGGLY TREES PUTTING OUT SUSPICIOUS FLOWERS.
BY RIGHTS, KING LIR SHOULD HAVE BEEN IN THE VAN, BEFORE MOLLY GRUE AND SCHMENDRICK THE MAGICIAN.
BUT HE KEPT FALLING BEHIND.
IS IT BECAUSE UNICORNS HAVE PASSED HERE? IS THAT WHY IT FEELS THIS WAY?
IT'S NOT ONE SPRING, BUT FIFTY, MOLLY.

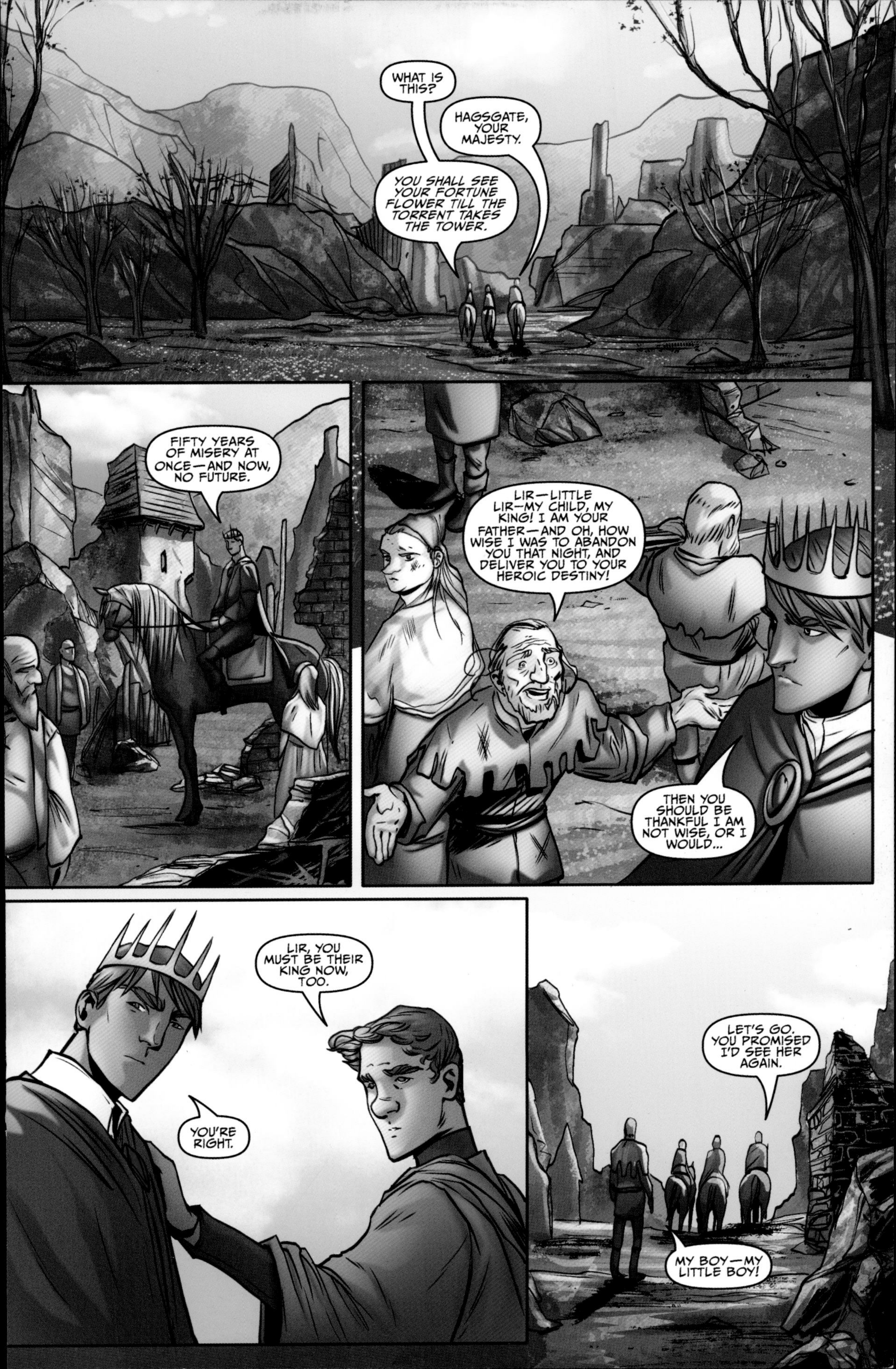
WHAT IS THIS?
HAGSGATE, YOUR MAJESTY.
YOU SHALL SEE YOUR FORTUNE FLOWER TILL THE TORRENT TAKES THE TOWER.
FIFTY YEARS OF MISERY AT ONCE—AND NOW, NO FUTURE.
LIR—LITTLE LIR—MY CHILD, MY KING! I AM YOUR FATHER—AND OH, HOW WISE I WAS TO ABANDON YOU THAT NIGHT, AND DELIVER YOU TO YOUR HEROIC DESTINY!
THEN YOU SHOULD BE THANKFUL I AM NOT WISE, OR I WOULD...
LIR, YOU MUST BE THEIR KING NOW, TOO.
YOU'RE RIGHT.
LET'S GO. YOU PROMISED I'D SEE HER AGAIN.
MY BOY—MY LITTLE BOY!

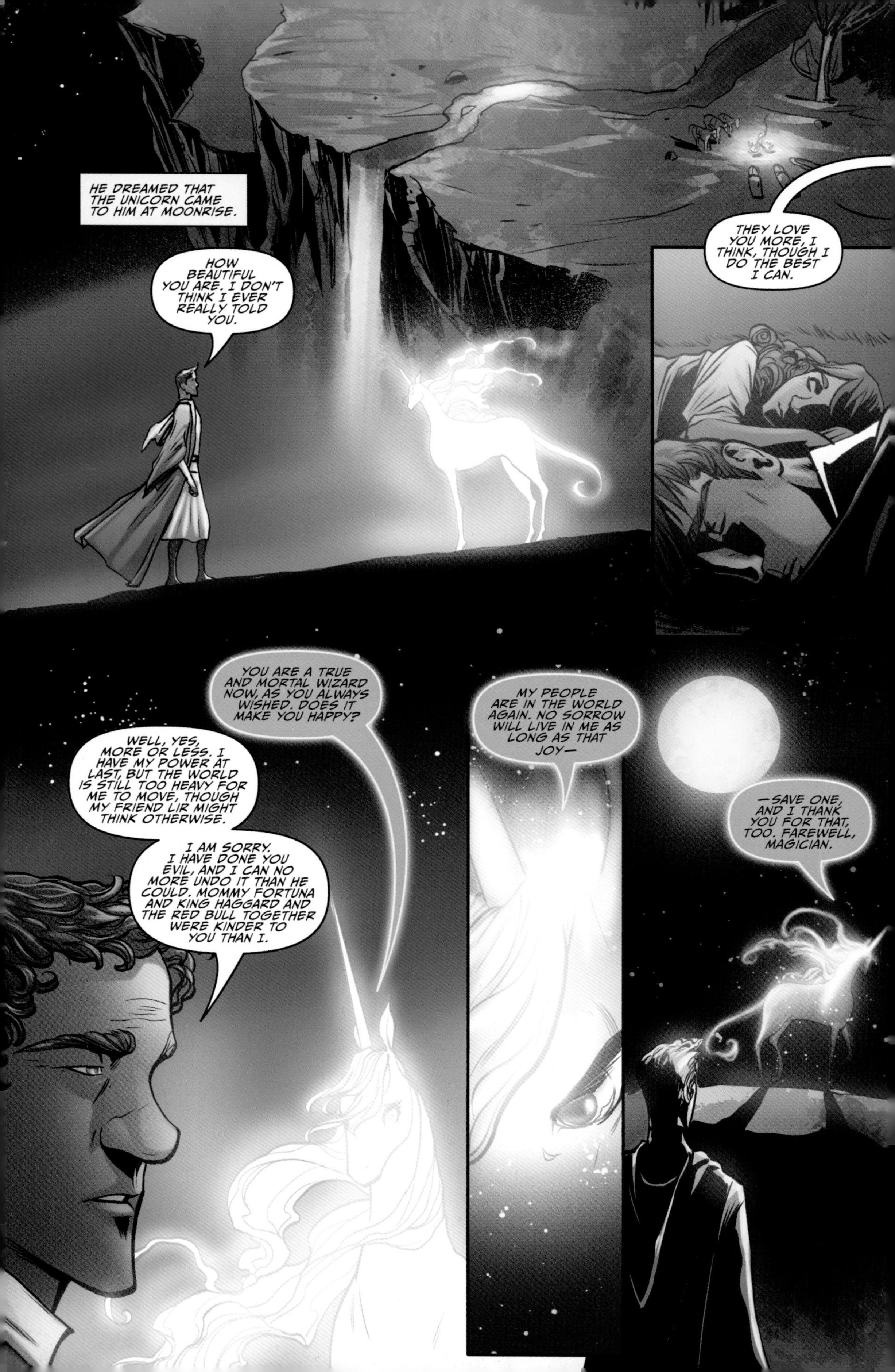
HE DREAMED THAT THE UNICORN CAME TO HIM AT MOONRISE.
HOW BEAUTIFUL YOU ARE. I DON'T THINK I EVER REALLY TOLD YOU.
THEY LOVE YOU MORE, I THINK, THOUGH I DO THE BEST I CAN.
YOU ARE A TRUE AND MORTAL WIZARD NOW, AS YOU ALWAYS WISHED. DOES IT MAKE YOU HAPPY?
WELL, YES, MORE OR LESS. I HAVE MY POWER AT LAST, BUT THE WORLD IS STILL TOO HEAVY FOR ME TO MOVE, THOUGH MY FRIEND LIR MIGHT THINK OTHERWISE.
I AM SORRY. I HAVE DONE YOU EVIL, AND I CAN NO MORE UNDO IT THAN HE COULD. MOMMY FORTUNA AND KING HAGGARD AND THE RED BULL TOGETHER WERE KINDER TO YOU THAN I.
MY PEOPLE ARE IN THE WORLD AGAIN. NO SORROW WILL LIVE IN ME AS LONG AS THAT JOY—
—SAVE ONE, AND I THANK YOU FOR THAT, TOO. FAREWELL, MAGICIAN.

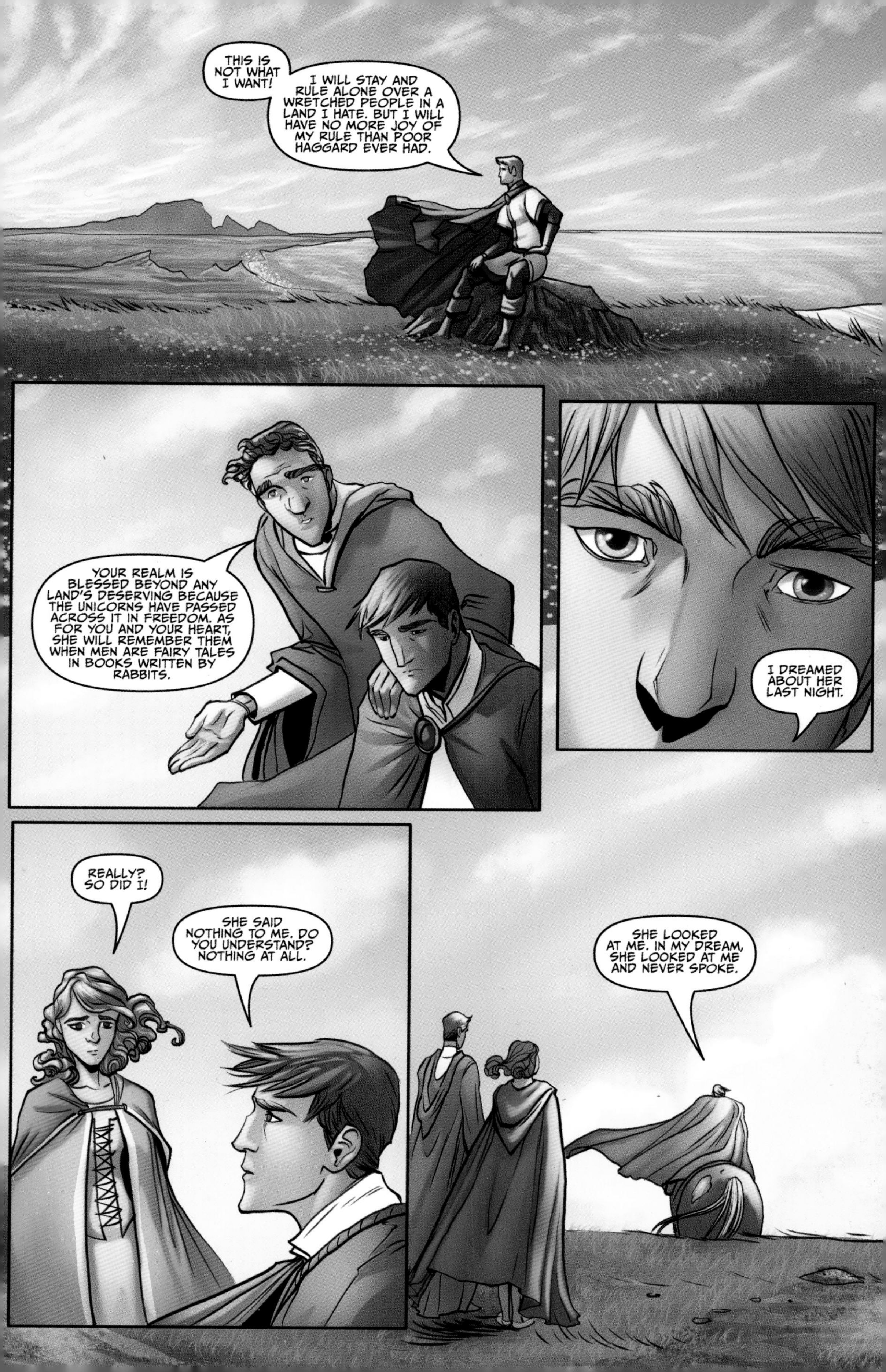
THIS IS NOT WHAT I WANT!
I WILL STAY AND RULE ALONE OVER A WRETCHED PEOPLE IN A LAND I HATE. BUT I WILL HAVE NO MORE JOY OF MY RULE THAN POOR HAGGARD EVER HAD.
YOUR REALM IS BLESSED BEYOND ANY LAND'S DESERVING BECAUSE THE UNICORNS HAVE PASSED ACROSS IT IN FREEDOM. AS FOR YOU AND YOUR HEART, SHE WILL REMEMBER THEM WHEN MEN ARE FAIRY TALES IN BOOKS WRITTEN BY RABBITS.
I DREAMED ABOUT HER LAST NIGHT.
REALLY? SO DID I!
SHE SAID NOTHING TO ME. DO YOU UNDERSTAND? NOTHING AT ALL.
SHE LOOKED AT ME. IN MY DREAM, SHE LOOKED AT ME AND NEVER SPOKE.

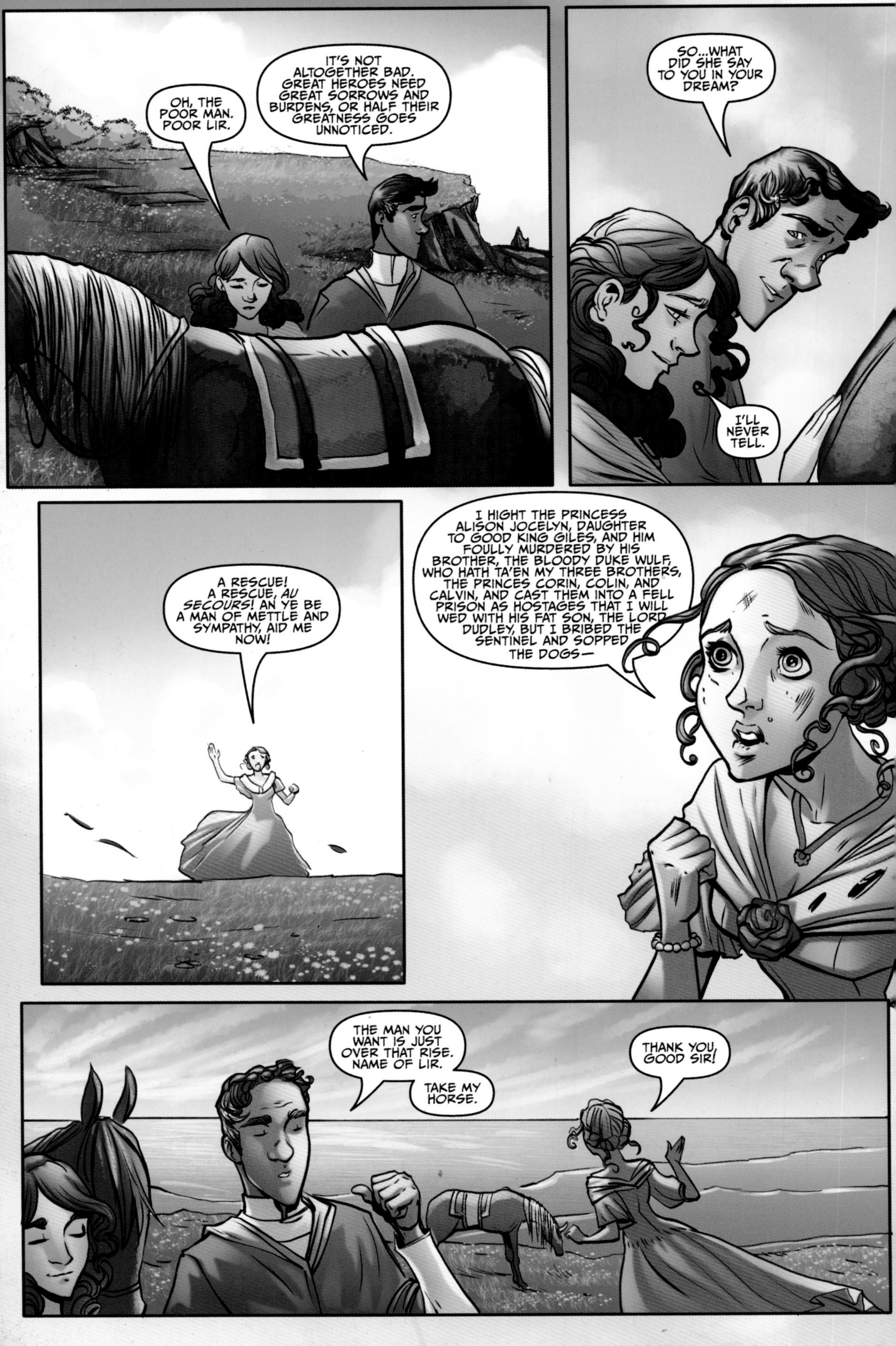

OH, THE POOR MAN. POOR LIR.
IT'S NOT ALTOGETHER BAD. GREAT HEROES NEED GREAT SORROWS AND BURDENS, OR HALF THEIR GREATNESS GOES UNNOTICED.
SO...WHAT DID SHE SAY TO YOU IN YOUR DREAM?
I'LL NEVER TELL.
A RESCUE! A RESCUE, *AU SECOURS*! AN YE BE A MAN OF METTLE AND SYMPATHY, AID ME NOW!
I HIGHT THE PRINCESS ALISON JOCELYN, DAUGHTER TO GOOD KING GILES, AND HIM FOULLY MURDERED BY HIS BROTHER, THE BLOODY DUKE WULF, WHO HATH TA'EN MY THREE BROTHERS, THE PRINCES CORIN, COLIN, AND CALVIN, AND CAST THEM INTO A FELL PRISON AS HOSTAGES THAT I WILL WED WITH HIS FAT SON, THE LORD DUDLEY, BUT I BRIBED THE SENTINEL AND SOPPED THE DOGS—
THE MAN YOU WANT IS JUST OVER THAT RISE. NAME OF LIR.
TAKE MY HORSE.
THANK YOU, GOOD SIR!

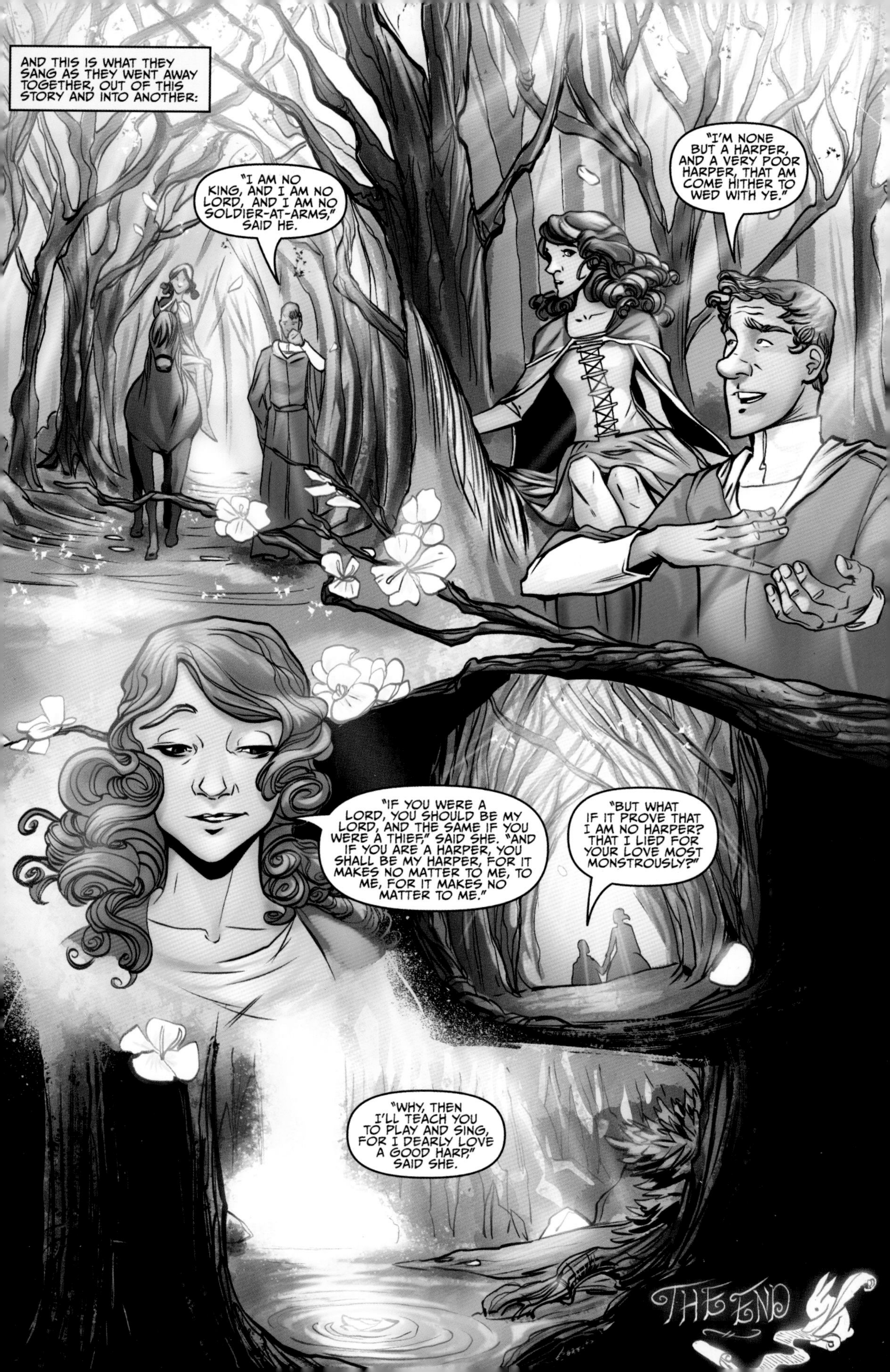
AND THIS IS WHAT THEY SANG AS THEY WENT AWAY TOGETHER, OUT OF THIS STORY AND INTO ANOTHER:
"I AM NO KING, AND I AM NO LORD, AND I AM NO SOLDIER-AT-ARMS," SAID HE.
"I'M NONE BUT A HARPER, AND A VERY POOR HARPER, THAT AM COME HITHER TO WED WITH YE."
"IF YOU WERE A LORD, YOU SHOULD BE MY LORD, AND THE SAME IF YOU WERE A THIEF," SAID SHE. "AND IF YOU ARE A HARPER, YOU SHALL BE MY HARPER, FOR IT MAKES NO MATTER TO ME, TO ME, FOR IT MAKES NO MATTER TO ME."
"BUT WHAT IF IT PROVE THAT I AM NO HARPER? THAT I LIED FOR YOUR LOVE MOST MONSTROUSLY?"
"WHY, THEN I'LL TEACH YOU TO PLAY AND SING, FOR I DEARLY LOVE A GOOD HARP," SAID SHE.
THE END

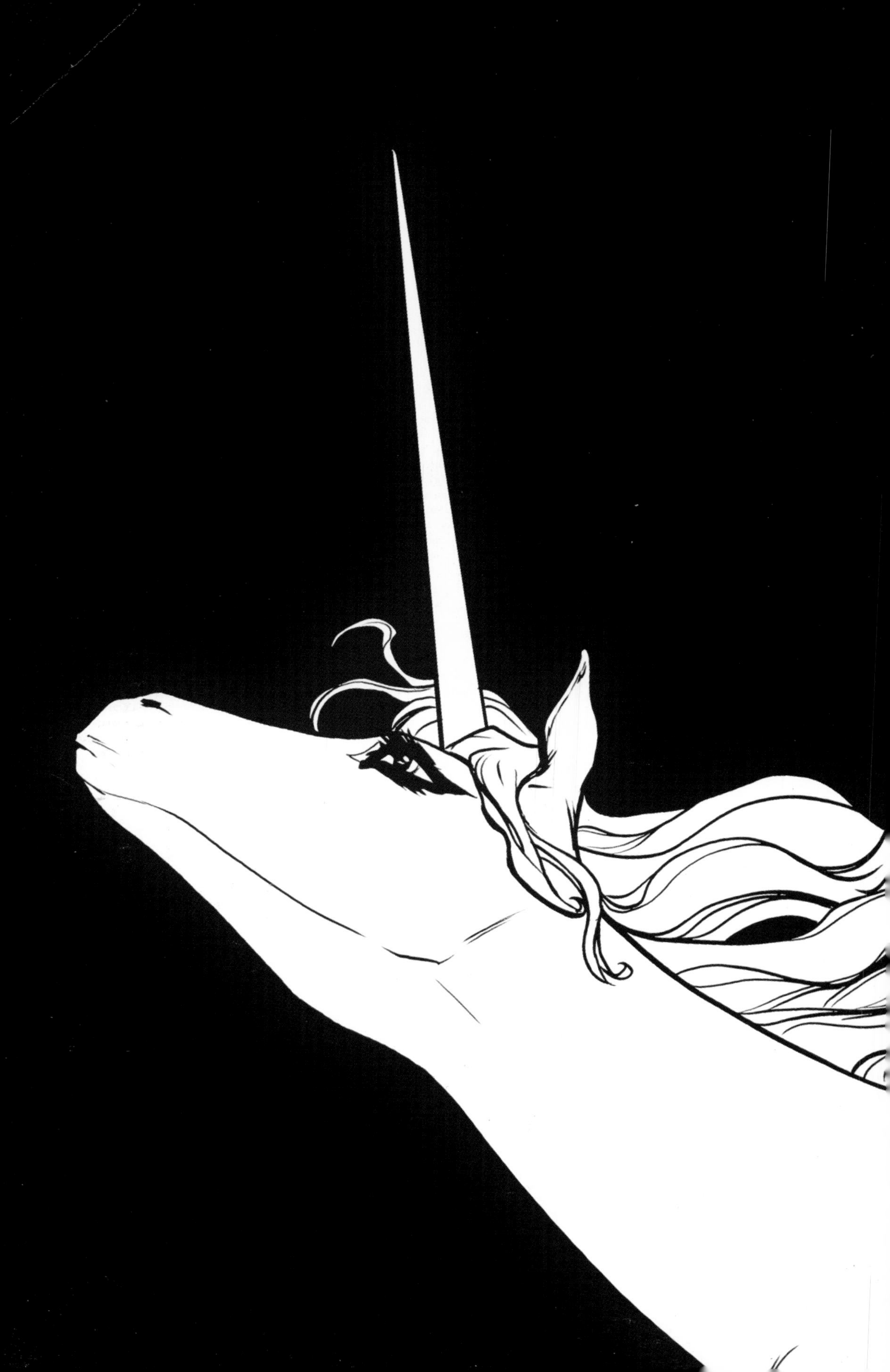

A CONVERSATION WITH
PETER S. BEAGLE

Connor Cochran: What's the most wonderful thing that writing *The Last Unicorn* has brought into your life?

Peter S. Beagle: If I had to say one thing, it would be all the people who come up and tell me, out of nowhere, how much the book meant to them, and how much it changed their lives. I hadn't bargained for that at all.

Connor: Does this happen often?

Peter: It happens a good deal. Certainly more than I could possibly expect. All writers live with the fact that you do your work, and it's out there, and maybe your publisher puts it in the stores and maybe they don't, maybe people find their way to it and maybe they don't... so the one thing you learn, if you stay with this, is not to hold your breath, not to expect that anything you do will ever affect any one particular person in any particular way. So the response to *The Last Unicorn* on an individual basis has been nothing I could ever have imagined. For example, there were the two Latino brothers I met at Wondercon a few years ago. They were very big guys, very dangerous looking, with huge weightlifter arms and lots of tattoos, and if I were making a movie I could easily cast them as leg-breakers for the Mob. Anyway, when they spotted my table they jumped at it, pointing at the DVD of *The Last Unicorn* and saying "Is this your movie?" When I confessed that I'd written the screenplay, one of them literally grabbed my arm and said, "Your movie saved our lives, man." What can you say to something like that? And then he explained that when he and his brother were small, their parents were going through one of those horrendous divorces where things smash and there's blood and cops get called. Every time a new mom-and-dad fight would break out the brothers would run into the living room, shove a VHS cassette of *The Last Unicorn* into the player, and watch it for as many times as it would take for things to finally quiet down. And then the second one gave me this absolutely wonderful smile, and he said "We are sane, functioning human beings today, with families of our own, because we had your world to hide out in. Thank you." I was speechless.

Connor: Over the years I've watched hundreds of people at cons and store appearances tell you that the book or film changed their lives.

Peter: Well, I've been speechless a lot.

Connor: When *The Last Unicorn* came out in 1968, it was your third published book. I'd like to put it in context by going back earlier than that, all the way to your first novel, *A Fine and Private Place*.

Peter: I always think of that as my "state of grace" book. When I look at it now, I see a lot of things that are wrong with it technically, and I see mistakes I'd never make today... and yet, somehow, I got away with it.

Connor: I know that you wrote *A Fine and Private Place* in college, when you were only 19 years old, and that you sold it to the Viking Press when you were 20. I know that when copies first landed in bookstores you were off spending a year in Europe, following graduation from the University of Pittsburgh. But what happened after the book was published and you came home to New York?

Peter: That was the fall of 1960. I didn't get to spend a great deal of time at home because my agent had put me up for a Wallace Stegner Fellowship at Stanford University, and to my utter shock they accepted me. So shortly after coming back I was on my way out again. I have very clear memories of landing at the airport in San Francisco, looking around, and thinking "Well, here I am in California and it really is sunny, just like the pictures. Now I have to get to Palo Alto. Where's the subway?"

Connor: I presume you eventually gave up looking for a subway. Who was your agent?

Peter: Elizabeth Otis, who was also John Steinbeck's agent and Harper Lee's agent. Steinbeck was her first client; she'd literally gone into business in 1929 with him, back when he was just a guy who had never sold a book, not a world-famous Pulitzer and Nobel Prize winner. I was recommended to Elizabeth by the poet-anthologist Louis Untermeyer, and his wife Bryna Ivens, who was editor of *Seventeen* magazine. A couple of years before, when I was 14 or 15, I'd sent a story in to *Seventeen*. The magazine didn't buy it, of course, but Bryna thought it was interesting and decided to track me down—something I'd accidentally made difficult by forgetting to put a return address on the envelope. Luckily for me the Bronx postmark was readable, and in those days all the Beagles in the borough were related to one another. She called the first one listed in the phone book and pretty soon she found me.

Connor: Your short story must really have been something. That's not a typical reaction to get from a magazine editor.

Peter: I don't really remember it now—I think it might have been a Western with some fantasy elements. What matters is that Bryna and Louis took me under their wing and introduced me to all the people they knew. I was just a kid in high school and I was meeting Norman Mailer, and Charles G. Jackson—he wrote *The Lost Weekend*—and even Arthur Miller and his brand-new bride, Marilyn Monroe, who never took her eyes off Miller and smelled wonderful. They also introduced me to Elizabeth, who took me on as a client when I was 17. We became so close that she was practically another aunt. Elizabeth loved young writers, and she spent a good deal of time with me, taking me out to lunch, looking at my latest story or poem or whatever I'd come up with. She knew I was still a long way from being someone she could sell, but she treated me like a real author anyway. That was very important.

Connor: It wasn't *that* long before you went pro. You placed a couple of stories during your first years in college, and Elizabeth sold *A Fine and Private Place* for you right away once you finished it.

Peter: She looked out for me, is what she did. I remember that Doubleday made the first bid, but Elizabeth, who was a bit of a proper lady, waited and didn't accept it. She didn't think Doubleday was the right house for a *very* young writer. She wanted a bid from Viking instead, because she thought they'd be more serious about the book and about me. And somehow she got it. Elizabeth usually found a way to get her authors what she wanted. I certainly would never have been a Stegner Fellow without her. It would never even have occurred to me to apply.

Connor: What was the Stegner Fellowship like?

Peter: First thing on the list was just getting to the University! It took me forever, that first day, to find

my way to Palo Alto, and ultimately to Stanford Village, which was old Army housing from the '40s that had long since supposed to be destroyed, but hadn't been. They were stashing foreign students there, and odd people like me. As for the Fellowship itself, which began with a big outdoor welcoming reception, the class that year was remarkable for who was in it—it's been written about more than once. A few years ago I actually got interviewed for a doctoral dissertation all about our group.

Connor: Who was in the session with you?

Peter: An amazing gang. I admit that at times I felt completely overwhelmed. There was Larry McMurtry, the first friend I made there, known now for *Lonesome Dove* and *The Last Picture Show* and the screenplay to *Brokeback Mountain*. He was a only a couple of years older than I was, and really talented. He wrote most of *Leaving Cheyenne* during our session. There was a 25-year-old Ken Kesey, at that point working on *One Flew Over the Cuckoo's Nest*. There was Judith Rascoe, who was the niece or great-niece of a very influential critic named Burton Rascoe; Judith went on to write stories and some very good screenplays. There was a Scottish guy named Robin MacDonald, whose wife, Joanna Ostrow, was Bronx Jewish like me. Robin was the one with the fellowship, but Joanna turned out to be the real writer. She would sit in on the class and years later, after the class was long over, she published an excellent novel called *In the Highlands Since Time Immemorial*. There was Chris Koch, an Australian writer whose best-known work over here is probably *The Year of Living Dangerously*. He started that one while he was at Stanford. But my closest friend in the class was Gurney Norman, from Hazard, Kentucky. Gurney and I took to each other immediately. As we've often said, he was my first redneck and I was his first City Jew. We used to sit up nights comparing childhoods. We're still in touch today. In fact, I visited him in Kentucky a few years ago and wrote all about it in the forward to *The Rhinoceros Who Quoted Nietzsche*, my first collection from Tachyon Publications.

Connor: How long did the Fellowship run?

Peter: Now it's a two-year session, but back then it only lasted one. We had two six-month semesters, each run by a different visiting writer. During the first half, while Malcolm Cowley ran the class, nobody missed anything. Every time Malcolm lectured, the room was so full that people were literally sitting on the sills of the open windows, or leaning in through them. Not only did Malcolm *know* stuff, but if he could help you, he would. Of course, if you could figure out a way to do the story on your own, that was also fine—Malcolm's ego was not tied up in this, just so long as the story worked.

Connor: He sounds like an extraordinary teacher.

Peter: He was a fine writer and editor, too—without Malcolm Cowley, Viking would never have published Jack Kerouac, and William Faulkner might have been completely forgotten. I was very fond of Malcolm. I didn't have a beard in those days, just a moustache, and so did he. We used to walk over the campus together, talking, with me mostly asking questions, and a time or two we were taken for father and son.

Connor: That year was the start of many big changes in your life. You discovered California, where you now live, and in particular you fell in love with Berkeley. You met a lot of people who would eventually be important to you.

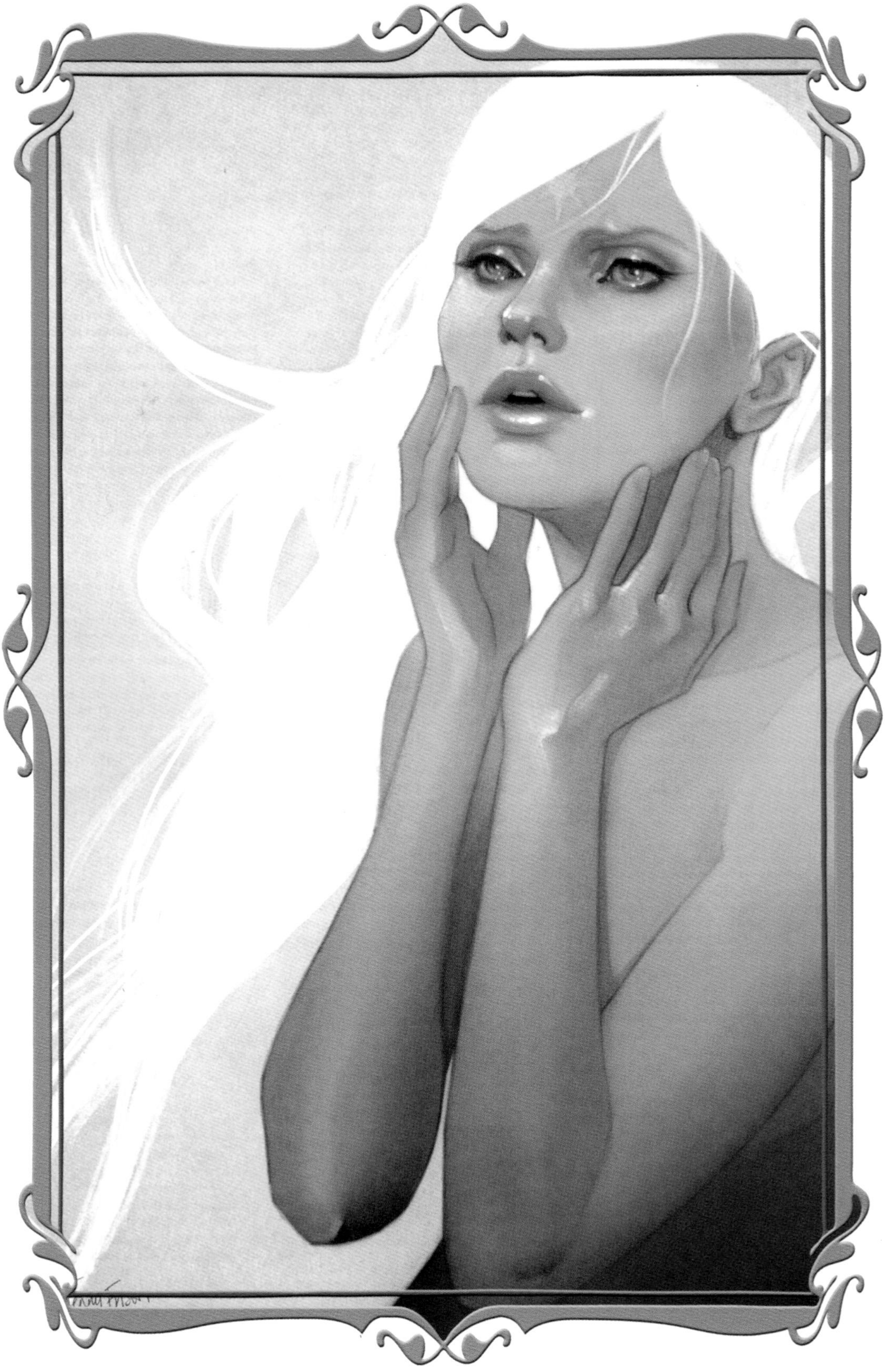

ART BY JENNY FRISON

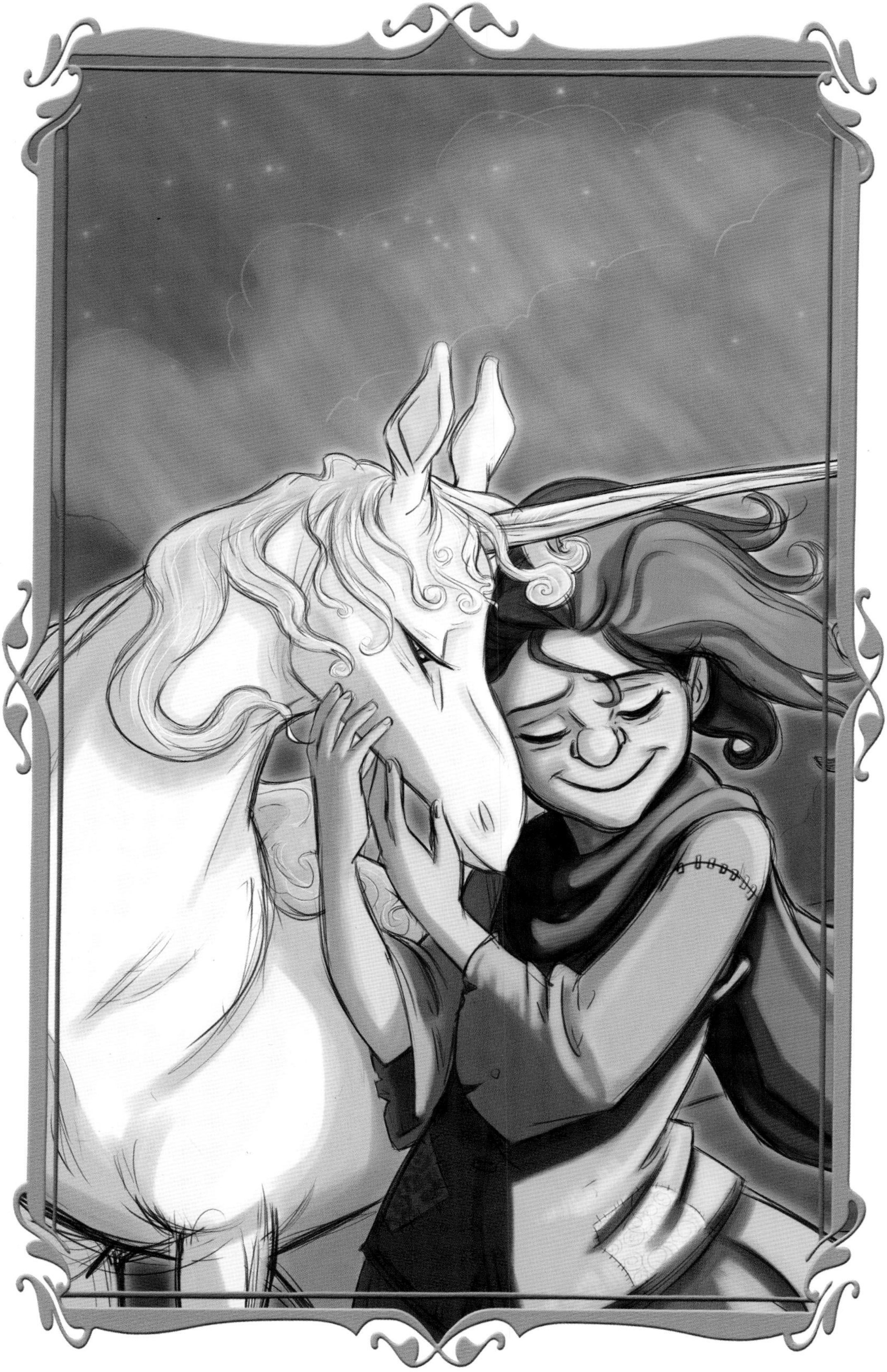

ART BY LEIGH DRAGOON

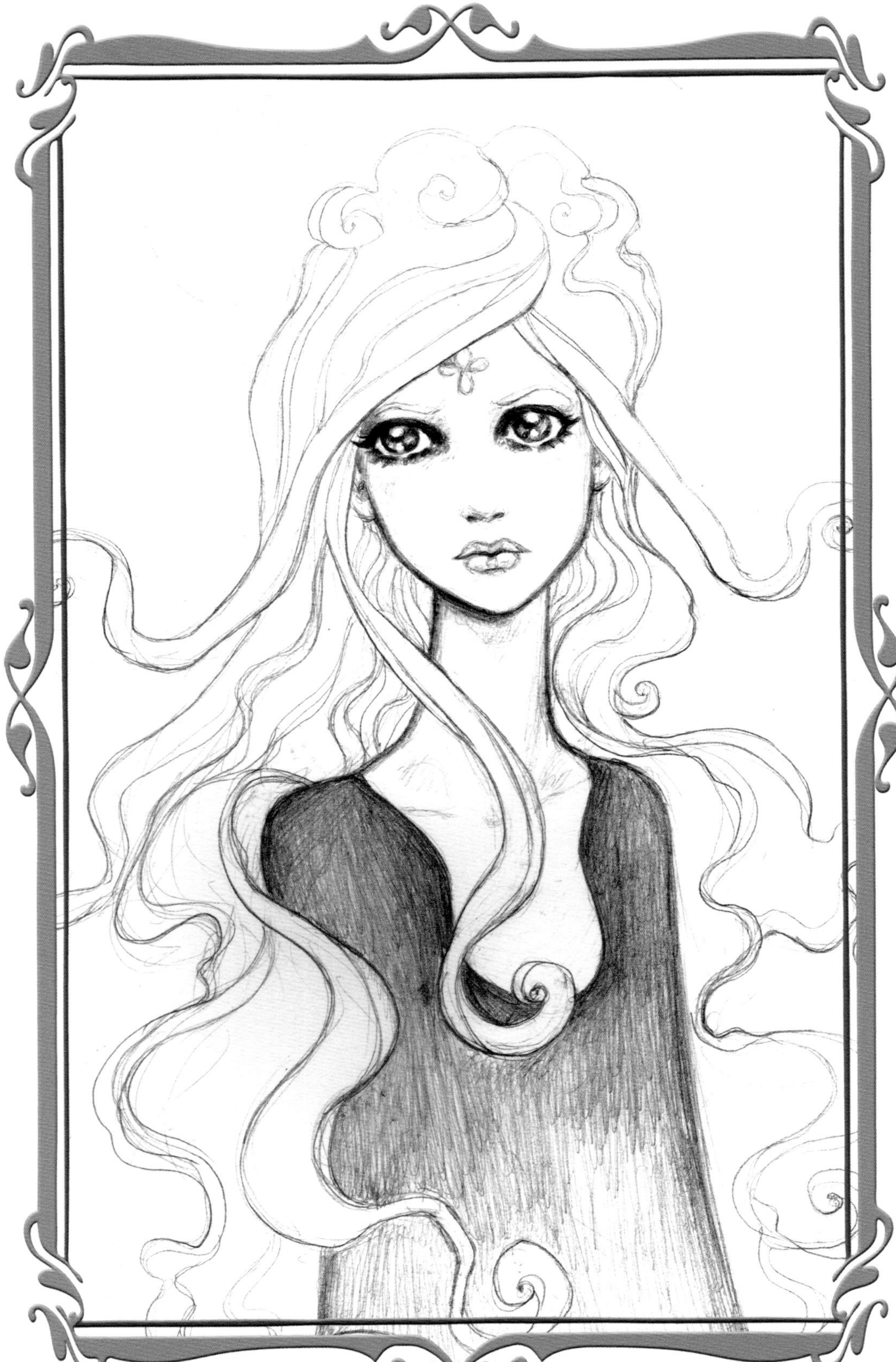

ART BY MARIAH MCCOURT

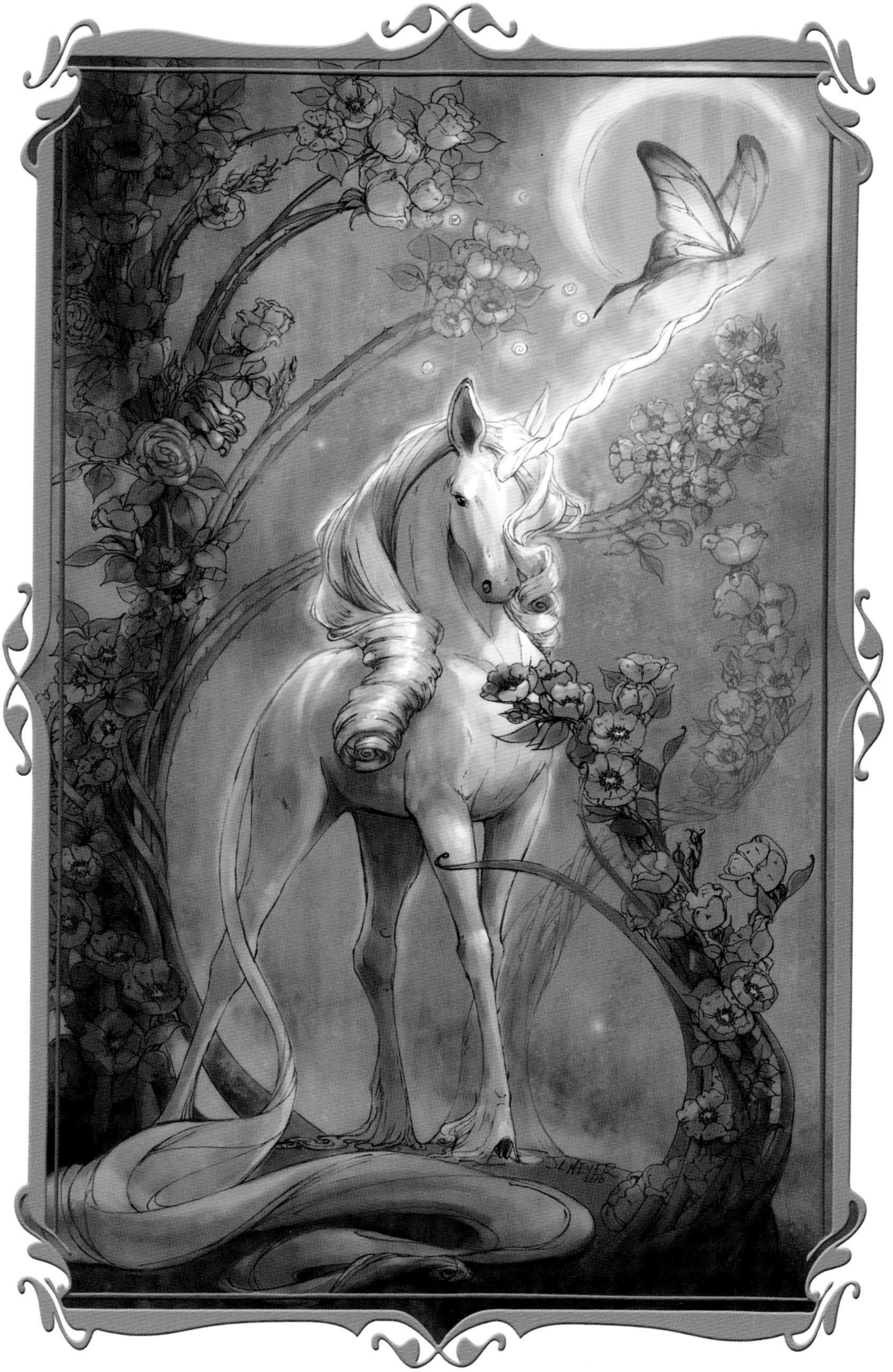
J.L. MEYER
2010

ART BY JENNIFER L. MEYER

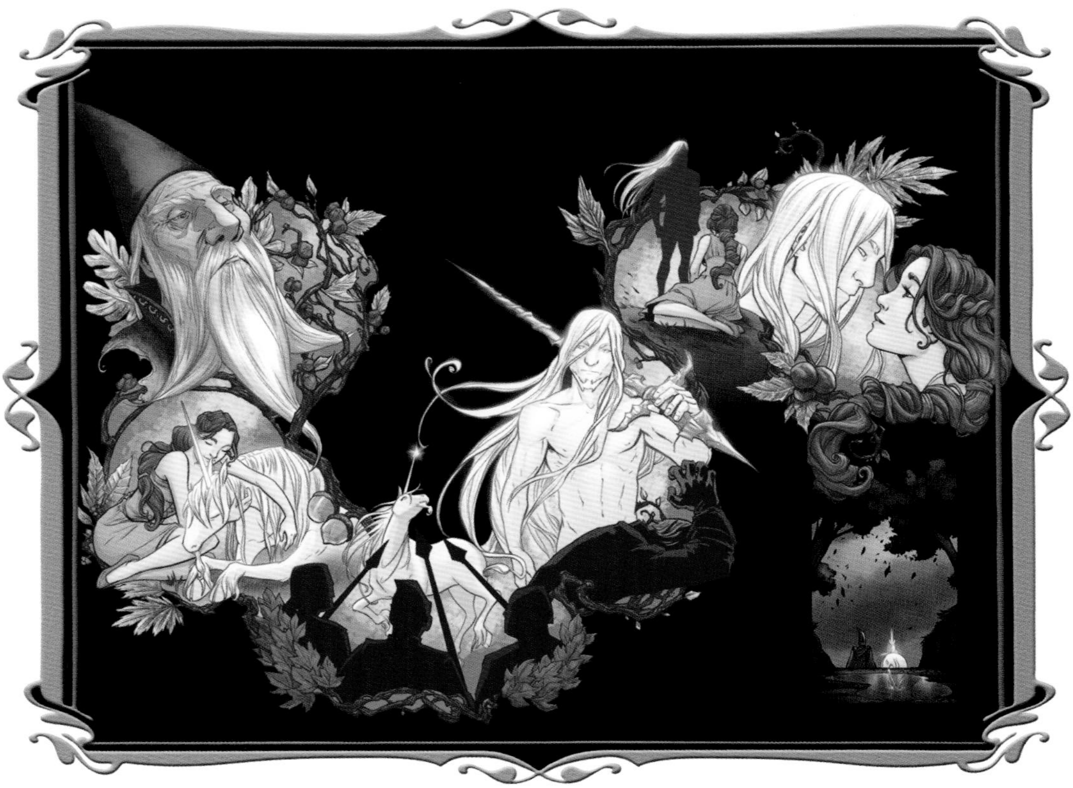

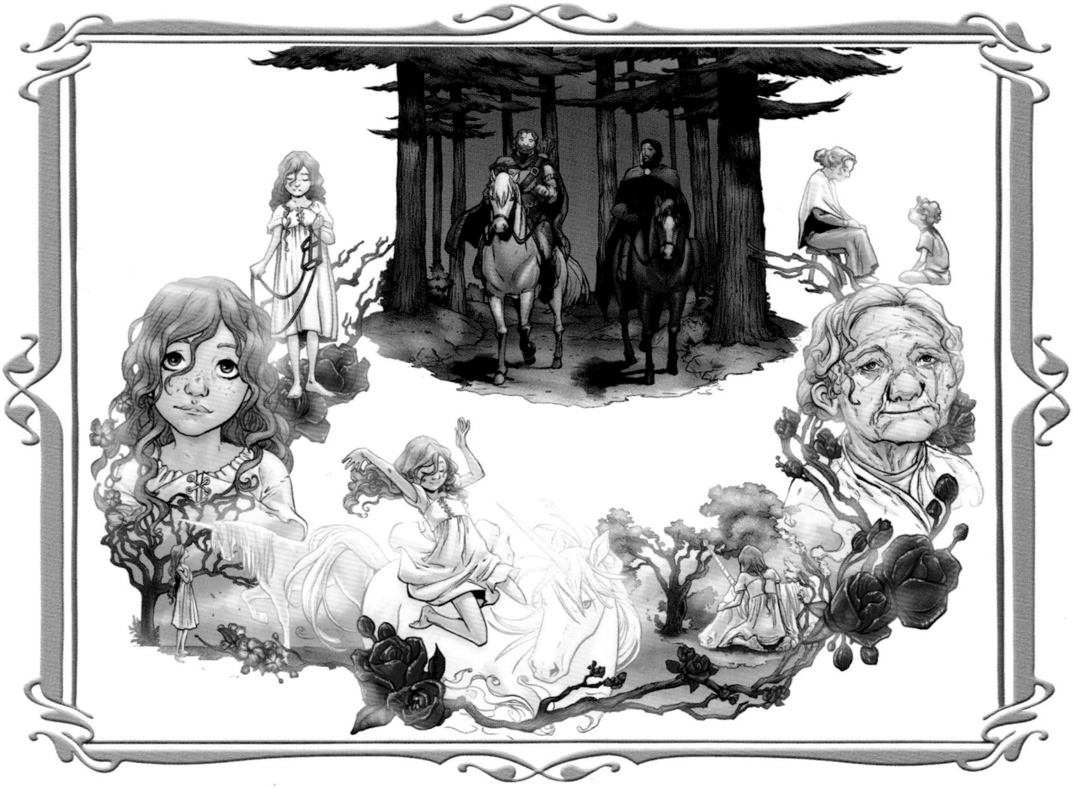

ART BY RENE DE LIZ

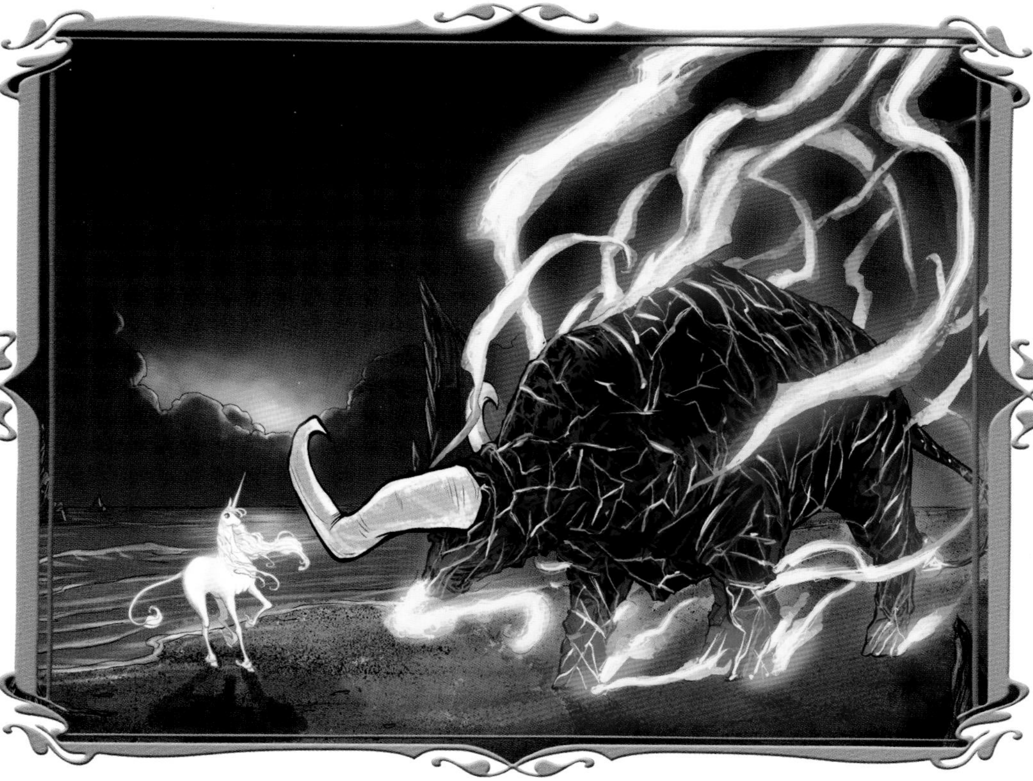

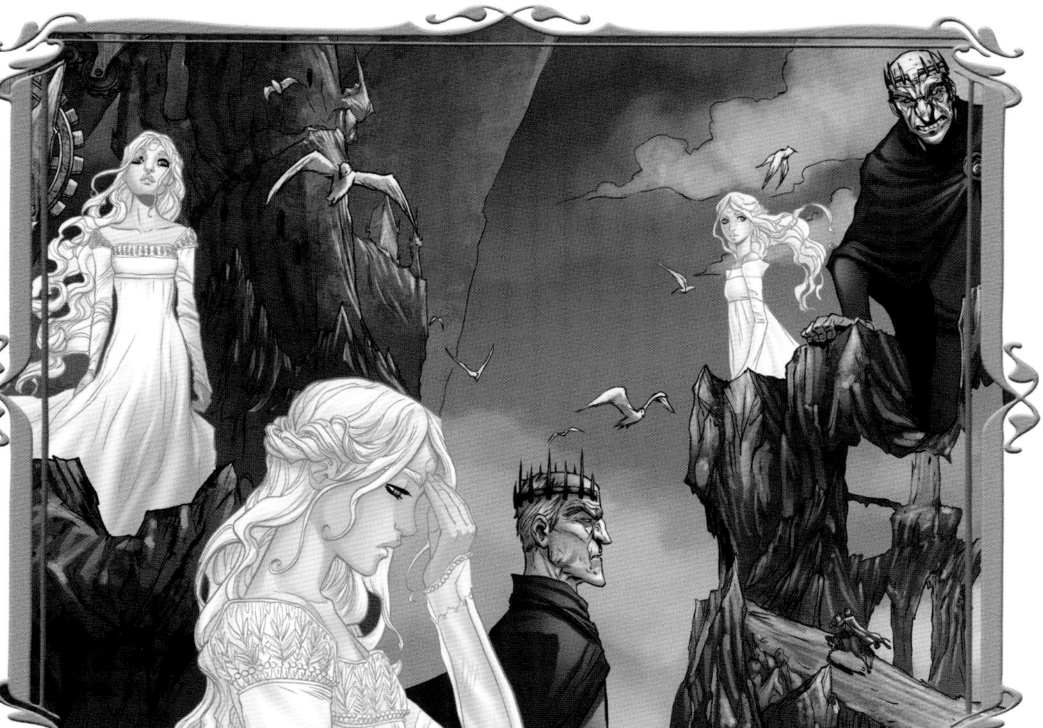

ART BY RENE DE LIZ

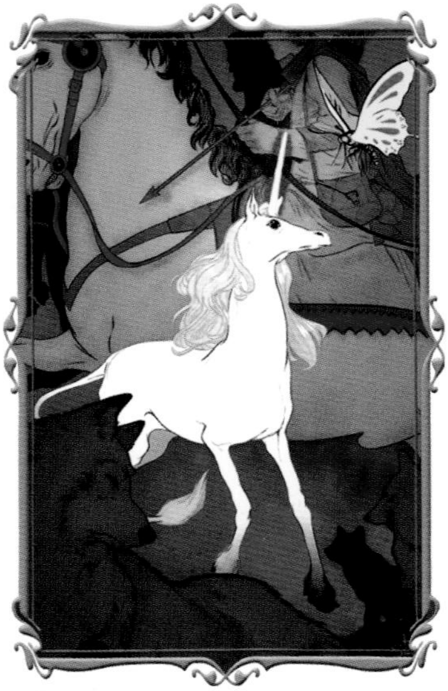
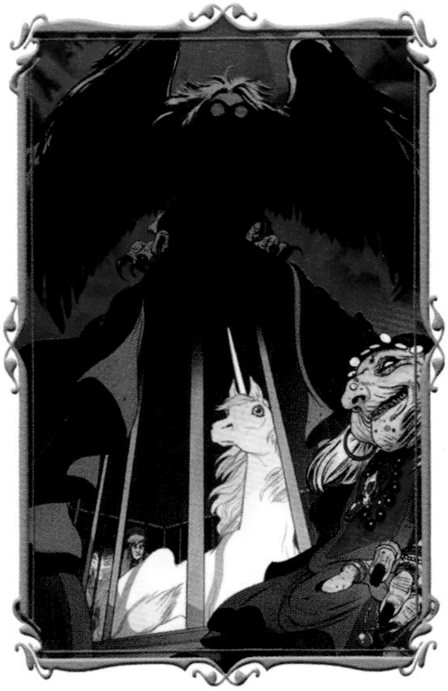
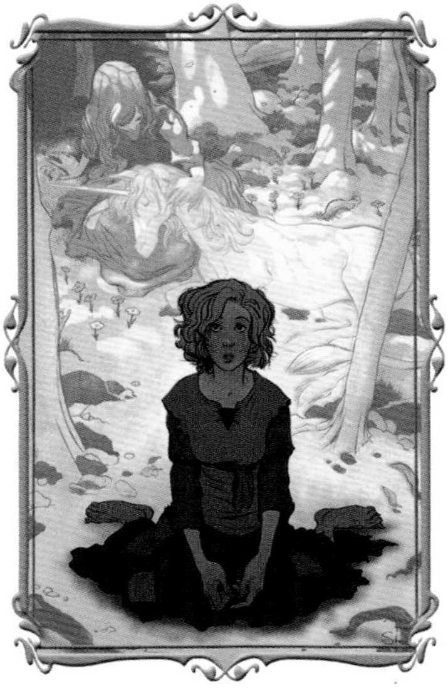
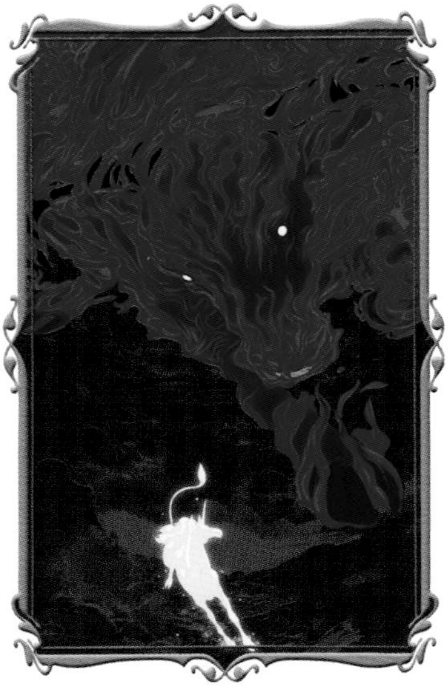
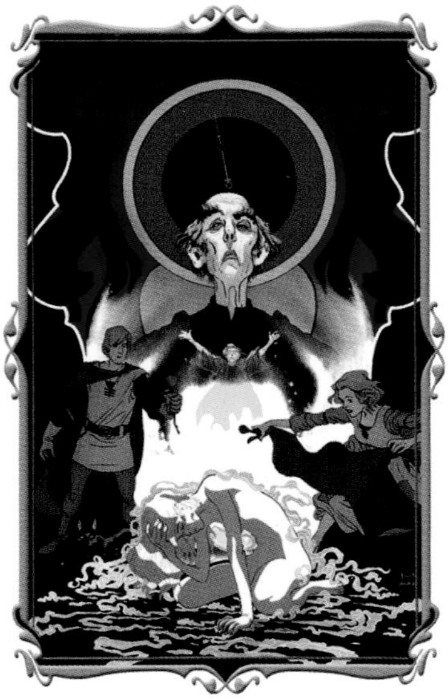
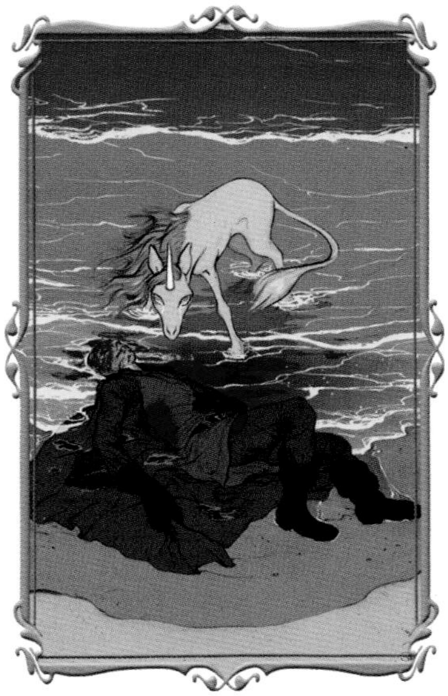

ART BY FRANK STOCKTON

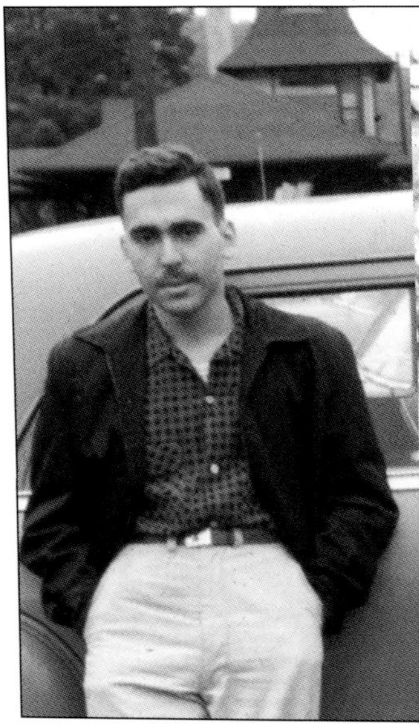 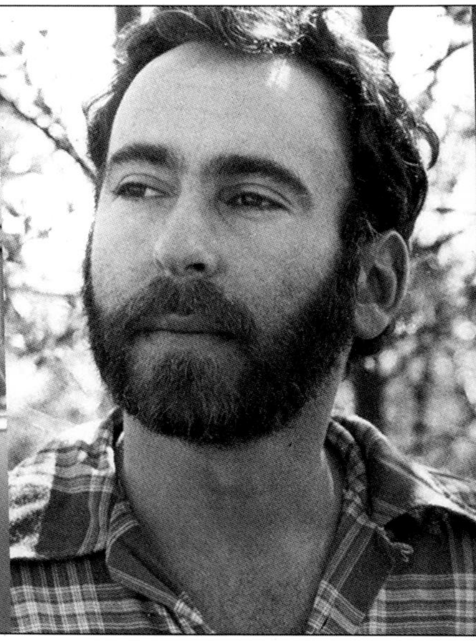 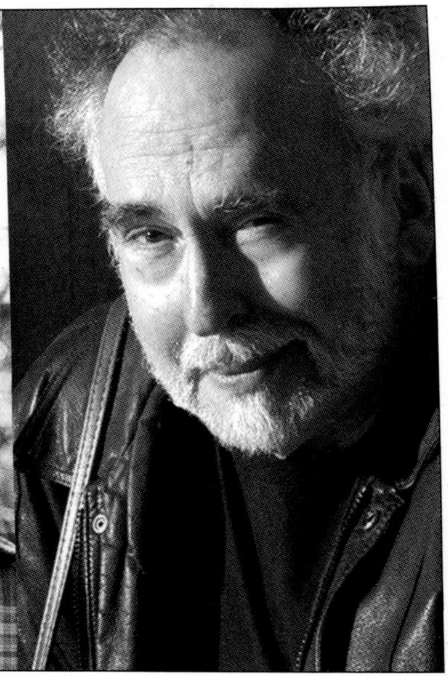

PETER S. BEAGLE

Peter S. Beagle, author of *The Last Unicorn*, is America's greatest living fantasist, and his work has won him fans all around the world.

His grandfather, Avram Soyer, was a celebrated Jewish immigrant author and journalist whose stories and folktales were published in America, Europe, and eventually Israel. His uncles (Moses, Raphael, and Isaac) became famous and successful realist painters with works in the permanent collection of more than a hundred major museums.

He was conceived in Mexico City when his parents, founders of the New York Teacher's Union, were visiting a Mexican branch of the family and socializing with a group that included Diego Rivera, Frieda Kahlo, and Leon Trotsky. He was then born in New York City in 1939 and raised in the Bronx, where he grew up surrounded by the arts and education. As a child Peter used to sit by himself in the stairwell of his apartment building, making up stories. As a young teenager he appeared on a regular New York weekend radio show, reviewing and discussing books. By the time he was 15 one of his story submissions caught the eye of Bryna Ivins, fiction editor of *Seventeen* magazine, who took him under her wing. Together she and her husband, the poet, critic, and anthologist Louis Untermeyer, introduced the talented young man to many of the famous writers, editors, and personalities of the day, including Arthur Miller, Marilyn Monroe, Norman Mailer, and Charles G. Jackson. They also connected him with his first literary agent, Elizabeth Otis, who at the time represented Harper Lee (*To Kill a Mockingbird*) and John Steinbeck (*The Grapes of Wrath, Of Mice and Men*).

Peter was 16 when he graduated from the Bronx High School of Science in 1955, a feat he says he managed only with the help of friends ("I loved history and English, and got good grades in those. At everything else I was dismal to the point of embarrassment.") Fortunately for Peter, a poem he'd written the year before won "best in America" from the Scholastic Art and Writing Awards. The prize: a full scholarship to the Creative Writing Program at the University of Pittsburgh.

While there Peter wrote and sold his first novel, the remarkable graveyard fantasy *A Fine and Private Place*, while still only 19 years old. This led to him being named to a Wallace Stegner Fellowship at Stanford University, where he participated in a program that included such future literary luminaries as Ken Kesey (*One Flew Over the Cuckoo's Nest*), Larry McMurtry (*The Last Picture Show, Lonesome Dove*), and Christopher Koch (*The Year of Living Dangerously*).

During that fellowship he met the woman who would become his first wife. He later moved from New York to California permanently to be with her: his 1963 cross-country motor scooter trip became the subject of second published book, *I See By My Outfit*, which has been continuously in print since 1965 and still wins awards. (Most recently, *Conde Nast Traveler* magazine named it one of the greatest 88 travel books of all time; and the new 2007 paperback edition won a Bronze medal for its publisher from the Independent Publishers Association.)

Peter followed this up in 1968 with his second (and best-known) novel, *The Last Unicorn*, which has sold more than 6 million copies worldwide and has been translated into more than 20 languages. In 1982 an animated version of *The Last Unicorn* was released, based on Peter's own screenplay, and with a voice cast that included Alan Arkin, Jeff Bridges, Mia Farrow, Angela Lansbury, and Christopher Lee. The film has established a huge following via subsequent cable, videotape, and DVD releases: since 2004 it has sold nearly two million DVDs in America alone.

Peter also wrote the screenplay for the 1978 animated version of *The Lord of the Rings*, and the teleplay for "Sarek" a fan-favorite episode of *Star Trek: The Next Generation*.

His other books include the novels *The Folk of the Air, The Innkeeper's Song*, and *Tamsin*; the short story collections *Giant Bones, The Rhinoceros Who Quoted Nietzsche, The Line Between, We Never Talk About My Brother; Mirror Kingdoms*, and the nonfiction books *The California Feeling, The Lady and Her Tiger, In the Presence of Elephants*, and *The Garden of Earthly Delights*. In 2002 he came roaring back on the scene with an extraordinary run of short fiction—over 60 stories, novelettes, and novellas—including a sequel to *The Last Unicorn* called "Two Hearts," which won both the Hugo and Nebula Awards.

Now 71, he continues to write steadily and has more than a dozen books in the publishing pipeline, including new novels (*Summerlong* and *I'm Afraid You've Got Dragons*); new collections (*Sleight of Hand, The First Last Unicorn & Other Beginnings, Green-Eyed Boy: New Schmendrick Stories, 3 Unicorns*); revised and updated edition of older works (*The Innkeeper's Song, Th Magician of Karakosk*); new nonfiction book (*Sméagol, Déagol, and Beagle: Essays from t Headwaters of My Voice*); and his first t children's books.

He is also a gifted poet, lyricist, singer/songwriter, with several recordings i works. To celebrate his 70th birthday he lau the subscriber-only *52/50 Project*, in wh wrote a new song lyric or poem every wee year. All 52 pieces from that series are no recorded by Peter himself and a startlin professional singers and musicians who of his work.

Since late 2001 he has made his home i California. For more information on Pe works, go to www.conlanpress.com.

The Last Unicorn

Peter S. Beagle

he
s
he
wo

and
n the
nched
ch he
k for a
y being
g mix of
are fans

Oakland,
ter and his

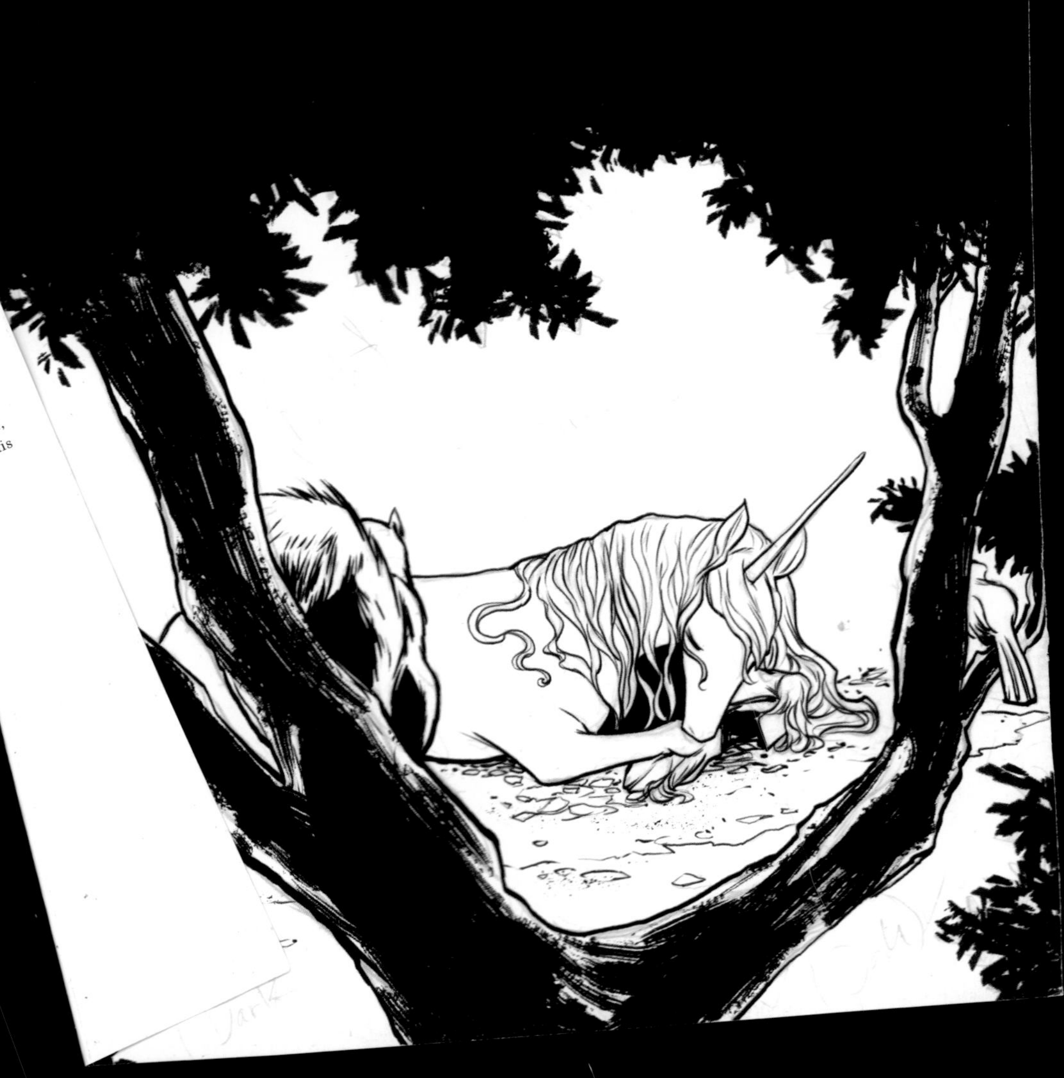